AMERICAN EDUCATION

Featuring current information and challenging perspectives on the latest issues and forces shaping the American educational system—with scholarship that is often cited as a primary source—Joel Spring introduces readers to the historical, political, social, and legal foundations of education and to the profession of teaching in the United States. In his signature straightforward, concise approach to describing complex issues, he illuminates events and topics that are often overlooked or whitewashed, giving students the opportunity to engage in critical thinking about education. Students come away informed on the latest topics, issues, and data and with a strong knowledge of the forces shaping the American educational system.

Thoroughly updated throughout, the new edition of this clear, authoritative text remains fresh and up-to-date, reflecting the many changes in education that have occurred since the publication of the previous edition. Topics and issues addressed and analyzed include:

- The decline of the Common Core State Standards, particularly as a result of a Republican-controlled administration currently in place
- Increasing emphasis on for-profit education, vouchers, charter schools, and free-market competition between schools, expected to surge with the appointment of the new U.S. Secretary of Education Betsy DeVos
- Current debates about immigration and "Dreamers"—new statistics on immigrant education, discussion of education proposals to accommodate the languages, cultures, and religions of newly arrived immigrants
- New education statistics on school enrollments, dropouts, education and income, school segregation, charter schools, and home languages
- The purposes of education as presented in the 2016 platforms of the Republican, Democratic, Green, and Libertarian parties
- Discussions around transgender students

Joel Spring is Professor Emeritus at Queens College and the Graduate Center of the City University of New York, USA.

Sociocultural, Political, and Historical Studies in Education
Series Editor: Joel Spring

This series focuses on studies of public and private institutions, the media, and academic disciplines that contribute to educating—in the broadest sense—students and the general public. The series welcomes volumes with multicultural perspectives, diverse interpretations, and a range of political points of view from conservative to critical. Books accepted for publication in this series will be written for an academic audience and, in some cases, also for use as supplementary readings in graduate and undergraduate courses.

Topics to be addressed in this series include, but are not limited to, sociocultural, political, and historical studies of:

- Local, state, national, and international educational systems
- Elementary and secondary schools, colleges, and universities
- Public institutions of education such as museums, libraries, and foundations
- Computer systems and software as instruments of public education
- The popular media as forms of public education
- Content areas within the academic study of education, such as curriculum and instruction, psychology, and educational technology

Chet A. Bowers • *A Critical Examination of STEM: Issues and Challenges*

Edited by Joel Spring, John Eric Frankson, Corie A. McCallum, Diane Price Banks • *The Business of Education: Networks of Power and Wealth in America*

Timothy Reagan • *Non-Western Educational Traditions: Indigenous Approaches to Educational Thought and Practice, Fourth Edition*

Joel Spring • *Political Agendas for Education: From Make America Great Again to Stronger Together, Sixth Edition*

Joel Spring • *The American School, Tenth Edition*

Joel Spring • *Global Impacts of the Western School Model: Corporatization, Alienation, Consumerism*

For more information about this series, please visit: www.routledge.com/ Sociocultural-Political-and-Historical-Studies-in-Education/book-series/ LEASPHSES

AMERICAN EDUCATION

19th Edition

Joel Spring

Routledge
Taylor & Francis Group
NEW YORK AND LONDON

Nineteenth edition published 2020
by Routledge
52 Vanderbilt Avenue, New York, NY 10017

and by Routledge
2 Park Square, Milton Park, Abingdon, Oxon, OX14 4RN

Routledge is an imprint of the Taylor & Francis Group, an informa business

© 2020 Taylor & Francis

The right of Joel Spring to be identified as author of this work has been asserted by him in accordance with sections 77 and 78 of the Copyright, Designs and Patents Act 1988.

First edition published by Longman 1978
Eighteenth edition published by Routledge 2018

Library of Congress Cataloging-in-Publication Data
A catalog record for this book has been requested

ISBN: 978-0-367-22264-2 (hbk)
ISBN: 978-0-367-22265-9 (pbk)
ISBN: 978-0-429-27413-8 (ebk)

Typeset in Sabon
by Apex CoVantage, LLC

BRIEF CONTENTS

CONTENTS

PREFACE

The goal of this book is to critically describe the goals, laws, structure, and issues related to the American educational system. Many of these aspects of American schooling are controversial and involve social and political values. Regarding controversial issues, I discuss a range of possible opinions so the reader can formulate his or her own conclusions. Controversial issues cover a broad range of topics, such as the role and content of civic education, the content of sex and health education, the goal of providing equal educational opportunity, the role of schools in ending poverty, the protection family languages, the role of multicultural curricula, the expansion of for-profit and charter schools, the role of the federal government in schools, the role of strikes and teacher unions, and the consequences of globalizing the Western school model.

In this 19th edition, the following changes were made to each chapter. Tables used throughout the book have been updated, with dated material being cut.

Chapter 1
a. Discussion of recent court suit regarding schools not providing a civic education.
b. Updated court cases about the Pledge of Allegiance.
c. Comparison of voter turnout in the United States with other industrialized countries.
d. Reorganized for clarity.

Chapter 2
a. Added discussion of multicultural aspect of character education.
b. Discussion of religion and LGBTQ.
c. Updated discussion of school crime and shootings.
d. Updated discussion of bullying and cyberbullying.
e. Discussion of Melania Trump's Be Best campaign against bullying.

Chapter 3
a. Updated PISA scores.
b. New inequality of income statistics.

Chapter 4
a. Added discussion of teaching skills needed to prepare students as workers in the global economy.
b. Added discussion of the Asia Society's Center for Global Education, which takes a broader view of the skills needed for a global society by recommending that students learn about world cultures and histories.

Chapter 5
a. Addition of time line of African American desegregation of schools.
b. Updated discussion of racial classifications used by the U.S. census bureau.
c. Added discussion of controversy about census question dealing with citizenship.
d. Discussion of current controversy over student survivors of sexual assault and harassment to exclude much of the abuse students experienced and altering how schools will respond to reports of sexual harassment and violence.

Chapter 6
a. Added section: Native Americans and Mexican Americans as Native-Born Citizens and Immigrants.
b. Updated statistics on percentage of foreign born in the United States.
c. Expanded discussion of Dreamers and DACA (Deferred Action for Childhood Arrivals).
d. Section added about children of illegal immigrants being separated from their parents and held in government shelters.
e. Added discussion of 2018 suit against Harvard University for discrimination against Asian Americans in the admissions process.
f. Added discussion of teachers in Los Angeles, the second largest school district in the United States, going on strike in 2019 for more school funding.

Chapter 7
a. Updated world migration statistics.

Chapter 8
a. Added section on U.S. Secretary of Education Betsy DeVos.

Chapter 9

a. Discussion of U.S. Secretary of Education DeVos's use of the bully pulpit to persuade states to adopt school choice plans.

b. Expanded discussion of Every Student Succeeds Act (ESSA).

Chapter 10

a. Discussion of recent teacher strikes in Los Angeles, Arizona, West Virginia, Kentucky, and Oklahoma.

Chapter 11

a. Added an extended discussion of the negative impact of the globalization of the Western school model.

PART 1

SCHOOL AND SOCIETY

CHAPTER 1

The History and Political Goals of Public Schooling

"Are Civics Lessons a Constitutional Right? These Students Are Suing for Them" was the startling 2018 title of a *New York Times* article. Preparing students to vote and understand the workings of government was a central reason for establishing public schools in the nineteenth century. What happened? Aleita Cook, 17, the plaintiff in the suit, had never taken a class in government, civics, or economics in the four years she attended a technical high school in Providence, Rhode Island. She brought the lawsuit hoping her younger brothers could "have a really good education, and go into adulthood knowing how to vote, how to do taxes, and learning basic things that you should know going into the real world."

In the same article, Luther Spoehr, a professor of history and education at Brown University, argues that history and civics "have become curricular 'stepchildren' because of the pressure on schools to raise test scores in reading and math and prepare children for work in an unforgiving economy." And the subtitle to the news article asserted: "Many see the lack of civics in schools as a national crisis."

In a similar concern that schools are not preparing students in life skills, a 2018 report, "Respected Perspectives of Youth on High School and Social and Emotional Learning," concluded that "current and recent high school students . . . see a big missing piece in their education—a lack of social and emotional skills development—and most recent students feel unprepared for life after high school." Students and teachers in the study believe that social and emotional learning will reduce bullying and prepare them for postsecondary education, work, and life.

As I later discuss, civic education was a major goal in the establishment of public schools in the nineteenth century. By the end of the nineteenth century and in the early twentieth century, educational goals focused on the whole child and added social skills to the curriculum. Today the major educational goal is preparation for work. Changes in educational goals are reflected in what students study (the curriculum).

THE IMPORTANCE OF THE GOALS OF EDUCATION

Aleita Cook claims the shifting goals of education deprived her of an education in civics and what she called the "basic things that you should know going into the real world." What she discovered was that learning goals and instructional methods are determined by a political process involving local, state, and federal officials and, as illustrated by Aleita Cook's case, the courts. Even when a student or parent chooses a themed public or charter school, such as ones focused on art education or technical training, they don't have direct control over what they will be taught.

Imagine public or charter school principals greeting each parent at the beginning of the school year with the question: "What do you want your child to learn, and how do you want it to be taught?" Of course, that seldom happens. What is to be taught and how are usually decided by the time children begin the school year. Politically determined goals of public education guide what is taught and how it is taught. When students enter a public school, they are submitting to the will of the public as determined by local, state, and federal governments. The goals of American schools are politically determined.

To distinguish between educational goals, I have divided them into political, social, and economic. In this chapter I focus on the issues surrounding the political goals of education. In Chapter 2, I discuss the social goals of schooling. In Chapter 3, I consider one of the most important and complex goals of education: equality of opportunity. Chapter 4 continues the discussion of equality of opportunity in the context of economic goals.

This chapter introduces readers to:

- The goals and history of U.S. public schools
- Debates about the political goals of public schools
- A discussion about whether these goals have been achieved
- Questions designed to help readers formulate their own opinions about the purposes of American education

EDUCATION GOALS ARE CONTROVERSIAL

What type of goals spark public controversy? Consider the goal of educating patriotic citizens. Should teaching patriotism consist of saluting the flag and reciting the Pledge of Allegiance, which contains a reference to God? Some religious groups criticize flag salutes as worshiping false gods while others complain about the reference to God in the

Pledge. Also, social goals can stimulate debates such as those related to instruction in abstinence or birth control as means of reducing teenage pregnancy. An important traditional goal of schooling is reducing crime through instruction in moral and social values. But whose social values or morality should form the basis of instruction in public schools? Today, the economic goals of schooling primarily center on educating workers to help the U.S. economy compete in the global economy. But will this goal increase or decrease economic inequalities in society?

The previous questions do not have right or wrong answers. They are questions that reflect real debates about the role of U.S. public schools. The questions also provide insight into the historical evolution of American education. For instance, what are your answers to the following questions?

- Do you think there are public benefits from education that should override the objections of parents and other citizens regarding the teaching of particular subjects, attitudes, or values?
- Should elected representatives determine the subject matter, attitudes, and values taught in public schools?
- What should public-school teachers do if they are asked to teach values that are in conflict with their own personal values?

In answering the preceding questions, remember that public schools do not always operate for the general good of society. Most people assume that public schooling is always a social good. However, public schools are used to advance political and economic ideologies that do not improve the condition of human beings. For instance, in the 1930s Nazis enlisted schools in a general campaign to educate citizens to believe in the racial superiority of the German people, to support fascism, and to be willing to die at the command of Hitler. Racial biology and fascist political doctrines were taught in the classroom; patriotic parades and singing took place in the schoolyard. A similar pattern occurred in South African schools in attempts to maintain a racially divided society. In the United States, racial segregation and biased content in textbooks was used to maintain a racial hierarchy. Consequently, the reader should be aware that "education" does not always benefit the individual or society. Public and personal benefits depend on the content of instruction.

Educational goals are a product of what people think schooling should do for the good of society. Consequently, they often reflect opinions and beliefs about how people should act and how society should be organized. Since there is wide variation in what people believe, educational goals often generate a great deal of debate. I'm sure that in reading this book you will find yourself taking sides on issues.

HISTORICAL GOALS OF SCHOOLING

The historical record provides insight into current controversies surrounding public-school goals. As indicated in Figure 1.1, the founding of public schools from the 1820s to the 1840s had as a goal the uniting of Americans by instilling in students common moral and political values. It was believed that if all children were exposed to a common instruction in morality and politics the nation might become free of crime, immoral behavior, and the possibility of political revolution. These educational goals have persisted into the twenty-first century with government policies still calling upon schools to instill in students moral values, a common cultural identity, and civic values. A later section of this chapter discusses the problems associated with the continuing political education mission of schools. Chapter 2 discusses the enduring problems in attempting to form the moral character of the American population through public schooling.

A persistent educational goal from these early days of schooling is providing equality of opportunity, which is discussed in more detail in Chapter 3. Horace Mann referred to this goal as the "great balance wheel of society." Worried about conflicts between the rich and poor, education was believed to be the key in giving everyone an equal opportunity to gain wealth. Equality of opportunity refers to everyone having the same chance to pursue wealth. It does not mean everyone will have equal status or income, but just an equal chance to economically succeed. It was hoped that the poor would not resent the rich when they realized they had an equal opportunity through schooling to become rich. Today, a major goal of schooling remains providing everyone with equality of opportunity to succeed.

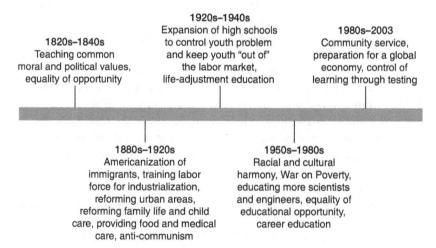

Figure 1.1 Goals of Public Schools in the United States, 1820–2003

As indicated in Figure 1.1, industrialization, urbanization, and increased immigration from the 1880s to the 1920s turned public schools into welfare agencies that extended their reach to something called the "whole child." This included concerns about the health, family, and neighborhood conditions affecting students and resulted in school cafeterias, school nurses, playgrounds, extracurricular activities, after-school programs, and intervention into families, and kindergartens became part of the expanded goals of schooling. Like political and moral education and equality of opportunity, these concerns extended into the 21st century. For instance, school cafeterias were originally introduced to ensure children received proper nutrition. Today, this concern persists in the battle against childhood obesity.

The teaching of multiculturalism and racial harmony was highlighted in schools, as indicated in Figure 1.1, during the civil rights movement from the 1950s to the 1980s. Prior to this period, schools attempted to strip Native Americans, African Americans, Asian Americans, and Mexican Americans of their languages and cultures and replace them with the dominant Anglo-Saxon culture. The result, as I discuss in Chapters 5, 6, and 7, is a continuing struggle over the language and culture of schooling.

After the 1960s, an important goal of education has been to increase economic growth and prepare students for jobs in the global economy. During the period from the 1820s to the 1840s, champions of public school argued that mass schooling would end poverty and increase national wealth. This argument persisted into the period from the 1880s to the 1920s, when schools introduced vocational education, vocational guidance, and high school programs designed to educate students for particular jobs in the labor market. Today, mass testing and national standards are considered the key to global economic competition.

In summary, schools are the focus of many hopes for political, social, and economic improvement. The dreams of public-school advocates of the early nineteenth century persist in the form of civic education, patriotic school exercises, and character education. Providing equality of opportunity to pursue wealth remains a dream of school people. Growing the economy and preparing students for work are central to political policies affecting schools. "Reform the individual rather than society" is the message of those who trust the school to end crime, poverty, broken families, drug and alcohol abuse, and myriad other social troubles.

PROTECTED OR PREPARED CHILDHOOD?

Social concepts of childhood are another way of thinking about educational goals. Is the educational goal designed to protect or prepare children for some future life? In *Huck's Raft: A History of American Childhood*,

Steven Mintz argues there was a transition in American thought from the concept of "protected" childhood to "prepared childhood." "Protected childhood" focuses on the happiness and well-being of the child. In "prepared childhood" attention is given to the child's future as an adult rather than concern about the child's immediate happiness.

Public schools are traditionally concerned with both protected and prepared childhood. For instance, schools reflect the concept of protected childhood by providing opportunities to play, be healthy, use imagination, and be happy. Educational practices that traditionally reflect protected childhood include:

- Recess
- Availability of playgrounds
- Emphasis in instruction on intellectual enjoyment and interest of the student
- Gym
- School clubs
- Extracurricular activities
- Health care and instruction
- Kindergarten for imagination and personal development in contrast to preparation for the first grade
- Education for enjoyment of arts
- Personal development for a happy life

Preparation for work or college affects many of the practices associated with prepared childhood, including:

- As early as preschool, learning skills for work and later schooling
- Kindergarten as preparation for first grade in contrast to time for social and imaginative development
- Reduction of arts programs and recess time for more class time and test preparation
- Career education

POLITICAL GOALS OF SCHOOLING

The major political goals of American schools are:

- Teaching a common set of political beliefs
- Learning to obey the law by obeying school rules
- Providing an equal opportunity for all to be elected to political positions
- Emphasizing voting as the key to political and social change

- Learning about the workings of government
- Educating patriotic citizens
- Educating students to be involved in community activities

Before the actual establishment of public schools, American political leaders wanted schooling to create a national culture and to educate qualified politicians for a republican government. The role of schools in determining national culture continues into the twenty-first century, particularly as a result of increased immigration. The concern about education focusing on American nationalism appeared in the 2012 Republican platform with its call for a "renewed focus on the Constitution and the writings of the Founding Fathers, and an accurate account of American history that celebrates the birth of this great nation." This renewal focused in American schools was to be accompanied by the idea of American exceptionalism as stated in the same national platform: "Professing American exceptionalism—the conviction that our country holds a unique place and role in human history—we proudly associate ourselves with those Americans of all political stripes who, more than three decades ago in a world as dangerous as today's, came together to advance the cause of freedom." In contrast, the 2012 Democratic platform mentioned nothing about teaching American nationalism and focused on education for improving the economy and increasing incomes.

After the American Revolution, many worried about national unity and the selection of political leaders. In his first message to Congress in 1790, President George Washington proposed a national university for training political leaders and creating a national culture. He wanted it to be attended by students from all areas of the country. It was hoped that a hereditary aristocracy of the British would be replaced by an aristocracy of the educated. Washington's proposal was criticized as elitist. Requiring a college education, some protested, would result in politicians being primarily recruited from the elite. If none but the rich had access to higher education, then the rich could use higher education as a means of perpetuating and supporting their social status. To avoid the problem of elitism, Thomas Jefferson suggested that education could provide an equal opportunity for all nonslave citizens to gain political office. All citizens were to be given an equal chance to develop their abilities and to advance in the political hierarchy.

Jefferson was concerned with finding the best politicians through a system of schooling. In the 1779 Bill for the More General Diffusion of Knowledge, Jefferson proposed three years of free education for all nonslave children. The most talented of these children were to be selected and educated at public expense at regional grammar schools. From this select group, the most talented were to be chosen for further education.

Jefferson wrote in *Notes on the State of Virginia,* "By this means twenty of the best geniuses will be raked from the rubbish annually, and be instructed, at the public expense."

The details of Jefferson's plan are not as important as the idea, which has become ingrained in American social thought, that schooling is the best means of identifying democratic leadership. This idea assumes that the educational system is fair in its judgments. Fairness of selection assumes that judgment is based solely on talent demonstrated in school and not on other social factors such as race, religion, dress, and social class.

Besides educating political leadership, schools were called on to educate future citizens. However, opinions were divided on how this should be accomplished. Jefferson proposed a very limited education for the general citizenry. The three years of free education were to consist of instruction in reading, writing, and arithmetic. He did not believe people needed to be educated to be good citizens. He believed in the guiding power of natural reason to lead citizens to correct political decisions. Citizens were to receive their political education from reading newspapers published under laws protecting freedom of the press. Citizens would choose between competing political ideas found in newspapers. For Jefferson the most important political function of schools was teaching reading.

Interestingly, while Jefferson wanted political opinions to be formed in a free marketplace of ideas, he advocated censorship of political texts at the University of Virginia. These contradictory positions reflect an inherent problem in the use of schools to teach political ideas. There is always the temptation to limit political instruction to what one believes are correct political ideas.

In contrast to Jefferson, Horace Mann, often called the father of public schools, wanted to instill a common political creed in all students and an obligation and desire to vote as part of maintaining a republican form of government. Mann developed his educational ideas and his reputation as America's greatest educational leader while serving as secretary of the Massachusetts Board of Education from 1837 to 1848. Originally a lawyer, Mann gave up his legal career because he believed schooling and not law was the key to creating a good society.

Without commonly held political beliefs, Mann believed, society was doomed to political strife and chaos. According to Mann, it is necessary to teach the importance of using the vote, as opposed to revolution and violence, to bring about political change. This was an important issue during Mann's time because the extension of universal male suffrage took place in the 1820s. Before that time, the vote was restricted by property requirements. In reference to the vote replacing political violence, Mann stated: "Had the obligations of the future citizen been sedulously inculcated upon all children of this Republic, would the patriot have had to mourn over so many instances, where the voter, not being able to accomplish his purpose by voting, has proceeded to accomplish it by violence."

Also, Horace Mann worried that growing crime rates and social class conflict would lead to violence and mob rule. Commonly held political values along with belief in the power of the vote, Mann hoped, would maintain political order. For Mann, the important idea was that all children in society attend the same type of school. The school was to be common to all children. Within the public or common school, children of all religions and social classes were to share in a common education. Basic social disagreements would vanish as rich and poor children, and children whose parents were supporters of different political parties, mingled in the schoolroom.

Within the walls of the public schoolhouse students were to be taught the basic principles of a republican form of government. Mann assumed there was general agreement about the nature of these general political values and that they could be taught without objection from outside political groups. In fact, he opposed teaching politically controversial topics because he worried that conflicting political forces would destroy the public-school idea. The combination of social mingling in school and the teaching of a common political philosophy would establish, Mann hoped, shared political beliefs that would ensure the survival of the U.S. government. Political liberty would be possible, according to Mann's philosophy, because it would be restrained and controlled by the ideas students learned in public schools.

Is there a common set of political values in the United States? Since the nineteenth century, debates over the content of instruction have rocked the schoolhouse. Throughout the twentieth and twenty-first centuries, conservative and liberal political groups pressured local public schools to teach their respective political viewpoints.

SHOULD SCHOOLS TEACH POLITICAL VALUES AND PATRIOTISM?
There is a strong tradition of dissent to public schools teaching any political doctrines. Some argue that teaching of political ideas is a method of maintaining the political power of those in control of government. In the late eighteenth century, English political theorist William Godwin warned against national systems of education because they could become a means by which those controlling the government could control the minds of future citizens. Writing in 1793, Godwin stated, "Their views as institutors of a system of education will not fail to be analogous to their views in their political capacity: the data upon which their instructions are founded."

In addition to teaching political doctrines, the organizational features of schools were to instill political values. Simply defined, *socialization* refers to what students learn from following school rules, interacting with other students, and participating in school social events. Socialization can be contrasted with academic learning, which refers to classroom instruction, textbooks, and other forms of formal learning.

For some educational leaders, socialization is a powerful means of political control. Learning to obey school rules is socialization for obedience to government laws. Advocating the use of schools for political control, Johann Fichte, a Prussian leader in the early nineteenth century, wanted schools to prepare students for conformity to government regulations by teaching obedience to school rules and developing a sense of loyalty to the school. He argued that students will transfer their obedience to school rules to submission to government laws. According to Fichte, loyalty and service to the school and fellow students prepares citizens for service to the country. The school, according to Fichte, is a miniature community where children learn to adjust their individuality to the requirements of the community. The real work of the school, Fichte said, is shaping this social adjustment. A well-ordered government requires citizens to go beyond mere obedience to written constitutions and laws. Fichte believed children must see the government as something greater than the individual and must learn to sacrifice for the good of the social whole.

To achieve these political goals, Fichte recommended teaching patriotic songs, national history, and literature to increase a sense of dedication and patriotism to the government. This combination of socialization and patriotic teachings, he argued, would produce a citizen more willing and able to participate in the army and, consequently, would reduce the cost of national defense.

In the United States, patriotic exercises and fostering school spirit were emphasized after the arrival of large numbers of immigrants from southern and eastern Europe in the 1890s. In 1892, Francis Bellamy wrote the Pledge of Allegiance and introduced it in the same year to educators attending the annual meeting of the National Education Association (NEA). A socialist, Bellamy wanted to include the word "equality" in the Pledge, but this idea was rejected because state superintendents of education opposed equality for women and African Americans. The original Pledge of Allegiance was: "I pledge allegiance to my Flag and to the Republic for which it stands, one nation, indivisible, with liberty and justice for all." Bellamy's Pledge of Allegiance became popular classroom practice as educators worried about the loyalty of immigrant children.

In the 1920s, the American Legion and the Daughters of the American Revolution thought the Pledge's phrase "I pledge allegiance to my Flag" would be construed by immigrants to mean they could remain loyal to their former nations. Consequently, "my Flag" was replaced by "the flag of the United States." It was during this period that schools initiated Americanization programs that were precursors to current debates about immigrant education. Americanization programs taught immigrant children the laws, language, and customs of the United States. Naturally, this included teaching patriotic songs and stories. With the coming of World War I, the recitation of the Pledge of Allegiance, the singing of patriotic songs, participation in student government, and other patriotic exercises became a part of the American school. In addition, the development of extracurricular activities led to an emphasis on school spirit. The formation of football and basketball teams, with their accompanying trappings of cheerleaders and pep rallies, was to build school spirit and, consequently, prepare students for service to the nation.

In the 1950s, the Pledge of Allegiance underwent another transformation when some members of the U.S. Congress and religious leaders campaigned to stress the role of religion in government. In 1954, the phrase "under God" was added to the Pledge. The new Pledge referred to "one nation, under God." Congressional legislation supporting the change declared that the goal was to "acknowledge the dependence of our people and our Government upon . . . the Creator. . . [and] deny the atheistic and materialistic concept of communism." For similar reasons, Congress added the words "In God We Trust" to all paper money in 1955.

Reflecting the continuing controversy over the Pledge, a U.S. Court of Appeals ruled in 2002 that the phrase "one nation, under God" violated the U.S. Constitution's ban on government-supported religion. The decision was later dismissed by the U.S. Supreme Court because the father in the case did not have legal custody of his daughter for whom the case was originally brought. The suit was filed by Michael Newdow, the father of a second-grade student attending California's Elk Grove Unified School District. Newdow argued his daughter's First Amendment rights were violated because she was forced to "watch and listen as her state-employed teacher in her state-run school leads her classmates in a ritual proclaiming that there is a God, and ours is 'one nation under God.'" While the issue remains unresolved, the suit raised important questions about the Pledge of Allegiance.

In reaction to the Court's decision, Anna Quindlen wrote in the July 15, 2002, edition of *Newsweek*, "His [Bellamy's] granddaughter said he would have hated the addition of the words 'under God' to a statement he envisioned uniting a country divided by race, class and, of course, religion." Another dimension of the story was that Bellamy was a socialist during a period of greater political toleration than today. In contrast to the 1890s, today it would be difficult to find a professional educational organization that would allow an outspoken socialist to write its patriotic pledge.

On May 9, 2014, the Massachusetts Supreme Court ruled that "under God" in the Pledge of Allegiance did not discriminate against non-religious students. However, the ruling did recognize that the Pledge was voluntary according to a 1942 U.S. Supreme Court Decision *West Virginia State Board of Education v. Barnette.* In the 1942 decision a group of students refused to say the Pledge because it violated their religious beliefs against worshiping graven images. The U.S. Supreme court ruled that students could not be forced to say the Pledge and that it had to be voluntary. Many students are not told about this constitutional right in which they do not have to participate in saying the Pledge.

But the controversy over the Pledge has not ended. In 2017, a 17-year-old at Houston's Windfern High School was expelled for refusing to stand for the daily Pledge of Allegiance. The student's parents sued, and she was allowed to return to school. In 2018, a Waterbury, Connecticut, student sued her teacher for mocking and shaming her for refusing to stand for the Pledge of Allegiance in protest over racial injustice in the United States.

In conclusion, political education in American schools has consisted of teaching a national culture, performing patriotic exercises, political socialization through the life of the school, the study of government and national history, and the teaching of a dedication to voting as a means of social change. Like any other political agenda, political education in public schools is surrounded by controversy.

CENSORSHIP AND AMERICAN POLITICAL VALUES

What political values should be taught in public schools? Horace Mann assumed schools could just teach the basic principles of government free from controversy. Time has proved his assumption naïve as the schools became embroiled in censorship issues, textbook struggles, and court decisions about freedom of speech.

Textbooks are a traditional means of instilling political values. But, as I will describe, textbook content is highly politicized, with many conflicts over what values should appear on their pages. These controversies are highlighted by the state adoption policies in California and Texas and pressures on textbook publishers by special-interest groups. Oddly, given the struggle over their content, textbooks appear bland; history and civics texts often seem just plain boring and are often seen as compendiums of facts containing no political messages. In part, this appearance is caused by the wish of textbook publishers to avoid controversy. But embedded in the blandness are facts and ideas that are the product of a whole host of political debates and decisions.

Texas's textbook hearings are extremely important for publishers. This situation has changed in recent years as California is replacing textbooks with open source readers. This action is making Texas the major determiner of the content of textbooks. Texas represents 8 percent of the $2.2 billion national market in textbooks.

Texas's selection of textbooks is the most controversial. Writing for the *Washington Post* in 2014, Valerie Strauss stated, showing her bias against the board's actions, "Back in 2010, we had an uproar over proposed changes to social studies standards by religious conservatives on the State Board of Education, which included a bid to calling the United States' hideous slave trade history as the 'Atlantic triangular trade.' There were other doozies, too, such as one proposal to remove Thomas Jefferson from the Enlightenment curriculum and replace him with John Calvin."

Exemplifying the problem of finding common political values, the Texas State School Board was sued in 2003 for rejecting the textbook *Environmental Science: Creating a Sustainable Future* (sixth edition) by David D. Chiras. The board rejected the book for "promoting radical policies" and being "anti–free enterprise, and anti-American." In its place, the board chose a science textbook partially financed by a group of mining companies, according to the suit filed by Trial Lawyers for Public Justice, a Washington, DC-based public-interest law firm. The suit claimed the board's actions violated the free speech rights of Texas schoolchildren.

The suit reflects the continuing censorship issues surrounding the actions of the Texas State School Board. For instance, during the hot summer of 2002, the board began public hearings to select textbooks in history and social studies for its four million students. Texas's textbook hearings are notorious for their strident demands by opposing interest groups to add and delete material from textbooks. At the opening of the hearings in 2002, there already seemed to be agreement among board members not to select Pearson Prentice Hall's history text *Out of Many: A History of the American People* for advanced-placement classes despite its being a national best seller. The problem was two paragraphs dealing with prostitution in late-nineteenth-century cattle towns. "It makes it sound that every woman west of the Mississippi was a prostitute," said Grace Shore, the Republican chairwoman of the Texas State Board of Education. "The book says that there were 50,000 prostitutes west of the Mississippi. I doubt it, but even if there were, is that something that should be emphasized? Is that an important historical fact?"

During the hearings, *Out of Many: A History of the American People* was criticized not only for its section "Cowgirls and Prostitutes" but also for its mention of Margaret Sanger and the development of contraception and the gay rights movement. Complaining about the book's content, Peggy Venable, director of the Texas chapter of Citizens for a Sound Economy, said, "I don't mean that we should sweep things under the rug. But the children should see the hope and the good things about America."

In 2014, these concerns were answered by the Texas Freedom Network: Education in its report "Writing to the Standards: Reviews of Proposed Social Studies Textbooks for Texas Public Schools." The report criticized the Texas State Board of Education, citing a review from the "conservative" Thomas B. Fordham Institute that the Texas State Board of Education's guidelines for U.S. history provided a " 'politicized distortion of history' filled with 'misrepresentations at every turn.' " The report stated that these charges were collaborated by the Texas Higher Education Coordinating Board's Social Studies Faculty. Working with faculty and graduate students at Southern Methodist University in reviewing the work of the Texas State Board of Education and history textbooks, the Texas Freedom Network issued these concerns:

- A number of government and world history textbooks exaggerate Judeo-Christian influence on the nation's founding and Western political tradition.
- Two government textbooks include misleading information that undermines the constitutional concept of the separation of church and state.
- Several world history and world geography textbooks include biased statements that inappropriately portray Islam and Muslims negatively.
- All the world geography textbooks inaccurately downplay the role that conquest played in the spread of Christianity.
- Elements of the Texas curriculum standards give undue legitimacy to neo-Confederate arguments about "states' rights" and the legacy of slavery in the South.

In 2018, the Texas State Board of Education initially decided to eliminate discussions of Helen Keller and Hillary Clinton and retain an emphasis on how the biblical figure Moses influenced the founding fathers. After a firestorm of criticism, the board reversed its decision and kept lessons on Keller and Clinton along with Moses's influence. The Texas controversies highlight attempts to censor textbooks and ensure that the teaching of history reflects a particular political point of view.

COURTS AND POLITICAL VALUES

As noted in the previous section, teaching political values can generate conflict. Sometimes these issues have ended up in the courts. Court cases involve the "Free Speech Clause" of the First Amendment to the United States Constitution. As I discuss throughout this book, court decisions have a significant role in shaping school policies. The First Amendment states:

> Congress shall make no law respecting an establishment of religion [Establishment Clause], or prohibiting the free exercise [Free Exercise Clause] thereof; or abridging the freedom of speech [Free Speech Clause], or of the press; or the right of the people peaceably to assemble, and to petition the Government for a redress of grievances.

Our interest is the Free Speech Clause and its applicability to teaching political values.

One court case, *Board of Island Union Free School District v. Steven A. Pico* (1982), involved using a political agenda to remove books from the school library by the local board of education. Several board members attended a conference of a politically conservative organization concerned with school legislation in New York State. While they were at the conference, the board members received a list of books considered morally and politically inappropriate for high school students. Upon returning from the conference, the board members investigated the contents of their high school library and discovered nine books that were on the list. Subsequently, the board ordered the removal of the books from the library shelves. The books included *Best Short Stories of Negro Writers* edited by Langston Hughes, *Down These Mean Streets* by Piri Thomas, *The Fixer* by Bernard Malamud, *Go Ask Alice* of anonymous authorship, *A Hero Ain't Nothin' but a Sandwich* by Alice Childress, *Naked Ape* by Desmond Morris, *A Reader for Writers* by Jerome Archer, *Slaughterhouse Five* by Kurt Vonnegut Jr., and *Soul on Ice* by Eldridge Cleaver.

In its decision the U.S. Supreme Court gave full recognition to the power of school boards to select books for school libraries and to the importance of avoiding judicial interference in the operation of local school systems. On the other hand, the court recognized its obligation to ensure that public institutions do not suppress ideas. Here, there was a clear intention to suppress ideas by making decisions about book removal based on a list from a political organization.

The Supreme Court's method of handling this dilemma was to recognize the right of the school board to determine the content of the library if its decisions on content were not based on partisan or political motives. In the words of the court, "If a Democratic school board, motivated by party affiliation, ordered the removal of all books written by or in favor of Republicans, few would doubt that the order violated the constitutional rights of the students denied access to those books." In another illustration, the court argued, "The same conclusion would surely apply if an all-white school board, motivated by racial animus, decided to remove all books authored by blacks or advocating racial equality and integration." Or, as the court more simply stated, "Our Constitution does not permit the official suppression of ideas."

On the other hand, the court argued that books could be removed if the decision was based solely on their educational suitability. In summary, the court stated:

> We hold that local school boards may not remove books from school library shelves simply because they dislike the ideas contained in those books and seek by their removal to prescribe what shall be orthodox in politics, nationalism, religion, or other matters of opinion.

What about upholding the free speech rights of students? Certainly free speech is an important political value in the United States. *Tinker v. Des Moines Independent School District* (1969) is the landmark case involving free speech rights for students. The *Tinker* case originated when a group of students decided to express their objections to the war in Vietnam by wearing black armbands. School authorities in Des Moines adopted a policy that any student wearing an armband would be suspended. When the case was decided by the U.S. Supreme Court, clear recognition was given to the constitutional rights of students. The court stated that a student "may express his opinion, even on controversial subjects like the conflict in Vietnam. . . . Under our Constitution, free speech is not a right that is given only to be so circumscribed that it exists in principle but not in fact."

One extremely important condition placed on the right of free speech of students a is the possibility of disruption of the educational process. The court does not provide any specific guidelines for interpreting this condition and limitation. What it means is that school authorities have an obligation to protect the constitutional rights of students and, at the same time, an obligation to ensure there is no interference with the normal activities of the school.

In recent years, student rights were limited by claims of interference with the educational purposes and activities of schools. A federal appellate court ruled that a school administration can disqualify a student campaigning for student body president because of remarks about the vice principal and school administration. The appellate court reasoned that the administration's educational concerns allowed it to censor comments that might hurt the feelings of others. This form of censorship taught students to respect others.

In *Hazelwood School District v. Kuhlemier* (1988), the U.S. Supreme Court ruled that school administrators have the right to control the content of school-sponsored publications because they are part of the curriculum. The case involved a newspaper published by the journalism class at Missouri's Hazelwood High School. The newspaper contained articles about student pregnancies and students from divorced families. False names were used to protect the students interviewed for the articles. The school's principal objected to the articles because the interviewed students might be identifiable to other students, and he considered the sexual discussions inappropriate for high school students. The authors of the articles responded that both divorce and pregnancy were appropriate topics for modern youth and that they were widely discussed among students.

The right of school administrators to censor student publications was expanded to include all school activities. School administrators have the right to refuse to produce student plays, to prohibit student publication of articles that are poorly written or vulgar, and to ban student expression that advocates drugs, alcohol, or permissive sex. In censorship cases of this type, the legal test is whether the school administration's actions are based on legitimate educational concerns.

School authorities are allowed to punish student speech they consider to be lewd and indecent. In *Bethel v. Fraser* (1986), the U.S. Supreme Court ruled that school administrators in the Bethel, Washington, school system could punish a high school senior, Matthew Fraser, for giving a nominating speech at a school assembly that used an "elaborate, graphic, and explicit sexual metaphor." The court said that school officials have the right to determine what is vulgar and offensive in the classroom and at school activities and to prohibit vulgar and offensive speech. This decision did not apply to speech about political, religious, educational, and public policy issues; it was limited to the issue of indecent speech.

Even patriotic exercises are subject to court rulings. Some religious groups object to pledging allegiance to a flag because they believe it is worship of a graven image. In *West Virginia State Board of Education v. Barnette* (1943), the U.S. Supreme Court ruled that expelling children of Jehovah's Witnesses for not saluting the flag was a violation of their constitutional right to freedom of religion. Some teachers view patriotic exercises as contrary to the principles of a free society.

In summary, contrary to Horace Mann's original hope, finding common and agreed-upon political values to be taught in public schools has been difficult. As we shall see in the next section, this problem has extended to finding common political values to include in state and national education standards.

U.S. SECRETARY OF EDUCATION BETSY DEVOS: FREE ENTERPRISE AND EDUCATING FOR A MORAL SOCIETY

President Donald Trump's secretary of education, Betsy DeVos, exemplifies the effect of religious, political, and economic goals with how schools should be organized. DeVos wants a more moral society, which, she believes, can be achieved by allowing religious-oriented charter schools to compete in an unregulated education marketplace. Quality schools would emerge, according to her argument, as parents voted with their feet. Schools that didn't attract parental support would close, and those that were attractive would remain. Competition would teach children the value of the free market while allowing religious-oriented charter schools to expand.

The concern about religion and free enterprise in education were central to DeVos's education work prior to her appointment as U.S. secretary of education. Born Betsy Prince, she attended Michigan Christian schools: the Holland Christian School and Calvin College. The Holland Christian School's mission is to educate students to be:

> **"Biblically Discerning**—Possess a knowledge of God's Word; understand and are able to defend a Biblical worldview; able to critically evaluate the current culture in light of God's Word.
>
> **Spiritually Growing**—Have a vibrant, growing relationship with God the Father, Son, and Holy Spirit. Understand their God-given design and desire to serve Jesus Christ in whatever they do."

Calvin College proclaims: "Calvin's identity is a Christian academic community dedicated to rigorous intellectual inquiry."

Betsy and her husband, Richard DeVos, established the Dick and Betsy DeVos Family Foundation in 1992, which in turn created the American Foundation for Children. The major goal of the American Foundation for Children was supporting state legislators who advocate school choice plans using vouchers, tuition tax credits, education savings accounts, and the expansion of charter schools, especially for-profit charter schools.

School choice would allow parents to choose the schools their children attend and to pay for their children's education using either a voucher supplied by the state or local school system or money deposited by the state in an education savings account. Another option was getting education expenses returned to parents as a tuition tax credit on their state or federal taxes. Within this system, parents could choose a standard public school, a charter school, a private school, or a for-profit school. Charter schools are created by the state government and operate outside the control of local school districts and are an important element in most choice plans. Charter schools, depending on state regulations, can create their own curricula, including religious-oriented curricula—again limited by particular state regulations.

The couple's combined inheritances paid for the Dick and Betsy DeVos Family Foundation. Richard DeVos inherited part of the Amway fortune of $5.1 billion from his father, Richard DeVos Sr. Betsy (Prince) DeVos received an inheritance from her father's estate of $1.35 billion. "The couple," according to one report, "gave $5.2 million to the foundation in 2002, $10 million in 2003 and $14 million in 2004." Dick DeVos said, "We have not hidden the fact by laying out in our disclosure that we have been blessed financially. Part of that responsibility is to be a blessing to others."

The advocacy of school choice reflected Richard DeVos's dedication to free-market economics. In addition, school choice would, they hope, allow parents to choose Christian-oriented schools. Richard DeVos's support of school choice and for-profit schools is reflected in his attendance of Michigan's Northwood University, where he funded a school of management named after him. The stated mission of the university is: "To develop the future leaders of a global, free-enterprise society. We believe in: The advantages of an entrepreneurial, free-enterprise society. . . . The Northwood idea: Bringing the lessons of the America free-enterprise society into the college classroom."

The idea of for-profit schools competing in a marketplace supported by government funds, particularly as vouchers or as charter schools, was highlighted by President Donald Trump's speech on September 8, 2016, at the for-profit charter school Cleveland Arts and Social Science Academy. In the speech, President Trump praised the owner, Ron Packard, as representing the entrepreneurial spirit behind for-profit charter schools.

Describing Donald Trump's selection of Betsy DeVos as secretary of education, New York University historian Kim Phillips-Fein stated, "They [Betsy DeVos and husband Richard DeVos] have this moralized sense of the free market that leads to this total program to turn back the ideas of the New Deal, the welfare state." As reported in *New York* magazine, Betsy DeVos believes a free-market ideology can "advance God's kingdom."

U.S. Secretary of Education Betsy DeVos's advocacy of free markets for schools received support from Vice President Mike Pence, who, as governor of Indiana in 2012, greatly expanded the voucher system created by his predecessor, Governor Mitch Daniels. Under Daniels, a student receiving a voucher for 90 percent of a private school tuition had to be from a low-income family as determined by eligibility for free or reduced lunch. When Governor Pence took office, he worked to expand vouchers to cover 50 percent of private school tuition for families earning $67,000 to $90,000, with no limits on the number of private school vouchers that could be issued.

In keeping with free-market theory, Betsy DeVos supported unregulated charter schools in Detroit, Michigan. DeVos backed 2010 Michigan legislation expanding the number of charter schools. She helped block legislation that would have kept failing charter schools from expanding or being replicated. In 2016, Secretary DeVos was described as a chief force in defeating Michigan legislation for state standards to identify and close failing charter schools. DeVos's vision was of charter schools opening and closing according to the demands of parental choice in a free market.

This free-market vision included for-profit schools, with 80 percent of Detroit, Flint, and Grand Rapids charter schools operating in 2016 as for-profit. According to *New York Times* reporter Kate Zernike, in defeating Michigan legislation to regulated charter schools, "Ms. DeVos argued that this kind of oversight would create too much bureaucracy and limit choice. A believer in a freer market than even some free market economists would endorse, Ms. DeVos pushed back on any regulation as too much regulation. Charter schools should be allowed to operate as they wish; parents would judge with their feet."

The DeVos-Michigan model of unregulated free-market competition between charter schools would, of course, undermine traditional public schools referred to by President Trump as "failing government schools." Tonya Allen, the president of the Skillman Foundation, a nonprofit that works with Detroit children, described DeVos: "She is committed to an ideological stance that is solely about the free market, at the expense of practicality and the basic needs of students in the most destabilized environment in the country." This free-market position led Randi Weingarten, the president of the American Federation of Teachers, to call Ms. DeVos "the most ideological, anti-public education nominee" for education secretary since the position was first created in the 1970s.

THE FRUITS OF POLITICAL EDUCATION

Horace Mann considered voting the most important political act because it protected orderly change in contrast to revolution. It could be argued that the effect of citizenship education might be measured by the simple act of voting. Voting is the most fundamental act of political participation in a democracy. Has schooling increased political participation as reflected in voter turnout at elections?

Given its commitment to education, why does the United States have one of the lowest voter turnouts among industrialized nations? Is there a relationship between schooling and voting? In highly developed, democratic states, according to the Pew Research Center, the United States is

26th out of 32 countries in voter turnout. The countries with the highest turnouts of voting age populations are Belgium (87.2%), Sweden (82.6%), Denmark (80.3%), and Australia (78.9%). In comparison, only 55.7% of the United States' voting age population voted in 2016.

It is difficult to separate the effect of schooling on voter turnout rates from other influences such as media, family, friends, community, and other social organizations and groups. These other influences make it almost impossible to establish a causal relationship between the influence of a public-school education and voting or not voting. However, one could hypothesize that the expansion of public schools might lead to greater voter turnout rates.

In examining this issue, let's first look at the history of school attendance in the United States. Government records on school attendance are available since 1868 and are partially represented in Table 1.1. While the historical Table 1.1 only includes up to 2004–2005, the most recent figures provided by National Center for Education Statistics in *The Condition of Education 2016* is: "In 2014, some 93 percent of 5- to 6-year-olds and 98 percent of 7- to 13-year-olds were enrolled in elementary or secondary school." *The Condition of Education 2018* reported using different parameters: "Between October 2000 and October 2016, the enrollment rate for students ages 5–6, who are typically enrolled in kindergarten or grade 1, decreased from 96 to 93 percent. In contrast, the enrollment rate increased during this period for students ages 18–19 in secondary education (from 16 to 19 percent) and did not change measurably for students ages 3–4, 7–13, 14–15, and 16–17."

Table 1.1 School Enrollment and Average Days of Attendance, 1868–2004

Years	Enrollment as a Percentage of 5- to 17-Year-Olds (%)	Average Number of Days Attended per Pupil
1869–1870	64.7	78.4
1899–1900	71.9	99.0
1919–1920	78.3	121.2
1939–1940	84.4	151.7
1959–1960	82.2	160.2
1979–1980	86.6	160.8
1999–2000	88.7	169.2
2004–2005	91.9	Not Available

Source: Adapted from National Center for Education Statistics, *Digest of Education Statistics*, "Table 33: Historical Summary of Public Elementary and Secondary School Statistics for Selected Years 1868–70 through 2006–07." Retrieved from http://nces.ed.gov/programs/digest/d09/tables/dt09_033.asp on 5 August 2010.

Table 1.1, adapted from the historical statistics provided by the U.S. government's *Digest of Educational Statistics*, shows the percentage of 5- to 17-year-olds attending school and the average days of attendance. If public schools are actually educating students for political engagement, one might assume that as the number of 5- to 17-year-olds attending school increases and more time is spent in school, voter participation would also increase.

According to Table 1.1, there has been significant growth in school attendance and days in school since 1869, when 64.7 percent of 5- to 17-year-olds were in school for an average of 78.4 days. By 1999 the percentage of pupils in school jumped to 88.7 percent for 5- to 17-year-olds, and attendance increased to an average of 169.2 days. According to our hypothesis, increased school attendance and more days in school should result in larger voter turnout rates. But this doesn't seem to be the case according to voter turnout rates, as seen in Table 1.2.

While Table 1.2 only includes records up to 2004, the percentage of eligible voters voting in 2016 according to the United States Election Project was around 60 percent.

Table 1.2 Voter Turnout in Presidential Elections: Select Years 1824–2004

Year	Total Voting Age Population	Turnout	Percentage Voting of Voting Age Population (%)
1824			26.9
1828			57.6
1832			55.4
1840			80.2
1852			69.6
1860			81.2
1872			71.3
1880			79.4
1892			74.7
1900			73.2
1912			58.8
1920			49.2
1932			56.9
1940			62.5
1952			63.3
1960	109,672,000	68,838,204	62.77
1964	114,090,000	70,644,592	61.92

Year	Total Voting Age Population	Turnout	Percentage Voting of Voting Age Population (%)
1968	120,328,186	73,211,875	60.84
1972	140,776,000	77,718,554	55.21
1976	152,309,190	81,555,789	53.55
1980	. 164,597,000	86,515,221	52.56
1984	174,468,000	92,652,680	53.11
1988	182,630,000	91,594,693	50.15
1992	189,044,500	104,405,155	55.23
1996	196,511,000	96,456,345	49.08
2000	205,815,000	105,586,274	51.30
2004	221,256,931	122,295,345	55.27

Source: Adapted from the American Presidency Project, Voter Turnout in Presidential Elections. Retrieved from www.presidency.ucsb.edu/data/turnout.php on 5 August 2010.

Table 1.2, derived from the American Presidency Project (www.americanpresidency.org) at the University of California–Santa Barbara, compiles statistics on voter participation beginning in 1824. Of course, measuring voter participation before the Voting Rights Act of 1965, which eliminated barriers to voting by minority groups in the United States and particularly African Americans, is difficult. In addition, women did not gain the right to vote until 1920 with the ratification of the Nineteenth Amendment to the U.S. Constitution.

Keeping these issues in mind, it is possible to reach some tentative understanding of voter participation in national elections since 1824 as represented in Table 1.2. Surprisingly, only 26.9 percent of the voting age population participated in 1824. This figure jumped to 57.6 percent in 1828 with the largest percentage of voter participation in presidential elections occurring from 1840 (80.2 percent) to 1900 (73.2 percent). After 1900, voter participation plummeted to 49.2 percent in 1920 before rising to 62.77 percent in 1960. Again, it must be noted that these figures do not necessarily represent citizens interested in voting since many citizens were discouraged or kept from voting by discriminatory state laws until the 1965 Voting Rights Act. Despite this act, however, voter participation in presidential elections since 1965 fell from 60.84 percent in 1968 to 49.08 percent in 1996 before rising to 55.27 percent in 2004. This would indicate that a relatively high percentage of eligible voters during this period (from 50.92 percent to 44.73 percent) did not exercise their political right to vote for the president of the United States. Why? Did schools fail in their goal of political education? Or could it be that school attendance does *not* affect voter participation rates?

When combining some of the data in Tables 1.1 and 1.2, there appears to be little effect on voter participation rates from increased schooling. In fact, voter participation rates declined from 1900 as school attendance and days in school increased. Since 1900 voter participation rates declined from 73.2 percent to a low point of 49.08 percent in 1996 while school attendance for 5- to 17-year-olds increased from 71.9 percent in 1900 to 88.7 percent in 1999. During the same period the average number of days attended per pupil increased from 99 to 169.2.

In other words, voter participation rates actually declined as more people attended school for longer periods of time! A causal relationship cannot be established; there is no proof that attending school results in less political engagement through voting. However, there appears to be little effect from school attendance or time in school on increased citizen participation in voting.

What about the civic knowledge of public-school students? In 1999 the International Association for the Evaluation of Educational Achievement (IEA) assessed the civic knowledge of ninth-grade students in 29 countries. American students ranked sixth compared to students in the other nations. Table 1.3 provides the international rankings.

Table 1.3 Average Total Civic Knowledge Achievement of Ninth-Grade Students by Nation, 1999

Nation	Average Score
Poland	111
Finland	109
Cyprus	108
Greece	108
Hong Kong (SAR)	107
United States	106
Italy	105
Slovak Republic	105
Norway	103
Czech Republic	103
Hungary	102
Australia	102
Slovenia	101
International average	100
Denmark	100
Germany	100
Russian Federation	100
England	99

Nation	Average Score
Sweden	99
Switzerland	98
Bulgaria	98
Portugal	96
Belgium (French)	95
Estonia	94
Lithuania	94
Romania	92
Latvia	92
Chile	88
Colombia	86

Source: Stephane Baldi, et al., *What Democracy Means to Ninth-Graders: U.S. Results from the International IEA Civic Education Study* (Washington, DC: U.S. Department of Education, April 2001), p. 14.

This study demonstrates that American students do quite well when tested for civic knowledge. But does this create a disposition to actively engage in political activities? While ninth-grade American students affirmed the importance of voting, the study questioned this as an indicator of future voting. The study's report states, "Overall, most students thought that voting in every election and showing respect for government leaders were the two most important factors in being good citizens. . . . *These results seem at odds with the fact that a relatively low percentage of adults typically do vote in elections in the United States*" (emphasis in original).

The study also found that the majority of American students defined good citizenship as "respect for authority and obedience to the law." This is a passive concept of citizenship in contrast to an active concept of citizenship. Active citizenship involves participation in political movements and organizations and community activities.

What are the fruits of the political goals for American schools? There seems to be little relationship between school attendance and voter turnout. While American students compare well to other nations in civic knowledge, their concept of good citizenship is primarily passive— respect and obedience. Does this mean that American public schools are educating a large number of citizens who will not vote and who do not believe good citizenship involves active participation in civic and political life? Is the major accomplishment of the political goals of American schools an inactive citizen who demonstrates little civic responsibility but who is obedient to authority and the law? Is this the meaning of a democratic education?

CONCLUSION

Political education in American schools is plagued by controversies over its content. Also, a large percentage of school graduates do not vote despite this being a central creed of civic education. Many students seem to leave school with a concept of citizenship focused on obedience to the law and authority in contrast to community activism. In considering these issues, the reader might ask the following questions:

- Should there be a consensus of political values in the United States, and should public schools develop that consensus?
- Should the public schools develop emotional or patriotic attachments to symbols of the state through the use of songs, literature, and history?
- Should the purpose of teaching history be the development of patriotic feelings?
- Does the teaching of patriotism in schools throughout the world increase the potential for international conflict?
- Who or what government agency should determine the political values taught in public schools?

SUGGESTED READINGS AND WORKS CITED IN CHAPTER

American Presidency Project. www.presidency.ucsb.edu/. An important source of information on presidential elections, including party platforms, voter turnout, and speeches.

Baldi, Stephane, et al. *What Democracy Means to Ninth-Graders: U.S. Results from the International IEA Civic Education Study*. Washington, DC: U.S. Department of Education, April 2001. Important summary of the civic knowledge and attitudes among multinational students.

Borja, Rhea. "Pledge of Allegiance in the Legal Spotlight." *Education Week* (July 10, 2002). This article details the 2002 court decision that declared the phrase "one nation, under God" a violation of the ban on a government-established religion.

Calvin College. *Who We Are*. https://calvin.edu/about/who-we-are/ on November 29, 2016.

Cremin, Lawrence. *The Republic and the School*. New York: Teachers College Press, 1957. This is a good selection of Horace Mann's writings taken from his reports to the Massachusetts Board of Education and a good introduction to the social and political purposes of American education.

Delfattore, Joan. *What Johnny Shouldn't Read: Textbook Censorship in America*. New Haven, CT: Yale University Press, 1992. Delfattore discusses the Hawkins County, Tennessee, protest by evangelical Christians over the content of school textbooks. Her book also covers other major censorship conflicts.

DeSilver, Drew. "U.S. Trails Most Developed Countries in Voter Turnout." *Pew Research Center* (May 21, 2018). www.pewresearch.org/fact-tank/2018/05/21/u-s-voter-turnout-trails-most-developed-countries.

Fitzgerald, Frances. *America Revised: History Schoolbooks in the Twentieth Century*. Boston: Little, Brown, 1979. Fitzgerald depicts the major debates and changes in content of public-school history texts.

Goldstein, Dana. "Are Civics Lessons a Constitutional Right? These Students Are Suing for Them." *The New York Times* (November 28, 2018). www.nytimes.com/2018/11/28/us/

civics-rhode-island-schools.html. Many see the lack of civics in schools as a national crisis. A federal lawsuit says it also violates the law.

Greenberg, David. *History Lesson: The Pledge of Allegiance*. www.slate.msn.com (June 28, 2002). This article provides a history of the Pledge of Allegiance from its origin in 1892 to the present.

Hoffman, Kathy Barks. "Dick DeVos and Wife Give Millions to Own Foundation." *AP vis MLive* (April 21, 2006). http://209.157.64.200/focus/f-news/1618311/posts?page=1 on December 11, 2016.

Holland Christian Schools. *Mission and Beliefs*. www.hollandchristian.org/about-us/mission-and-beliefs/ on November 29, 2016.

Jefferson, Thomas. *Notes on the State of Virginia*. New York: Penguin Books, 1998. Contains Jefferson's proposal for schooling.

Kaestle, Carl. *Pillars of the Republic: Common Schools and American Society, 1780–1860*. New York: Hill and Wang, 1983. This is currently the best history of the common-school movement.

Lee, Gordon. *Crusade Against Ignorance: Thomas Jefferson on Education*. New York: Teachers College Press, 1961. This collection of statements by Jefferson on education has a good introductory essay.

McCready, Brian. "Student Protests Pledge of Allegiance, Sues Teacher." *Patch* (October 18, 2018). https://patch.com/connecticut/across-ct/student-protests-pledge-allegiance-sues-teacher-patch-pm. Continuing protests over the Pledge of Allegiance.

McInerny, Claire. "Five Years Later, Indiana's Voucher Program Functions Very Differently." *State Impact: A Reporting Project of WFIU & WTIU with Support from IPBS* (August 19, 2016). http://indianapublicmedia.org/stateimpact/2016/08/19/years-indianas-voucher-program-functions-differently/ on December 1, 2016.

McKinley, James C., Jr. "Texas Approves Curriculum Revised by Conservatives." *The New York Times on the Web* (March 12, 2010). www.nytimes.com. News article on Texas controversy over textbook contents.

———. "Texas Conservatives Seek Deeper Stamp on Texts." *The New York Times on the Web* (March 10, 2010). www.nytimes.com. News article on Texas controversy over textbook contents.

Mintz, Steven. *Huck's Raft: A History of American Childhood*. Cambridge, MA: Harvard University Press, 2004. This history of American childhood discusses the transition from concepts of "protected childhood" to "prepared childhood."

National Center for Education Statistics. *The Condition of Education 2016*. Washington, DC: U.S. Department of Education, 2016. Report gives current school enrollments.

———. *The Condition of Education 2018*. Washington, DC: U.S Department of Education, 2018. Report gives current school enrollments.

———. *Digest of Education Statistics*. http://nces.ed.gov/programs/digest/d09/tables/dt09_033.asp. The annual digest of education statistics is an important source of information about American schools.

Northwood University. *About Northwood*. www.northwood.edu/about/index.aspx on November 29, 2016.

Perkinson, Henry. *The Imperfect Panacea: American Faith in Education, 1865–1965*. New York: Random House, 1968. This is a study of attempts to use the school to solve major social problems in the United States.

Quindlen, Anna. "Indivisible? Wanna Bet?" *Newsweek* (July 15, 2002), p. 64. Quindlen argues that the phrase "under God" in the Pledge of Allegiance violates the original intention of its author, Francis Bellamy, and the First Amendment.

Reid, Brad. "Massachusetts Supreme Court Decides Pledge of Allegiance Case." *Huffington Post* (May 12, 2014). www.huffingtonpost.com/brad-reid/massachusetts-supreme-cou_b_5311538.html. This article discusses the Massachusetts decision on the Pledge of Allegiance and other associated cases, such as *West Virginia State Board of Education v. Barnette*.

Robelen, Erik W. "History a Flash Point as States Debate Standards." *Education Week on the Web* (March 25, 2010). www.edweek.org. A news article on the debate over history standards.

Rubin, David. *The Rights of Teachers*. New York: Avon, 1972. This is the American Civil Liberties Union handbook of teachers' rights.

Stille, Alexandra. "Textbook Publishers Learn to Avoid Messing with Texas." *The New York Times on the Web* (June 29, 2002). www.nytimes.com. This article discusses the struggle over the content of history and science textbooks before the Texas State Board of Education.

Strauss, Valerie. "Proposed Texas Textbooks Are Inaccurate, Biased and Politicized, New Report Finds." *Washington Post* (September 12, 2014). www.washingtonpost.com/blogs/answer-sheet/wp/2014/09/12/proposed-texas-textbooks-are-inaccurate-biased-and-politicized-new-report-finds/. This article details the censoring of textbooks in Texas.

Superville, Denisa R. "Amid Backlash, Colo. Board Rethinks U.S. History Review." *Education Week on the Web* (October 3, 2014). www.edweek.org/ew/articles/2014/10/03/07jeffco.h34.html?qs=amid+backlash. Story covers the controversy over the board of education's efforts to revise Advanced Placement U.S. History to include more patriotism and less about social action for change.

Tabor, Nick, and James Walsh. "Government by Gazillionaires: Betsy DeVos." *New York* (January 23–February 5, 2017), p. 31.

Texas Freedom Network. *Writing to the Standards: Reviews of Proposed Social Studies Textbooks for Texas Public Schools*. www.tfn.org/site/DocServer/FINAL_executivesummary.pdf?docID=4625. This report criticizes the history curriculum and textbook selections made by the Texas State Board of Education.

United States Election Project. *2016 November Election Turnout Rates*. www.electproject.org/2016g on March 5, 2017.

U.S. Department of Education. *A Guide to Education and No Child Left Behind*. Washington, DC: Education Publications Center, 2004. This is the official government guide to No Child Left Behind.

Weeks, J. Devereux. *Student Rights Under the Constitution: Selected Federal Decisions Affecting the Public School Community*. Athens: University of Georgia Press, 1992. This is a guide to student rights under the U.S. Constitution.

Zernike, Kate. "How Trump's Education Nominee Bent Detroit to Her Will on Charter Schools." *New York Times* (December 12, 2016). www.nytimes.com/2016/12/12/us/politics/betsy-devos-how-trumps-education-nominee-bent-detroit-to-her-will-on-charter-schools.html?rref=collection%2Fsectioncollection%2Fus&action=click&contentCollection=us&region=rank&module=package&version=highlights&contentPlacement=2&pgtype=sectionfront&_r=0 on December 14, 2016.

———. "Trump's Education Pick, Has Steered Money from Public Schools." *New York Times* (November 23, 2016). www.nytimes.com/2016/11/23/us/politics/betsy-devos-trumps-education-pick-has-steered-money-from-public-schools.html?ref=todayspaper&_r=0 on December 1, 2016.

CHAPTER 2

The Social Goals of Schooling

As I discussed in Chapter 1, the early goals of public schooling included moral instruction as a means of reducing crime. Horace Mann believed crime could be reduced by moral instruction in schools. He asserted that there was one experiment society had not tried in its attempt to control crime: "It is an experiment which, even before its inception, offers the highest authority for its ultimate success. Its formula is intelligible to all; and it is as legible as though written in starry letters on an azure sky." This formula, and the key to the good society, he stated, was "best expressed in these few and simple words:—*'Train up a child in the way he should go, and when he is old he will not depart from it.'*" Later, this approach to controlling crime was referred to as putting a police person in every child's heart. Mann even suggested that America might see the day when schooling would significantly reduce the number of police required by society.

Horace Mann also hoped to break down the barriers between the rich and poor by mixing students in a common classroom and school. Mann worried that the beginnings of industrial development in the early nineteenth century would create a major divide between the rich and poor. Writing in the Twelfth Annual Report about industrial development in Massachusetts, he wondered: "Are we not in danger of . . . those hideous evils which are always engendered between Capital and Labor, when all the capital is in the hands of one class and all the labor is thrown upon another?" He argued that if one class possesses all the wealth and education, and the other is poor and ignorant, then the latter will be "servile dependents and subjects of the former." Mann answered, "Now, surely nothing but Universal Education can counter-work this tendency to the domination of capital and servility of labor."

He believed two alternatives existed for eliminating antagonism between rich and poor. The first was to eliminate the friction between these two groups by mixing their children in the schoolhouse and classroom. The second was expanding a sense of community that would encompass the rich and poor. He wrote, "The spread of education, by enlarging the cultivated class or caste, will open a wider area over which the social feelings will expand; and, if this education should be universal and complete, it would do more than all things else to obliterate factitious distinctions in society."

At the time, Mann's idea of uniting the community through social mixing in classrooms and schools was seriously limited by the existence of slavery, the denial of citizenship to Native Americans, and discrimination against Mexican Americans after the Mexican-American War in 1848. These divisions in American society became a focus of school reform during the civil rights movement of the 1950s and 1960s. Prior to the civil rights era, the existence of school segregation and discrimination made it impossible to actually use the school to break down social divisions and create a sense of community.

As noted in Chapter 1, the social functions of the school expanded between the 1880s and the 1920s, turning it into a general welfare institution. Under the slogan "the whole child goes to school," public schools assumed responsibility for students' recreation by building playgrounds and creating after-school programs. Health issues became important, with schools hiring school nurses and, in some cases, doctors and dentists. Health concerns resulted in schools monitoring student cleanliness and even providing school showers. Diet became an important issue with schools creating cafeterias and providing instruction on healthy foods in home economics courses. Also, the initiations of home economics courses were to reform home life, providing a better climate for raising children. Schools attempted to control adolescent sexuality through the institution of sex education courses.

A great fear during this period was the breakdown of community in urban settings. School leaders called upon the school to become the new social center of community life, resulting in the building of school auditoriums that could be used for community events and the opening of schools to adult activities in the evening. In addition, junior and senior high schools in the 1920s organized extracurricular activities to create a spirit of school community. John Dewey, the great educational philosopher of the period, explained the new social functions of the school to educators who gathered in 1902 for the annual convention of the National Education Association. He told school people from around the country that education must provide a "means for bringing people and their ideas and beliefs together, in such ways as will lessen friction and instability, and introduce deeper sympathy and wider understanding." Using the schools as social centers, he argued, would morally uplift the quality of urban living by replacing brothels, saloons, and dance halls as centers of recreation. The school as social center, Dewey told his audience, "must interpret to [the worker] the intellectual and social meaning of the work in which he is engaged: that is, must reveal its relations to the life and work of the world." For Dewey, therefore, the new role of the school was to serve as an agency providing social services and a social center.

As a result of the school becoming a welfare agency, it became the symbol and hope for achieving the good society. This hope is best illustrated by a story told to kindergartners in the early twentieth century about two children who bring a beautiful flower from their school class to their dirty and dark tenement apartment. Their mother places the flower in a glass of water near a dirty window. She decides the flower needs more light to expose its beauty. The mother cleans the window, allowing more light into the apartment, which illuminates the dirty floors, walls, and furniture. The added light sends the mother scurrying around to clean up the now-exposed dirt. In the meantime, the father, who is unemployed because of a drinking problem, returns to the apartment and is amazed to find his grim dwelling transformed into a clean and tidy house. The transformation of the apartment results in the father wanting to spend more time at home and less time at the local bar. The father's drinking problem is solved, he is able to find work, and the family lives happily ever after. This story characterizes the hope that the social influence of the school will penetrate the homes and neighborhoods of America.

In summary, the social goals of American public schools include:

- Regulating sexuality through sex education courses
- Reducing crime through moral instruction and character education
- Improving children's health with school nurses, doctors, and dentists; regulating student's cleanliness; and providing health instruction
- Improving the nutrition of students with school cafeterias and home economics instruction
- Creating a sense of community through after-school programs and extracurricular activities and building school spirit

THE PROBLEM OF DETERMINING MORAL VALUES: RELIGION AND SECULARISM

If you want to start an argument in your local community, ask people what they think should be the treatment of transgender students and what should be taught in sex education. Most often, the answers reflect a person's religious orientation. For instance, consider the following situation that occurred in 2018 when a Virginia high school teacher was fired for refusing to use a transgender student's preferred pronoun. As reported in the *Virginian-Pilot*:

> After a contentious, five-hour hearing, the [West Point school] board voted 5–0 to support the school superintendent's recommendation, saying Peter Vlaming's actions harassed and discriminated against the student and were insubordinate. Vlaming had been on administrative leave since Oct. 31 [2018] for refusing to use the ninth-grade student's preferred male pronoun, citing his own religious beliefs. Vlaming, 47, taught French at the division for seven years.

Do you believe public-school teachers should be required to violate their religious beliefs to conform to school policies? Horace Mann proposed teaching the moral values common to most Christian denominations. A variety of religious groups disagreed with his ideas. The Catholic Church, the largest single religious group to reject Mann's plan, established its own system of schools. Catholic Church leaders argued that education was fundamentally religious when it involved shaping behavior and that it was impossible for public schools to teach moral values that reflected the views of all religious groups. Even if the public school eliminated all religious and moral teaching, this alternative could not be accepted because education would then become irreligious.

Mann's hope of eliminating crime through moral instruction in public schools received further support in the late nineteenth century. Writing in the 1890s, sociologist Edward Ross referred to education as a key mechanism for *social control*. Social control, as he used the term, referred to how a society maintained order and controlled crime and rebellion. He divided social control into external and internal. External social control involved the police and military regulating social behavior. Internal social control involved people controlling their own behaviors according to moral values. Traditionally, he argued, families, churches, and communities taught children moral values and social responsibility. In modern society, Ross declared, the family and church were being replaced by the school as the most important institution for instilling values. Ross saw reliance on education for control becoming characteristic of American society. "The ebb of religion is only half a fact," Ross wrote. "The other half is the high tide of education. While the priest is leaving the civil service, the schoolmaster is coming in. As the state shakes itself loose from the church, it reaches out for the school."

Essentially, Ross advocated teaching secular values that would not be associated with any religion. By the late twentieth and early twenty-first centuries some religious groups would object to this approach, calling it secular humanism. From the perspective of these groups, the teaching of moral values should not be separated from religious doctrine.

Until the 1960s many parents and school people assumed that moral and character education in public schools would be based on values related to Christianity. Many public schools prior to the 1960s began the school day with a prayer and a reading from the Bible. Things changed dramatically when the U.S. Supreme Court ruled that school prayer and Bible reading were unconstitutional. The result was a flurry of activity by those claiming that schools had become antireligious and those promoting secular values. The school prayer and Bible decisions spawned a religiously conservative movement focused on ensuring that religious values were reflected in school instruction.

The U.S. Supreme Court's 1962 school-prayer decision *Engel v. Vitale* denied the right of a public-school system to conduct prayer services within school buildings during regular school hours. The school-prayer case began when the New York Board of Regents granted a local school system the right to have a brief prayer said in each class at the beginning of the school day. The prayer, considered denominationally neutral, read, "Almighty God, we acknowledge our dependence upon Thee, and we beg Thy blessings upon us, our parents, our teachers and our country." The New York courts granted the right of local school systems to use this prayer. The one requirement was that they could not compel students to say the prayer if they or their parents objected.

The U.S. Supreme Court overturned the rulings of the New York courts in *Engel v. Vitale*. One major objection of the U.S. Supreme Court was that government officials wrote the prayer. This seemed to put the government directly in the business of establishing religion. The court stated that "in this country it is not part of the business of government to compose official prayers for any group of the American people to recite as a part of the religious program carried on by government." The court reviewed the early history of the United States and the struggle for religious freedom and the ending of government support of churches. The court argued: "By the time of the adoption of the Constitution, our history shows that there was a widespread awareness among many Americans of the dangers of a union of Church and State." The writing of a prayer by government officials ran counter to this long-standing struggle in the United States.

The U.S. Supreme Court rejected the argument that the school-prayer law did not violate any rights because it did not require students to recite the prayer and the prayer was nondenominational. The court argued that this confused the right of free exercise of religion with the prohibition against the state establishing and supporting religion. Excusing students from reciting the prayer might protect their free exercise of religion, but the very existence of the prayer involved the establishment of religion.

In 1963, the court applied the same reasoning to the issue of Bible reading in the public schools. In *Abington School District v. Schempp,* the issue was a Pennsylvania law that permitted the reading of 10 verses from the Bible at the opening of each public-school day. The verses were to be read without comment, and any child could be excused from reading the verses or attending the Bible reading upon the written request of the parents or guardians. Like the school-prayer issue, the court felt that a Bible reading service of this type involved the state in the establishment of religion. The court made it clear that it did not reject the idea of Bible reading as part of a study of comparative religion or the history of religion. Nor did the court exclude the possibility of studying the Bible as a piece of literature. What the court objected to was the reading of the Bible as part of a religious exercise.

To the consternation of some religious groups, the school prayer and Bible decisions seemed to remove religion from the public school except when the study of religion was part of an academic course like English or history. There began an unsuccessful political movement to return religion to public schools by adding an amendment to the U.S. Constitution that would allow prayers in schools.

Failing to achieve a school-prayer amendment, religious groups had to be content with a special section of the No Child Left Behind Act of 2002 titled "School Prayer" that gives the U.S. Department of Education an active role in ensuring that school districts allow for school prayer within the boundaries of the law. The legislation orders the U.S. secretary of education to provide guidance in writing and on the Internet to local schools "on constitutionally protected prayer in public elementary schools and secondary schools." The phrase *constitutionally protected prayer* includes the right for students to form religious clubs on campus where they can pray and read religious texts. This right is also extended to teachers who can meet on campus for prayers and religious readings. In addition, students can write about religious figures and themes in class assignments.

MORAL VALUES AND SEX EDUCATION

A topic that stirs a great deal of controversy is sex education. Sex education requirements vary between states. In 2018, the Center for American Progress reported that state sex education standards vary widely and that only about half of adolescent students receive school instruction about contraception before having sex. Only 20 states require contraception instruction while 27 states stress sexual abstinence before marriage and 18 states require instruction that sexual activity should only occur within marriage.

Conflicts over whether the values taught in school should be based on religious or secular morals in the late twentieth and early twenty-first centuries have included discussions of abstentious sex education, birth control, abortion, and gay and lesbian orientations. Originally sex education was promoted in 1926 by the National Education Association's Committee on Character Education as a means of combating the decline of the family and regulating sexual impulses for the good of society. The recommendation defined the purpose of human life as: "The creation of one's own home and family, involving first the choice and winning of, or being won by, one's mate." Sex education was to prepare youth to fulfill this purpose.

Similar to today's emphasis on sexual abstinence before marriage, these early sex education courses taught that sexual control was necessary for "proper home functioning, which includes the comfort and happiness of all, maximum development of the mates, proper child production, and effective personal and social education of children." Students were warned that sexual intercourse outside marriage should be avoided because of its potential threat to the stability of the family.

Ironically, mass enrollment in high schools heightened the possibility of early sexual activity by bringing large numbers of youth together within one institution. High school activities created a shared experience for youth. In *From Front Porch to Back Seat: Courtship in Twentieth-Century America*, Beth Bailey argues that the high school standardized youth culture and created ritualized dating patterns. High school marriage texts and manuals built sexual boundaries around dating. According to Bailey, early high school sex education books dealt with the issue of petting, which meant anything from hand-holding to sexual acts short of actual penetration. All the books warned against promiscuous petting. High school girls were cautioned that heavy petting would lead to a decline of their dating value in the marketplace. Women were given the task of ensuring that petting did not go too far. They were warned that boys tended to sit around and talk about their sexual exploits. The worst thing that could happen to a girl was to become an object of locker room discussions. Girls were told to achieve a balance between being known as an "icicle" and a "hot number."

By the 1930s, the senior prom was the pinnacle of the high school dating experience. In *Prom Night: Youth, Schools, and Popular Culture*, Amy Best argues that as a growing number of youth attended high school, "School clubs, school dances, and student government increasingly became a significant part of the kids' lives." Proms became widespread in the 1930s as the high school became a mass institution. They were considered a poor or middle-class version of the debutante ball, which instructed youth in proper dating and mating rituals. Best contends, "Proms were historically tied to a schooling project used to govern the uncontrollable youth. By enlisting you to participate in middle-class rituals like the prom, schools were able to advance a program that reigned in student's emerging and increasingly public sexualities."

By the 1940s, high schools had created a national youth culture, and school youth were given the name "teenagers." After World War II, spending patterns changed, as symbolized by the magazine *Seventeen* with its slogan, "Teena means business." The word "teenager," according to Kelly Schrum, was invented by advertisers. At first advertisers experimented with "teenster" and "petiteen"; "teenager" was popularized during the 1940s to mean a group defined by high school attendance. The institutionalization of youth in high schools and the creation of "teenager" as a separate age group heightened concerns about adolescent sexuality.

Today, the sexual education of teenagers is a controversial issue. Many people turn to the schools in efforts to exert control over adolescent sexual behavior. In recent years, the most heated value conflicts centered on AIDS education. These debates pitted those who believe in a strong moral code to control sexual behavior against those who believe in the right of free sexual activity between consenting adults. Those who believe in a strong moral code tend to support AIDS education programs that advocate sexual abstinence outside marriage and take a strong stand against homosexual activities. Those at the other end of the value spectrum emphasize educational programs that teach safe sexual procedures and advocate the dispensing of condoms in public schools.

For example, in 2018, Sex Respect claimed it was the world's leading abstinence program. The Sex Respect program began in 1983 with a curriculum guide designed to motivate teens to practice chastity. The program's current goal is "to enable each individual to progressively develop responsible behavior, positive self-esteem, and respect for others as he/she makes decisions involving the use of his/her sexual freedom." Sex Respect defines sexual freedom as the freedom to say no. Sex Respect teaches teens that saying "no" to premarital sex is their right, is in the best interest of society, and is in the spirit of true sexual freedom.

Programs like Sex Respect were made possible by Title V of the Welfare Reform Act of 1996 in which Congress authorized federal funds to be provided to the states in the form of block grants to promote chastity until marriage. Title V requires states to fund education that:

- Has as its exclusive purpose teaching the social, psychological, and health gains to be realized by abstaining from sexual activity
- Teaches abstinence from sexual activity outside marriage as the expected standard for all school-age children

- Teaches that abstinence from sexual activity is the only certain way to avoid out-of-wedlock pregnancy, sexually transmitted diseases, and other associated health problems
- Teaches that a mutually faithful monogamous relationship in the context of marriage is the expected standard of human sexual activity

The No Child Left Behind Act of 2001 reflects the values of religious conservatives in its prohibitions against using any money granted through the legislation that might promote birth control or homosexuality. Section 9526 specifically states:

'SEC. 9526. GENERAL PROHIBITIONS.

(a) PROHIBITION.—None of the funds authorized under this Act shall be used—

(1) to develop or distribute materials, or operate programs or courses of instruction directed at youth, that are designed to promote or encourage sexual activity, whether homosexual or heterosexual;

(2) to distribute or to aid in the distribution by any organization of legally obscene materials to minors on school grounds;

(3) to provide sex education or HIV-prevention education in schools unless that instruction is age appropriate and includes the health benefits of abstinence; or

(4) to operate a program of contraceptive distribution in schools.

These provisions restrict the use of federal funds under No Child Left Behind to discussions "of the health benefits of abstinence" sex education. It also eliminates any funds for use in providing contraceptive devices to students. There is also vague wording about not funding instruction that might promote heterosexual or homosexual activity. This provision eliminates discussion of sexual practices that might enhance sexual pleasure, certainly something about which many adults seek advice from physicians, which might be considered a factor in helping stabilize marriages.

How effective are sex education courses and abstinence education? The respected Guttmacher Institute, which is devoted to promoting sexual and reproductive health, reports annual rates of teenage pregnancy. From early 1986 to 2010, as indicated in Table 2.1, pregnancy rates among teenagers in the United States dropped from 106.7 per thousand to 57.4 per thousand in 2010.

Table 2.1 Pregnancy Rate of Women Aged 15 to 19 per 1,000 Women Aged 15 to 19

Year	Pregnancy Rate per 1,000 Women Aged 15 to 19
1986	106.7
1996	95.6
2006	70.1
2010	57.4

Source: Adapted from Kathryn Kost and Stanley Henshaw, *U.S. Teenage Pregnancies, Births and Abortions: National and State Trends and Trends by Race and Ethnicity 2010: National and State Trends by Age, Race and Ethnicity*, Guttmacher Institute, May 2014, p. 9. Retrieved from www.guttmacher.org/sections/pregnancy.php.

The Guttmacher Institute attributes this decline "to increased contraceptive use." The use of contraceptives, of course, is contrary to the official abstinence-only-based sex education. The increased use of contraception by teenagers was confirmed by a report from the U.S. Department of Health and Human Services' Centers for Disease Control and Prevention (CDC), which in a survey of teenagers asked if they had "used a condom during last sexual intercourse." In 1991, 46.2 percent answered yes, while in 2009, 61.1 percent answered yes.

Abstinence education appears effective when one considers the rate of sexual activity among teenagers. In response to the CDC's question, "Ever had sexual intercourse?" 54.1 percent responded yes in 1991, and 46.0 percent responded yes in 2009.

Sexually transmitted diseases remain a major problem among teenagers despite abstinence-only education and the increased use of condoms. While most sexually transmitted diseases are on the decline, such as gonorrhea and syphilis, chlamydia remains a major problem among teenage women. In fact, chlamydia is most prevalent among teenage girls in comparison to older women and men. The CDC reports that the "chlamydia case rate for females in 2007 was almost three times higher than for males (543.6 vs. 190.0 per 100,000 population). . . . *Young females 15 to 19 years of age had the highest chlamydia rate* (3,004.7 per 100,000 population), followed by females 20 to 24 years of age (2,948.8 per 100,000 population)" (emphasis in original). In 2013, the CDC reported that the rate of chlamydia for 15- to 24-year-olds had increased 63 percent and HPV (human papillomavirus) 49 percent. The increase of gonorrhea for this group was the largest at a whopping 70 percent.

While groups engaged in struggles over abstinence-only sex education versus sex education that teaches birth control and condom use, there was an actual decline in teenage pregnancies and teenage rates of intercourse while teenagers increased their use of condoms. However, high rates of teenage chlamydia cases indicate a major problem. The increasing rates of condom use, despite abstinence-only education, could be attributed to instruction about AIDS and HIV infection. The problem is that the CDC found an actual decline in instruction on this topic. Its survey asked, "Were [you] ever taught in school about AIDS or HIV infection?" The CDC reported that instruction on this topic "decreased, 1997–2009," from 91.5 to 87.0 percent.

An increasing issue in schools is sexual harassment, which can now begin as early as elementary school. In 2018, *Education Week* reported that a Los Angeles third-grade teacher created a chart to introduce her students to the concept without discussing sexual activity. The students were asked questions about what activities should require their consent. They responded by identifying hugs, kisses, and other physical touches. They were then asked how they should respond. This created a list that included "of course," "yes," "no," "I don't like that," and "maybe another time."

On November 16, 2018, U.S. Secretary of Education Betsy DeVos issued new guidelines for bringing charges of sexual harassment. Secretary DeVos worried that "far too many students have been forced to go to court to ensure their rights are protected because the Department has not set out legally binding rules that hold schools accountable for responding to allegations of sexual harassment in a supportive, fair manner." The new rules from the U.S. Department of Education would require schools to respond meaningfully to every known report of sexual harassment and to investigate every formal complaint; the proposed rule would require remedies for the survivor to restore or preserve access to the school's education program or activity and would require schools to apply basic due process protections for students, including a presumption of innocence throughout the grievance process; written notice of allegations and an equal opportunity to review all evidence collected; and the right to cross-examination.

SCHOOL VALUES: LGBTQ (LESBIAN, GAY, BISEXUAL, TRANSGENDER, AND QUESTIONING SEXUAL ORIENTATION)

Issues surrounding LGBTQ youth continue to highlight a major moral divide in American society. As mentioned at the beginning of this chapter, a Virginia high school teacher was fired for not using a student's preferred pronoun because it violated his religious beliefs. In 2016, North Carolina was embroiled in discussing laws requiring students to use bathrooms according to the gender stated on their birth certificates. A number of other states were considering similar legislation.

In 2018, the U.S. Supreme Court accepted a case where a group of Pennsylvania high school students backed by Alliance Defending Freedom filed suit against its district's policy allowing transgender students to use bathrooms and locker rooms reflecting their gender identity. The Alliance Defending Freedom is dedicated to helping school districts and students that have refused to adopt pro-transgender policies or object to sharing restrooms and locker rooms with transgender students. They want students to use restrooms and locker rooms according to the gender appearing on their birth certificates.

In contrast, Germany passed a 2018 law allowing parents to choose "diverse" as an option for their children's birth certificates. According to *New York Times* reporter Melissa Eddy, "The change came more than a year after Germany's highest court ruled that binary gender designations were discriminatory and in violation of guarantees of personal freedom. The court ordered legislators to change the law to include a third category or do away with gender classification altogether."

Gay-Straight Alliance Network and Crossroads Collaborative, a research organization led by University of Arizona faculty, issued a report "that LGBTQ youth of color and gender-nonconforming youth are frequently blamed for their own victimization and targeted for harsh and biased school discipline." This, the group claimed, was consistent with previous reports "illustrating race-based bias and criminalization of youth of color, but it is important to note that these students are also targeted due to sexual orientation and gender identity, expression, or presentation."

The Gay-Straight Alliance Network reported complaints by LGBTQ youth that they felt "a lack of support in school and a sense that they were being watched by educators," that "teachers frequently assumed a gender-nonconforming peer was 'acting up,'" and that LGBT and gender-nonconforming students started confrontations with peers who were bullying them or did not properly address the bullying. Most important, this research group recommended the inclusion "of actual or perceived sexual orientation as a protected class in school bullying and harassment policies."

CHARACTER EDUCATION

Despite the struggles over what values will be taught in schools, proponents of character education have kept alive Horace Mann's hope that schools can contribute to a crime-free and moral society. The 2002 federal legislation No Child Left Behind contains a section titled "Partnerships in Character Education" that calls for the integration of character education into classroom instruction.

Although many parents and teachers support the development of good character and citizenship, there is still the problem of defining its meaning. For instance, the No Child Left Behind Act refers to "integrating *secular* character education into curricula and teaching methods of schools [emphasis added]." The use of "secular" in the legislation is to make a distinction from character education based on religious values. As examples of the elements of secular character education, the legislation provides the following:

- Caring
- Civic virtue and citizenship
- Justice and fairness
- Respect
- Responsibility
- Trustworthiness
- Giving

These terms are vague. The substance of these desired character traits only takes on meaning when put in a political context. For instance, does "caring" mean an individual should support a strong welfare government that guarantees all citizens health care, shelter, and adequate nutrition? Or does "caring" mean eliminating welfare programs so the poor learn to be economically independent?

While character education is expected to be included in all school subjects, its values continue to be vague. For instance, the Character Education Partnership states:

Character education holds that widely shared, pivotally important, core ethical values—such as caring, honesty, fairness, responsibility, and respect for self and others—along with supportive performance values—such as diligence, a strong worth ethic, and perseverance—form the basis of good character. A school committed to character development stands for these values (sometimes referred to as "virtues" or "character traits"), defines them in terms of behaviors that can be observed in the life of the school, models these values, studies and discusses them, uses them as the basis of human relations in the school, celebrates their manifestations in the school and community, and holds all school members accountable to standards of conduct consistent with the core values.

Some religious leaders might claim that these ethical standards are meaningful only if they are interpreted within a religious framework. People who consider themselves political liberals might interpret the core values identified in the previous quote as requiring civic activism to ensure social justice. Self-identified conservatives might stress obedience to the law and authority rather than civic activism. Probably, there will continue to be problems in reaching a consensus on values that will achieve Horace Mann's dream of the school reducing crime and achieving a moral society.

There is also a multicultural aspect to character education. University of Minnesota Professor Kate Walker argues that character education involves social-emotional education. Professor Walker writes, "To be successful now and ready for college, careers, and civic responsibilities, today's young people need to develop a range of skills intermittently referred to as social-emotional, global, 21st-century, or character skills." However, she writes, the concept of success, forms of communication, and expressions of emotions vary between cultures. Therefore, character education should include instruction on recognizing and accommodating cultural differences. Professor Walker proposes that character education include global competence in recognizing differing global perspectives. Of course, this assumes that teachers are also trained to understand cultural differences.

DO PUBLIC SCHOOLS REDUCE CRIME?

Horace Mann's dream of ending crime through the education of children in public schools has not proved a reality. Similar to the problem of voter turnout discussed in Chapter 1, there may be no causal relationship between school attendance and crime rates. However, one might predict that if schooling is related to crime rates then increased school attendance might be accompanied with a reduction in crime rates. According to Table 1.1 in Chapter 1 and the National Center for Education Statistics' *The Condition of Education 2016* (updated historical attendance statistics are not available in *The Condition of Education 2018*), the percentage of 5- to 17-year-olds in school increased from 82.2 percent in 1959–1960 to 88.7 percent in 1999–2000 and 91.9 percent in 2004–2005, and in 2016 93 percent of 5- to 6-year-olds and 98 percent of 7- to 13-year-olds were enrolled in elementary or secondary school. Average days of attendance increased from 160.2 in 1959–1960 to 169.2 in 1999–2000 (average days of attendance was not available for 2004–2005).

According to Table 2.2, as the percentage of 5- to 17-year-olds in school and number of days in school increased from 1960 to 2004, so did the crime rate. In fact, violent crimes increased rapidly from 1960 to 2000 from 160.9 to 506.5 per 100,000 inhabitants, respectively. There was a decline in violent crimes which by 2012 was 386.9 per 100,000 inhabitants. However, the 2012 violent crime rate was significantly higher than the 160.9 per 100,000 inhabitants recorded in 1960. Crimes involving property increased from 1,726.3 per 100,000 inhabitants in 1960 to 3,658.1 per 100,000 inhabitants before dropping to 2,859.2 per 100,000 inhabitants in 2012.

The FBI crime report for 2016 stated that the 2015 violent crime total was 0.7 percent lower than 2014.

Table 2.2 U.S. Crime Rate Index per 100,000 Inhabitants, 1960–2000

Year	No. of Violent Crimes	No. of Property Crimes
1960	160.9	1,726.3
1970	363.5	3,621.0
1980	596.6	5,353.3
1990	731.8	5,088.5
2000	506.5	3,658.1
2004	463.2	3,514.1
2012	386.9	2,859.2

Source: The Disaster Center, *United States Crime Rates 1960–2008*. Retrieved from www.disaster center.com/crime/uscrime.htm.

These statistics indicate an error in Horace Mann's dream of schooling reducing crime by expanding the schooling of the population. However, and this is important to understand, these statistics do not establish a causal relationship between schooling and crime. In other words, it cannot be concluded from the data that expanded schooling increases or decreases crime rates. All that can be said is that expanded schooling has not resulted in a decline in crime rates.

However, a relationship does exist between level of educational attainment and criminal convictions. The higher a person's educational attainment, the less likely he/she is to be in prison.

Table 2.3 Educational Attainment for Correctional Populations and the General Population

Educational Attainment	Total Incarcerated (%)	Prison Inmates				
		State (%)	Federal (%)	Local Jail (%)	Probationers (%)	General Population (%)
Some high school or less	41.3	39.7	26.5	46.5	30.6	18.4
GED*	23.4	28.5	22.7	14.1	11.0	N/A
High school diploma	22.6	20.5	27.0	25.9	34.8	33.2
Postsecondary	12.7	11.4	23.9	13.5	23.6	48.4

Source: Caroline Wolf Harlow, *Education and Correctional Populations*, Bureau of Justice Statistics Special Report (Washington, DC: U.S. Department of Justice, Office of Justice Programs, 2003), p. 1.

* GED refers to General Educational Development (GED), which was first administered in 1942 to World War II military personnel who had not graduated from high school. Initiated by the U.S. Armed Forces, the testing program was extremely helpful to war veterans returning to civilian life. In 1963, the GED program was expanded to serve more civilians and nonveteran adults.

As shown in Table 2.3, the higher the level of educational attainment, the less likely a person is to be in jail. According to Table 2.3, 41.3 percent of Americans in prison have some high school or less as compared to 12.7 percent of the prison population with some postsecondary education. Caroline Wolf Harlow, in *Education and Correctional Populations*, found the following:

> Young inmates less well educated than older inmates were more likely than older inmates to have failed to complete high school or its equivalent. Over half of inmates 24 or younger had not completed the 12th grade or the GED (52%), while just over a third of those 35 or older did not have a high school diploma or GED (34% for those 35–44 and 35% for those 45 or older).

It is difficult to determine the importance of educational attainment in predicting the likelihood of being in prison given other social factors, such as neighborhood conditions, peer groups, family wealth, and employment opportunities. For instance, Wolf Harlow's report suggests a relationship between education, unemployment, and imprisonment.

Approximately 38% of inmates who completed 11 years or less of school were not working before entry to prison. Unemployment was lower for those with a GED (32%), a high school diploma (25%), or education beyond high school (21%). About 20% without a high school diploma, 19% with a GED, 14% with a high school diploma, and 13% with training beyond high school were not looking for work.

As I discuss later in this book, educational attainment is related to neighborhood conditions, peer groups, and family wealth. It could be that increasing family wealth, improving neighborhood conditions, and changing peer groups will increase educational attainment and, consequently, reduce the prison population. In other words, improving social and economic conditions for all people might result in lower rates of unemployment and a smaller prison population.

SCHOOL CRIME: STUDENT VIOLENCE

School crime was one thing Horace Mann did not consider in his quest for a crime-free society through instilling moral values in students in school. Could schools become crime centers?

On February 14, 2018, heavily armed Nikolas Cruz arrived at the Marjory Stoneman Douglas High School shortly before dismissal time. Cruz shot people in the hallways and inside classrooms. Before the shooting rampage ended 17 people were dead and 14 wounded. In protest against school shootings, students at Marjory Stoneman Douglas High

School led a national movement for stricter gun control laws and held a Washington, DC, rally.

Reporting on the rally, Michael D. Shear wrote, "They led a crowd that filled blocks of Pennsylvania Avenue between the White House and Capitol Hill. Thousands more rallied at about 800 'sibling' marches around the country and abroad, where students, like those in the capital, made eloquent calls for gun control and pledged to exercise their newfound political power in the midterm elections this fall." The result of the protests was that in 2018 state legislators passed 69 gun control laws.

The response of President Trump's administration was contained in a 2018 report on school safety. Nothing in the report spoke directly to the demands by student protesters for tighter gun control laws. *Education Week* reporter Madeline Will described one of the recommendations as, "There should be more military veterans and law enforcement officers in schools, and all teachers should be versed in what to do if there were an active shooter, the Trump administration has said."

Writing in *USA Today*, reporter Greg Toppo recalled one of the most infamous school massacres at Denver's Columbine High School on April 20, 1999:

> They weren't goths or loners. The two teenagers who killed 13 people and themselves at suburban Denver's Columbine High School 10 years ago next week weren't in the "Trenchcoat Mafia," disaffected videogamers who wore cowboy dusters. The killings ignited a national debate over bullying, but the record now shows Eric Harris and Dylan Klebold hadn't been bullied—in fact, they had bragged in diaries about picking on freshmen and "fags."

While Columbine became the most infamous school massacre, there were other incidents that sparked federal action to make schools safe.

On December 14, 2012, at Sandy Hook Elementary School in Newtown, Connecticut, as reported in *Education Week*: "Adam Lanza, 20, acted alone when he gunned down 26 people at the school, the summary report released last month says, and he used weapons and ammunition that were legally purchased by his mother. While State's Attorney Stephen Sedensky III found no clear motive, he found items that suggest Lanza had a fascination with mass killings, including a computer game called School Shooting that was found in his home."

Despite these gruesome massacres, school crimes have declined. The U.S. Department of Education's *The Condition of Education 2018* reported, "Between 2000 and 2016, the rates of nonfatal victimization both at school and away from school declined for students ages 12–18.

The rate of victimization at school declined 65 percent, and the rate of victimization away from school declined 72 percent. In 2016, students ages 12–18 reported 749,000 nonfatal victimizations at school and 601,000 nonfatal victimizations away from school. Nonfatal victimizations include theft and all violent crime. Violent crime includes serious violent crime (rape, sexual assault, robbery, and aggravated assault) and simple assault." Regarding violent crime, *The Condition of Education 2018* reported the rates of specific types of victimization—thefts, violent victimizations, and serious violent victimizations—both at school and away from school all declined between 2000 and 2016.

As a result of school crime, schools implemented policies to prevent violence, including emergency lockdowns in cases of mass killings. The National Crime Prevention Council recommends the following safety tips for school administrators:

- Enforce zero-tolerance policies toward the presence of weapons, alcohol, and illegal drugs.
- Establish and enforce drug- and gun-free zones.
- Establish policies that declare that anything that is illegal off campus is illegal on campus.
- Engage students in maintaining a good learning environment by establishing a teen court.
- Develop protocols between law enforcement and the school about ways to share information on at-risk youth.
- Develop resource lists that provide referral services for students who are depressed or otherwise under stress.
- Involve teens in designing and running programs such as mediation, mentoring, peer assistance, School Crime Watch, and graffiti removal.
- Insist that all students put outerwear in their lockers during school hours.
- Require all students to tuck in their shirts to keep them from hiding weapons.
- Develop and enforce dress codes that ban gang-related and gang-style clothing.
- Establish a policy of positive identification such as ID badges for administrators, staff, students, and visitors.
- Deny students permission to leave school for lunch and other non-school-related activities during school hours.

These procedures and the attention given to the problem may have contributed to curbing some school crime. According to the National Center for Education Statistics, *The Condition of Education 2016*:

Between 1992 and 2014, the rates of total nonfatal victimization of 12- to 18-year-old students declined both at school and away from school. During these years, the rates of theft, violent crime, and serious violent crime—subsets of total nonfatal victimization—against 12- to 18-year-old students also generally declined. Nonfatal victimizations include theft and all violent crime. Violent crime includes serious violent crime (rape, sexual assault, robbery, and aggravated assault) and simple assault.

SCHOOL CRIME: BULLYING AND CYBERBULLYING

In August 2018, *Education Week* reported, "Teenagers are experiencing cyberbullying on Instagram more than on any other social-media platform. That's what Ditch the Label, an international anti-bullying organization, discovered from its survey of more than 10,000 young adults, ages 12 to 20, in the United Kingdom, about their experiences with bullying, both online and in person." Of these 10,000, "69 percent admitted that they had done something abusive toward another person online."

In 2018, First Lady Melania Trump launched the Be Best campaign, which aims to teach children about the importance of social, emotional, and physical health, with a concentration on social media. "Social media is an inevitable part of our children's daily lives," she said at a conference on cyberbullying. "This is why Be Best chooses to focus on the importance of teaching our next generation how to conduct themselves safely and in a positive manner in an online setting."

The White House's Be Best Website explains the mission of Melania Trump's campaign against bullying.

The mission of BE BEST is to focus on some of the major issues facing children today, with the goal of encouraging children to BE BEST in their individual paths, while also teaching them the importance of social, emotional, and physical health. BE BEST will concentrate on three main pillars: well-being, social media use, and opioid abuse.

BE BEST will champion the many successful well-being programs that provide children with the tools and skills required for emotional, social, and physical health. The campaign will also promote established organizations, programs, and people who are helping children overcome some of the issues they face growing up in the modern world.

Bullying received major national attention in January 2010, when Phoebe Prince, 15, hanged herself as a result of a relentless, months-long bullying campaign that included threats of physical harm. Some of the bullying was cyberbullying that occurred online on Facebook. According to *New York Times* reporters Erik Eckholm and Katie Zezima, Prince was insulted and called a whore after dating a popular high school football player who had also dated one of the accused girls. Allegations that school officials knew of the bullying but failed to intervene sparked outrage.

What is bullying and cyberbullying? In 2014 U.S. government's Center for Disease Control offered this definition that includes online actions:

- **Are unwanted aggressive behaviors.** This behavior could be online or in person, and it is committed by another youth or group of youths who are not siblings or current dating partners of the victim.
- **Involve an observed or perceived power imbalance.** This power imbalance between the perpetrator and the victim could involve factors like social stature, resources, physical size, or influence.
- **Are repeated multiple times or are likely to be repeated.**

The case of Phoebe Prince highlights one of the toxic aspects of school life, namely bullying. The Bureau of Justice Statistics reported in *Indicators of School Crime and Safety: 2013* that "in 2011, about 28 percent of 12- to 18-year-old students reported being bullied at school, and 9 percent reported being cyber-bullied during the school year."

Cyberbullying became widespread among students with the rapid growth in the use of text messaging, instant messaging, and the Internet. The Fight Crime Invest in Kids highlighted the story of Vermont teenager Kylie Kenney, who was harassed by a Website calling for her death and threatening and embarrassing phone calls from other students. Kenney stated, "No child should have to endure the cyber bullying I endured. I was scared, hurt and confused. I didn't know why it was happening to me. I had nowhere to turn except to my mom. I am speaking out now because I want other kids who are bullied online or on their cell phones to know that they should tell their parents or other adults." The organization's report included these other findings:

- 10 percent of the teens and 4 percent of the younger children were threatened online with physical harm.
- 16 percent of the teens and preteens who were victims told no one about it. About half of children aged 6 to 11 told their parents. Only 30 percent of older kids told their parents.

- Preteens were as likely to receive harmful messages at school (45 percent) as at home (44 percent). Older children received 30 percent of harmful messages at school and 70 percent at home.
- 17 percent of preteens and 7 percent of teens said they were worried about bullying as they start a new school year.

PROMOTING NATIONAL HEALTH: NUTRITION

Beginning in the late nineteenth century, schools took on the goal of improving national health through classroom instruction and school cafeterias. Key to this effort was the early development of home economics. The home economics profession, currently called "family and consumer sciences," called upon schools to play a major role in improving the quality of American families, changing the lifestyles of women, bettering urban conditions, and reforming the American diet. Schools responded by providing home economics courses for girls and adding school cafeterias. Founded in 1909, the American Home Economics Association spearheaded the creation of educational goals linked to home and urban improvement projects.

Home economics courses were designed to train women to be scientific housekeepers who would free themselves from kitchen drudgery by relying on packaged and processed foods. Home economics courses taught cooking, household budgeting, sewing, and scientific methods of cleaning. The goal was providing housewives with more free time for education and working to improve municipal conditions. The family model was of wives as consumers of household products and educators and husbands as wage earners. By teaching women household budgeting, families were to learn how to live within their means, which would reduce worker discontent about wages. A clean and cheerful house, it was believed, would reduce alcoholism because husbands would want to hurry home from work rather than stop at a tavern. Teaching women how to cook healthy meals would give their husbands more energy at work. And, of course, freed to receive more education, the housewives would improve the political and cultural level of the American home.

In *Perfection Salad: Women and Cooking at the Turn of the Century*, Laura Shapiro credits home economists with the development of a distinctive American cuisine. She argues that during the latter part of the nineteenth-century, home economists "made American cooking American, transforming a nation of honest appetites into an obedient market for instant mashed potatoes." Jell-O and Wonder Bread, a factory-baked white bread, became symbols of American cuisine. These home economists paved the way for America's greatest contributions to global cuisine, the fast-food franchise.

School cafeterias were intended to reform American eating habits. Home economists made school and hospital cafeteria food healthy, inexpensive, and bland. Through the school cafeteria, home economists hoped to persuade immigrant children to abandon the diet of their parents for the new American cuisine. A founder of the home economics movement, Ellen Richards projected a liberating role for prepared food in a 1900 article titled "Housekeeping in the Twentieth Century." In her dream home, where the purchase of cheap, mass-produced furniture allowed more money for "intellectual pleasures," the pantry was filled with a large stock of prepared foods—mainly canned foods and bakery products. A pneumatic tube connected to the pantry sped canned and packaged food to the kitchen, where the wife simply heated up the meal. In addition, the meal would be accompanied by store-bought bread. Besides being unsanitary, home economists believed homemade bread and other bakery goods required an inordinate amount of preparation time and therefore housewives should rely on factory-produced bread products. Richards dismissed the issue of taste with the comment, "I grant that each family has a weakness for the flavor produced by its own kitchen bacteria, but that is a prejudice due to lack of education." People would stop worrying about taste, she argued, when they fully realized the benefits of the superior cleanliness and consistency of factory kitchens and bakeries.

Continuing the efforts to use schools to improve the nation's health and eating habits, the U.S. Congress considered passage of the Child Nutrition Bill. Following in the tradition of nineteenth-century home economists, First Lady Michelle Obama dedicated herself to improving the nutrition of children and initiated the Website Let's Move: America's Move to Raise a Healthier Generation of Kids. First Lady Obama commented on the Child Nutrition Bill working its way through the U.S. Congress in 2010:

> The bill will make it easier for the tens of millions of children who participate in the National School Lunch Program and the School Breakfast Program—and many others who are eligible but not enrolled—to get the nutritious meals they need to do their best. It will set higher nutritional standards for school meals by requiring more fruits, vegetables and whole grains while reducing fat and salt. It will offer rewards to schools that meet those standards. And it will help eliminate junk food from vending machines and a la carte lines—a major step that is supported by parents, health-experts, and many in the food and beverage industry.

In a controversial 2018 decision, according to *Education Week*, the U.S. Department of Agriculture released its final school rule on school meals that "will ease requirements related to flavored milk, whole grains, and sodium in meals served through the National School Lunch and breakfast programs." "If kids are not eating what is being served, they are not benefiting, and food is being wasted," agriculture secretary Sonny Perdue said in a statement announcing the relaxed rule. "We all have the same goals in mind—the health and development of our young people. USDA trusts our local operators to serve healthy meals that meet local preferences and build bright futures with good nutrition."

PROMOTING NATIONAL HEALTH: DRUG AND ALCOHOL ABUSE

Since the nineteenth century, class instruction, school activities, and teachers' warnings have attempted to curb the use of alcohol, tobacco, and illegal drugs. The 2002 No Child Left Behind Act's section Safe and Drug-Free Schools and Communities Act provided federal funds to prevent student use of illegal drugs.

Probably the best-known antidrug program is the Drug Abuse Resistance Education (D.A.R.E.) program that conducts police officer–led classroom lessons to teach kids from kindergarten through 12th grade to resist peer pressure and live drug- and violence-free lives. D.A.R.E. describes itself as follows: "D.A.R.E. was founded in 1983 in Los Angeles and has proven so successful that it is now being implemented in 75 percent of our nation's school districts and in more than 43 countries around the world."

Efforts to curb drug usage among students have encountered some legal problems, however. In 1998, the Tecumseh, Oklahoma, school district required students to submit to a urinalysis for illegal drugs—for example, amphetamines, marijuana, cocaine, opiates, and barbiturates—prior to participating in competitive extracurricular activities. The extracurricular activities included in the school district policy were the Academic Team, Future Farmers of America, Future Homemakers of America, band, choir, pom pom, cheerleading, and athletics. Two students at Tecumseh High School, Lindsay Earls and Daniel James, and their parents claimed that students' Fourth Amendment rights to protection from "unreasonable searches" and the requirement of "probable cause" were being violated. In other words, was the urinalysis an "unreasonable search"? Was there a "probable cause" of drug usage by students engaged in competitive extracurricular activities?

The Fourth Amendment states:

The right of the people to be secure in their persons, houses, papers, and effects, against unreasonable searches and seizures, shall not be violated, and no warrants shall issue, but upon probable cause, supported by oath or affirmation, and particularly describing the place to be searched, and the persons or things to be seized.

In *Board of Education of Independent School District No. 92 of Pottawatomie County et al. v. Earls et al.*, the U.S. Supreme Court ruling stated that students in school are in "temporary custody of the state," that "student privacy interest is limited in a public school environment," and that students participating in extracurricular activities, such as athletics or those requiring travel, involve "communal undress." In addition, the manner in which the school district collected the urine samples was not an invasion of privacy. The U.S. Supreme Court decision provided the following description of the Tecumseh school district's collection of urine samples:

> A faculty monitor waits outside the closed restroom stall for the student to produce a sample and must listen for the normal sounds of urination in order to guard against tampered specimens and to insure an accurate chain of custody. The monitor then pours the sample into two bottles that are sealed and placed into a mailing pouch along with a consent form signed by the student. This procedure . . . additionally protects privacy by allowing male students to produce their samples behind a closed stall.

Based on the school's custodial care of the student, "communal undressing," and "given the minimally intrusive nature of the sample collection," the U.S. Supreme Court concluded that "the invasion of students' privacy is not significant."

Is there a probable cause requiring drug testing? Are students using drugs while engaging in extracurricular activities? First, the U.S. Supreme Court decision declares, based on previous cases, that "a warrant and finding of probable cause are unnecessary in the public school context because such requirements would unduly interfere with the maintenance of the swift and informal disciplinary procedures needed." In other words, school authorities do not have to prove probable cause before searching a student's possessions as long as the search is conducted in a reasonable manner. Also, school authorities can test for drugs even though there is no suspicion the student has actually used drugs.

The U.S. Supreme Court ruled that the Tecumseh school district's Student Activities Drug Testing Policy was not a violation of the Fourth Amendment's prohibition of unreasonable searches and the requirement of probable cause. The result of this decision means that any public school district can legally adopt a drug policy modeled on that of the Tecumseh school district.

Many school districts adopted the Tecumseh school district's stated policies to avoid any future legal problems. "I tell districts," said Paul Lyle, a lawyer representing 50 Texas school districts, "that if they adopt the same verbatim policy as Tecumseh that would be safe. But I tell them, if you change a comma, it could open the door to something." Raymond Lusk, superintendent of the Lockney, Texas, school district, commented, "We'll probably get 85 percent of the kids in extracurriculars. I think it would be fairer to test everybody, because why are some kids more important than others?"

What has been the result of drug education and testing? According to the Bureau of Justice statistics: "The percentage of students in grades 9–12 who reported that illegal drugs were offered, sold, or given to them decreased from 32 percent in 1995 to 26 percent in 2011."

What about the D.A.R.E. program? *New York Times* reporter Marc Kaufman cited a *Journal of Consulting and Clinical Psychology* study funded by the National Institutes of Health that found that "children who took the 17-week D.A.R.E. course in elementary school used drugs and alcohol at the same rate 10 years later as children who learned about them in traditional health classes."

CONCLUSION

Attempts to use public schools to solve social problems will continue to raise problems about what values should dominate character education and how to reconcile secular and religious values. Consider the following questions:

- What are legitimate areas of social concern for public schools?
- Should public schools attempt to solve social problems, such as the AIDS epidemic or other epidemics, the destructive use of drugs and alcohol, teenage pregnancy, and rising crime rates?
- What government agency, organization, or group of individuals should decide the moral values to be taught in public schools?

SUGGESTED READINGS AND WORKS CITED IN CHAPTER

Aarons, Dakarai I. "The Experience of Lesbian, Gay, Bisexual and Transgender Middle School Students." *Education Week*, Vol. 29, no. 6 (October 7, 2009), p. 5. An exploration of the problems faced by lesbian, gay, bisexual, and transgender youth in school.

Almukhtar, Sarah, K. K. Rebecca Lai, Anjali Singhvi, and Karen Yourish. "What Happened in the Parkland School Shooting." *New York Times* (April 24, 2018). Describes school shootings at the Marjorie Stoneman High School.

Astor, Maggie, and Karl Russell. "After Parkland, a New Surge in State Gun Control Laws." *The New York Times* (December 14, 2018). www.nytimes.com/interactive/2018/12/14/us/politics/gun-control-laws.html on December 14, 2018. The results of national protests over school shootings.

Bailey, Beth L. *From Front Porch to Back Seat: Courtship in Twentieth-Century America.* Baltimore: Johns Hopkins University Press, 1988. Bailey presents a history of twentieth-century dating, including high school dating.

Best, Amy L. *Prom Night: Youth, Schools, and Popular Culture.* New York: Routledge, 2000. Best offers a historical and sociological study of the high school prom.

Blad, Evie. "LGBT and Gender-Nonconforming Youth Target of Unfair Discipline, Groups Say." *Education Week* (October 8, 2014). http://blogs.edweek.org/edweek/rulesforengagement/2014/10/lgbt_and_gender_non-conforming.html. Research group highlights discrimination and offers solutions related to LBGTQ youth.

———. "New Teacher-Preparation Standards Focus on Sex Education: Teachers Often Lack Training, Experts Say." *Education Week* (May 6, 2014). www.edweek.org/ew/articles/2014/05/07/30sexed.h33.html?qs=sex+education. Discussion of recent sex education standards.

———. "Researchers and Schools Diverge in Definitions of Bullying." *Education Week* (October 7, 2014). www.edweek.org/ew/articles/2014/10/08/07bullying.h34.html. This article discusses the Center for Disease Control's definition of bullying and cyberbullying.

———. "Sandy Hook Elementary School Officially Confirms Some Widely Reported Details of the December 14, 2012, Massacre at Newtown, Conn." *Education Week* (December 3, 2013). www.edweek.org/ew/articles/2013/12/04/13report-1.h33.html?qs=sandy+hook.

———. "Trump Administration Further Relaxes School Lunch Rules." *Education Week* (December 6, 2018). https://blogs.edweek.org/edweek/rulesforengagement/2018/12/trump_administration_further_relaxes_school_lunch_rules.html on December 14, 2018. Discusses new federal government regulations governing school lunches. This article details new teacher education standards for sex education.

Bureau of Justice Statistics. *Indicators of School Crime and Safety: 2013, U.S Department of Education and U.S Department of Justice* (June 2014). http://nces.ed.gov/pubs2014/2014042.pdf. This report provides statistics on bullying and cyberbullying.

Center for Consumer Freedom. www.consumerfreedom.com/. Founded in 1996, the Center for Consumer Freedom is a nonprofit organization devoted to promoting personal responsibility and protecting consumer choices. It opposes any government ban on food that might contribute to childhood obesity.

Character Education Partnerships. www.character.org/. Character Education Partnership (CEP) is a national advocate and leader for the character education movement.

Commission on the Reorganization of Secondary Education, National Education Association. *Cardinal Principles of Secondary Education, Bureau of Education Bulletin.* Washington, DC: U.S. Government Printing Office, 1918. Publication that outlined the goals of modern comprehensive high school.

Cremin, Lawrence. *The Republic and the School.* New York: Teachers College Press, 1957. This is a good selection of Horace Mann's writings taken from his reports to the Massachusetts Board of Education and a good introduction to the social and political purposes of American education.

Dewey, John. "The School as Social Center." *National Education Association Proceedings.* Washington, DC: National Education Association, 1902, pp. 373–383.

Drug Abuse Resistance Education (D.A.R.E.). www.dare.com/home/default. asp. Organization conducts police officer–led classroom lessons to teach kids from kindergarten through 12th grade to resist peer pressure and live drug- and violence-free lives.

Eddy, Melissa. "Not Male or Female? Germans Can Now Choose 'Diverse'." *The New York Times* (December 14, 2018). www.nytimes.com/2018/12/14/world/europe/transgender-germany-diverse.html?rref=collection%2Fsectioncollection%2Fworld&action=click&contentCollection=world&region=rank&module=package&version=highlights&contentPlacement=10&pgtype=sectionfront on December 14, 2018. One resolution of the debate about gender shown on birth certificate determining use of bathrooms and locker rooms.

Federal Bureau of Investigation. *Latest Crime Statistics Released* (September 26, 2016). www.fbi.gov/news/stories/latest-crime-statistics-released on March 5, 2017. Crime statistics for 2015.

Fight Crime: Invest in Kids. www.fightcrime.org/. This organization is composed of law enforcement officers dedicated to reducing crime, including cyberbullying, through education of children and parents.

Future of Sex Education. *National Teacher Preparation Standards for Sexuality Education*. www.futureofsexed.org/documents/teacher-standards.pdf. Guidelines for preparing teachers of sex education.

Gewertz, Catherine. "Poll: Building Character More Important Goal of K-12 Ed. Than Building Economy." *Education Week* (February 19, 2014 4:43 PM). http://blogs.edweek.org/edweek/curriculum/2014/02/americans_rank_building_charac.html?qs=character+education. Poll reports that Americans place character education over other educational goals.

Glsen, the Gay, Lesbian and Straight Education Network. www.glsen.org/cgi-bin/iowa/all/home/index.html. This organization is the leading national education organization focused on ensuring safe schools for all students. Established in 1990, GLSEN envisions a world in which every child learns to respect and accept all people, regardless of sexual orientation or gender identity/expression.

Guttmacher Institute. *U.S. Teenage Pregnancies, Births and Abortions: National and State Trends and Trends by Race and Ethnicity* (January 2010). www.guttmacher.org. This organization is dedicated to issues of family planning.

Harlow, Caroline Wolf. *Education and Correctional Populations, Bureau of Justice Statistics Special Report*. Washington, DC: U.S. Department of Justice, Office of Justice Programs, 2003. This is a study of educational attainment of prisoners.

Jones, Sasha. "Looking for Cyberbullies? Try Instagram." *Education Week* (August 28, 2018). www.edweek.org/ew/articles/2018/08/29/looking-for-cyberbullies-try-instagram.html on November 21, 2018. Discussion of latest method for cyberbullying.

Kaestle, Carl. *Pillars of the Republic: Common Schools and American Society, 1780–1860*. New York: Hill and Wang, 1983. This is currently the best history of the common-school movement.

Kaufman, Marc. "Study Fails to Find Value in Dare Program." *The Washington Post* (August 3, 1999). www.mapinc.org/drugnews/v99.n797.a09.html. Reports study on ineffectiveness of D.A.R.E. program.

Let's Move: America's Move to Raise a Healthier Generation of Kids. www.letsmove.gov/index.php. First Lady Michelle Obama's U.S. government Website for fighting childhood obesity.

Lewin, Tamar. "With Court Nod, Parents Debate School Drug Tests." *The New York Times on the Web* (September 29, 2002). www.nytimes.com. Lewin presents a survey of the reaction of local school districts to the U.S. Supreme Court decision to allow drug testing of students involved in extracurricular activities.

Lickona, Tom, Eric Schaps, and Catherine Lewis. *CEP's Eleven Principles of Effective Character Education*. Washington, DC: Character Education Partnership, 2007. A guide to character education.

Luck, Ashley. "Virginia High School Teacher Fired for Refusing to Use Student's Preferred Pronoun." *The Virginian-Pilot* (December 7, 2018). https://pilotonline.com/news/nation-world/virginia/article_f5654b02-fa31-11e8-8660-2f7abd41e8dd.html on December 13, 2018. This article highlights the conflict between religious values and recognition of transgender students.

National Center for Chronic Disease Prevention and Health Promotion. *Childhood Obesity*. www.cdc.gov/HealthyYouth/obesity/. Information available on childhood obesity.

National Center for Education Statistics. *The Condition of Education 2018*. Washington, DC: U.S Department of Education, 2018. Report gives statistics on school crime.

National Crime Prevention Council. *School Safety Tips for Administrators*. www.ncpc.org/topics/school-safety/school-safety-tips-for-administrators. Guide for school administrators to combat school crime.

National Education Association. *Report of the Committee on Character Education of the National Education Association.* Washington, DC: U.S. Government Printing Office, 1926. This report recommended the teaching of sex education in high schools.

No Child Left Behind Act of 2001. *Public Law 107-110 (8 January 2002).* Washington, DC: U.S. Government Printing Office, 2002.

Olweus. *The Olweus Bullying Prevention Program.* www.fightcrime.org/cyberbullying/10steps long.pdf. This is a widely recognized program to counter school bullying, including cyber-bullying.

Perkinson, Henry. *The Imperfect Panacea: American Faith in Education, 1865–1965.* New York: Random House, 1968. This is a study of attempts to use the school to solve major social problems in the United States.

Rodman, Hyman, Susan Lewis, and Saralyn Griffith. *The Sexual Rights of Adolescents.* New York: Columbia University Press, 1984. This book provides information on the legal, social, and psychological aspects of adolescent sexuality.

Ross, Edward A. *Social Control.* New York: Palgrave Macmillan, 1906. Ross is the sociologist who declared that schools were the best instrument for controlling the public.

Schrum, Kelly. "Teena Means Business: Teenage Girls' Culture and 'Seventeen Magazine,' 1944–1950." In *Delinquents & Debutantes: Twentieth-Century American Girls' Cultures.* New York: New York University Press, 1998. This chapter discusses the origin of the word "teen-ager" and the development of teenage commercial markets.

Schwartz, Sarah. "How One Teacher Explains Consent to Her 3rd Grade Students." *Education Week* (October 9, 2018). https://blogs.edweek.org/teachers/teaching_now/2018/10/how_one_teacher_explains_consent.html on November 18, 2018. How one teacher introduces students to sexual harassment issues.

Sex Respect. www.sexrespect.com. This organization is playing a leading role in advocating absti-nence via sexual education for public schools.

Shapiro, Laura. *Perfection Salad: Women and Cooking at the Turn of the Century.* New York: Random House, 2001. Shapiro gives a history of the role of home economics in the devel-opment of American cuisine.

Shapiro, Sarah, and Catherine Brown. "Sex Education Standards Across the States." *American Progress Organization* (May 9, 2018). www.americanprogress.org/issues/education-k-12/reports/2018/05/09/450158/sex-education-standards-across-states/ on December 2, 2018. Survey of sex education standards.

Shear, Michael. "Students Lead Huge Rallies for Gun Control Across the U.S." *New York Times* (March 24, 2018). www.nytimes.com/2018/03/24/us/politics/students-lead-huge-rallies-for-gun-control-across-the-us.html on December 5, 2018. Description of student rallies demanding changes in gun control after school shootings.

Spring, Joel. *The American School Tenth Edition.* New York: Routledge, 2018. This history of U.S. schools emphasizes multiculturalism and critical thinking.

Stage, Sarah. "Ellen Richards and the Social Significance of the Home Economics Movement." In *Rethinking Home Economics: Women and the History of the Profession,* edited by Sarah Stage, and Virginia B. Vincenti. Ithaca, NY: Cornell University Press, 1997. This chapter outlines the social purposes of home economics education.

Stage, Sarah, and Virginia Vincenti, eds. *Rethinking Home Economics: Women and the History of a Profession.* Ithaca, NY: Cornell University Press, 1997. This is a collection of essays on the history of home economics.

Toporek, Bryan. "Youth-Obesity Rate Plunged by 43 Percent Over Past Decade, CDC Finds." *Education Week* (February 26, 2014). http://blogs.edweek.org/edweek/schooled_in_sports/2014/02/youth-obesity_rate_plunged_by_43_percent_over_past_decade_cdc_finds.html?qs=obesity.

Toppo, Greg. "10 Years Later, the Real Story Behind Columbine." *USA Today* (April 14, 2009). www.usatoday.com/news/nation/2009-04-13-columbine-myths_N.htm.

U.S. Department of Education. *Be Best First Lady Melania Trump's Initiative.* www.whitehouse.gov/bebest/ on December 6, 2018. First Lady Melania Trump's campaign against bullying.

————. *Condition of Education 2014.* http://nces.ed.gov/pubs2014/2014083.pdf. Contains recent statistics on school crimes.

————. *A Guide to Education and No Child Left Behind.* Washington, DC: Education Publications Center, 2004. This is the official government guide to No Child Left Behind.

————. *Secretary DeVos: Proposed Title IX Rule Provides Clarity for Schools, Support for Survivors, and Due Process Rights for All* (November 16, 2018). www.ed.gov/news/press-releases/secretary-devos-proposed-title-ix-rule-provides-clarity-schools-support-survivors-and-due-process-rights-all on December 1, 2018. New U.S. guidelines for legal cases involving sexual harassment.

U.S. Department of Health and Human Services, Centers for Disease Control and Prevention. *Control and Prevention, Trends in Reportable Sexually Transmitted Diseases in the United States, 2007 and Trends in the Prevalence of Sexual Behaviors National YRBS: 1991–2009.* www.cdc.gov. National surveillance data on chlamydia, gonorrhea, and syphilis.

U.S. Office of Adolescent Health in the U.S. Department of Health and Human Services. www.hhs.gov/ash/oah/oah-initiatives/teen_pregnancy/db/tpp-searchable.html. Website for programs to reduce teenage pregnancy.

Walker, Kate. "Resources to Support Social-Emotional Learning." *Education Week* (November 28, 2018). https://blogs.edweek.org/edweek/global_learning/2018/11/resources_to_support_social_emotional_learning.html on December 10, 2018. Discussion of resources for social and emotional instruction.

Walsh, Mark, and Laura Miller. "Challenge to District's Pro-Transgender Policy Reaches U.S. Supreme Court." *Education Week* (November 20, 2018). https://blogs.edweek.org/edweek/school_law/2018/11/challenge_to_pa_districts_pro-.html on November 24, 2018.

————. "Court Upholds Drug Tests for Student Athletes." *Education Week on the Web* (July 12, 1995). www.edweek.org. The recent ruling on drug tests for school athletics is reported.

————. "Students Claiming Sex Harassment Win Right to Sue." *Education Week* (March 4, 1992), pp. 1, 24. This article discusses the U.S. Supreme Court ruling in *Franklin v. Gwinnett County Public Schools* (1992), which provides students with protection from sexual harassment by teachers.

————. "Supreme Court Lets Stand Rulings on Drug Tests, Teaching Materials." *Education Week on the Web* (September 14, 1998). www.edweek.org. Walsh reports on the U.S. Supreme Court decision to uphold the right of school districts to perform random drug tests on students participating in extracurricular activities.

————. "White House Backs Wider Drug Testing in Schools." *Education Week on the Web* (September 11, 2002). www.edweek.org. This article discusses the booklet issued by the White House Office of National Drug Control Policy urging drug testing of students involved in extracurricular activities.

Will, Madeline. "What the Trump School Safety Report Says About Teachers." *Education Week,* (December 18, 2018). http://blogs.edweek.org/edweek/teacherbeat/2018/12/trump_safety_report_train_teachers.html on December 17, 2018. A controversial report because it avoided tackling the issue of gun control.

Yettick, Holly. "Website and Review Identify Sex-Ed. Programs with Proven Track Records." *Education Week* (March 18, 2014). http://blogs.edweek.org/edweek/inside-school-research/2014/03/sex_ed.html?qs=sex+education. This article details the new government Website dedicated to programs to reduce teenage pregnancies.

CHAPTER 3

Education and Equality of Opportunity

This chapter examines the differing models and problems associated with school efforts to educate for equality of opportunity. In the 1830s, Horace Mann declared schools the great balance wheel of society by providing graduates with equality of opportunity to pursue wealth. In this context, *equality of opportunity means all members of a society are given equal chances to pursue wealth and enter any occupation or social class.* Sometimes people think equality of opportunity means equal incomes and status. Therefore, it is important to emphasize what it is not: *Equality does not mean everyone will have equal incomes and equal status.*

I first describe the different educational models for achieving equality of opportunity. Second, I analyze problems in schools and society in attempting to achieve equality of opportunity—namely, educational advantages and disadvantages given to the child and future worker by family income and cultural background.

In summary, this chapter explores the continuing hope that schools can provide equality of opportunity for all people by discussing:

- The relationship between schooling and the concept of equality of opportunity
- School models for achieving equality of opportunity, including the common-school, sorting-machine, and testing models
- The relationship between family income and educational achievement
- The relationship between a student's cultural background and educational achievement
- Discriminatory factors in the labor market that hinder the achievement of equality of opportunity, including gender, race, and cultural background
- Inequalities between schools that contribute to *inequality* of opportunity

SCHOOLS AND EQUALITY OF OPPORTUNITY

Equality of opportunity is based on the idea of an *un*equal society in which individuals compete with one another, with some becoming wealthy and some falling to the bottom of the economic scale. In Horace Mann's vision, schools will ensure everyone receives an education that allows them to compete for wealth on equal terms. Life is a competitive race, and school is the starting point.

What about the meaning of equality of opportunity and the wording of the 1776 American Declaration of Independence, which declared, "All men are created equal." In *The Pursuit of Equality in American History*, J. R. Pole argues that promoting equality of opportunity was America's way of balancing the ideal of equality with a society riddled with inequality. After the American Revolution, the ideal of equality was compromised by women not being able to vote, slavery, legal racial segregation, exploitation of Native Americans, and differences in wealth and status. Even many of the signers of the Declaration of Independence, including Thomas Jefferson, owned enslaved Africans and later denied U.S. citizenship to Native Americans. Did the Declaration's statement of equality exclude women since women did not gain the right to vote until the twentieth century? Apparently, given the historical circumstances, the phrase "All men are created equal" applied only to white men at the time of the signing of the Declaration. Limiting full citizenship rights to white men was highlighted by the Naturalization Act of 1790. Passed by the U.S. Congress, this legislation restricted the granting of citizenship to "free white persons" only. Under this law, Native Americans were excluded from citizenship because they were classified as domestic foreigners. Until the 1940s and 1950s, this 1790 law was used to deny citizenship to Asian immigrants.

An emphasis on equality of opportunity through schooling seemed to resolve the conflict between the use of the word "equality" and the existence of widespread inequality. Education would provide everyone with an equal chance to pursue wealth. Ideally, equality of opportunity through education would ensure that citizens occupied their particular social positions because of merit and not because of family wealth, heredity, or special cultural advantages.

Equality of opportunity can be thought of as a contest where everyone is competing for jobs and income. To provide everyone with an equal chance in the competition, all participants must begin at the same starting line. During the contest, some people will succeed and others will fail. In this concept, it is the role of the school to ensure that everyone begins the race for riches on an equal footing.

In declaring schools the great balance wheel of society, Mann believed equality of opportunity would reduce tensions between the rich and poor. The poor could believe their children had an equal chance to compete with the children of the rich. Rather than feeling antagonistic toward the wealthy, the poor could believe they had the opportunity to join the rich. By believing schools could give everyone an equal opportunity to achieve wealth and power, one could ignore blatant social, economic, and political inequalities. Faced with obvious inequalities, people could now argue, "Hey, everyone is given a chance to get ahead. Those without money or power just didn't work hard enough. They had all the chances. They could have done well in school and gotten into a good college." This reasoning stabilized the social system by shifting the causes of inequality onto the shoulders of the individual. People seeking rectification of unequal conditions could call for more and better schools rather than demanding major political and economic changes. Schools promised to be the gateway to equal opportunity.

Can schools provide equality of opportunity to pursue wealth? How can schools be structured to provide graduates with equality of opportunity? Can they simultaneously compensate for differences in students' family income, race, ethnic background, languages spoken at home, cultural capital, and gender to provide equality of opportunity after graduation to compete for income and property? These questions are central to current discussions about school organization, curriculum, and methods of instruction.

SCHOOL MODELS FOR EQUALITY OF OPPORTUNITY

Debate about equality of opportunity is centered on three major models. These models overlap and sometimes operate simultaneously and are associated with particular historical periods. However, like other things in American education, nothing ever seems to disappear; a new model or educational practice is simply added onto an older one. Just as U.S. schools in the twenty-first century are a patchwork of educational goals from different historical periods, the schools are also a patchwork of attempts to ensure equality of opportunity.

I call these attempts to provide equality of opportunity the common-school model, the sorting-machine model, and the high-stakes testing model. Today, all three models are present in public schools, with the high-stakes testing model receiving the greatest attention. Interestingly, all these models assume schools can provide equality of opportunity. But can they?

THE COMMON-SCHOOL MODEL

In the common-school model, illustrated in Figure 3.1, everyone receives an equal and common education. Theoretically, this will ensure everyone begins the economic race on equal footing. Children from all social backgrounds attend school and receive an education that will prepare them to compete on equal terms in the economic system. Upon graduation, all students have an equal chance to succeed; thus, competition for socioeconomic standing occurs *outside* the schoolhouse.

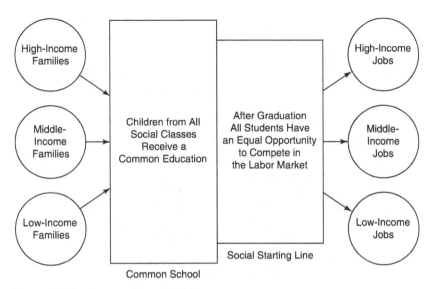

Figure 3.1 The Common-School Model

Nineteenth-century advocates of common schools believed differences of social class and special advantages would disappear as everyone was given an equal chance to get an equal education. During the 1830s, workingmen's parties wanted publicly supported common schools, believing that if the children of rich and poor families were mixed in the same schoolhouse there would be greater equality of opportunity. But what about before children entered schools? Were there advantages to growing up in a rich household as opposed to a poor one?

The most extreme answer to these questions came from one faction of the New York Workingman's Party. This group argued that sending students to a common school would not in itself eliminate differences in social background because the well-to-do child would return from school to a home richly furnished and full of books, whereas the poor child would return to a shanty barren of books and opportunities to learn. School, in the opinion of these workingmen, could never eliminate these differences. Their solution was that all children in New York should be removed from their families and placed in state boarding schools, where they would all live in the same types of rooms, wear the same types of clothes, and eat the same food. In this milieu, education would truly allow all members of society to begin school on equal terms. This extreme solution to the problem did not receive wide support, and debates about it eventually led to the collapse of the New York Workingman's Party.

However, the common-school model continues to be plagued by differences in family backgrounds. Children with parents who read to them and expose them to a variety of cultural events are probably better prepared to learn than children whose parents are illiterate. Also, wealthy parents can provide their children with special advantages such as tutors and learning aids, while poor parents might have to struggle just to feed their children. After graduation, children might receive uneven support in pursuing a career. We explore these issues later in the chapter.

THE SORTING-MACHINE MODEL

In the sorting-machine model, as depicted in Figure 3.2, the school attempts to overcome the influence of family background. Here, equality of opportunity is guaranteed by impartial decisions of teachers, counselors, and standardized tests. Students from all social backgrounds enter school and are classified and placed in ability groups and tracks that will lead to jobs appropriate to student abilities. Unlike the common-school model, students receive unequal and different educations. Some students graduate with vocational training while others prepare to enter college. In this model, competition for social positions takes place *within* the school.

Figure 3.2 The Sorting-Machine Model

As it developed in the early twentieth century, students entered the first grade and were placed by their teachers in different reading and math ability groups. During junior high, or what is now called middle school, students were to be tested and evaluated to find out what types of jobs they might be able to do after graduation or whether they should go on to college. An important addition to both middle and high schools was the guidance counselor. Students were to meet with counselors who would help them select a future career and an educational program leading to that career.

Why did educational leaders assume they could fairly provide equality of opportunity by sorting students according to their future positions in the job market? In part, it was a result of a belief that ability or intelligence could be scientifically determined at an early age. Intelligence testing promised to eliminate the effect of social backgrounds. Some believed intelligence tests could be an objective measure to determine what type of occupation a person should enter.

Another approach is to reject inherited intelligence and place emphasis on the effect of the child's environment. This is the famous nurture versus nature debate. Those who see nurture as more important argue that differences in measured intelligence between social and racial groups primarily reflect differences in social conditions. The poor grow up in surroundings limited in intellectual training: an absence of books and magazines in the home; poor housing, diet, and medical care; and lack of peer-group interest in learning all might account for their poor performance on intelligence tests. This approach suggests the school can act positively to overcome differences caused by social and cultural conditions.

Most recently, school programs try to overcome inequalities caused by differences in preparation for school learning. Preschool is used to overcome inadequate learning opportunities for children in some families. Compensatory education is designed to provide special instruction in reading and other skills to offset disadvantages in preparation for formal schooling.

THE HIGH-STAKES TESTING MODEL

The high-stakes testing model is a variation on the sorting-machine model (see Figure 3.3). A "high-stakes test" refers to an achievement examination that determines a person's future academic career and job opportunities. These are not tests of innate qualities, as are intelligence tests, but tests of what a person has learned. High-stakes testing begins in elementary school, where the results determine promotion from one grade to another. High-stakes tests then determine graduation from high school; admission to undergraduate, graduate, and professional schools; and professional licenses and employment credentials. In Chapter 9, I analyze the educational ramifications of high-stakes testing.

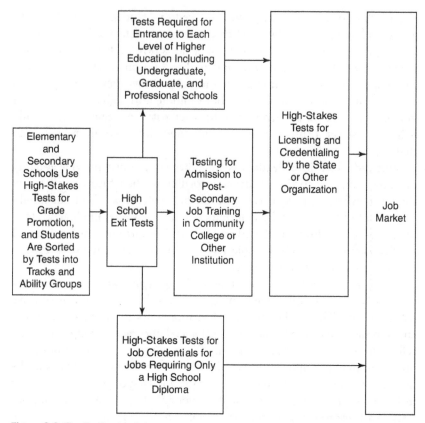

Figure 3.3 The Testing Model

How is equality of opportunity to be achieved? Imagine a society where complete regulation of employment is based on high-stakes testing. Tests are the basis for issuing diplomas, certificates for job skills, and licenses. Educational institutions become well-oiled machines processing children using a variety of tests and training to receive particular credentials for jobs ranging from childcare provider to auto mechanic to real estate salesperson to accountant to college professor. When applying for any job, people are asked to submit proof of their qualifications. This proof would be their credentials. A society organized around high-stakes testing is advantageous to employers because they are presented with immediate evidence of a person's abilities to perform a job.

Throughout the twentieth century, there existed many forms of high-stakes testing used for granting licenses for careers ranging from physician to beautician. Most of these licenses required a combination of educational achievement and state testing, such as attending medical school and then taking a state examination. In the twenty-first century, the labor market has been swamped with calls for greater testing and certification. Consider the history of the licensing of teachers. In the nineteenth century, a person applying for a teaching position was simply evaluated by a local school board using whatever method it felt adequate. Then, in the early twentieth century, state governments required local school systems to hire only those teachers licensed by the state. To obtain these licenses teachers had to take college courses in education. In the second half of the twentieth century, state governments began to require both college courses and the passing of a state examination.

Most school systems are test driven. In the United States, life-determining standardized testing begins in elementary school and extends into the workplace. Most states now require passing a state test before receiving a high school diploma. Of course, standardized testing does not end in high school but extends through a person's college career. Test centers and test courses exist for the sole purpose of preparing people to take tests. It is now a test-happy world!

In a society organized around high-stakes testing, people can undergo a variety of examinations to gain credentials that provide proof of their ability to perform a job. For instance, some employers might just be interested in a job applicant having a high school or college diploma. Another employer might want to see a college transcript to ensure the applicant received a particular type of education, such as engineering. Another employer might want to see a diploma plus test scores qualifying the applicant for the job. Another employer might want a diploma, test scores, and a license.

In a society organized around high-stakes tests, the school becomes a crucial institution for determining economic success. To ensure equality of opportunity in the high-stakes testing model, the school must give everyone an equal chance to learn and to be tested without cultural bias. Is this possible?

TESTING AND SKILLS AS PREDICTORS OF ECONOMIC CONDITIONS

Since the 1990s, two international tests have ranked countries according to their scores. This creates an international academic Olympiad with nations competing for top results. The two tests are Organization for Economic Co-operation and Development (OECD)'s Programme for International Student Assessment (PISA) and the International Association for the Evaluation of Educational Achievement (IEA)'s Trends in International Mathematics and Science Study (TIMSS). The scores from these tests are considered so important in evaluating national school systems and the skills of the workforce that economists Eric A. Hanushek and Ludger Woessman and political scientist Paul E. Peterson argue in *Endangering Prosperity: A Global View of the American School* that "the gains in test scores over time are strongly related to [economic] gains over time."

Consequently, PISA and TIMSS scores are used to measure the quality of a nation's labor force without using predictions of the number of possible college and high school graduates needed to meet future manpower requirements. In the most recent 2015 report, the 10 countries with the highest PISA scores were, in order, Singapore, Japan, Estonia, Chinese Taipei, Finland, Macao (China), Canada, Vietnam, Hong Kong (China) and Beijing, Shanghai, Jiangsu, Guangdong (China). The United States was ranked 25th behind Portugal and Norway.

An important aspect of these tests is that they are designed to measure student skills needed in the workplace. PISA and TIMSS are supposed to measure cognitive skills wanted by employers. "Skills have become the global currency of twenty-first century economies," declared OECD's publication *Trends Shaping Education*.

EDUCATION AND INCOME

What is the relationship between education and income? This is a crucial question in considering the school's ability to provide equality of opportunity. The preceding three models assume a close relationship between education and income. Studies show that years of schooling are associated with income levels. These findings suggest that achievement in school is the road to economic success. However, a comparison of educational attainment, gender, and race suggests that other social factors affect the role of schools in determining personal income.

To illustrate the relationship between schooling and income, I use the National Center for Education Statistics report *The Condition of Education 2018*.

Table 3.1 Mean Annual Earnings of 25- to 34-Year-Olds by Educational Attainment

Educational Attainment	Annual Earnings 2016 ($)	Annual Earnings 2014 ($)
Less than high school completion	25,400	25,000
High school completion	31,800	30,000
Attained bachelor's degree	50,000	52,000

Source: National Center for Education Statistics, *The Condition of Education 2018* (Washington, DC: U.S Department of Education, 2018), p. 251.

Table 3.2 indicates gender is a factor in the relationship between education attainment and income. Simply stated, even with equal educational attainments, men earn more than women. As Table 3.2 shows, there is a steady increase in annual median income with educational attainment.

Please note that Table 3.2 and the following tables are taken from the 2010 U.S. census statistics. The census is taken every 10 years, with the next one scheduled for 2020. However, regarding the relationship between gender and earnings, the U.S. Department of Labor Bureau of Labor Statistics reported:

> In 2014, women who worked full time in wage and salary jobs had median usual weekly earnings of $719, which was 83 percent of men's median weekly earnings ($871). Women's earnings as a percentage of men's varied by occupation. Women's median usual weekly earnings in construction and extraction occupations ($691) were 91 percent of the earnings of their male counterparts.

For men, the increase in annual median earnings from no high school diploma ($24,985) to a bachelor's degree ($70,898) is $45,913. The difference for women with no high school diploma ($15,315) to a bachelor's degree ($43,127) is $27,812.

LABOR MARKET BIAS: WHITE PRIVILEGE: GENDER, RACE, EDUCATIONAL ATTAINMENT, AND INCOME

Can schools provide equality of opportunity? Are there bias factors in society that limit the ability of schools to ensure everyone an equal chance to attain wealth?

Table 3.2 Mean Earnings for Highest Degree Earned for Persons 18 Years Old and Older with Earnings

Gender	Total Persons ($)	Not a High School Graduate ($)	High School Completion ($)	Bachelor's Degree ($)	Master's Degree ($)	Professional Degree ($)
Male	50,110	24,985	36,985	70,898	86,966	142,282
Female	32,899	15,315	24,234	43,127	54,772	83,031

Source: U.S. Census Bureau, *The 2010 Statistical Abstract: The National Data Book*, Table 227.

Table 3.3 shows the ratio of female earnings by racial classification to those of white males. For all racial categories, white men earn more than females. White females (white alone, not Hispanic) with a high school diploma earn 70 percent in lifetime wages of what white males with a high school diploma earn in lifetime wages. However, some of this difference declines with educational attainment except for professional degrees. For instance, white females over a lifetime with a doctorate degree earn 80 percent of a male's lifetime income. Hispanic females with a high school diploma earn 60 percent in lifetime wages of what white males with a high school diploma earn in lifetime wages, while for Hispanic females with a doctorate it is 71 percent.

White males, as indicated in Table 3.3, have lifetime earnings higher than all males except Asians (Asian alone, not Hispanic) with master's degrees (1.04 percent) and Asians with professional (0.99 percent) and doctorate degrees (0.98 percent), who are almost equal to white males in lifetime income. However, at all levels of educational attainment men earn more than women.

Table 3.3 Ratio of Synthetic Work-Life Earnings to White Males by Level of Education

Female	High School Graduate	Bachelor's Degree	Master's Degree	Professional Degree	Doctorate Degree
Hispanic	0.60	0.60	0.68	0.49	0.71
White alone, not Hispanic	0.70	0.71	0.71	0.67	0.80
Black alone, not Hispanic	0.63	0.65	0.70	0.60	0.78
Asian alone, not Hispanic	0.63	0.72	0.82	0.77	0.85
Other, not Hispanic	0.67	0.66	0.67	0.61	0.73
Male					
Hispanic	0.77	0.73	0.84	0.66	0.84
Black alone, not Hispanic	0.79	0.74	0.76	0.74	0.79
Asian alone, not Hispanic	0.76	0.86	1.04	0.99	0.98
Other, not Hispanic	0.87	0.84	0.89	0.86	0.90

Source: Tiffany Julian and Robert Kominski, *Education and Synthetic Work-Life Earnings Estimates*, U.S. Department of Commerce Economics and Statistics Administration, U.S. Census Bureau, September 2011, p. 10. Retrieved from www.census.gov/prod/2011pubs/acs-14.pdf.

In 2018, the U.S. Department of Labor reported:

Hispanics and Blacks continued to have considerably lower earnings than Whites and Asians. The median usual weekly earnings of full-time wage and salary workers in 2017 were $655 for Hispanics, $682 for Blacks, $890 for Whites, and $1,043 for Asians. Among men, the earnings for Whites ($971), Blacks ($710), and Hispanics ($690) were 80 percent, 59 percent, and 57 percent, respectively, of the earnings of Asians ($1,207). The median earnings of White women ($795), Black women ($657), and Hispanic women ($603) were 88 percent, 73 percent, and 67 percent, respectively, of the earnings of Asian women ($903).

In conclusion, the preceding statistics indicate that in the United States income is related to educational attainment, but discriminatory factors related to gender and race in the labor market negate some of the advantages gained through increased education. Simply stated, equality of opportunity depends on equality of opportunity in the labor market.

ARE SCHOOLS CONTRIBUTING TO THE RICH GETTING RICHER AND THE POOR GETTING POORER?

A current reality is that American workers compete with workers from other nations. If a company can find less expensive workers in another country, it might move to that country. If a company needs highly educated workers that are available in the United States, the company might remain. The result is the increasing income of Americans with skills needed for high-paying jobs in the global economy and a decline in wages for those competing for low-wage jobs.

Is this global competition contributing to income inequality? Are the rich getting richer and the poor getting poorer? In 2018, the Pew Research Center released information of growing inequality in U.S. incomes. Income inequality has increased steadily since the 1970s. According to the Pew report written by Rakesh Kochhar and Anthony Cilluffo: "The gap between Americans at the top and the bottom of the income ladder increased 27% from 1970 to 2016." While the causes of inequality are debated and there are other causes than global labor market competition, the reality is that income inequality is growing. Another Pew research report written by Drew Desilver found: "More than half (61%) of Americans said the U.S. economic system favors the wealthy, while just 35% said it's fair to most people . . . A similar share (66%) of Americans said the gap between rich and poor had increased in the past five years; nearly three-quarters of respondents said the rich-poor gap was either a 'very big' (47%) or 'moderately big' (27%) problem."

Table 3.4 Share of Aggregate Income Received by Each Fifth of Households in 2017

Year	Lowest Fifth	Second Fifth	Third Fifth	Fourth Fifth	Top Fifth
2017	3.1%	8.2%	14.3%	22.9%	51.5%

Source: Statista, *Shares of Household Income of Quintiles in the United States from 1970 to 2017*. Retrieved from www.statista.com/statistics/203247/shares-of-household-income-of-quintiles-in-the-us/ on December 17, 2018.

Table 3.4 indicates the share of household income in 2017 for each 20 percent of the population. For instance, the lowest 20 percent of the population by income received only 3.1 percent of the total income in the United States in contrast to the top 20 percent in income with 51.5 percent of the total U.S. income. These statistics highlight the large inequality of income existing in the United States. It has been the hope of human capital economists that increased schooling would reduce inequalities in incomes, but this has not occurred.

Why the increase in the percentage of total household income of the upper class? The U.S. Census Bureau explains, "Increasing income inequality is believed to be related to changes taking place in the labor market and in the composition of the households in the United States." The composition of households is an important factor with a decline in married couple households and an increase in single-parent and nonfamily households, which typically have lower incomes.

On the other hand, the National Education Summit on High Schools blames the failure of schools to prepare youth for competition in the global labor market. As stated before, the labor market's contribution to income inequality is the result of increasing wages paid to well-educated or highly skilled workers and declining wages for poorly educated or low-skilled workers. Workers now compete in an international labor market. U.S. companies will move if they can find cheaper labor and production costs in another country. U.S. workers must compete with the wages paid in other countries. This results in a decline in real wages for unskilled labor in the United States.

RICH AND POOR SCHOOL DISTRICTS

Ask any real estate agent in your area to name the best local school district. Most likely the real estate agent will name school districts with wealthy households and a high percentage of college graduates. Often the housing in these districts, which may vary in large cities, is beyond the purchasing power of low-income families. This is a form of economic segregation in schooling that contributes to inequalities in educational outcomes.

Table 3.5 Percentage Distribution of Aggregate Income by Each Fifth and Top 5 Percent of Households

Year	Lowest Fifth (%)	Second Fifth (%)	Third Fifth (%)	Fourth Fifth (%)	Highest Fifth (%)	Top 5 Percent (%)
1990	3.8	9.6	15.9	24.0	46.6	18.5
2000	3.6	8.9	14.8	23.0	49.8	22.1
2007	3.4	8.7	14.8	23.4	49.7	21.2
2017	3.1	8.2	14.3	23.0	51.5	22.3

Source: U.S. Census Bureau, *Historical Income Tables: Households*. Retrieved from www.census.gov/data/tables/time-series/demo/income-poverty/historical-income-households.html.

Imagine that you and your spouse are setting out to buy a house and that your primary concern is settling in an area with good schools. Your dream is for your children to attend college and, thereby, gain access to high-paying jobs. Recognizing the important influence of peers on your children's academic future, you want to live in a community where most students plan to attend college. In other words, you want the best for your children. According to Horace Mann's dream, all school districts should be equal. But this is not the case when you consider expenditures per child, test scores, and college attendance. Communities in the United States are not equal in the wealth and educational attainment of their students.

Many of the wealthy districts are located in suburbs near major cities. The U.S. Census Bureau's "The Geographic Concentration of High-Income Households: 2007–2011" reported that most wealth is concentrated in areas outside the central cities. It states: "Central cities had lower concentrations [of the top 5 percent income earners] than the suburbs, as 4.9 percent of households in the central city were among the top 5 percent, compared to 6.1 percent of outside central cities."

As shown in Table 3.6, there is wide disparity in per-pupil funding between states and between districts within states with differing concentrations of poverty. Regarding disparities in per-pupil revenues by state, Maine had revenues per pupil of $12,880 in districts with 0 percent poverty while Florida had revenues per pupil of $9,230 in districts with 0 percent poverty. In all the states in Table 3.6, the amount of revenue per pupil declines as the concentration of poverty increases. For instance, in Pennsylvania the amount of revenue per pupil in districts with 0 percent poverty was $13,675 declining to $12,373 for districts with a 30 percent concentration of poverty, and in Colorado the amount declined for the same levels of poverty from $9,478 to $8,961.

Table 3.6 Cost-Adjusted (Predicted) Local and State Revenues per Pupil in the Eight Least Equitable States by Child Poverty Rate

State	0% Poverty	10% Poverty	20% Poverty	30% Poverty
Maine	$12,880	$12,373	$11,418	$11,418
Pennsylvania	13,675	13,226	12,792	12,373
Missouri	9,509	9,251	9,000	8,756
Idaho	7,783	7,591	7,404	7,221
Nebraska	10,542	10,337	10,136	9,939
Florida	9,230	9,036	8,847	8,661
Colorado	9,478	9,303	9,139	8,961

Source: Adapted from Table 1 in Bruce D. Baker and Sean P. Corcoran, *The Stealth Inequities of School Funding: How State and Local School Finance Systems Perpetuate Inequitable Student Spending*, Center for American Progress, September 2012, pp. 7–8. Retrieved from www.americanprogress.org/issues/education/report/2012/09/19/38189/the-stealth-inequities-of-school-funding/.

Another source of unequal funding is local fundraising groups that add extra revenue to local school budgets. These fundraising groups are primarily located in wealthy school districts. In 2014, the *New York Times* reported that school districts with high median incomes had the most fundraising groups and collected more money per pupil than districts with low-income families. These fundraising groups raised $880 million in 2010. *New York Times* reporter Motoko Rich provided this example of the work of these fundraising groups;

> In Coronado, Calif., a wealthy enclave off the coast of San Diego, for example, local education groups, which support about 3,200 students in five schools, raised more than $1,500 per student in 2010. These private funds helped pay for arts and music classes at all grade levels, sports medicine courses at the high school and a digital media academy at the middle school, where students are learning animation and designing buildings with 3-D printers. By contrast, the combined fund-raising of groups affiliated with schools in the San Diego Unified School District—where the median household income is about two-thirds that of Coronado—amounted to $19.57 per student.

There are other factors besides educational expenditures that determine the educational quality of the school district, including college attendance and test scores. Some parents use reports of test scores and college attendance rates when shopping for a new home. Where do home buyers get their information on schools? They usually get the data from real estate brokers or online services. Using these sources, home buyers can collect information on schools, neighborhood characteristics, and housing for any place in the United States. Some might consider real estate agents and Websites the best guide to quality public education in the United States.

SOCIAL CLASS AND AT-RISK STUDENTS

During the last century, many terms, including "disadvantaged," "urban," and "culturally deprived," were used to characterize students who might have academic problems. The latest descriptor is "at risk." Many students classified as at risk experience few academic problems. Being at risk is only an indication of *potential* academic problems. The National Center for Education Statistics (NCES) found that 35 percent of students with risk factors finished high school and enrolled in a four-year college or university within two years of high school graduation.

Poverty is high on the list of factors that put students at risk. The NCES report *The Condition of Education 2002* lists the factors that might indicate a student is at risk of academic failure. In this list, the NCES uses socioeconomic status (SES) rather than the U.S. Census Bureau's income classifications. The SES of students is determined by parental education level, parental occupation, family income, and household items. In the following list of at-risk factors, low SES refers to students from the bottom 25 percent of households on a socioeconomic scale. These are families in which the parents have minimum levels of educational attainment, low income, and poor job status. The report's list of at-risk factors is:

- Being in the lowest SES
- Changing schools two or more times from grades 1 to 8 (except for transitions to middle school or junior high school)
- Having average grades of C or lower from grades 6 to 8
- Being in a single-parent household during grade 8
- Having one or more older siblings who left high school before completion
- Being held back one or more times from grades 1 to 8

The best predictor of whether a student will drop out of school is if a student repeated a grade in elementary or middle school, conclude sociologists Karl Alexander and Doris Entwistle in "Signs of Early Exit for Dropouts Abound" in *Education Week*'s special 2006 report "Diplomas Count: An Essential Guide to Graduation Policy and Rates." Studying students in Baltimore public schools revealed that 64 percent of those who repeated a grade in elementary school and 63 percent of those who repeated a grade in middle school eventually left school without a high school diploma. Russell Rumberger, in the same report, concludes from his national study that students who move twice during high school are twice as likely to drop out. A Gates Foundation survey tied dropping out to excessive absenteeism.

Raising female incomes to the level of males would appear to be one means of reducing the number of at-risk students. Poverty combined with being raised in a single-parent family appears to put a student at risk for school failure.

THE END OF THE AMERICAN DREAM: SCHOOL DROPOUTS

Dropping out of school before high school graduation results, as shown in previous tables, in a lower lifetime income compared to school graduates. However, the number of dropouts has decreased in the twenty-first century. Graduation rates vary between ethnic groups, as revealed in the following findings from the U.S. Department of Education's *The Condition of Education 2018*. It reported:

> The overall status dropout rate decreased from 10.9 percent in 2000 to 6.1 percent in 2016. During this time, the Hispanic status dropout rate decreased by 19.2 percentage points, while the Black and White status dropout rates decreased by 6.9 and 1.7 percentage points, respectively. Nevertheless, in 2016 the Hispanic status dropout rate (8.6 percent) remained higher than the Black (6.2 percent) and White (5.2 percent) status dropout rates.

A status dropout is the percentage of 16- through 24-year-olds who are not enrolled in school and have not earned a high school credential (either a diploma or an equivalency credential such as a General Educational Development [GED] certificate).

National school dropouts are denied the dream of equality of opportunity through schooling. However, conditions are improving, but racial disparities continue.

THE DIGITAL GAP BETWEEN RICH AND POOR

No one knows for sure the effect of screen time on children's brains. In the past, the worry was about equal access to computers. Now many parents are worried as children spend more time looking at computer and smartphone screens. This concern, as reported by Nellie Bowles, has created a new social class divide. Upper-class families and the schools that serve them are limiting the time their children spend staring at screens. Bowles writes, "America's public schools are still promoting devices with screens—even offering digital-only preschools. The rich are banning screens from class altogether." She found that parents and schools serving low-income children are not limiting screen time. On the other hand, upper-class families often have rules limiting screen time. Bowles reports, "Lower-income teenagers spend an average of eight hours and seven minutes a day using screens for entertainment, while higher income peers spend five hours and 42 minutes. Two studies that look at race have found that white children are exposed to screens significantly less than African-American and Hispanic children."

Will less screen time mean more intellectual growth? There are no clear answers to this question. However, it might indicate a future divide between social classes.

SOCIAL REPRODUCTION

The discussion so far in this chapter suggests that schools might play a role in maintaining differences between social classes through economic segregation. This argument is called *social reproduction*. Simply defined, social reproduction means that the schools reproduce the social class structure of society. Economists Samuel Bowles and Herbert Gintis are the major proponents of the concept of social reproduction. They contend that the school causes occupational immobility. This argument completely reverses the idea that the school creates occupational mobility. Bowles and Gintis, in constructing this thesis, accept the findings that mobility rates are consistent throughout Western industrialized countries and that family background is one major factor in determining economic and social advancement. What they argue is that the school is a medium through which family background is translated into occupational and income opportunities.

This translation occurs in personality traits relevant to the work task; modes of self-presentation such as manner of speech and dress; ascriptive characteristics such as race, sex, and age; and the level and prestige of an individual's education. Bowles and Gintis insist that the four factors—personality traits, self-presentation, ascriptive characteristics, and level of educational attainment—are all significantly related to occupational success. They also are all related to the social class of the family. For instance, family background is directly related to the level of educational attainment and the prestige of that attainment. Here the economic level of the family determines educational attainment. Children from low-income families do not attain as high a level of education as children from rich families. From this standpoint the school reinforces social stratification and contributes to intergenerational immobility. For ascriptive characteristics such as race, the social advantages or disadvantages of a particular racial group are again related to levels of educational attainment.

As discussed in previous sections on cultural capital, personality traits and self-presentation are, according to Bowles and Gintis, important ingredients in occupational success. In *Schooling in Capitalist America*, Bowles and Gintis support these findings on cultural capital. Child-rearing, they declare, is important in developing personality traits related to entrance into the workforce. Personalities evidencing a great deal of self-direction tend to have greater success in high-status occupations. The differences in child-rearing patterns, the authors state, are reflected in the schools attended by different social classes. Schools with populations from lower-income families tend to be more authoritarian and require more conformity than schools attended by children from higher-income families. This is often reflected in the differences between educationally innovative schools in high-income suburbs and the more traditional schools in low-income, inner-city neighborhoods. In some cases, parents place pressure on local schools either to be more authoritarian or to allow more self-direction. The nature of this pressure tends to be related to the social class of the parents.

In this manner, Bowles and Gintis argue, the child-rearing patterns of the family are reflected in the way schools treat children. Children from authoritarian families are prepared by authoritarian schools to work at low-paying jobs that do not require independent thinking and decision making. The reverse is true for children coming from upper-income families and schools; they are socialized to high-paying jobs that require independent thinking. In this manner, education reproduces social classes. One problem with the social reproduction argument is the treatment of students as passive recipients of knowledge.

CONCLUSION

Can schools provide equality of opportunity? Or does equality of opportunity depend on economic circumstances outside the power of the school? Does the school reduce social differences or heighten them through ability grouping, tracking, teacher expectations, counseling, and inequalities in school financing? Will the equalizing of school finances ensure an equal education for children from all social classes? These questions reflect the major problems confronting a public-school system that professes equal educational opportunity and tries to provide an education that will guarantee equality of opportunity.

SUGGESTED READINGS AND WORKS CITED IN CHAPTER

Baker, Bruce, and Sean Corcoran. *The Stealth Inequities of School Funding: How State and Local School Finance Systems Perpetuate Inequitable Student Spending*, Center for American Progress (September 2012). www.americanprogress.org/issues/education/report/2012/09/19/38189/the-stealth-inequities-of-school-funding/. This study provides tables showing unequal funding of schools between states and between districts with different concentrations of poverty.

Bee, Charles Adam. "The Geographic Concentration of High-Income Households: 2007–2011." *U.S. Census Bureau: American Community Survey Briefs* (February 2013). www.census. gov/prod/2013pubs/acsbr11-23.pdf. The report provides statistics on the geographical areas with concentrations of wealth. This is important regarding rich and poor school districts.

Binet, Alfred. *The Intelligence of the Feeble-Minded*. Baltimore: Williams & Wilkins, 1916. Alfred Binet's pioneering work on developing measurements of intelligence.

Bowles, Nellie. "The Digital Gap Between Rich and Poor Kids Is Not What We Expected." *The New York Times* (October 26, 2018). www.nytimes.com/2018/10/26/style/digital-divide-screens-schools.html on December 4, 2018.

Bowles, Samuel, and Herbert Gintis. *Schooling in Capitalist America*. New York: Basic Books, 1976. This classic book by two neo-Marxist economists argues that schooling in the United States maintains the existing social class structure for the benefit of an economic elite.

Carey, Kevin. *The Funding Gap 2004: Many States Still Shortchange Low-Income and Minority Students*. Washington, DC: Education Trust, 2004. Carey shows disparities in funding based on level of poverty in school districts.

Day, Jennifer, and Eric Newburger. *The Big Payoff: Educational Attainment and Synthetic Estimates of Work-Life Earnings*. Washington, DC: U.S. Census Bureau, July 2002. This is an important study on the relationship between income and educational attainment.

Giroux, Henry. *Theory of Resistance: A Pedagogy for the Opposition*. South Hadley, MA: Bergin and Garvey, 1983. In this book, Giroux criticizes reproduction theorists and presents his theories of resistance.

Kochhar, Rakesh, and Anthony Cilluffo. *Key Findings on the Rise in Income Inequality Within America's Racial and Ethnic Groups* (July 12, 2018). www.pewresearch.org/fact-tank/2018/07/12/key-findings-on-the-rise-in-income-inequality-within-americas-racial-and-ethnic-groups/ on December 2, 2019. Recent data on income inequality in the United States.

National Center for Education Statistics. *The Condition of Education 2018*. Washington, DC: U.S. Government Printing Office, 2018. This excellent annual report on the conditions of schools in the United States is an invaluable source for educational statistics ranging from test scores to school finance.

———. *Digest of Education Statistics 2007*. Washington, DC: U.S. Department of Education, 2008. Introduction to data on U.S. schools.

———. "Indicator 6: Family Characteristics of 5- to 17-Year-Olds." *The Condition of Education 2008*. Washington, DC: U.S. Government Printing Office, 2008. Provides data on poverty and family structures.

———. "Special Section: High-Poverty Schools and the Students Who Attend Them." *The Condition of Education 2010*. Washington, DC: U.S. Government Printing Office, 2010. Reports the degree of economic segregation in public schools.

Oakes, Jeannie. *Keeping Track: How Schools Structure Inequality*. New Haven, CT: Yale University Press, 1985. This book explores the issue of tracking as a source of inequality.

Organization for Economic Co-operation and Development (OECD). *PISA 2015. Results in Focus*. PISA 2015. www.oecd.org/pisa/pisa-2015-results-in-focus.pdf. This publication provides the international ranking of education systems based on PISA scores.

———. *Trends Shaping Education 2013*. Paris: OECD Publishing, 2013. This publication argues for emphasizing skill-based education.

Pole, J. R. *The Pursuit of Equality in American History*, second edition, revised and enlarged. Berkeley: University of California Press, 1993. This is the best history on the concept of equality in U.S. history and the importance of the idea of equality of opportunity.

Ratter, Michael, et al. *Fifteen Thousand Hours*. Cambridge, MA: Harvard University Press, 1979. This is a study of the differences among 12 inner-city schools in London and how those differences are related to behavior and academic achievement.

Rich, Motoko. "Nation's Wealthy Places Pour Private Money into Public Schools, Study Finds." *The New York Times* (October 21, 2014). www.nytimes.com/2014/10/22/us/nations-wealthy-places-pour-private-money-into-public-schools-study-finds.html?ref=us&_

r=0www.nytimes.com/2014/10/22/us/nations-wealthy-places-pour-private-money-into-public-schools-study-finds.html?ref=us&_r=0. This article highlights how local fundraising groups in high-income school districts increase the disparity of spending between school districts.

Rosenthal, Robert, and Lenore Jacobson. *Pygmalion in the Classroom: Teacher Expectation and Pupils' Intellectual Development.* New York: Irvington, 1988. The authors study the effects of teacher expectations.

Spring, Joel. *Education and the Rise of the Global Economy.* Mahwah, NJ: Lawrence Erlbaum, 1998. Spring studies the development of education in the context of global economics.

———. *Economization of Education: Human Capital, Global Corporations, Skill-Based Schooling.* New York: Routledge, 2015. This book describes the development of skill-based curricula and international testing.

Statista: The Statistics Portal. *Shares of Household Income of Quintiles in the United States from 1970 to 2017.* www.statista.com/statistics/203247/shares-of-household-income-of-quintiles-in-the-us/ on December 17, 2018. Gives the distribution of income in the United States.

Tiffany, Julian, and Robert Kominski. *Education and Synthetic Work-Life Earnings Estimates.* U.S. Department of Commerce Economics and Statistics Administration, U.S. Census Bureau, September 2011, p. 10. www.census.gov/prod/2011pubs/acs-14.pdf. This study provides comparison of lifetime earnings by race, gender, and educational attainment.

U.S. Census Bureau. *The 2010 Statistical Abstract: The National Data Book*, Table 227. www.census.gov/compendia/statab/2010/cats/education/educational_attainment.html. This table provides statistics on the relationship between educational attainment and income.

———. *United States Census Bureau Historical Income Tables: Households.* www.census.gov/data/tables/time-series/demo/income-poverty/historical-income-households.html on November 15, 2018. Provides data on household incomes and the growing inequality of income in the United States.

U.S. Department of Labor, Bureau of Labor Statistics. *Earnings and Unemployment Rates by Educational Attainment* (2013). www.bls.gov/emp/ep_chart_001.htm. Statistics showing relationship between educational attainment and earnings.

———. *Women's Earnings 83 Percent of Men's, But Vary by Occupation* (January 2016). www.bls.gov/opub/ted/2016/womens-earnings-83-percent-of-mens-but-vary-by-occupation.htm on March 6, 2017. Shows the continuing pay gap between males and females.

CHAPTER 4

The Economic Goals of Schooling
Human Capital, Global Economy, and Preschool

Economic goals are a primary influence on public-school policies, curricula, and standardized testing. As mentioned in Chapter 1, a current goal of schooling is educating students to compete in a global labor market. Politicians and policy leaders claim educating students for work in the global economy will result in economic growth and help the United States compete in the global economy.

Current global economic goals are based on what economists call human capital theory, which assumes that money spent on education will cause economic growth, reduce poverty, and improve personal incomes. Human capital arguments currently justify the expansion and funding of preschool education from zero to four years of age to improve their chances for employment.

For example, the link between human capital theory, the global economy, and preschool was highlighted in a speech by Montana governor Brian Schweitzer at a three-day Partnership for America's Economic Success Economic Summit on Early Childhood Investment held in September 2007. He told the gathering of education leaders, politicians, and business groups: "We're no longer competing just with Colorado; we're competing with China. We need to challenge every single educator to create the next engineer." Reporting on the conference for *Education Week*, Linda Jacobson gave her article the descriptive human capital title "Summit Links Preschool to Economic Success." She reported, "Hoping to win over skeptical policymakers, leaders from the business, philanthropic, and political arenas gathered here this week to strengthen their message that spending money on early-childhood education will improve high school graduation rates and help keep the United States economically strong."

In summary, this chapter discusses:

1. Human capital theory as related to the role of education in:
   a. Growing the economy
   b. Reducing poverty
   c. Raising personal income
2. Education for the global economy
3. School curriculum and the global economy
4. Criticisms of human capital theory
   a. Can investment in schools grow the economy?
   b. Does increasing school attendance reduce the value of academic diplomas?
5. Preschool education
   a. Human capital theory and the education of zero- to four-year-olds
   b. Preschool education and the teaching of social skills
6. Child-rearing and social and cultural capital
7. Family learning and school success

HUMAN CAPITAL THEORY

The idea of educating for economic growth and competition is not new. Since the nineteenth century, politicians and school leaders have justified schools as necessary for economic development. Originally, Horace Mann proposed two major economic objectives. One was what we now call *human capital*. Simply stated, human capital theory contends that investment in education will improve the quality of workers and, consequently, increase the wealth of the community.

Mann, often called the father of American schools, used human capital theory to justify community support of schools. For instance, why should an adult with no children be forced to pay for the schooling of other people's children? Mann's answer was that public schooling increased the wealth of the community and that, therefore, even people without children economically benefited from schools. Mann also believed schooling would eliminate poverty by raising the wealth of the community and preparing everyone to be economically successful. The current concepts of human capital and the knowledge economy can be traced to the work of economists Theodore Schultz and Gary Becker. In 1961, Theodore Schultz pointed out that "economists have long known that people are an important part of the wealth of nations." Schultz argued that people invested in themselves through education to improve their job opportunities. In a similar fashion, nations could invest in schools as a stimulus for economic growth.

In his 1964 book *Human Capital*, Becker asserts that economic growth depends on the knowledge, information, ideas, skills, and health of the workforce. Investments in education, he argued, could improve human capital, which would contribute to economic growth. Later, he used the phrase knowledge economy: "An economy like that of the United States is called a capitalist economy, but the more accurate term is human capital or *knowledge* capital economy." Becker claimed that human capital represented three-fourths of the wealth of the United States and that investment in education would be the key to further economic growth. Following a similar line of reasoning, Daniel Bell in 1973 coined the term "post-industrial" and predicted that there would be a shift from blue-collar to white-collar labor requiring a major increase in educated workers. This notion received support in the 1990s from Peter Drucker, who asserted that knowledge rather than ownership of capital generates new wealth and that power was shifting from owners and managers of capital to knowledge workers. During the same decade, Robert Reich claimed that inequality between people and nations was a result of differences in knowledge and skills. Invest in education, he urged, to reduce these inequalities. Growing income inequality between individuals and nations, according to Reich, was a result of differences in knowledge and skills.

It was human capital theory that provided arguments to support expanding preschool education and the 1960s War on Poverty which resulted in Head Start, the television program *Sesame Street*, and compensatory school programs to eliminate poverty. Based on human capital theory, the economic model of the War on Poverty in Figure 4.1 exemplifies current and past ideas about schooling and poverty. Notice that poor-quality education is one element in a series of social factors that tend to reinforce other social conditions. Moving around the inner part of the diagram, an inadequate education is linked to low-income jobs, low-quality housing, poor diet, poor medical care, health problems, and high rates of absenteeism from school and work. This model suggests eliminating poverty by improving any of the interrelated points. For instance, the improvement of health conditions will mean fewer days lost from school and employment, which will mean more income. Higher wages will mean improved housing, medical care, diet, and education. These improved conditions will mean better jobs for those of the next generation. Antipoverty programs include Head Start, compensatory education, vocation and career education, public housing, housing subsidies, food stamps, and medical care.

Today, preschools for low-income families and Head Start programs are premised on the idea that some children from low-income families begin school at a disadvantage compared to children from middle- and high-income families. Head Start programs provide early childhood education to give poor children a head start on schooling, allowing them to compete on equal terms with other children. Job-training programs are designed to end teenage and adult unemployment. Compensatory education in fields such as reading is designed to ensure the success of low-income students.

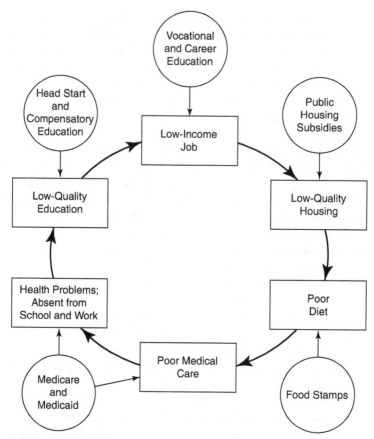

Figure 4.1 War on Poverty

Besides the issue of poverty, human capital arguments directly influenced the organization of schools. In the twentieth and twenty-first centuries, the dominant model for linking schools to the labor market is the sorting machine, as I discussed in Chapter 3. The image of the sorting machine is that of pouring students—called human capital or human resources—into schools, where they are separated by abilities and interests. Emerging from the other end of the machine, school graduates enter jobs that match their educational programs. In this model, the school counselor or other school official uses a variety of standardized tests to place the student into an ability group in an elementary school classroom and later in high school into a course of study. Ideally, a student's education will lead directly to college or a vocation. In this model, there should be a correlation among students' education, abilities, and interests and their occupations. With schools as sorting machines, proponents argue, the economy will prosper and workers will be happy because their jobs will match their interests and education.

SCHOOLING AND THE GLOBAL KNOWLEDGE ECONOMY

In the twenty-first century, American workers are competing in a global knowledge economy. As U.S. companies seek cheaper labor in foreign countries, American workers are forced to take reductions in benefits and wages to compete with foreign workers. The only hope, it is argued, is to train workers for jobs that pay higher wages in the global labor market. Preparation for the global economy shifts the focus from service to a national economy to a global economy by preparing workers for international corporations and for competition in a world labor market. American workers' income supposedly will rise because they will be educated for the highest-paying jobs in the world knowledge economy.

The global knowledge economy is linked to new forms of communication and networking. Referring to the new economy of the late twentieth century, Manuel Castells states in *The Rise of the Network Society*: "I call it informational, global, and networked to identify its fundamental distinctive features and to emphasize their intertwining." By informational, he meant the ability of corporations and governments to "generate, process, and apply efficiently knowledge-based information." It is global because capital, labor, raw materials, management, consumption, and markets were linked through global networks. "It is networked," he contends, because "productivity is generated through and competition is played out in a global network of interaction between business networks." Information or knowledge, he claims, is now a product that increases productivity.

The human capital and knowledge economy argument became a national issue in 1983 when the federal government's report *A Nation at Risk* blamed the allegedly poor academic quality of American public schools for causing lower rates of economic productivity than those of Japan and West Germany. In addition, it blamed schools for reducing the lead of the United States in technological development. The report states, "If only to keep and improve on the slim competitive edge we still retain in world markets, we must rededicate ourselves to the reform of the educational system for the benefit of all." Not only was this argument almost impossible to prove, but some have claimed it was based on false data and assumptions, as captured in the title of David Berliner and Bruce Biddle's *The Manufactured Crisis: Myths, Fraud and the Attack on America's Public Schools*.

In the 1990s, President Bill Clinton used the rhetoric of human capital and the knowledge economy. When Clinton ran for the presidency in 1992, the Democratic platform declared: "A competitive American economy requires the global market's best educated, best trained, most flexible work force." Education and the global economy continued as a theme in President Clinton's 1996 reelection: "Today's Democratic Party knows that education is the key to opportunity. In the new global economy, it is more important than ever before. Today, education is the fault line that separates those who will prosper from those who cannot."

The architect of educational policies for the global economy, former labor secretary Robert Reich, writes in *The Work of Nations*, "Herein lies the new logic of economic capitalism: The skills of a nation's workforce and the quality of its infrastructure are what make it unique, and uniquely attractive, in the world economy." Reich draws a direct relationship between the type of education provided by schools and the placement of the worker in the labor market. He believes many workers will be trapped in low-paying jobs unless their employment skills are improved. Reich argues, "There should not be a barrier between education and work. We're talking about a new economy in which lifelong learning is a necessity for every single member of the American workforce."

Human capital and global competitiveness are used to justify No Child Left Behind, the most important federal legislation affecting schools in the twenty-first century. The opening line to the official U.S. Department of Education's *A Guide to Education and No Child Left Behind* declares, "Satisfying the demand for highly skilled workers is the key to maintaining competitiveness and prosperity in the global economy." In his 2006 State of the Union Address, President George W. Bush declared, "Keeping America competitive requires us to open more markets for all that Americans make and grow. One out of every five factory jobs in America is related to global trade . . . we need to encourage children to take more math and science, and to make sure those courses are rigorous enough to compete with other nations."

In 2012, at the Second Annual International Summit of the Teaching Profession, education ministers, national union heads, and teacher leaders from over 20 countries discussed teaching skills needed to prepare students to work in a twentieth-century economy. The summit concluded that teacher-preparation programs should not only incorporate, but demand, "more focus on critical thinking, STEM, foreign language, collaborative problem-solving, and technology literacy."

Asia Society's Center for Global Education takes a broader view of the skills needed for a global society by recommending that students learn about world cultures and histories. This goes beyond skills needed for work. The center lists as global competences:

Investigate the World

Globally competent students are aware, curious, and interested in learning about the world and how it works.

Recognize Perspectives

Globally competent students recognize that they have a particular perspective, and that others may or may not share it.

Communicate Ideas

Globally competent students can effectively communicate, verbally and non-verbally, with diverse audiences.

TAKE ACTION

Globally competent students have the skills and knowledge to not just learn about the world, but also to make a difference in the world.

Combining learning skills for work with the Center for Global Education competencies would prepare workers for a variety of foreign settings. This would be truly preparing students to work in a global economy.

THE HUMAN CAPITAL EDUCATION PARADIGM AND LIFELONG LEARNING

Human capital arguments contain an educational agenda of standardization of the curriculum; accountability of students and school staff based on standardized-test scores; and the deskilling of the teaching profession. What is meant by *deskilling* is that in some cases teaching involves following a scripted lesson created by some outside agency or sometimes teachers are forced to teach to the requirements of standardized tests. The deskilling of teaching includes the disappearance of teacher-made tests and lesson plans and the inability of teachers to select the classroom's instructional methodology.

Following is the list of features of the human capital education paradigm.

- The value of education measured by economic growth
- National standardization of the curriculum
- Standardized testing for promotion, entrance, and exiting from different levels of schooling
- Performance evaluation of teaching based on standardized testing of students
- Mandated textbooks
- Scripted lessons
- Lifelong learning

In recent years, there has been discussion of the school's role in promoting a learning society and lifelong learning so that workers can adapt to constantly changing needs in the labor force. A learning society and lifelong learning are considered essential parts of global educational systems. Both concepts assume a world of constant technological change, which will require workers to continually update their skills. This assumption means schools will be required to teach students how to learn so they can continue learning throughout their lives. These two concepts are defined as follows:

- In a learning society, educational credentials determine income and status. Also, all members in a learning society are engaged in learning to adapt to constant changes in technology and work requirements.
- Lifelong learning refers to workers engaging in continual training to meet the changing technological requirements of the workplace.

In the context of education for the global economy, the larger questions include the following:

- Should the primary goal of education be human capital development?
- Should the worth of educational institutions be measured by their contribution to economic growth?
- Will a learning society and lifelong learning to prepare students for technological change increase human happiness?

CAN INVESTMENT IN SCHOOLS GROW THE ECONOMY?

There are criticisms regarding human capital theory and the ability of schools to educate students for occupations in the global economy and end economic inequality. What happens if there are not enough jobs in the knowledge economy to absorb school graduates into skilled jobs or if the anticipated demand for knowledge workers has not occurred? One result might be the declining economic value of high school and college diplomas, or what is called "educational inflation." Are employers, who in the past would hire a high school graduate for a job, now seeking college graduates for the same job because of an overabundance of college graduates?

An important effect of the labor market on the value of academic diplomas is the routinization of so-called knowledge work that allows for the hiring of less-skilled workers. "It is, therefore," Phillip Brown and Hugh Lauder conclude, "not just a matter of the oversupply of skills that threatens the equation between high skills and high income, where knowledge is 'routinized' it can be substituted with less-skilled and cheaper workers at home or further afield."

Brown and Lauder argue that multinational corporations are able to keep salaries low by encouraging nations to invest in schools that prepare for the knowledge economy. An oversupply of educated workers depresses wages to the advantage of employers. This could be occurring in the United States, as suggested by Brown and Lauder, through a combination of immigration of educated workers from other countries and the increased emphasis on college education for the workforce. In fact, Brown and Lauder argue there has been no real increase in income for college graduates since the 1970s except for those entering "high earner" occupations. However, college graduates still earn more than noncollege graduates.

Economist Andrew Hacker criticizes the very foundation of human capital arguments. Human capital economists premise their arguments on the fact that growth in school attendance parallels the growth of the economy. But it is a big leap from this fact to say that increased education causes economic growth. Hacker flips the causal relationship around and argues that economic growth provides the financial resources to fund educational expansion and offer youth an entertaining interlude in life. Hacker notes that much of the original funding of higher education came from innovative industrialists who were not college graduates. Today, college dropouts lead the list of innovative developers, such as Larry Ellison (Oracle), Bill Gates (Microsoft), Steve Jobs and Steve Wozniak (Apple), and Michael Dell (Dell).

Hacker's argument does not mean schooling is not important for jobs. However, human capitalists may have oversold their argument about education causing economic growth and being necessary for global competition. First, the state of the global economy and jobs is uncertain and constantly changing. Second, there may be an overeducation of the population causing educational inflation. *Inflation* refers to employers increasing the educational requirements of jobs when there is an overabundance of graduates. In this situation, the economic value of a high school or college degree declines when there is an overabundance of well-schooled workers.

Are jobs really tied to more schooling? Not according to economist Andrew Hacker. In a review of *The Race between Education and Technology* by Claudia Goldin and Lawrence Katz, Hacker questions the argument that more schooling, particularly more higher education, is necessary for employment in today's job markets.

Hacker's question is legitimate when you examine a 2012 U.S. Bureau of Labor Statistics report, which found, "The most new jobs from 2012 to 2022 are projected to be in occupations that typically can be entered with a high school diploma." Also, the statistics revealed there would be more jobs for those with less than a high school diploma than for those with bachelor's degrees. The job projections show the number of occupations requiring a high school diploma or its equivalent growing by 4,630,800 and those occupations requiring less than a high school diploma increasing by 4,158,400. In contrast, the job projections for those with bachelor's degrees show an increase in number of jobs by 3,143,600, with those for occupations requiring a doctoral or professional degree increasing by 638,400, master's degree by 448,500, associate's degree by 1,046,000, and some college, no degree by 225,000.

In practice some business enterprises disregard the quality of workers' schooling when they train employees at the work site. Consider the decision by foreign auto manufacturers to locate in states with low wages and no unions but with high dropout rates: Nissan, Coffee County, Tennessee, 26.3 percent school dropout rate; BMW, Spartanburg County, South Carolina, 26.9 percent school dropout rate; Honda, St. Clair County, Alabama, 28.7 percent school dropout rate; and Toyota, Union County, Mississippi, 31.5 percent school dropout rate. Hacker argues that these companies didn't care about local school quality because worker training was on the job. Based on these arguments, more schooling may *not* result in higher-paying jobs or economic growth.

There are also questions about investing in education to reduce income inequality. From the 1970s to the present, U.S. income inequality increased so that inequality, according to one report, was greater in 2010 than in 1913. The Pew Research Center claimed, "U.S. income inequality has been increasing steadily since the 1970s, and now has reached levels not seen since 1928." Economist Theodore Schultz argued that "changes in the investment in human capital are a basic factor reducing the inequality in the personal distribution of income." Schultz's argument appears wrong when compared to the reality of increasing differences in income.

PRESCHOOL, HUMAN CAPITAL THEORY, AND SOFT SKILLS
A recent argument for expanding preschool is that it can teach the "soft" skills needed by global employers. Human capital theorists make a distinction between soft and hard skills needed for work. Hard skills refer to such things as literacy instruction and numeracy along with specific job skills, and soft skills refer to character traits that will help the worker succeed in the workplace.

Preschool has been a concern of educators since the nineteenth century. Originally it was mainly focused on the hard and soft skills students brought to school and how it affected the school achievement. Nineteenth-century common-school advocates worried that children entered school with different social experiences and knowledge—a situation members of the New York Workingman's Party wanted to correct by placing children in state residential institutions. Today, the focus is on preschool education to provide all children with similar access to social experiences and knowledge as preparation for schooling and employment. The most well-known of the federal preschool programs are Early Head Start and Head Start—which, as indicated by their names, are designed to give children from low-income families a head start on schooling so they reach the same level of educational achievement as children from high-income families.

In the twenty-first century, human capital economists argue that preschool education is the most efficient way for the government to invest its money to support economic growth by providing young children the hard and soft skills needed for success in primary school and later in employment. Investing in preschool education to reduce poverty is recommended by Nobel economist James J. Heckman. Heckman's major concern is the soft skills learned in preschool. His recommendation is based on research studies regarding the Perry Preschool. Before considering the results of research on the Perry Preschool, I discuss the current approach of human capitalist economists like Heckman compared to the early human capital economists like Gary Becker.

When Gary Becker did his work in the 1960s, he primarily thought of investment in human capital as involving knowledge, information, ideas, skills, and the health of the workforce. One distinction between Becker and Heckman is the focus on early investments in human capital that enhance the development of later skills and employability: namely, preschool education. In their 2005 book *Inequality in America: What Role for Human Capital Policies?* Pedro Carneiro and James J. Heckman assert: "This dynamic complementarity in human investment was ignored in the early work on human capital. Learning beget learning, skills (both cognitive and noncognitive) acquired early on facilitate later learning."

Today, human capital economists like Heckman focus on soft skills, such as motivation, self-discipline, stability, dependability, perseverance, self-esteem, optimism, future orientation, and other related skills that affect learning and job performance. Many researchers argue that there is a strong relationship between family background and academic success. Economists like Heckman now argue that family background provides the noncognitive skills needed for school and job achievement. Families "fail" when these noncognitive skills are not taught to their children.

Carneiro and Heckman stress the importance of noncognitive abilities: "Noncognitive abilities [soft skills] matter for success both in the labor market and in schooling." In fact, they argue, the success of people with high cognitive abilities is dependent on their noncognitive abilities. Simply stated, a smart person without motivation, perseverance, dependability, trustworthiness, and self-esteem may not do well in school or in the labor market. On the other hand, a person with low cognitive abilities but high noncognitive abilities might succeed at school and work. Carneiro and Heckman assert, "Numerous instances can be cited of high-IQ people who fail to achieve success in life because they lack self-discipline and low-IQ people who succeed by virtue of persistence, reliability, and self-discipline."

If noncognitive abilities are important for future school and work success, and early learning of skills helps in gaining future skills, then, according to Heckman, money spent on preschool education provides a greater economic rate of return than increased spending on primary, secondary, and higher education or on job training. This is Heckman's major conclusion.

For instance, consider the investment in financial aid for college. Family income is related to college attendance and completion. But is it the major factor? The answer, according to Heckman, is no. Admittedly, the wealthy have an easier time paying for higher education than the poor. However, college readiness and success in college are dependent on noncognitive abilities like motivation, self-discipline, stability, dependability, perseverance, and self-esteem. Without these attributes both rich and poor students will fail. Heckman argues that enough funding sources are available for students from low-income families who are college ready and have the right noncognitive abilities to complete their college educations.

What about increasing spending per public-school student and reducing class size? Carneiro and Heckman conclude that "the United States may be spending too much on students given the current organization of educational production." Spending too much? Also, they argue that spending more money on schools and lowering class size will not improve American education. The same arguments are made regarding investment in job training and high school intervention programs. In the end, success in work and high school depends on noncognitive abilities learned at an early age.

What about reducing the racial and ethnic gaps in school achievement? "A major conclusion," Carneiro and Heckman state, "is that the ability that is decisive in producing schooling differentials is shaped early in life. If we are to substantially eliminate ethnic and income differentials in schooling, we must start early. We cannot rely on tuition policy applied in the child's adolescent years, job training, or GED programs to compensate for the neglect the child experienced in the early years."

THE PERRY PRESCHOOL STUDY

The Perry Preschool study is often cited as proof of the value of preschool in fostering soft skills for success in school and employment. After reviewing a Perry Preschool report, Heckman concluded, "This report substantially bolsters the case for early interventions in disadvantaged populations. More than 35 years after they received an enriched preschool program, the Perry Preschool participants achieve much greater success in social and economic life than their counterparts who are randomly denied treatment."

Beginning in 1962, the Perry Preschool study began with 123 African American children from low-income families who were considered at risk for school failure. They had low IQs (this measure was later rejected and not used in later studies) and were borderline mentally impaired with no organic deficiencies that might cause impairment. During the first phase, from 1962 to 1967, the children attended what was considered a high-quality early childhood education program with teachers visiting their homes. Children attended the preschool for 2.5 hours per day Monday through Friday for a two-year period with a staff ratio of one adult for every five or six children. The staff did home visits for 1.5 hours each week. During this first phase the principle concern was improving the cognitive abilities of the children. In 1970, the research became the principle project of the High/Scope Foundation, which today claims it "is perhaps best known for its research on the lasting effects of preschool education and its preschool curriculum approach."

A longitudinal follow-up tracked students through the third grade or age 8 for intellectual development, school achievement, and "social maturity." Another study included the children and families in the cohort group from age 8 to age 15 with an emphasis on intellectual development, school achievement, and family attitudes. Participants were studied after leaving school until age 19 with the research described as follows:

> Instead of an intelligence or traditional achievement test, study participants took a test of functional competence that focused on information and skills used in the real world. *Other measures focused on social behavior in the community at large, job training, college attendance, pregnancy rates, and patterns of crime.* For the first time, the cost-benefit analysis is based on actual data from complete school records, police reports, and state records of welfare payments. . . . While projections of lifetime earnings are still necessary, the basic patterns of the subjects' adult lives are beginning to unfold.

> (emphasis in original)

As indicated in Table 4.1, researchers found that those attending Perry Preschool as compared to those who didn't attend who were from a similar economic and social background were less likely to commit crimes and, if female, become pregnant. They were also more likely to be employed, graduate from high school, and attend college or receive vocational training. In addition, Perry Preschool graduates were less likely to be placed in special education. Regarding cost-benefit analysis, the researchers concluded, "These benefits considered in terms of their economic value make the preschool program a worthwhile investment for society. Over the lifetimes of the participants, preschool is estimated to yield economic benefits with an estimated present value that is over seven times the cost of one year of the program."

A 2000 report by the Office of Juvenile Justice and Delinquency Prevention Project reported that Perry Preschool graduates had significantly lower crime, delinquency, teenage pregnancy, and welfare dependency rates than the no-preschool group. The report concluded that "the program group has demonstrated significantly higher rates of prosocial behavior, academic achievement, employment, income, and family stability as compared with the control group. The success of this and similar programs demonstrates intervention and delinquency prevention in terms of both social outcome and *cost effectiveness*" (emphasis in original).

Table 4.1 Report Findings at Age 19 of the Perry School Cohort Group

Category	Number Responding	Preschool Group (%)	No-Preschool Group (%)
Employed	121	59	32
High school graduation (or its equivalent)	121	67	49
College or vocational training	121	38	21
Ever detained or arrested	121	31	51
Females only: teen pregnancies, per 100	49	64	117
Percentage of years in special education	112	16	28

Source: Adapted from John R. Berrueta-Clement, Lawrence J. Schweinhart, W. Steven Barnett, Ann S. Epstein, and David P. Weikart, *Changed Lives: The Effects of the Perry Preschool Program on Youths through Age 19* (Ypsilanti, MI: Monographs of the High/Scope Educational Research Foundation, 1984), p. 20.

In 2004, High/Scope researchers reported the continued educational success of Perry Preschool. Of particular importance for human capital economists were the reported economic benefits:

- More of the group members who received high-quality early education than the nonprogram group was employed at age 40 (76 vs. 62 percent).
- Group members who received high-quality early education had median annual earnings more than $5,000 higher than the nonprogram group ($20,800 vs. $15,300).
- More of the group members who received high-quality early education owned their own homes.
- More of the group members who received high-quality early education had a savings account than the nonprogram members (76 vs. 50 percent).

The findings concluded, "Overall, the study documented a return to society of more than $16 for every tax dollar invested in the early care and education program."

All these studies reinforce the claim that investment in preschool yields high rates of economic returns for the participants and nation. They also suggest that preschool will reduce the cost to the public of special education programs, the criminal justice system, unemployment, and losses to crime victims. Table 4.2 shows the cost-benefit data reported by Carneiro and Heckman.

However, there are some issues regarding the replication of the Perry Preschool study. One is the sample size and location. The sample size for the study is small, with only 123 low-income African American children between ages three and four who were considered at high risk of school failure. Only 58 attended the Perry Preschool program while the other 65 received no preschool. Can a study using only 58 preschool students justify the economic value of preschool?

The research group High/Scope suggests another limitation on its applicability to other contexts. The study specifically uses low-income African American students in Ypsilanti, Michigan. In answering the question about generalizability, High/Scope researchers state, "The external validity or generalizability of the study findings extends to those programs that are reasonably similar to the High/Scope Perry Preschool program." By reasonable similarity they mean a preschool taught by certified early childhood teachers that serves low-income families, enrolls children three to four years old, and meets daily for two and a half hours.

Table 4.2 Perry Preschool: Costs versus Benefits through Age 27

Costs and Benefits	Increased (1) and Decreased (2) Costs ($)
Cost of preschool for each child aged 3–4	(1) 12,148
Decrease cost of special education for Perry Preschool graduates	(2) 6,365
Decrease criminal justice system cost for ages 15 to 28	(2) 27,378
Projected decrease criminal justice system cost for ages 29 to 44	(2) 22,817
Income from increased employment ages 19 to 27	(2) 28,380
Projected income from increased employment ages 28 to 65	(2) 27,565
Decrease in losses to crime victims	(2) 210,690
Total benefits or decreased costs to public	43,195
Total benefits or decreased costs to public without projections for criminal justice costs and income	32,047
Benefits minus cost of preschool	31,047
Benefits minus cost of preschool without projections for criminal justice costs and income	20,665

Source: Adapted from Pedro Carneiro and James J. Heckman, "Human Capital Policy," in *Inequality in America: What Role for Human Capital Policies?* ed. James J. Heckman and Alan Krueger (Cambridge, MA: MIT Press, 2005), Table 2.7, p. 168.

In conclusion, the Perry Preschool study is used to support arguments on the economic value of preschool. However, as mentioned previously, there are issues about sample size and applicability in other cultural contexts. In recent studies the emphasis has been on noncognitive abilities or soft skills in contrast to the early concern with intellectual development. The 2004 study of the Perry Preschool graduates relates their school achievement to noncognitive abilities and attitudes: "The program group spent more time on homework and demonstrated more positive attitudes toward school at ages 15 and 19. More parents of program group members had positive attitudes regarding their children's educational experiences and were hopeful that their children would obtain college degrees."

CHILD-REARING AND SOCIAL AND CULTURAL CAPITAL

Do different family environments for preschool children affect children's school achievement and, consequently, their economic futures? In other words, do children enter school with differing abilities as a result of dissimilar family backgrounds? Do these differences in family background continue to affect learning throughout the student's school years, and do they have an effect on the level of a student's educational attainment, such as graduating from high school or college, and their future employment?

There are a number of studies purporting to show the importance of particular types of families in determining academic success. Like the Perry Preschool studies, these other studies can be questioned regarding their relevance to different forms of family lifestyles. Should the findings discussed in this section be used to try and change family structures to ensure success in school?

The key to answering the preceding questions is the concept of *social and cultural capital*, which refers to the economic value of a person's behaviors, attitudes, knowledge, and cultural experiences. It can be argued that education, which provides a person with particular knowledge and attitudes, is related to income and therefore has economic value when seeking employment. Also, behaviors learned in the home contribute to soft skills. Experiences in the home might provide the social knowledge that will help the child later climb the occupational ladder. Do the behaviors learned in the home prepare the child to interact with professionals and managers, or do they prepare the child to feel comfortable only in social situations with blue-collar workers? Visits to museums, concerts, stage performances, and similar experiences increase children's cultural capital, which might make them better prepared to interact with elite groups. In other words, what social and cultural experiences do the family provide that will help the child succeed in school and in later employment?

Variations in social and cultural capital affect the ability of children to learn in school and gain future employment. In *Unequal Childhoods: Class, Race, and Family Life*, Annette Lareau writes:

Many studies have demonstrated that parents' social structural location has profound implications for their children's life chances. Before kindergarten, for example, children of highly educated parents are much more likely to exhibit "educational readiness" skills, such as knowing their letters, identifying colors, counting up to twenty, and being able to write their first names.

Lareau demonstrates that educational readiness is affected by differences in child-rearing practices. She distinguishes child-rearing practices by the terms "concerted cultivation" and "accomplishment of natural growth." Concerted cultivation is practiced by what she calls "middle-class" families and accomplishment of natural growth by "working-class" families.

The terms "middle class" and "working class" have a special meaning in Lareau's work. Throughout this chapter, I highlight differing definitions of social class. For Lareau's purposes, a middle-class family is one where one or both parents have supervisory or managerial authority in the workplace and are required to have stringent educational credentials. In working-class families, parents' occupations are without supervisory authority and do not require a high level of educational credentials.

Differences in child-rearing between working- and middle-class families are summarized in Table 4.3. Lareau concludes that middle-class families consciously intervene (concerted cultivation) in their children's lives to develop their talents. In contrast, working-class families have a more laissez-faire attitude, allowing their children to grow without much intervention (accomplishment of natural growth) except for attending to their basic needs.

Table 4.3 Differences in Child-Rearing between Working- and Middle-Class Families

	Middle-Class Concerted Cultivation	Working-Class Accomplishment of Natural Growth
General	Parents involve children in multiple organized activities such as sports, music and dance lessons, and arts, crafts, and hobby groups.	Children "hang out" with siblings, friends, and relatives while parents involve them in a minimum of organized activities.
Speech	Parents reason with their children, allowing them to challenge their statements and negotiate.	Parents issue directives and seldom allow their children to challenge or question these directives.
Dealings with institutions	Parents criticize and intervene in institutions affecting the child, such as school, and train their children to assume a similar role.	Parents display power-lessness and frustration toward institutions, such as school.
Results	Children gain the social and cultural capital to deal with a variety of social situations and institutions.	Children develop social and cultural capital that results in dependency on institutions and jobs where they take orders rather than manage others.

Source: Adapted from Annette Lareau, *Unequal Childhoods: Class, Race, and Family Life* (Berkeley: University of California Press, 2003), p. 31.

Imagine the life of middle-class children as detailed in Table 4.3. Their parents spend time chauffeuring them from training events and competitions in organized sports, to music and dance lessons, to an art, craft, or hobby group. After-school time and weekends are packed with events as parents try to develop their children's various talents. If their children encounter any problems in these activities, parents quickly intervene and discuss the situation with the coach, trainer, or teacher. These middle-class parents influence their children's behavior through reasoned discussion in which their children learn to question their parents' arguments if they think their parents are wrong.

According to Lareau, the result of concerted cultivation is the development of the social and cultural capital that allows the children, and later as adults, to feel comfortable and know how to act in a variety of social and institutional situations; this is a result of all those after-school activities. Middle-class children learn to interact, challenge, and reason with authority; this is learned through their interaction with their parents and the model of their parents questioning institutional authority. Their cultural capital is increased through participation in activities such as dance and music lessons and attendance at cultural institutions.

In contrast, working-class parents, Lareau argues, allow their children to spend unstructured time with their friends and relatives in their yards, in local parks, on the street, or in another home. The most frequently planned activity for children is some form of organized sports. Working-class parents tell their children what to do and don't allow the children to be sassy and talk back. When problems occur at school or other institutions their children might encounter, the parents act powerless.

Working-class accomplishment of natural growth, according to Lareau, results in social capital that does not contain the skills to interact in a variety of social and institutional situations. The children lack the verbal ability and behavioral skills needed to become managers and supervisors. They primarily assume jobs where they take orders rather than give orders. They lack the verbal skills, social graces, and dress to interview for jobs as bank managers, but they do have the social capital to accept low-paying jobs where they are given orders. Without exposure to museums, lessons in art and dance, and attendance at concerts and stage performances, these children do not gain the cultural capital to move easily among the social elite.

The social and cultural capital developed in middle- and working-class families has different economic value. First, middle- and working-class children have different social and cultural capital when interacting with schools. These forms of capital are needed for educational success and, consequently, have economic value when educational achievement helps people gain higher-paying jobs. Middle-class children have learned the verbal and social skills to advantage themselves when interacting with teachers and school staff. If something negative happens to them at school, their parents are quick to intervene on their behalf. The opposite is true of working-class children. Their social and cultural capital hinders their ability to succeed at school. The social and cultural capital of middle-class children increases their possibilities of gaining jobs high on the income scale while working-class children have the social and cultural capital to work in jobs low on the income scale.

In conclusion, the promise of schooling providing equality of opportunity to compete for income and wealth is seriously compromised before the child even enters the classroom. Parents develop different forms of social and cultural capital that advantage or disadvantage their children in school and in the labor market. In the next section, I discuss how family background is related to the actual reading and math skills of children as they enter kindergarten and advantages or disadvantages them throughout their school careers.

FAMILY LEARNING AND SCHOOL SUCCESS

Valerie Lee and David Burkham's report *Inequality at the Starting Gate: Social Background Differences in Achievement as Children Begin School* confirms the fears of early common-school advocates that family background would compromise the ability of schools to provide equality of opportunity. Students entering kindergarten have significantly different reading and ability skills as measured by tests given as part of the U.S. Department of Education's Early Childhood Longitudinal Study, Kindergarten Cohort. Test results show differences that are correlated with social class and race, with social class being the most important factor.

What are the preschool family factors affecting reading and math skills of children entering kindergarten? The following could be considered a parental guide for ensuring children have high reading and math skills as measured by tests on entering kindergarten. Lee and Burkham found the strongest correlation between family factors and reading skills on entering kindergarten to be:

1. Frequency of reading (including parents reading to their children)
2. Ownership of home computer
3. Exposure to performing arts
4. Preschool

Other factors weakly correlated with reading skills are:

5. Educational expectations of family
6. Rules limiting television viewing

7. Number of tapes, records, CDs
8. Sports and clubs
9. Arts and crafts activities

For math scores, the most strongly correlated family factors are:

1. Ownership of computer
2. Exposure to performing arts
3. Preschool

Other factors weakly correlated with math skills are:

4. Educational expectations
5. Frequency of reading (including parents reading to their children)
6. Number of tapes, records, CDs
7. Sports and clubs
8. Arts and crafts activities

Therefore, parents planning to prepare their child to enter kindergarten with high reading and math scores would read to their child, own a computer, take their child to performing arts events, and send their child to preschool. In addition, they should have high expectations for their child's education; have rules governing television viewing; have a large amount of media in the home, such as tapes, records, and CDs; and involve their child in sports, clubs, and arts and crafts.

Social class is directly related to kindergarten entrance test scores and family factors correlated with high reading and math scores. Using a different definition of social class than Lareau's separation of families into middle and working class, Lee and Burkham divide families by SES, or socioeconomic status, which is determined by a combination of occupation, income, educational attainment, and wealth. They divide SES into quintiles or gradations of 20 percent. Those in the lowest SES represent the 20 percent at the bottom of the SES scale in occupation, income, education, and wealth while the highest are in the top 20 percent. Table 4.4 reports math and reading achievement at the beginning of kindergarten by SES. Test scores are those used by Lee and Burkham in analyzing the Early Childhood Longitudinal Study, Kindergarten Cohort.

As noted in Table 4.4, reading and math skills on entering kindergarten are closely related to the family SES as measured by tests in the Early Childhood Longitudinal Study: The higher the SES of the family, the higher the test scores; the lower the SES of the family, the lower the test scores.

Table 4.4 Socioeconomic Status and Math and Reading Scores at the Beginning of Kindergarten

Socioeconomic Status of Family	Reading Scores	Math Scores
Highest 20%	27.2	24.1
Next-highest 20%	23.6	21.0
Middle 20%	21.3	19.1
Next-lowest 20%	19.9	17.5
Lowest 20%	17.4	15.1

Source: Adapted from Valerie E. Lee and David Burkham, *Equality at the Starting Gate: Social Background Differences in Achievement as Children Begin School* (Washington, DC: Economic Policy Institute, 2002), p. 18.

Table 4.5 Socioeconomic Status and Family Activity Correlated with Math and Reading Scores at the Beginning of Kindergarten

Socioeconomic Status of Family	Percentage of Kindergartners with a Computer in the Home (%)	Percentage of Kindergartners Whose Parents Read to Them at Least Three Times a Week (%)	Percentage of Kindergartners Who Attend Preschool (%)	Percentage of Kindergartners Who Attend Performing Arts Events (play/concert/show) (%)
Highest 20%	84.7	93.9	65.0	48.4
Next-highest 20%	71.5	87.3	52.2	43.0
Middle 20%	54.7	80.7	41.7	38.9
Next-lowest 20%	38.3	76.6	31.2	33.9
Lowest 20%	19.9	62.6	20.1	27.1

Source: Data are from Valerie E. Lee and David Burkham, *Equality at the Starting Gate: Social Background Differences in Achievement as Children Begin School* (Washington, DC: Economic Policy Institute, 2002), pp. 24–25.

Is there a relationship between family SES and activities that are correlated with high test scores? Table 4.5 shows the relationship found by Lee and Burkham.

As indicated in Table 4.5, upper-SES families are more likely than lower-SES families to expose their children to factors that are correlated with high math and reading scores on entering kindergarten. No wonder children from higher-SES families have higher scores on tests measuring math and reading skills when entering kindergarten. Simply stated, families provide their children with differing cultural capital needed to succeed in school. Lee and Burkham's study seems to confirm fears that family background could hinder the ability of schools to provide equality of opportunity.

In 2015, the Economic Policy Institute issued the report "Inequalities at the Starting Gate: Cognitive and Noncognitive Skills Gaps between

2010–2011 Kindergarten Classmates" by Emma García. In its follow-ing conclusions, "SES" stands for socioeconomic status as a measure of social class. The report concluded:

> Inequalities based on socioeconomic status (SES) are very signifi-cant. Cognitive and noncognitive skills are least developed among those with the lowest socioeconomic status and sharply increase as one ascends the socioeconomic ladder, as these examples show: The relative advantage of a child in the top fifth of the SES distribution (referred to in this report as "high SES") relative to a child in the bottom fifth ("low SES") is of 0.8 standard deviations in reading and math, and 0.4 standard deviations in persistence in completing tasks. Middle-socioeconomic-status children have a relative disad-vantage with respect to children in the top SES.

In addition, the report found:

> There are statistically significant education inequalities by race and ethnicity before accounting for the circumstances in which children live (i.e., their social class). After these factors are taken into con-sideration, race-based gaps shrink (and even vanish, in some cases). Importantly, this supports other evidence that *education gaps are driven by socioeconomic differences* (i.e., racial gaps reflect that racial minorities have lower socioeconomic status).

(emphasis in original)

Table 4.6 2018 Poverty Guidelines for the 48 Contiguous States and the District of Columbia

Persons in Family/household	Poverty Guideline
1	$12,140
2	16,460
3	20,780
4	25,100
5	29,420
6	33,740
7	38,060
8	42,380

Source: U.S. Department of Health and Human Services, *U.S. Federal Poverty Guidelines Used to Deter-mine Financial Eligibility for Certain Federal Programs.* Retrieved from https://aspe.hhs.gov/pover-ty-guidelines on December 21, 2018.

As discussed throughout this chapter, there are many indicators that family income is related to school achievement. What about children living in poverty? Most evidence shows that the conditions surrounding childhood poverty hinder school achievement. Table 4.6 provides the official 2018 U.S. government definition of poverty based on income and size of household. For instance, according to Table 4.6 a single person living alone is poor if his or her annual income is below $12,140. A family of four is poor if their household income is below $25,100.

As indicated in Table 4.7, the percentage of children living in poverty has decreased for all racial/ethnic groups from 2010 to 2016. The percentage of all 5- to 17-year-olds living in poverty has decreased from 21 percent in 2010 to 19 percent in 2016. The highest poverty rate for children in this age range is found among those classified as black, with 38 percent living in poverty in 2010 and 34 percent in 2016.

Children living in poverty are often concentrated in high-poverty schools. *The Condition of Education 2018* uses eligibility for "free or reduced-price lunch" (FRPL) to determine the concentration of poverty in a school. The report states:

> The percentage of students eligible for free or reduced-price lunch (FRPL) under the National School Lunch Program provides a proxy measure for the concentration of low-income students within a school. Children from families with incomes at or below 130 percent of the poverty level are eligible for free meals. Those from families with incomes that are between 130 percent and 185 percent of the poverty level are eligible for reduced-price meals.

Table 4.7 Percentage of 5- to 17-Year-Olds Living in Poverty, by Race/Ethnicity: 2010 and 2016 (%)

	2010	2016
Total	21	19
White	13	11
Black	38	34
Hispanic	32	28
Asian	12	11
Pacific Islander	22	23
American Indian/Alaska Native	34	34
Two or more races	21	19

Source: National Center for Education Statistics, *The Condition of Education 2018* (Washington, DC U.S. Department of Education, 2018), p. 37.

Table 4.8 Percentage of Public-School Students in High-Poverty Schools, by Race/Ethnicity and School Level: School Year 2015–2016

Race/Ethnicity	Percentage of Public-School Students in High-Poverty Public Schools (%)
White	8
Black	45
Hispanic	45
Asian	15
Pacific Islander	25
American Indian/Alaska Native	18

Source: National Center for Education Statistics, *The Condition of Education 2018* (Washington, DC U.S. Department of Education, 2018), p. 82.

Table 4.9 Percentage of Public-School Students in Low-Poverty Schools, by Race/Ethnicity and School Level: School Year 2015–2016

Race/Ethnicity	Percentage of Public-School Students in Low-Poverty Schools (%)
White	28
Black	7
Hispanic	8
Asian	37
Pacific Islander	12
American Indian/Alaska Native	9

Source: National Center for Education Statistics, *The Condition of Education 2018* (Washington, DC U.S. Department of Education, 2018), p. 82.

The Condition of Education 2018 defines high-poverty and low-poverty schools as: "Low-poverty schools are defined as public schools where 25 percent or less of the students are eligible for free or reduced-price lunch (FRPL). A high-poverty school is defined as a public school where more than 75 percent of the students are eligible for FRPL."

As indicated in Tables 4.8 and 4.9, those students classified as Asian (37%) were most likely to be in schools with the lowest student populations living in poverty, followed by whites (28%). In contrast, those students classified as black (45%), Hispanic (45%), and American Indian (37%) were most likely in schools with a high concentration of students living in poverty.

If peer groups affect learning, these figures suggest Asians and whites are advantaged by going to school with more prosperous students in contrast to black, Hispanic, and Native American students. However, and this is important to note, attending a school with a high concentration of students living in poverty does not mean a lack of opportunity to earn a quality education. The author of this book grew up poor, and schools helped him succeed.

An important factor in raising school achievement could be reducing childhood poverty. However, reduction of childhood poverty is not something schools can achieve directly. Reduction of childhood poverty depends on other government social and economic policies.

CONCLUSION

Human capital economics is a driving force in public-school policies. As indicated in this chapter, not all economists agree with the idea that investment in schooling will result in economic growth and higher personal incomes. In fact, increasing the number of school graduates might decrease the economic value of academic diplomas or, as it is called, cause educational inflation. For instance, many college graduates might be unable to obtain jobs that are related to their academic studies. Some areas of the labor market might be flooded with college graduates, which, because of the oversupply of those seeking employment in that particular occupational field, might drive down salaries and force some educated for that occupation to seek other types of employment.

A more basic issue is whether or not public-school policies, including curriculum, methods of instruction, and testing, should be determined by the economic goal of growing the economy and educating workers for global economic competition. It could be argued that given the uncertainty of future labor market needs, students should be given a general education that would prepare them for all aspects of living, including any type of employment. Others could argue that schooling should prepare students to improve the quality of society and their own happiness. Transmitting culture, including history, literature, and the arts, could be another goal of public schooling. In other words, should human capital economics dominate public-school policies?

SUGGESTED READINGS AND WORKS CITED IN CHAPTER

Achieve, Inc. *About Achieve*. www.achieve.org. This organization is composed of members of the National Governors Association and leading members of the business community dedicated to shaping the direction of U.S. schools.

———. *America's High Schools: The Front Line in the Battle for Our Economic Future*. www. achieve.org. This document issued for the 2005 National Education Summit on High Schools stresses the importance of changing the high school curriculum to ensure the success of the United States in the global economy.

———. *National Education Summit on High Schools Convenes in Washington*. www.achieve. org/node/93. This is a report on the opening of the 2005 National Education Summit on High Schools.

Achieve, Inc., and the National Governors Association. *An Action Agenda for Improving America's High Schools: 2005 National Education Summit on High Schools*. Washington, DC:

Achieve, Inc. and the National Governors Association, 2005. This official report of the high school summit calls for a core high school curriculum of four years each of English and math.

Becker, Gary. *Human Capital*. New York: Columbia University Press, 1964. The original explanation of the relationship between schooling and economic growth.

Bell, Daniel. *The Coming of the Post-Industrial Society*. New York: Basic Books, 1973. One of the early books describing the transition to a knowledge economy.

Berrueta-Clement, John R., et al. *Changed Lives: The Effects of the Perry Preschool Program on Youths Through Age 19*. Ypsilanti, MI: Monographs of the High/Scope Educational Research Foundation, 1984. One of the early studies of the Perry Preschool program.

Brown, Phillip, and Hugh Lauder. "Globalization, Knowledge and the Myth of the Magnet Economy." In *Education, Globalization & Social Change*, edited by Hugh Lauder, Phillip Brown, Jo-Anne Dillabough, and A. H. Halsey. Oxford: Oxford University Press, 2006, pp. 317–340. This article is critical of human capital arguments.

Carneiro, Pedro, and James J. Heckman. "Human Capital Policy." In *Inequality in America: What Role for Human Capital Policies?* edited by James J. Heckman, and Alan Krueger. Cambridge, MA: MIT Press, 2005. This chapter describes current concerns of human capital economists with the economic value of preschool.

Castells, Manuel. *The Rise of the Network Society*. Oxford: Blackwell, 2000. This book describes the relationship between new information technology and the knowledge society.

Center for Global Education: Asia Society. *What Is Global Competence?* https://asiasociety.org/education/what-global-competence on December 20, 2018. Global competence is defined in this document as knowing about the world's peoples and cultures.

García, Emma. *Economic Policy Institute: Inequalities at the Starting Gate: Cognitive and Noncognitive Skills Gaps Between 2010–2011 Kindergarten Classmates*. http://files.eric.ed.gov/fulltext/ED560407.pdf on March 6, 2017. This report highlights the growing inequality of incomes in the United States.

Hacker, Andrew. "Can We Make America Smarter?" *The New York Review of Books* (April 30, 2009). Economist Hacker disputes the basic ideas of human capital education and suggests that many occupations needing workers will primarily train them at the workplace.

Heckman, James J., and Alan Krueger, eds. *Inequality in America: What Role for Human Capital Policies?* Cambridge, MA: MIT Press, 2005. This book contains articles claiming that preschool education is the best educational investment for reducing poverty.

High/Scope Foundation. *High/Scope Perry Preschool Study*. www.highscope.org/. This Website provides current information on Perry Preschool graduates.

Keeley, Brian. *Human Capital: How What You Know Shapes Your Life*. Paris: OECD Publishing, 2007. Provides a simple explanation of how human capital economics can influence schooling.

Lareau, Annette. *Unequal Childhoods: Class, Race, and Family Life*. Berkeley: University of California Press, 2003. This is a study of differing child-rearing methods between middle- and working-class families and their effect on the development of cultural capital.

Lee, Valerie E., and David T. Burkham. *Inequality at the Starting Gate: Social Background Differences in Achievement as Children Begin School*. Washington, DC: Economic Policy Institute, 2002. This book reports the impact of preschool experiences on math and reading tests at the beginning of kindergarten.

Parks, Greg. "The High/Scope Perry Preschool Project." *Juvenile Justice Bulletin*. Washington, DC: U.S. Department of Justice, Office of Juvenile Justice and Delinquency Prevention, 2000. This study found positive results, particularly regarding reduced crime rates, among Perry Preschool graduates.

Partnership for America's Economic Success. *Telluride Economic Summit on Early Childhood Investment*. www.partnershipforsuccess.org/index.php?id518. Conference advocated investment in early childhood education to stimulate economic growth.

Reich, Robert. *The Work of Nations*. New York: Vintage Books, 1992. This is one of the major forecasts regarding the nature of work in the global knowledge economy.

Schultz, Theodore. *The Economic Value of Education.* New York: Columbia University Press, 1963. Schultz provides economic arguments that investment in education will grow the economy and reduce income inequality.

Schweinhart, Lawrence, et al., "The High/Scope Perry Preschool Study Through Age 40: Summary, Conclusions, and Frequently Asked Questions." *High/Scope Press* (2005). www. highscope.org/file/Research/PerryProject/specialsummary_rev2011_02_2.pdf. This study includes questions about sample size and cultural context related to the Perry Preschool study.

U.S. Bureau of Labor Statistics. *Education and Training Outlook for Occupations, 2012–22* (2012). www.bls.gov/emp/ep_edtrain_outlook.pdf. This statistical report projects future jobs and their educational requirements.

U.S. Department of Education. *21st Century Skills: A Global Imperative.* https://blog.ed.gov /2012/03/21st-century-skills-a-global-imperative/ on December 1, 2018. A discussion of skills needed for a global economy.

———. *The Condition of Education 2018.* Washington, D.C. U.S. Department of Education, 2018. This report contains the characteristics of school students, including the number in poverty and attending high-poverty schools.

U.S. Department of Health and Human Services. *U.S. Federal Poverty Guidelines Used to Determine Financial Eligibility for Certain Federal Programs.* https://aspe.hhs.gov/poverty-guidelines on March 6, 2017.

———. *U.S. Federal Poverty Guidelines Used to Determine Financial Eligibility for Certain Federal Programs.* https://aspe.hhs.gov/poverty-guidelines on December 21, 2018. U.S. government's official definition of poverty levels.

CHAPTER 5

Equality of Educational Opportunity

Race, Gender, and Special Needs

This chapter focuses on *equality of educational opportunity*. In contrast to "equality of opportunity" to compete in the labor market, *equality of educational opportunity* refers to giving everyone an *equal chance to receive an education*. When defined as an equal chance to attend school, equal educational opportunity is primarily a legal issue. In this context, the provision of equal educational opportunity can be defined solely on the grounds of justice: If government provides a service like education, all classes of citizens should have equal access to that service.

Another aspect of equality of educational opportunity is the treatment of students in schools. Are all students given an equal chance to learn in schools? Do students of different races and genders receive equal treatment in schools? Is there equality of educational opportunity for students with special needs? This chapter discusses the following issues regarding equality of educational opportunity.

- The legal issues in defining race
- The major court decisions and laws involving equality of educational opportunity
- Current racial segregation in schools
- The struggle for equal educational opportunity for women
- Students with disabilities and equality of educational opportunity

THE LEGAL PROBLEM IN DEFINING RACE

The problems courts have defining race is illustrated by the famous 1896 U.S. Supreme Court case *Plessy v. Ferguson*, which allowed segregation of public schools (I discuss the details of this case in the next section). According to the lines of ancestry as expressed at that time, Plessy was one-eighth African American and seven-eighths white. Was Homer Plessy white or black? What was the meaning of the term "white"? Why wasn't Plessy classified as white since seven-eighths of his ancestry was white and only one-eighth was black? Why did the court consider him black?

Plessy v. Ferguson highlights the principle that race is a social and legal construction. The U.S. legal system was forced to construct a concept of race because the 1790 Naturalization Law limited naturalized citizenship to immigrants who were free white persons. This law did not define "white," and it excluded Native Americans from citizenship. The limitation on being "white" for naturalized citizenship remained until 1952. Because of the law, U.S. courts were forced to define the meaning of white persons. Adding to the legal problem was that most southern states in the nineteenth and early twentieth centuries adopted the so-called one drop of blood rule, which classified anyone with an African ancestor, no matter how distant, as African American. Under the one drop of blood rule, Homer Plessy was considered black.

The startling fact about the many court cases dealing with the 1790 law was the inability of the courts to rely on scientific evidence in defining white persons. Consider two of the famous twentieth-century court cases. The first, *Takao Ozawa v. United States* (1922), involved a Japanese immigrant who graduated from high school in Berkeley, California, and attended the University of California. He and his family spoke English and attended Christian churches. A key issue in *Takao Ozawa v. United States* was whether "white persons" referred to skin color. Many Japanese are fair skinned. The court responded to this issue by rejecting skin color as a criterion. The court stated:

> The test afforded by the mere color of the skin of each individual is impracticable, as that differs greatly among persons of the same race, even among Anglo-Saxons, ranging by imperceptible gradations from the fair blond to the swarthy brunette, *the latter being darker than many of the lighter hued persons of the brown and yellow races.*

> (emphasis added)

Rejecting the idea of skin color, the court recognized the term "Caucasian" to define white persons—and denied citizenship to Takao Ozawa.

However, the following year the U.S. Supreme Court rejected Caucasian as a standard for defining white persons in *United States v. Bhagat Singh Thind* (1923). In this case, an immigrant from India applied for citizenship as a Caucasian. According to the scientific rhetoric of the time, Thind was a Caucasian. Faced with this issue, the court suddenly dismissed Caucasian as a definition of white persons. The court argued, "It may be true that the blond Scandinavian and the brown Hindu have a common ancestor in the dim reaches of antiquity, but the average man knows perfectly well that there are unmistakable and profound differences between them today." Therefore, rather than relying on a scientific definition, as it had in *Takao Ozawa v. United States*, the U.S. Supreme Court declared, "What we now hold is that the words 'free white persons' are words of common speech, to be interpreted in accordance with the understanding of the common man." The court never specified who was to represent this common man. Thind was denied citizenship.

U.S. court histories are filled with efforts to define race. My nineteenth-century ancestors on my father's side were denied U.S. citizenship and were recognized as having only tribal citizenship despite the fact that many of their ancestors were European. Until Native Americans were granted U.S. citizenship in 1924, many so-called mixed-blood Native Americans were limited to tribal citizenship. The confusion over legal racial categories was exemplified by an 1853 California court case involving the testimony of immigrant Chinese witnesses regarding the murder of another Chinese immigrant by one George Hall. The California Supreme Court overturned the murder conviction of Hall by applying a state law that disallowed court testimony from blacks, mulattos, and Native Americans. California's chief justice ruled that the law barring the testimony of Native Americans applied to all "Asiatics" since, according to theory, Native Americans were originally Asians who crossed into North America over the Bering Straits. Therefore, the chief justice argued, the ban on court testimony from Native Americans applied to "the whole of the Mongolian race."

The effect of this questionable legal construction of race was to heighten tensions among different groups of Americans. Many of those classified as African American have European and Native American citizenship. However, because of the one drop of blood rule and legal support of segregation, the possibilities for continuing assimilation and peaceful coexistence between so-called whites and blacks were delayed and replaced by a tradition of hostility between the two groups.

DEFINING RACE AFTER THE 1965 IMMIGRATION ACT

The 1965 Immigration Act shifted the bias of immigration laws from favoring European immigrants to a broader acceptance of immigrants from all the world's regions. However, this new immigration law did little to define the meaning of race. According to the 2010 census (the reader is reminded that an official census is required by the U.S. Constitution to be taken every 10 years), being classified as African American is problematic, as only 1 in 10 blacks are foreign born and Africa accounts for only 1 in 3 of foreign-born blacks. Is an African American a person with ancestry that can be traced to American slavery or any person with ancestors from Africa? Is it any person with African ancestry even if he/she was born in Africa, the Caribbean, or Central or South America? In 2014, the U.S. Census Bureau announced that the African-born population of the United States had doubled every decade since 1970. The Census Bureau reported: "The foreign-born population from Africa has grown rapidly in the United States during the last 40 years, increasing from about 80,000 in 1970 to about 1.6 million in the period from 2008 to 2012, according to a U.S. Census Bureau brief released today [October 1, 2014]."

What about the racial category of white? In all, 87 percent of Americans born in Cuba and 53 percent born in Mexico identify themselves as white. However, many immigrants from Cuba and Mexico identify themselves as Hispanic or Latino and Latina. Adding to confusion about racial labels, 1 in 50 Americans identify themselves as "multiracial." Immigrants from the Dominican Republic and El Salvador describe themselves as neither black nor white. Rather than race, many immigrants identify themselves by their countries of origin or world regions, such as Africa and Asia.

Concerning the racial identity of students, the 2008 book *Inheriting the City: The Children of Immigrants Come of Age* reports a survey of racial concepts in New York City schools. When asked their race, first- and second-generation immigrants used a variety of descriptors, including nationality, ethnicity, culture, and language. In other words, racial identity varied among new immigrant groups. There were also variations of the concept of race within each immigrant group. In contrast, more than 90 percent of native-born African Americans and whites express a clear racial identity as black or white. The range of racial identifiers among other groups, even among nonimmigrant groups such as Puerto Ricans, is amazing and highlights variations in the social meaning of race. The majority of Puerto Ricans identify their race in either ethnic or group concepts. For instance, 30.4 percent of Puerto Ricans gave their racial identity as Puerto Rican and 26 percent as Hispanic. Other racial identities among Puerto Ricans include white, black, American, indigenous Indian, human, Latin American, Latino, mixed, and Spanish.

First- and second-generation immigrants provide a similar range of racial concepts. For instance, 95 percent of first- and second-generation Chinese immigrants gave their race as Chinese while others gave their racial identity as American, Asian, or don't know. Some Chinese identified their race according to country of origin—there are many Chinese communities around the world—such as Vietnamese, Burmese, and Malay. In these countries, they are considered ethnic Chinese. The largest range of racial identifiers are among first- and second-generation immigrants from the Dominican Republic and South America. Among Dominicans racial identifiers include white, black, Indian, American, Dominican, Hispanic, human, Latin American, Latino, mixed, Spanish, and West Indian. Some people state they don't know their race. For South Americans, the range was even greater and includes countries from which people originally immigrated to South America, such as Japan. South Americans identified their race as white, black, Indian, Japanese, American, Asian, Colombian, Ecuadoran, Hispanic, human, Latin American, Latino, South American, and Spanish.

Table 5.1 What Does "Race" Mean? Varieties of Racial Identities among Native and Immigrant Groups (%)

Race Given	Native Black	Native White	West Indian	South American	Chinese
White		95.9	0.2	19.5	0.5
Black	99.5	0.2	92.9	3.7	
Native American	0.2				
Chinese			0.2		95.0
Indian				0.2	
Japanese				0.2	
Vietnamese					0.2
American		1.0		3.2	0.2
Asian					3.3
Burmese					0.2
Colombian				5.2	
Dominican					
Ecuadoran				4.7	
Hispanic		0.2	0.5	36.9	
Hunan			0.2	0.5	0.2
Indigenous Indian				1.0	
Latin American				1.7	
Latino		0.2	0.2	4.7	
Mixed	0.2		0.5		
Peruvian				2.0	
Puerto Rican				0.7	
South American				0.5	
Spanish				5.0	
West Indian			3.9		
Malay					0.2
Other race		0.2	0.2	0.5	
Don't know		0.5	0.7	8.5	0.3
Refused to answer		1.7	0.2	0.5	

Source: Adapted from "Racial Identification by Group," in *Inheriting the City: The Children of Immigrants Come of Age,* ed. Philip Kasinitz, John Mollenkopf, Mary C. Waters, and Jennifer Holdaway (Cambridge, MA: Harvard University Press, 2008), Table 3.1, p. 71.

The variety of responses from first- and second-generation immigrants regarding race indicates the changing character of racial concepts since earlier in American history when they were defined by American law and judicial rulings. The only ones who continue to think in former legal and judicial racial concepts are native-born African Americans and whites. Table 5.1 provides a short summary of the racial identities of first- and second-generation immigrants in New York City (a more complete table of racial identities can be found in *Inheriting the City: The Children of Immigrants Come of Age*). Are U.S. citizens in transition to a society where concepts of race are less important in determining social status? One indication of this possibility is those people who give their racial identity as human.

THE CENSUS AND RACE

As mentioned previously, the U.S. Census is taken every 10 years and uses the racial classifications adopted by the U.S. Office of Management of Budget in 1997 that there be "five minimum categories for data on race: American Indian or Alaska Native, Asian, Black or African American, Native Hawaiian or Other Pacific Islander, and White. There will be two categories for data on ethnicity: 'Hispanic or Latino' and 'Not Hispanic or Latino'."

For the 2020 census a proposed controversial question about citizenship was to be asked by census takers: "Is this person a citizen of the United States?" The choices to this question included four categories of yes (Born in U.S.; Born in Puerto Rico, Guam, the U.S. Virgin Islands, or Northern Marianas; Born abroad of U.S. Citizen parent or parents; Citizen by naturalization) and one category of no (Not a U.S. citizen). Many worried this question would keep noncitizens from answering census questions.

To resolve problems in defining a person's race, the U.S. Census Bureau uses personal self-identification. As indicated by the 2020 census, the concept of "race" includes nationality (such as Japanese), skin color (such as white or black), and tribal affiliation (American Indian or Alaskan Native).

The proposed 2020 census expands on the 1997 racial categories by asking the person identifying themselves as "White" if they are "German, Irish, English, Italian, Lebanese, Egyptian, etc." Of course, this raises the historically unanswered question of the meaning of the racial classification "White" since Egyptians are classified as white: does this mean all Arabs are white? Those selecting "Black" are asked if they are asked if they are "African American, Jamaican, Haitian, Nigerian, Ethiopian, Somali, etc." Also, on the 2020 census "American Indians" are asked to identify their tribe. The broad category of Asian is broken down into Chinese, Filipino, Asian Indian, Vietnamese, Korean, Japanese, and other Asian. The final blank allows for entering "some other race."

There is a separate question that asks, "Is this person of Hispanic, Latino, or Spanish origin?" This is a complex issue because of problems inherent in the terms "Hispanic" and "Latino," which might encompass only Spanish speakers from the Caribbean or Central and South America. However, there are peoples from these regions who speak English (such as Jamaica, Barbados, Belize, and Guyana), French (such as Haiti and Martinique), Portuguese (such as Brazil), and a variety of Native Americans speaking indigenous languages. To guide the responder, there are six choices.

- No, not of Hispanic, Latino, or Spanish Origin
- Yes, Mexican, Mexican Am., Chicano
- Yes, Puerto Rican
- Yes, Cuban
- Yes, another Hispanic, Latino, or Spanish origin—Print, for example, Salvadoran, Dominican, Colombian, Guatemalan, Spaniard, Ecuadorian, etc.

These options gloss over the fact that some immigrants from the Caribbean and Central and South America are not Spanish speakers. What happens to non-Spanish speakers, such as tribal members from these regions? They are not identified in the census. In other words, indigenous peoples from Central and South American have no way of identifying themselves in the 2020 census, nor do non-Spanish speakers from the Caribbean and Central and South America.

Racial classifications are complicated when considered against the background of nationality. For instance, how do you classify those Mexicans whose ancestors were African? A 2014 *New York Times* article posed the question in its title: "Negro? Prieto? Moreno? A Question of Identity for Black Mexicans." Mexico at one time had enslaved Africans. Their descendants worry about their identity in a society dominated by mestizos, with many terms being used, such as "Afromexican," "moreno," "mascogo," "jarocho," and "costeño." How should this population of African descendants from Mexico be classified if they immigrate to the United States?

Today, the issue of racial classification is tied to the concept of equality of educational opportunity. In addition, current school policies are trying to reduce the gap in test scores between so-called minority groups. But how are these minority groups classified—skin color, national origin, or tribal affiliation? While racial identification is a problematic concept, the public schools, as I discuss in the next section, must provide equal educational opportunity.

THE FOURTEENTH AMENDMENT AND EQUALITY OF EDUCATIONAL OPPORTUNITY

Equal treatment by the law is the great legal principle underlying the idea of equality of educational opportunity. This concept is embodied in the Fourteenth Amendment to the U.S. Constitution and provides that everyone should receive equal treatment by the law and no one should receive special privileges or treatment because of race, gender, religion, ethnicity, or wealth. This means that if a government provides a school system, everyone should be treated equally by that system; everyone should have equal access to that educational system.

Added in 1868, the purpose of the Fourteenth Amendment was to protect the basic guarantees of the Bill of Rights against laws passed by state and local governments. The Fourteenth Amendment guarantees that states cannot take away any rights granted to an individual as a citizen of the United States; this means that although states have the right to provide schools, they cannot in their provision of schools violate citizen rights granted by the Constitution. The wording of Section 1 of the Fourteenth Amendment is extremely important in a variety of constitutional issues related to education, particularly equality of educational opportunity.

Fourteenth Amendment

All persons born or naturalized in the United States, and subject to the jurisdiction thereof, are citizens of the United States and of the State wherein they reside. No State shall make or enforce any law which shall abridge the privileges or immunities of citizens of the United States; nor shall any State deprive any person of life, liberty, or property without due process of law [Due Process Clause]; nor deny to any person within its jurisdiction the equal protection of the laws [Equal Protection Clause].

These few lines of the Fourteenth Amendment are important for state-provided and state-regulated schools. For instance, "no state shall make or enforce any law which shall abridge the privileges or immunities of citizens of the United States" means the courts can protect the constitutional rights of students and teachers particularly with regard to freedom of speech and issues related to religion. The Due Process Clause is invoked in cases that involve student suspensions and teacher firings. Since states provide schools to all citizens, they cannot dismiss a student or teacher without due process. As we shall see later in this chapter, the courts established guidelines for student dismissals.

All the protections of the Fourteenth Amendment depend on the states making some provision for education. Once a state government provides a system for education, it must provide it equally to all people in the state. The Equal Protection Clause is invoked in cases that involve equal educational opportunity and is central to cases that involve school segregation, non-English-speaking children, school finance, and children with special needs.

Originally, the U.S. Supreme Court in 1896 interpreted equal protection as allowing for "separate but equal." In other words, segregated education based on race could be legal under the Fourteenth Amendment if all the schools were equal. The separate but equal ruling occurred in the previously mentioned 1896 U.S. Supreme Court decision *Plessy v. Ferguson*. The U.S. Supreme Court's decision was that segregated facilities could exist if they were equal. This became known as the separate but equal doctrine.

The 1954 desegregation decision, *Brown v. Board of Education of Topeka*, overturned the separate but equal doctrine by arguing that segregated education was inherently unequal. This meant that even if school facilities, teachers, equipment, and all other physical conditions were equal between two racially segregated schools, the two schools would still be unequal because of the racial segregation.

DESEGREGATING SCHOOLS

In 1964, Congress took a significant step toward speeding up school desegregation by passing the important Civil Rights Act. Title VI of the 1964 Civil Rights Act provided a means for the federal government to force school desegregation. In its final form, Title VI required the mandatory withholding of federal funds from institutions that practiced racial discrimination. Title VI states that no person, because of race, color, or national origin, can be excluded from or denied the benefits of any program receiving federal financial assistance. It required all federal agencies to establish guidelines to implement this policy. Refusal by institutions or projects to follow these guidelines was to result in the "termination

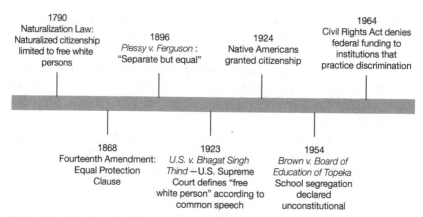

Figure 5.1a Timeline: Equality of Educational Opportunity

of or refusal to grant or to continue assistance under such program or activity."

Title VI of the 1964 Civil Rights Act remains important for two reasons. First, it established a major precedent for federal control of American public schools by making it explicit that the control of money would be one method used by the federal government to shape local school policies. (This aspect of the law will be discussed in more detail in Chapter 9.) Second, it turned the federal Office of Education into a policing agency with the responsibility of determining whether school systems were segregated and, if they were, of doing something about the segregated conditions.

Title VI sped up the process of school desegregation in the South, particularly after the passage of federal legislation in 1965 that increased the amount of money available to local schools from the federal government. In the late 1960s, southern school districts rapidly began to submit school desegregation plans to the Office of Education.

In the North, prosecution of inequality in educational opportunity as it related to school segregation required a different approach from that used in the South. In the South, school segregation existed by legislative acts that required separation of the races. There were no specific laws requiring separation of the races in the North. But even without specific laws, racial segregation existed. Therefore, it was necessary for individuals bringing complaints against northern school districts to prove the existing patterns of racial segregation were the result of purposeful action by the school districts. It had to be proved that school officials intended racial segregation to be a result of their educational policies.

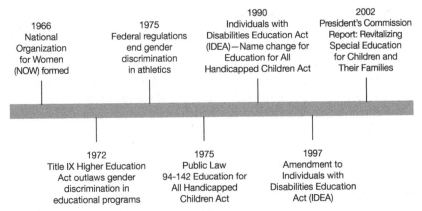

Figure 5.1b Timeline: Equality of Educational Opportunity

The conditions required to prove segregation were explicitly outlined in 1974 in the Sixth Circuit Court of Appeals case *Oliver v. Michigan State Board of Education*. The court stated, "A presumption of segregative purpose arises when plaintiffs establish that the natural, probable and foreseeable result of public officials' action or inaction was an increase or perpetuation of public school segregation." This did not mean individual motives or prejudices were to be investigated but that the overall pattern of school actions had to be shown to increase racial segregation; that is, in the language of the court, "the question whether a purposeful pattern of segregation has manifested itself over time, despite the fact that individual official actions, considered alone, may not have been taken for segregative purposes."

SCHOOL SEGREGATION TODAY

In 2014, 60 years after the 1954 Brown desegregation ruling by the Supreme Court, the UCLA Civil Rights project founded by Gary Orfield and Christopher Edley Jr. released its report on current school segregation. The report noted that since the court decision there has been a 30 percent drop in white students and an increase of close to 500 percent in Latino students. Its major conclusions are:

- Black and Latino students are an increasingly large percentage of suburban enrollment, particularly in larger metropolitan areas, and are moving to schools with relatively few white students.
- Segregation for blacks is the highest in the Northeast, a region with extremely high district fragmentation.
- Latinos are now significantly more segregated than blacks in suburban America.

- Black and Latino students tend to be in schools with a substantial majority of poor children, while white and Asian students typically attend middle-class schools.
- Segregation is by far the most serious in the central cities of the largest metropolitan areas; the states of New York, Illinois, and California are the top three worst for isolating black students.
- California is the state in which Latino students are most segregated.

In these findings it is important to note the increasing numbers of black and Latino students in suburban school districts reflecting a general movement of minority populations out of central cities. And, unlike the past, Latino students are now more segregated in schools than black students. Also, Latino and black students are economically segregated and are more likely to attend schools with a high concentration of low-income students. Also, Latinos are more segregated in California schools, while central cities in New York, Illinois, and California have the greatest segregation of black students.

In 2017, the UCLA Civil Rights Project warned that there was increasing segregation in the South. Since 1980 the percentage of black students in intensely segregated was 35.8 percent. The report states, "Latino students, who make up 27 percent of students in the South, surpasses that of Black students . . . with more than 40 percent of Latino students in the South attending intensely segregated schools as of 2014."

TITLE IX

The reader should check the Websites of the following organizations for current issues, policies, and the history of struggle regarding women's education: American Association of University Women (www.aauw.org), National Organization for Women Foundation (www.nowfoundation. org), and Education Equality of the Feminist Majority Foundation (www.feminist.org/education). These organizations are in the forefront in protecting women's rights in education. Given the space limitations of this book, I will only be dealing with issues surrounding Title IX of the 1972 Higher Education Act.

Since the nineteenth century, the struggle for racial justice paralleled that of justice for women. Demands for equal educational opportunity pervaded both campaigns for civil rights. In the second half of the twentieth century the drive for equal educational opportunity for women was led by the National Organization for Women (NOW), which was organized in 1966. The founding document of the organization declared, "There is no civil rights movement to speak for women as there has been for Negroes and other victims of discrimination."

NOW's activities and that of other women's organizations turned to legal action with the passage of Title IX of the 1972 Higher Education Act. Title IX states: "No person in the United States shall, on the basis of sex, be excluded from participation in, be denied the benefits of, or be subjected to discrimination under any education program or activity receiving federal financial assistance." The legislation applied to all educational institutions, including preschool, elementary and secondary schools, vocational and professional schools, and public and private undergraduate and graduate institutions. A 1983 U.S. Supreme Court decision, *Grove City College v. Bell*, restricted the application of Title IX to specific educational programs within institutions. In the 1987 Civil Rights Restoration Act, Congress overturned the court's decision and amended Title IX to include *all* activities of an educational institution receiving federal aid. Armed with Title IX, NOW and other women's organizations placed pressure on local school systems and colleges to ensure equal treatment of women in vocational education, athletic programs, textbooks and the curriculum, testing, and college admissions.

In 2014, the federal government updated the coverage of Title IX to extends to all students, regardless of sexual orientation or gender identity. The U.S. Department of Education released the following guidelines for Title IX:

> Title IX protects all students at recipient institutions from sex discrimination, including sexual violence. Any student can experience sexual violence: from elementary to professional school students; *male and female students; straight, gay, lesbian, bisexual, and transgender students*; part-time and full-time students; students with and without disabilities; and students of different races and national origins.
>
> (emphasis in original)

Also, under these guidelines, gay, lesbian, bisexual, and transgender students are protected against discrimination and sexual harassment and violence. These guidelines broaden the scope of Title IX and allow the federal Office of Civil Rights (OCR) to handle complaints about bullying of lesbian, gay, bisexual, and transgender students.

Title IX's sex discrimination prohibition extends to claims of discrimination based on gender identity or failure to conform to stereotypical notions of masculinity or femininity. OCR accepts complaints about these issues and can launch an investigation. Similarly, the actual or perceived sexual orientation or gender identity of the parties does not change a school's obligations. Indeed, lesbian, gay, bisexual, and transgender (LGBT) youth report high rates of sexual harassment and sexual violence. A school should investigate and resolve allegations of sexual violence regarding LGBT students using the same procedures and standards it uses in all complaints involving sexual violence.

In addition, the new guidelines require schools to investigate any negative comments about a student's sexual orientation: "The fact that incidents of sexual violence may be accompanied by anti-gay comments or be partly based on a student's actual or perceived sexual orientation does not relieve a school of its obligation under Title IX to investigate and remedy those instances of sexual violence."

Providing an example of discrimination against transgender youth, *Education Week* reporter Evie Blad wrote in 2014, "I've written previously about a transgender student suing her school when administrators refused to let her use girls' restrooms because she was born a boy. In January, a new California law went into effect that allows transgender students to use single-sex facilities and join sex-segregated teams that match their gender identities. Supporters of that law have pushed for federal guidance that addresses such issues."

However, all this began to change after the 2016 presidential election. The Republican Party gained control of the federal government and opposed extending Title IX rights to LGBT students as discussed in Chapter 2. The 2016 Republican platform specifically supports Title IX with limitations. The platform states: "We emphatically support the original, authentic meaning of Title IX of the Education Amendments of 1972." However, the 2016 platform accuses President Obama's administration of distorting the meaning of the law:

> That same provision of law is now being used by bureaucrats—and by the current President of the United States [Obama]—to impose a social and cultural revolution upon the American people by wrongly redefining sex discrimination to include sexual orientation or other categories. Their agenda has nothing to do with individual rights; it has everything to do with power. They are determined to reshape our schools—and our entire society—to fit the mold of an ideology alien to America's history and traditions.

In 2018, the American Association of University Women and other groups complained about the weakening of protections related to sexual assault and harassment. Under the heading "The Attack on Title IX," the organization declared:

> Make no mistake—the Department of Education's actions amount to a blatant rollback of strong and necessary protections for

students, and particularly for student survivors of sexual assault. Specifically, the November 2018 NPRM would weaken Title IX's protections by narrowing the definition of sexual harassment to potentially exclude much of the abuse students experience and altering when schools will respond to reports of sexual harassment and violence. In addition, the rule would put in place school processes that make it harder for students to come forward and receive the support they need when they experience sexual harassment or assault. Title IX protects all students from discrimination—students of all genders, from kindergarten through college—and these expansive changes would put those protections at risk.

This will continue to be an ongoing topic.

STUDENTS WITH DISABILITIES

By the 1960s, the civil rights movement encompassed students with disabilities. Within the context of equality of educational opportunity, students with special needs could participate equally in schools with other students only if they received some form of special help. Starting in the nineteenth century, many of the needs of these students were neglected by local and state school authorities because of the expense of special facilities and teachers. In fact, many people with disabilities were forced to live in state institutions for persons with mental illness or retardation. For instance, consider "Allan's story," a case history of treatment prior to the 1970s, provided by the U.S. Office of Special Education Programs:

> Allan was left as an infant on the steps of an institution for persons with mental retardation in the late 1940s. By age 35, he had become blind and was frequently observed sitting in a corner of the room, slapping his heavily callused face as he rocked back and forth humming to himself.

In the late 1970s, Allan was assessed properly for the first time. To the dismay of his examiners, he was found to be of average intelligence; further review of his records revealed that by observing fellow residents of the institution, he had learned the self-injurious behavior that had caused his total loss of vision. Although the institution then began a special program to teach Allan to be more independent, a major portion of his life was lost because of a lack of appropriate assessments and effective interventions.

The political movement for federal legislation to aid students with disabilities followed a path similar to the rest of the civil rights movement. First, finding themselves unable to change educational institutions by pressuring local and state governments, organized groups interested in improving educational opportunities for students with special needs turned to the courts. This was the path taken in the late 1960s by the Pennsylvania Association for Retarded Children (PARC). PARC was one of many associations organized in the 1950s to aid citizens with disabilities. These organizations were concerned with state laws that excluded children with disabilities from educational institutions because they were considered uneducable and untrainable. State organizations like PARC and the National Association for Retarded Children campaigned to eliminate these laws and to demonstrate the educability of all children. But, as the civil rights movement discovered throughout the century, local and state officials were resistant to change, and relief had to be sought through the judicial system.

In *Pennsylvania Association for Retarded Children (PARC) v. Commonwealth of Pennsylvania*, a case that was as important for the rights of children with disabilities as the *Brown* decision was for African Americans, PARC objected to conditions in the Pennhurst State School and Hospital. In framing the case, lawyers for PARC focused on the legal right to an education for children with disabilities. PARC, working with the major federal lobbyist for children with disabilities, the Council for Exceptional Children (CEC), overwhelmed the court with evidence on the educability of children with disabilities. The state withdrew its case, and the court enjoined the state from excluding children with disabilities from a public education and required that every child be allowed access to an education. Publicity about the PARC case prompted other lobbying groups to file 36 cases against different state governments. The CEC prepared model legislation and lobbied for its passage at the state and federal levels.

PUBLIC LAW 94-142: EDUCATION FOR ALL HANDICAPPED CHILDREN ACT

In 1975, Congress passed Public Law 94-142, the Education for All Handicapped Children Act, which guaranteed equal educational opportunity for all children with disabilities. In 1990, Congress changed the name of this legislation to the Individuals with Disabilities Education Act (IDEA). In 2010, the 20th anniversary of IDEA was commemorated by U.S. Secretary of Education Arne Duncan with the statement:

The Americans with Disabilities Act is a landmark piece of civil rights legislation. It protects individuals with disabilities from discrimination and promotes their full inclusion into education and all other aspects of our society. I want to celebrate the progress that we've made and highlight our commitment to continuing the work of providing equal access for all Americans. I acknowledge we still have work to do and renew my commitment to ensuring that individuals of all ages and abilities have an equal opportunity to realize their full potential.

The major provisions in Public Law 94-142 provided for equal educational opportunity for all children with disabilities. This goal included the opportunity for all children with disabilities to attend regular school classes. As stated in the legislation, "all children with disabilities [should] have available to them . . . a free appropriate public education which emphasized special education and related services designed to meet their unique needs."

In 2010, the U.S. Department of Education released its report "Thirty-Five Years of Progress in Educating Children with Disabilities through IDEA," which listed the following four purposes:

1. to assure that all children with disabilities have available to them . . . a free appropriate public education which emphasizes special education and related services designed to meet their unique needs
2. to assure that the rights of children with disabilities and their parents . . . are protected
3. to assist States and localities to provide for the education of all children with disabilities
4. to assess and assure the effectiveness of efforts to educate all children with disabilities

In celebrating 35 years of the legislation, the report declared: "During these last 35 years, IDEA also has developed a national infrastructure of supports that are improving results for millions of children with dis-abilities, as well as their nondisabled friends and classmates."

DISABILITY CATEGORIES

The Condition of Education 2018 provides a listing of disability categories. The percentage of students in schools in 2015–2016 for each recognized disability in that list is given in Table 5.2.

Table 5.2 Percentage Distribution of Students Ages 3–21 Served under the Individuals with Disabilities Education Act (IDEA), Part B, by Disability Type: School Year 2015–2016

Disabilities	Percentage with Disability (%)
Specific learning disability	34
Speech or language impairment	20
Other health impairment	14
Autism	9
Developmental delay	6
Intellectual disability	6
Emotional disturbance	5
Multiple disabilities	2
Hearing impairment	1
Orthopedic impairment	1

Source: National Center for Education Statistics, The Condition of Education 2018 (Washington, DC: U.S. Department of Education, 2018), p. 74.

WRITING AN IEP

One of the issues confronting Congress during legislative debates was that of increased federal control over local school systems. Congress resolved this problem by requiring that an *individualized education plan (IEP)* be written for each student with disabilities. This reduced federal control since IEPs would be written in the local school systems. IEPs are now a standard part of education programs for children with disabilities. Public Law 94-142 requires that an IEP be developed for each child jointly by the local educational agency and the child's parents or guardians. This gives the child or the parents the right to negotiate with the local school system about the type of services to be delivered.

According to U.S. guidelines, after a student is identified as having a disability, the school schedules and conducts the IEP meeting. Official U.S. Department of Education Regulations give these steps in providing an IEP:

1. Identify the members of the IEP Team.
2. The public agency must ensure that the IEP Team for each child with a disability includes:

    a. The parents of the child;
    b. Not less than one regular education teacher of the child (if the child is, or may be, participating in the regular education environment);

c. Not less than one special education teacher of the child, or where appropriate, not less than one special education provider of the child;
d. A representative of the public agency (who has certain specific knowledge and qualifications);
e. An individual who can interpret the instructional implications of evaluation results and who may also be one of the other listed members;
f. At the discretion of the parent or the agency, other individuals who have knowledge or special expertise regarding the child, including related services personnel as appropriate;
g. And whenever appropriate, the child with a disability.

3. The public agency must invite a child with a disability to attend the child's IEP Team meeting if a purpose of the meeting will be the consideration of the postsecondary goals for the child and the transition services needed to assist the child in reaching those goals.

INCLUSION

The term "inclusion" is the most frequently used word to refer to the integration of children with disabilities into regular classrooms. The phrase "full inclusion" refers to the inclusion of all children with disabilities. The 1975 Education for All Handicapped Children Act called for the integration of children with disabilities into regular classes. Similar to any form of segregation, the isolation of children with disabilities often deprives them of contact with other students and denies them access to equipment found in regular classrooms, such as scientific equipment, audiovisual aids, classroom libraries, and computers. Full inclusion, it is believed, will improve the educational achievement and social development of children with disabilities. Also, it is hoped, bias against children and adults with disabilities will decrease because of the interactions of students with disabilities with other students. The integration clause of the Education for All Handicapped Children Act specified that to the maximum extent appropriate, handicapped children, including children in public and private institutions and other care facilities, are to be educated with children who are not handicapped, and that special classes, separate schooling, or other removal of handicapped children from the regular educational environment should occur only when the nature or severity of the handicap is such that education in regular classes with the use of supplementary aids and services cannot be achieved satisfactorily.

In 1990, advocates of full inclusion received federal support with the passage of the Americans with Disabilities Act (ADA). This historic legislation bans all forms of discrimination against people who are disabled. The ADA played an important role in the 1992 court decision *Oberti v. Board of Education of the Borough of Clementon School District*, which involved an eight-year-old, Rafael Oberti, classified as educable mentally retarded. U.S. District Court Judge John F. Gerry argued that the ADA requires that people with disabilities be given equal access to services provided by any agency receiving federal money, including public schools. Judge Gerry decided Oberti could manage in a regular classroom with special aides and a special curriculum. In his decision Judge Gerry wrote, "Inclusion is a right, not a privilege for a select few."

The 1997 congressional amendments to this legislation, now called the Individuals with Disabilities Education Act (IDEA), emphasized the importance of including children with disabilities in regular classes. In the text of the 1997 amendments, it was claimed that since the passage of the original legislation research, inclusion in regular classes improved the academic performance of children with disabilities. In the words of the amendments, "Over 20 years of research and experience has demonstrated that the education of children with disabilities can be made more effective by . . . having high expectations for such children and ensuring their access in the general curriculum to the maximum extent possible."

The inclusion of children with disabilities in regular classrooms creates a challenge for regular teachers. Classroom teachers, according to the legislation, are to be provided with "appropriate special education and related services and aids." The legislation specified that teachers should receive extra training to help children with disabilities. In the words of the legislation, school districts must provide "high-quality, intensive professional development for all personnel who work with such children in order to ensure that they have the skills and knowledge necessary to enable them to meet developmental goals." Also, teacher-education programs are to give all student teachers training in working with students with disabilities.

UNESCO AND INCLUSION

In 2005, the United Nations Educational, Scientific, and Cultural Organization (UNESCO) issued its "Guidelines for Inclusion: Ensuring Access to Education for All." A global organization, UNESCO is particularly concerned with the inclusion of students in education in developing nations. The organization estimates that globally over half a billion persons are disabled and excluded not only from schools but also from fully participating in local economies and political systems. It estimates that 80 percent of the disabled live in developing countries. The guidelines state, "Today there are an estimated 140 million children who are out of school, a majority being girls and children with disabilities. Among them, 90% live in lower middle-income countries and over 80% of these children are in Africa."

UNESCO's supports of inclusion as a human right are based on Article 26 of the Universal Declaration of Human Rights:

Everyone has the right to education . . . Education shall be free, at least in the elementary and fundamental stages. Elementary education shall be compulsory. Education shall be directed to the full development of human personality and to the strengthening of respect for human rights and fundamental freedoms. It shall promote understanding, tolerance and friendship among all nations, racial or religious groups, and shall further the activities of the United Nations for the maintenance of peace.

In the context of Article 26 of the Universal Declaration of Human Rights, UNESCO's concept of inclusion includes not only students with disabilities but also children from differing cultures and religions. Thus, UNESCO's definition is:

Inclusion is seen as a process of addressing and responding to the diversity of needs of all learners through increasing participation in learning, cultures and communities, and reducing exclusion within and from education. It involves changes and modifications in content, approaches, structures and strategies, with a common vision which covers all children of the appropriate age range and a conviction that it is the responsibility of the regular system to educate all children.

In other words, UNESCO is actively making inclusion a global education doctrine that includes not only students with disabilities but also all children.

CHARTER SCHOOLS AND PUBLIC LAW 94-142

The federal government has issued guidelines for protecting the rights of students with disabilities in charter schools. Schools receiving federal funds must comply with Public Law 94—142. Since state governments and local school districts receive federal funds, any charter school created by these government units must comply with the law. The federal guidelines state:

Local educational agencies (LEAs) that receive Federal financial assistance either directly from ED or indirectly, e.g., through a State educational agency (SEA), must comply with the requirements . . . Federally-assisted LEAs, including both traditional LEAs (i.e., traditional school district LEAs) and charter school LEAs (i.e., public charter schools that operate as LEAs under State law) from discriminating against current and prospective students on the basis of disability.

CONCLUSION

Unequal educational opportunities continue to plague American schools. Even though the civil rights movement was able to overturn laws requiring school segregation, second-generation segregation continues to be a problem. Differences between school districts in expenditures per student tend to increase the effects of segregation. Many Hispanic, African American, and Native American students attend schools where per-student expenditures are considerably below those of elite suburban and private schools. These reduced expenditures contribute to unequal educational opportunity that, in turn, affects a student's ability to compete in the labor market.

However, the advances resulting from the struggle for equal educational opportunity highlight the importance of political activity in improving the human condition. In and out of the classroom, teachers assume a vital role in ensuring the future of their students and society. In the areas of race, gender, and children with disabilities, there have been important improvements in education since the nineteenth century. The dynamic of social change requires an active concern about the denial of equality of opportunity and equality of educational opportunity.

SUGGESTED READINGS AND WORKS CITED IN CHAPTER

American Association of University Women. *Attack on Title IX* (November 15, 2018). www.aauw.org/article/the-attack-on-title-ix/ on December 17, 2018. Article reflects concerns about changes in Title IX regulations by the Trump administration.

———. *What We Do.* www.aauw.org/what-we-do/ on December 13, 2018. This organization plays a major role in protecting women's rights in education. The reader should check the organization's annual reports on current issues.

Anderson, James. *The Education of Blacks in the South, 1860–1935.* Chapel Hill: University of North Carolina Press, 1988. Best history of early education of African Americans and their struggles to receive equal educational opportunities.

Archibald, Randal. "Negro? Prieto? Moreno? A Question of Identity for Black Mexicans." *The New York Times* (October 25, 2014). www.nytimes.com/2014/10/26/world/americas/negro-prieto-moreno-a-question-of-identity-for-black-mexicans.html?ref=world&_r=0 on January 17, 2019. This article describes the problem of classifying Mexican who are descendants of enslaved Africans.

Balfanz, Robert, and Nettie Legters. *Locating the Dropout Crisis: Which High Schools Produce the Nation's Dropouts? Where Are They Located? Who Attends Them?* Baltimore: Center for Social Organization of Schools, Johns Hopkins University, 2004. This study shows that a majority of African American and 40 percent of Hispanic students attend high schools where the majority of students do not graduate.

Carey, Kevin. *The Funding Gap 2004: Many States Still Shortchange Low-Income and Minority Students.* Washington, DC: Education Trust, 2004. Carey shows disparities in funding based on racial concentrations in school districts.

The Civil Rights Project UCLA. *New Research Shows Reversal of Civil Rights Era Gains, Increase in School Segregation in the South* (May 24, 2017). www.civilrightsproject.ucla.edu/news/press-releases/2017-press-releases/southern-schools-83-press-release/CRP-Southern-seg-report-news-release-7-dist-5–23.pdf on November 20, 2018. Report highlights increasing school segregation in Southern schools, particularly among Latinos.

———. *Report Finds Changing U.S. Demographics Transform School Segregation Landscape 60 Years After Brown v Board of Education* (May 15, 2014). http://civilrightsproject.ucla.edu/news/press-releases/2014-press-releases/ucla-report-finds-changing-u.s.-demographics-transform-school-segregation-landscape-60-years-after-brown-v-board-of-education/National-report-press-release-draft-3.pdf. Study of school segregation since 1954 showing the increasing segregation of Latinos.

Feminist Majority Foundation. *Education Equality: Threats to Title IX.* www.femist.org/education/ThreatstoTitleIX.asp on September 7, 2008. This site provides information on the continuing struggle for gender equality in the schools.

Kluger, Richard. *Simple Justice.* New York: Random House, 1975. Kluger provides a good history of *Brown v. Board of Education* and the struggle for equality.

Lemann, Nicholas. *The Promised Land: The Great Black Migration and How It Changed America.* New York: Vintage Books, 1991. This is a definitive history of African American migration from the South to the urban North.

Lopez, Ian F. Haney. *White by Law: The Legal Construction of Race.* New York: New York University Press, 1996. Legal cases involved in defining the legal meaning of "white" are discussed.

Lopez, Nancy. *Hopeful Girls, Troubled Boys: Race and Gender Disparity in Urban Education.* New York: Routledge, 2003.

Meier, Kenneth, Joseph Stewart, Jr., and Robert England. *Race, Class, and Education: The Politics of Second-Generation Discrimination.* Madison: University of Wisconsin Press, 1989. This book studies the politics of second-generation segregation.

National Organization for Women Foundation. www.nowfoundation.org. The annual reports of NOW's foundation list current educational issues involving gender equity.

Orfield, Gary. *Schools More Separate: Consequences of a Decade of Resegregation.* Cambridge, MA: Harvard University Press, The Civil Rights Project, 2001. Details of the resegregation of American schools in the last quarter of the twentieth century are presented.

———. *The Reconstruction of Southern Education: The Schools and the 1964 Civil Rights Act.* New York: Wiley-Interscience, 1969. Orfield presents a study of the desegregation of southern schools following the passage of the 1964 Civil Rights Act.

Philip, John Mollenkopf, Mary C. Waters, and Jennifer Holdaway. *Inheriting the City: The Children of Immigrants Come of Age.* Cambridge, MA: Harvard University Press, 2008. A study of immigrant students in New York City.

Republican Platform 2016. https://gop.com/platform/ on November 23, 2016. Discusses its political position on Title IX and LGBT students.

Rist, Ray. *Desegregated Schools: Appraisals of an American Experiment.* New York: Academic Press, 1979. This book provides many examples of second-generation segregation.

Roberts, Sam. "Census Figures Challenge Views of Race and Ethnicity." *The New York Times on the Web* (January 22, 2010). www.nytimes.com. Report on the complexity of identifying race and ethnicity in the 2010 census report.

United Nations Educational, Scientific and Cultural Organization. *Guidelines for Inclusion: Ensuring Access to Education for All.* Paris: UNESCO, 2005. These UNESCO guidelines declare inclusion to be a human right under the Universal Declaration of Human Rights.

U.S. Census Bureau. *Census Bureau Statement on 2020 Census Race and Ethnicity Questions* (January 26, 2018). www.census.gov/newsroom/press-releases/2018/2020-race-questions.html on December 20, 2018. Proposed census questions related to race and ethnicity.

———. *Questions Planned for the 2020 Census and American Community Survey* (March 2018). https://www2.census.gov/library/publications/decennial/2020/operations/planned-questions-2020-acs.pdf on December 21, 2018. Proposed census questions related to race and ethnicity.

U.S. Department of Education. *The Condition of Education 2018.* National Center for Education Statistics, 2018. Provides statistical information on race, disabilities, school enrollments, and teachers.

———. *Frequently Asked Questions About the Rights of Students with Disabilities in Public Charter Schools Under Section 504 of the Rehabilitation Act of 1973.* https://www2.ed.gov/about/offices/list/ocr/docs/dcl-faq-201612-504-charter-school.pdf on March 1, 2017. Discusses the policies regarding disabilities and charter schools.

———. *IDEA Regulations Individualized Education Program (IEP) Team Meetings and Changes to the IEP.* https://sites.ed.gov/idea/files/policy_speced_guid_idea_iep-qa-2010.pdf on November 14, 2018. Updated regulations on writing IEPs.

———. *Questions and Answers on Individualized Education Programs (IEPs), Evaluations, and Reevaluations Revised* (June 2010). https://sites.ed.gov/idea/files/policy_speced_guid_idea_iep-qa-2010.pdf on November 15, 2018. Answers basic questions about IEPs.

———. *Thirty-Five Years of Progress in Educating Children with Disabilities Through IDEA.* http://www2.ed.gov/about/offices/list/osers/idea35/history/idea-35-history.pdf on January 17, 2019. This report describes the progress made in implementation of IDEA.

U.S. Office of Management and Budget. *Revisions to the Standards for the Classification of Federal Data on Race and Ethnicity Federal Register*, Vol. 62, no. 210 (October 30, 1997). www.govinfo.gov/content/pkg/FR-1997-10-30/pdf/97-28653.pdf on December 20, 2018. These are the original racial classifications to be used in the U.S. census.

Wolf, Carmen, et al. *Income, Poverty, and Health Insurance Coverage in the United States: 2003.* Washington, DC: U.S. Census Bureau, August 2004. The authors provide important census material on the relationship between race and income.

Wollenberg, Charles. *All Deliberate Speed: Segregation and Exclusion in California Schools, 1855–1975.* Berkeley: University of California Press, 1976. This is a good history of segregation in California. It includes a discussion of the important Court decision regarding Mexican Americans, *Mendez et al. v. Westminster School District of Orange County*, and of the segregation of Asian Americans.

CHAPTER 6

Student Diversity

This chapter focuses on the diverse cultures and languages of students attending American schools. Often the United States is referred to as the "land of immigrants." But not all citizens of the country willingly became part of the country. Some were forced, such as Native Americans and enslaved Africans. Others joined the country because of conquest or annexation, such as Mexicans living in territories conquered by the United States in the nineteenth century, Puerto Ricans, Hawaiians, and Alaskan Natives. Often these groups were subject to deculturalization, or an attempt to destroy their cultures and languages. These groups are often called "dominated cultures" because they were forced to become part of the United States. Along with the vast number of immigrants, these dominated cultures are an important part of the U.S. population.

Cultural and language conflicts for dominated groups date back to the nineteenth century. This chapter, along with a discussion of the language and cultural issues of recent immigrants, will discuss two of these dominated groups, namely Mexican Americans and Native Americans. I will also discuss the early issues surrounding Asian immigration to the United States.

In 2014, for the first time, the "nonwhite" population of U.S. public schools exceeded the number of whites. Writing in *Education Week*, Lesli A. Maxwell reports:

> The new collective majority of minority schoolchildren—projected to be 50.3 percent by the National Center for Education Statistics—is driven largely by dramatic growth in the Latino population and a decline in the white population, and, to a lesser degree, by a steady rise in the number of Asian-Americans. African-American growth has been mostly flat.

In addition, the foreign-born population of the United States has increased rapidly over the last three decades. The U.S. Census Bureau defines foreign born as "anyone who is not a U.S. citizen at birth. This includes naturalized U.S. citizens, lawful permanent residents (immigrants), temporary migrants (such as foreign students), humanitarian migrants (such as refugees and asylees), and persons illegally present in the United States."

A 2018 U.S. Census Bureau report stated that the number of foreign born in the United States had become the largest share in over a century. In 2017, the foreign born were 13.7 percent of the U.S. population, the highest since 1910, when the foreign born were 14.7 percent of the population.

Also, as reported for Reuters by Jason Lange and Yeganeh Torbati:

> The data also showed that an increasing number of immigrants were Asian or had advanced university degrees, extending a trend that has been in place for over a decade during which immigration from Mexico slowed. The share of immigrants from Mexico fell to 25.3 percent last year from 26.5 percent in 2016, while the share from China rose to 6.4 percent from 6.2 percent.

A major issue, which will be discussed in this chapter, is teaching English to the foreign born.

This chapter will discuss:

- Dreamers and the Trump administration
- The effect of the 1965 Immigration Act on student diversity in U.S. schools
- The history of cultural and language conflicts in U.S. schools for dominated groups such as Mexican Americans and Native Americans
- Early educational and language discrimination experienced by Asian Americans
- The educational experiences of immigrants in U.S. schools
- Language issues in U.S. schools

DREAMERS AND DACA

The 2016 election caused concern among illegal immigrants and Dreamers. Dreamers are those children brought illegally into the United States. They attended American schools and are integrated into U.S. society. Unless they applied for citizenship, Dreamers remain illegal immigrants. Illegal students do have the right to attend public schools, according to the U.S. Supreme Court 1982 ruling *Plyler vs. Doe*. Washington State outlined the rights under the *Plyler* ruling for undocumented students. Public schools cannot:

- Deny admission to a student during initial enrollment or at any other time on the basis of undocumented status
- Treat a student differently to determine residency
- Engage in any practices to "chill" the right of access to school
- Require students or parents to disclose or document their immigration status
- Make inquiries of students or parents that may expose their undocumented status

However, the 2016 Republican platform and President Donald Trump's concerns about protecting U.S. borders against illegal immigrants sent chills through the immigrant community with fears that undocumented immigrant parents might be sent home, leaving their children behind. The 2016 Republican platform warned:

> With all our fellow citizens, we have watched, in anger and disgust, the mocking of our immigration laws by a president [Obama] who made himself superior to the will of the nation. We stand with the victims of his policies, especially the families of murdered innocents. Illegal immigration endangers everyone, exploits the taxpayers, and insults all who aspire to enter America legally.

Also complicating the picture was the future of these noncitizens who had been brought illegally as children into the United States. Many of these children reached adulthood without knowing the languages or cultures of the countries from which they had been brought illegally. How could these children, many of them now adults, be returned to countries they knew nothing about even though they resided illegally in the United States. This population became known as Dreamers.

The 2016 Republican platform rejected the idea of giving special rights to Dreamers. The platform stated: "We oppose any form of amnesty for those who, by breaking the law, have disadvantaged those who have obeyed it." Sounding the drum beat of fear about illegal immigrants, the platform continued:

> In a time of terrorism, drug cartels, human trafficking, and criminal gangs, the presence of millions of unidentified individuals in this country poses grave risks to the safety and sovereignty of the United States. Our highest priority, therefore, must be to secure our borders and all ports of entry and to enforce our immigration laws.

Under the previous Obama administration, legal protections had been provided under what was called the Deferred Action for

Childhood Arrivals, or DACA. DACA protected 250,000 school-age children and about 9,000 educators. In 2018, federal legislation dealing with the plight of Dreamers was defeated, leaving them in an uncertain status. (The Dream Act was an acronym for the Development, Relief, and Education for Alien Minors Act). It is unclear what will happen if the U.S. government attempts to deport Dreamers.

ILLEGAL IMMIGRANT CHILDREN IN SHELTERS

In 2017, the federal government adopted a "zero tolerance" policy for those illegally entering the United States. This meant that all adults entering illegally would be prosecuted. Any children accompanying illegal immigrants were to be put in shelters or foster homes. In 2018, a federal court order required that the children be reunified with their parents. The federal government identified 2,737 children who needed to be reunited.

However, there were complaints that the federal government did not keep accurate records and that shelters housed thousands of other children, including infants and toddlers. In addition, the government did not maintain a data system that would link parents with the children being held in shelter centers and foster homes. Some parents were deported without their children, causing a humanitarian crisis.

The situation of children illegally brought into the United States continues to be a major issue for Dreamers and children housed in detention shelters.

GLOBAL MIGRATION AND THE IMMIGRATION ACTS OF 1965 AND 1990

Globalization of the labor market and the Immigration Acts of 1965 and 1990 are increasing the diversity of the U.S. student population. This phenomenon is not limited to the United States. Most nations face multicultural educational issues as families move, searching for better economic and political conditions. With the ease of travel, there are now transnational families moving back and forth between their host countries and their countries of origin. Some ethnic Indian families in the United States travel back frequently to India to visit relatives, and others with relatives and friends in Central and South America make similar trips. Some even maintain homes in two different countries. As a result, U.S. classrooms host transnational students. For example, there is the little girl with aunts and uncles still in India whose parents dream of eventually finding her a husband from back home and the Mexican boy whose family frequently takes him to Mexico, where he hangs out with cousins and friends.

There is also the worldwide phenomenon of illegal immigration. Countries have a shadow population of students whose parents worry that sending their children to school might alert authorities to their illegal status. Global population movement is restricted by each country's immigration laws. Yet workers and families from Africa risk their lives crossing the Mediterranean Sea to illegally enter Spain and Italy, while thousands from many different countries face dangerous temperatures and unforgiving deserts trying to illegally enter the United States and other countries.

The greatest influx of recent immigrants into the United States resulted from the U.S. Immigration Act of 1965. In the past, restrictions were placed on the immigration of "nonwhite" populations; the use of "white" in immigration laws created many problems of interpretation for U.S. courts. Originally, the Naturalization Act of 1790, which remained in effect until 1952, restricted naturalized citizenship to "whites only." This meant that many immigrants, particularly those from Asian countries, were not allowed to receive citizenship rights; naturalized citizenship refers to those who are not born in the United States but receive citizenship after immigration by fulfilling whatever legal requirements exist.

The 1965 Immigration Act overturned previous and more restrictive immigrant legislation designed to favor European populations. The 1924 Immigration Act, which established an annual quota limiting immigration by national origin, favored immigrants from Western Europe. As a consequence of the 1924 Immigration Act, the Depression of the 1930s, and World War II, immigration to the United States declined from the late 1920s through the early 1950s. Immigration began to increase again in the 1950s and underwent a dramatic change after passage of the 1965 Immigration Act. Before 1965, the proportion of immigrants from Europe remained approximately constant compared with those from Asia and the rest of the Americas. But after 1965, the proportion of emigrants

After the conquest of northern Mexico, state governments tried to use their school systems to replace the speaking of Spanish with English. In 1856, two years after the Texas legislature established public schools, a law was passed requiring the teaching of English as a subject. In 1870, at the height of the cowboy era, the Texas legislature passed a school law requiring English to be the language of instruction in all public schools. The same attempt to eradicate Spanish occurred in the conquered territory of California. The California Bureau of Instruction mandated in 1855 that all school classes be conducted in English. In *The Decline of the Californios: A Social History of the Spanish-Speaking Californios, 1846–1890*, Leonard Pitt and Ramon Gutierrez write about the English-only requirement in public schools: "This linguistic purism went hand in hand with the nativist sentiments expressed in that year's legislature, including the suspension of the publication of state laws in Spanish."

Mexican Americans in the last half of the nineteenth century tried to escape the anti-Mexican attitudes of public-school authorities by attending either Catholic schools or nonsectarian private schools. In California, some members of the Mexican community were interested in providing a bilingual education for their children. They wanted their children to improve their ability to read and write Spanish and become acquainted with the cultural traditions of Mexico and Spain at the same time as learning to speak English. In some places, such as Santa Barbara, California, local Mexican leaders were able to bypass the state requirement on teaching in English and were able to maintain a bilingual public school. But in most places, bilingual instruction could be had only through schools operated by the Catholic Church.

The patterns of discrimination and segregation established in the nineteenth century were accentuated during the great immigration of Mexicans into the United States in the early twentieth century. Between 1900 and 1909, a total of 23,991 Mexicans immigrated to the United States. Between 1910 and 1919 this figure increased dramatically to 173,663, and between 1920 and 1929 the number rose to 487,775. Anglo-American attitudes about the education of the children of immigrant Mexicans involved two conflicting positions. On the one hand, farmers did not want children of their Mexican laborers to go to school because school attendance meant they were not available for farm work. Likewise, many Mexican families were reluctant to send their children to school because of the loss of the children's contribution to the family income. On the other hand, many public officials wanted Mexican children in school so they could be Americanized.

These conflicting positions represent the two methods by which education can be used as a method of social control. One is to deny a population the knowledge necessary to protect its political and economic rights and to economically advance in society; the other is segregation. Farmers wanted to keep Mexican laborers ignorant as a means of ensuring a continued inexpensive source of labor. As one Texas farmer stated, "Educating the Mexicans is educating them away from the job, away from the dirt." Reflecting the values of the farmers in his district, one Texas school superintendent explained, "You have doubtless heard that ignorance is bliss; it seems that is so when one has to transplant onions. . . . So you see it is up to the white population to keep the Mexican on his knees in an onion patch or in new ground. This does not mix very well with education." A school principal in Colorado stated, "Never try to enforce compulsory attendance laws on the Mexicans. . . . The banks and the company will swear that the labor is needed and that the families need the money."

Therefore, according to Guadalupe San Miguel Jr., in *"Let All of Them Take Heed": Mexican Americans and the Campaign for Educational*

Equality in Texas, 1910–1981, one of the most discriminatory acts against the children of Mexicans was the non-enforcement of compulsory school laws. A survey of one Texas county in 1921 found only 30.7 percent of Mexican school-age children in school. In another Texas county in the 1920s, school authorities admitted they enforced school attendance on Anglo children but not on Mexican children. San Miguel Jr. quotes one school authority from this period: "The whites come all right except one whose parents don't appreciate education. We don't enforce the attendance on the whites because we would have to on the Mexicans." One school superintendent explained that he always asked the local school board if it wanted the Mexican children in school. Any enforcement of the compulsory-education law against the wishes of the school board, he admitted, would probably cost him his job.

Those Mexican children who did attend school faced segregation and an education designed to rid them of their native language and customs. School segregation for Mexican children spread rapidly throughout Texas and California. The typical pattern was for a community with a large Mexican school population to erect a separate school for Mexican children. For instance, in 1891 the Corpus Christi, Texas, school board denied admission of Mexican children to their Anglo schools and built a separate school.

In *Chicano Education in the Era of Segregation*, Gilbert Gonzalez finds the typical attitude in California schools reflected in the April 1921 minutes of the Ontario, California, Board of Education: "Mr. Hill made the recommendation that the board select two new school sites; one in the southeastern part of the town for a Mexican school; the other near the Central School." Gonzalez reports that a survey conducted in the mid-1930s found that 85 percent of the districts investigated in the Southwest were segregated. In *All Deliberate Speed: Segregation and Exclusion in California Schools, 1855–1975*, Charles M. Wollenberg quotes a California educator writing in 1920: "One of the first demands made from a community in which there is a large Mexican population is for a separate school." A Los Angeles school official admitted that pressure from white citizens resulted in certain neighborhood schools being built to contain the majority of Mexican students.

Mexican Americans experienced many years of segregation in schools before winning a series of important legal cases. The first major case occurred in Ontario, California, in 1945, when Mexican American parents demanded the school board grant all requests for transfer out of segregated Mexican schools. When the board refused this request, Gonzalo Mendez and William Guzman sued for violation of the Fourteenth Amendment to the Constitution. The school board responded to this suit by claiming that segregation was not based on race or national origins but on the necessity of providing special instruction. In other words, the school district justified segregation on the basis that Mexican American children required special instruction because they came from homes where Spanish was the spoken language.

In 1946, a U.S. District Court ruled in *Mendez et al. v. Westminster School District of Orange County* that the only possible argument for segregation was the special educational needs of Mexican American children. These needs involved the issue of learning English. Completely reversing the educational justification for segregation, the judge argued that "evidence clearly shows that Spanish-speaking children are retarded in learning English by lack of exposure to its use by segregation." Therefore, the court ruled segregation was illegal because it was not required by state law and because there was no valid educational justification for it.

Heartened by the *Mendez* decision, the League of United Latin American Citizens (LULAC) forged ahead in its legal attack on segregation in Texas. With support from LULAC, a group of parents in 1948 sued the Bastrop Independent School District, charging that local school authorities had no legal right to segregate children of Mexican descent and that segregation was solely because the children were of Mexican descent. In *Delgado v. Bastrop Independent School District*, the court ruled that segregating Mexican American children was illegal and discriminatory. The ruling required the local school district to end all segregation.

Although the *Mendez* and *Delgado* decisions held out the promise of ending segregation of Mexican Americans, local school districts used many tactics to avoid integration, including manipulation of school district lines, choice plans, and different forms of second-generation segregation. For instance, the California State Department of Education reported in 1966 that 57 percent of the children with Spanish surnames were still attending schools that were predominantly Mexican American. In 1973, a civil rights activist, John Caughey, estimated that two-thirds of the Mexican American children in Los Angeles attended segregated schools. In *All Deliberate Speed*, Wollenberg estimates that in California by 1973 more Mexican and Mexican American children attended segregated schools than in 1947.

In the Mexican American Legal Defense and Education Fund (MALDEF) case, *Cisernos v. Corpus Christi Independent School District* (1970), Mexican Americans were officially recognized by the federal courts as an identifiable group in the public schools. A central issue in the case was whether the 1954 school desegregation decision could be applied to Mexican Americans. The original *Brown* decision dealt specifically with African Americans who were segregated by state and local laws. In his final decision, Judge Owen Cox ruled that blacks and Mexican Americans were segregated in the Corpus Christi school system and that Mexican Americans were an identifiable dominated group because of their language, culture, religion, and Spanish surnames.

Tensions continue for Mexican American students in U.S. schools. In 2014, a federal appeals court upheld a ban on U.S. flag shirts worn by white students on Cinco de Mayo, a Mexican holiday, to antagonize Mexican students. The case originated in California's Live Oak High School. As described by *Education Week* reporter Mark Walsh, the legal case was caused by white students who purposely wore U.S. flag shirts to antagonize students of Mexican descent on Cinco de Mayo.

> During lunchtime, a group of students of Mexican descent gathered in the school's outdoor quad, court papers say. One asked Assistant Principal Daniel Rodriguez why the white students got to wear "their flag" while Mexican students could not wear "our flag." Rodriguez met with the white students and told them they had to turn their U.S. flag shirts inside out or else go home. Two students who were wearing shirts with less prominent flag designs were allowed to return to class.

NATIVE AMERICAN STUDENTS AND U.S. SCHOOLS

Originally, the U.S. government attempted to destroy the languages and cultures of Native American tribes. As indicated in Figure 6.1, these policies were not reversed until the civil rights movement of the 1950s and 1960s. The initial attempt by the U.S. government to destroy the cultures and languages of Native Americans was spearheaded by Thomas McKenney, the first head of the Office of Indian Affairs. In 1819, he convinced the U.S. Congress to pass the Civilization Fund Act, which authorized the president to "employ capable persons of good moral character, to instruct them [Indians] in the mode of agriculture suited to their situation; and for teaching their children in reading, writing, and arithmetic." Reflecting on his effort to gain approval of the legislation, McKenney wrote, "I did not doubt then, nor do I now, the capacity of the Indian for the highest attainments in civilization, in the arts and religion, but I was satisfied that no adequate plan had ever been adopted for this great reformation." The Civilization Act funded Christian missionaries to educate Native Americans. Typical of missionary attitudes was Reverend James Ramsey's speech at a Choctaw school in 1846. Ramsey described his initial lecture to students and trustees in the following words: "I showed them [on a map] that the people who speak the English language, and who occupied so small a part of the world, and possessed the greatest part of its wisdom and knowledge; that knowledge they could thus see for themselves was power; and that power was to be obtained by Christianity alone." Then he told them that the key to their success would be to continue the practice of establishing religious schools. In this way, they could share in the glory of Anglo-Saxon culture and Christianity.

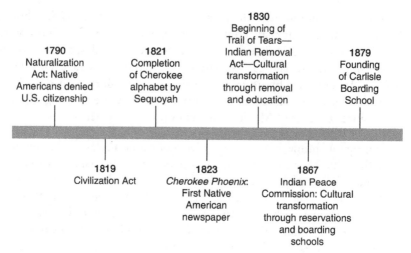

Figure 6.1 Timeline: Native American Equality of Educational Opportunity

In 1867, Congress created an Indian Peace Commission to deal with the warring tribes. The Peace Commission advocated using educational methods to convert Indians to Anglo-American civilization. Nathaniel Taylor, chair of the Peace Commission, told Crow Indians at Fort Laramie: "Upon the reservations you select, we . . . will send you teachers for your children." According to Jon Reyhner and Jeanne Eder, this promise was embodied in the Treaty of Fort Laramie with the Sioux and their allies. The members of the Peace Commission were not entirely satisfied with the traditional attempts to educate Indians, particularly with regard to language. The Indian Peace Commission report of 1868 stated that differences in language were a major source of the continuing friction between whites and Indians; therefore, emphasis on the teaching of English would be a major step in reducing hostilities and civilizing Native Americans. In the words of the report: "Through sameness of language is produced sameness of sentiment and thought; customs and habits are moulded [*sic*] and assimilated in the same way, and thus in process of time the differences producing trouble would have been gradually obliterated."

The first off-reservation boarding school was the Carlisle Indian School, established in Carlisle, Pennsylvania, in 1879. The founder of the school, Richard Pratt, wanted to instill a work ethic in Indian children, and as he told a Baptist group, he wanted to immerse "Indians in our civilization and when we get them under [hold] them there until they are thoroughly soaked." The slogan for the Carlisle Indian School reflected the emphasis on changing the cultural patterns of Indians: "To civilize the Indian, get him into civilization. To keep him civilized, let him stay."

Pratt attacked the tribal way of life as socialistic and contrary to the values of civilization. Reflecting the values of economic individualism, Pratt complained about missionary groups who did not "advocate the disintegration of the tribes and the giving to individual Indians rights and opportunities among civilized people." He wrote to the Commissioner of Indian Affairs in 1890, "Pandering to the tribe and its socialism as most of our Government and mission plans do is the principal reason why the Indians have not advanced more and are not advancing as rapidly as they ought."

Between the founding of the Carlisle Indian School in 1879 and 1905, 25 non-reservation boarding schools were opened throughout the country. It is important to emphasize the *non*-reservation location of the boarding schools because of the educational philosophy that Indian children should be removed from family and tribal influences.

Teaching English was an important issue for both non-reservation boarding schools and schools on reservations. As discussed previously, the attitude of many white educators in the latter part of the nineteenth century was that eliminating tribal languages and teaching English would lead to the absorption and practice of white values by Indians. In the Annual Report of the Commissioner of Indian Affairs in 1887, Commissioner J.D.C. Adkins ordered the exclusive use of English at all Indian schools. Atkins pointed out that this policy was consistent with the requirement that only English be taught in public schools in territories acquired by the United States from Mexico, Spain, and Russia.

In 1889, U.S. Commissioner of Indian Affairs Thomas J. Morgan wrote a bulletin on Indian education that outlined the goals and policies of Indian schools. The bulletin was distributed by the U.S. Bureau of Education with an introduction written by the commissioner of education, William T. Harris. In the introduction, Harris praised what he called "the new education for our American Indians," particularly the effort "to obtain control of the Indian at an early age, and to seclude him as much as possible from the tribal influences." Harris singled out the boarding school as an important step in changing the character of American Indians and argued that it was necessary to save the American Indian, but, he wrote, "We cannot save him and his patriarchal or tribal institution both together. To save him we must take him up into our civilization."

With regard to instruction in English, Morgan stressed in the bulletin, "Only English should be allowed to be spoken, and only English-speaking teachers should be employed in schools supported wholly or in part by the Government." Also, the general principles stressed the importance of teaching allegiance to the U.S. government.

Morgan also advocated early childhood education as a method of counteracting the influence of the Indian home. Similar to the boarding school, early childhood education would help strip away the influences of Indian culture and language. Morgan states, "Children should be taken at as early an age as possible, before camp life has made an indelible stamp upon them."

The conditions in boarding schools lived up to Morgan's edict: "In the sweat of their faces must they eat bread." During the 1920s, a variety of investigators of Indian schools were horrified by the conditions they found. At the Rice Boarding School in Arizona, Red Cross investigators found that children were fed "bread, black coffee, and syrup for breakfast; bread and boiled potatoes for dinner; more bread and boiled potatoes for supper." In addition to a poor diet, overcrowded conditions contributed to the spread of tuberculosis and trachoma.

Using a paramilitary form of organization, boarding schools were supported by the labor of the students. As early as the fifth grade, boys and girls attended classes for half the day and worked for the other half. Children raised crops and tended farm animals to learn agricultural methods. The paramilitary organization was reflected in the constant drilling of students. The children were given little time for recreation. They were awakened at five in the morning and marched to the dining room, then marched back to the dormitories and classrooms. At the Albuquerque Indian School, students marched in uniforms with dummy rifles. For punishment children were flogged with ropes, and some boarding schools contained their own jails. In the 1920s, anthropologist Oliver La Farge called the Indian schools "penal institutions—where little children were sentenced to hard labor for a term of years to expiate the crime of being born of their mothers."

The boarding schools and the long history of attempts to destroy their cultures led Native Americans to demand control of the education of their children and restoration of their cultural heritage and languages to the curriculum. The demand for self-determination by Native Americans received consideration in government decisions after the election of John F. Kennedy in 1960. The Kennedy administration advocated Indian participation in decisions regarding federal policies. Kennedy's secretary of interior, Stewart Udall, appointed a Task Force on Indian Affairs that, in its 1961 report, recommended that Native Americans be given full citizenship and self-sufficiency.

As a result, the Rough Rock Demonstration School was created in 1966. Established on a Navajo reservation in Arizona, the school was a joint effort of the Office of Economic Opportunity and the Bureau of Indian Affairs. One major goal of the demonstration school was for Navajo parents to control the education of their children and to participate in all aspects of their schooling. Besides tribal control, the Rough

Rock Demonstration School attempted to preserve the Navajo language and culture. In contrast to the attempts to destroy Native cultures and languages that took place in the nineteenth and early twentieth centuries, the goal of learning both Navajo and English was presented for preparing children to live in both cultures.

In 1969, the U.S. Senate Committee on Labor and Public Welfare issued the report *Indian Education: A National Tragedy—A National Challenge*. The report opened with a statement condemning previous educational policies of the federal government: "A careful review of the historical literature reveals that the dominant policy of the Federal Government toward the American Indian has been one of forced assimilation . . . [because of] a desire to divest the Indian of his land."

After a lengthy review of the failure of past educational policies, the report's first recommendation was for "maximum participation and control by Indians in establishing Indian education programs." In its second recommendation, the report called for maximum Indian participation in the development of educational programs in federal schools and local public schools. These educational programs were to include early childhood education, vocational education, work-study, and adult literacy education.

The congressional debates resulting from the report eventually culminated in the passage of the Indian Education Act in 1972. The declared policy of the legislation was to provide financial assistance to local schools to develop programs to meet the special educational needs of Native American students. In addition, the legislation created a federal Office of Indian Education.

In 1974, the Bureau of Indian Affairs issued a set of procedures for protecting student rights and due process. In contrast to the brutal and dictatorial treatment of Indian students in the boarding schools of the late nineteenth and early twentieth centuries, each Indian student was extended the right "to make his or her own decisions where applicable." And, in striking contrast to earlier deculturalization policies, Indian students were granted "the right to freedom of religion and culture."

The 1975 Indian Self-Determination and Education Assistance Act gave tribes the power to contract with the federal government to run their own education and health programs. The legislation opened with the declaration that it was "an Act to provide maximum Indian participation in the Government and education of Indian people; to provide for the full participation of Indian tribes in programs and services conducted by the federal government."

The Indian Self-Determination and Education Assistance Act strengthened Indian participation in the control of education programs. The legislation provided that a local school district receiving funds for the education of Indian students that did not have a school board composed of mostly Indians had to establish a separate local committee composed of parents of Indian students in the school. This committee was given the authority over any Indian education programs contracted with the federal government.

The principles embodied in the Indian Self-Determination and Education Assistance Act of 1975 were expanded upon in 1988 with the passage of the Tribally Controlled Schools Act. Besides the right to operate schools under a federal contract as provided in the 1975 legislation, the Tribally Controlled Schools Act provided for outright grants to tribes to support the operation of their own schools.

In 2014, Secretary of Education Arne Duncan warned of the problems facing Native American students:

> The President [Barack Obama] and I believe the future of Indian Country rests on ensuring that your children receive a high-quality education. Improving academic outcomes for Native American children has never been more important. Unfortunately, too many Native American children are not receiving an education that prepares them for college and career success, too few of them are going to college, and far too many of them drop out of high school. We need to do better.

Duncan's comments were part of the 2014 "Findings and Recommendations Prepared by the Bureau of Indian Education Study Group Submitted to the Secretaries of the Departments of the Interior and Education," which recommended the following:

- Highly Effective Teachers and Principals—Help tribes to identify, recruit, develop, retain, and empower diverse, highly effective teachers and principals to maximize the highest achievement for every student in all BIE [Bureau of Indian Education]-funded schools.
- Agile Organizational Environment—Build a responsive organization that becomes an expert in its field and provides resources, direction, and services to tribes so that they can help their students attain high levels of achievement.
- Promote Educational Self-Determination for Tribal Nations—Strengthen and support the efforts of tribal nations to directly operate BIE-funded schools.
- Comprehensive Supports through Partnerships—Foster parental, community, and organizational partnerships to provide the academic as well as the emotional and social supports BIE students need in order to be ready to learn.

- Budget that Supports Capacity-Building Mission—Develop a budget that is aligned with and supports BIE's new mission of tribal capacity-building and exchanging best practices.

ASIAN AMERICAN STUDENTS AND U.S. SCHOOLS

In a 2018 suit against Harvard University for discrimination of Asian Americans in the admissions process, one legal brief complained that Harvard officials repeatedly characterized Asian American applicants as "quiet, shy, science/math oriented, and hard workers." As I discuss, this was only one of many stereotypes faced by Asian Americans since the nineteenth century.

As with Mexican Americans, Asian Americans did not receive a warm welcome by many Anglo-American citizens. They were not eligible for citizenship because the 1790 Naturalization Law limited naturalized citizenship to "free white persons." Children born in the United States of Asian immigrant parents were U.S. citizens by birth. Figure 6.2 shows a time line of Asian Americans' struggle in the U.S. school system.

The first Chinese immigrants arrived in California in the 1850s to join the gold rush. In search of the Golden Mountain, these first arrivals were free laborers who paid their own transportation to the gold fields of California. By 1852, there were about 20,000 Chinese immigrants in California. By the 1860s, approximately 16,000 Chinese immigrants were working in the California gold fields. But as mining profits decreased, the Chinese immigrants found themselves without enough money to return to their homeland. Searching for work, these Chinese immigrants were hired to build the transcontinental railroad at wages that were about one-third less than would have been paid to white workers. In addition, Chinese workers filled low-wage jobs and built the agricultural industry in California. Racial hostility was highlighted in 1871 with the lynching of 22 Chinese men by Los Angeles mobs.

Japanese immigrated at a later date because a 1639 Japanese law forbade travel to foreign countries. Circumstances began to change in 1868 when Hawaiian planters were able to recruit 148 Japanese contract laborers, and, in 1869, 100 laborers were signed up for work in the California silk industry. By 1884, the Japanese government allowed open recruitment by Hawaiian planters. Between 1885 and 1920, as many as 200,000 Japanese immigrated to Hawaii and 180,000 to the U.S. mainland. Adding to the Asian population were 8,000 Koreans who immigrated, primarily to Hawaii, between 1903 and 1920. Between 1907 and 1917, when immigration from India was restricted, 6,400 Asian Indians came to the United States. In 1907, Filipinos, who incidentally were citizens of the U.S.-captured Philippine Islands, were recruited as laborers. By 1930, there were 110,000 Filipinos settled in Hawaii and 40,000 on the mainland.

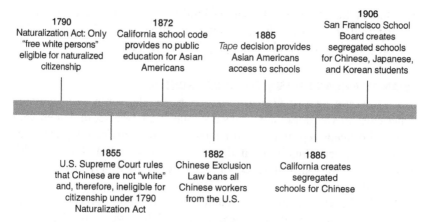

Figure 6.2 Timeline: Asian American Equality of Educational Opportunity

The white-only provisions of the 1790 Naturalization Law and other laws required U.S. courts to deal with the racial classification of Asian Americans. In the nineteenth century, California laws simply classified as Mongolian those immigrants from northern and southern Asia, Southeast Asia, and India. Later, despite the wide-ranging cultural and language differences among these regions, European Americans used the term "Asian" in reference to immigrants and their descendants from these differing areas. Unfortunately, while "Asian American" is now commonly used in the United States, the term tends to conceal the differences among peoples and countries, such as Korea, Japan, China, Cambodia, Indonesia, and India.

Confusion over the legal status of Asians was exemplified by the 1855 case of Chan Yong. A federal district court in California ruled that under the 1790 Naturalization Act citizenship was restricted to whites only and, consequently, immigrant Chinese such as Chan Yong were not eligible for U.S. citizenship. In the 1920s, laws were passed in California, Washington, Arizona, Oregon, Idaho, Nebraska, Texas, Kansas, Louisiana, Montana, New Mexico, Minnesota, and Missouri denying the right to own land to individuals who were ineligible for U.S. citizenship. The purpose of these laws was to deny land ownership to Asians.

Naturalization laws and court rulings underwent rapid changes during World War II. Prior to the outbreak of hostilities against Japan, most Anglo-Americans seemed to operate from the position that all Asians were the same and that it was difficult to discern physical differences. However, during World War II, China was a U.S. ally while Japan was the enemy. Consequently, popular media, including radio, movies, newspapers, and magazines, depicted Chinese, in contrast to images presented earlier in the century, as "hardworking, brave, religious,

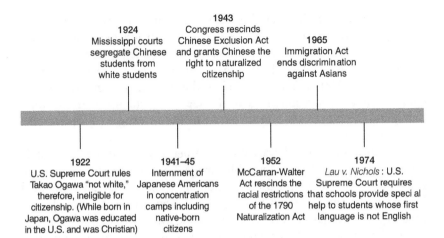

1924
Mississippi courts segregate Chinese students from white students

1943
Congress rescinds Chinese Exclusion Act and grants Chinese the right to naturalized citizenship

1965
Immigration Act ends discrimination against Asians

1922
U.S. Supreme Court rules Takao Ogawa "not white," therefore, ineligible for citizenship. (While born in Japan, Ogawa was educated in the U.S. and was Christian)

1941–45
Internment of Japanese Americans in concentration camps including native-born citizens

1952
McCarran-Walter Act rescinds the racial restrictions of the 1790 Naturalization Act

1974
Lau v. Nichols: U.S. Supreme Court requires that schools provide special help to students whose first language is not English

intelligent, and practical" while Japanese were depicted as "treacherous, sly, cruel, and warlike."

As a result of wartime conditions, the ban on naturalization of Chinese was ignored, and between 15,000 and 20,000 Chinese American men and women joined all branches of the military. In 1943, Congress rescinded the Chinese Exclusion Law and granted Chinese immigrants the right to become naturalized citizens but established a limited immigration quota[1] for Chinese of only 105 each year. Naturalization rights were not extended to immigrants from India and the Philippines until 1946, with each country being given a limited quota of 100 per year.

In contrast, Japanese American citizenship status was completely ignored, with the internment in concentration camps of more than 100,000 Japanese Americans during World War II. Many of these Japanese Americans were U.S. citizens because they had been born in the United States. Why were Japanese Americans interned in concentration camps but not the descendants of other U.S. enemies, such as German and Italian Americans? Because "the Occidental eye cannot rapidly distinguish one Japanese resident from another" argued three lawyers working for the U.S. Justice Department. Adding to the demands to place Japanese citizens in concentration camps were the conclusions of the U.S. government report on the bombing of Pearl Harbor, which called the Japanese an "enemy race" and claimed that despite many generations in the United States their "racial affinities [were] not severed by migration." The report recommended the removal of all people of Japanese ancestry from coastal areas of the United States.

The citizenship issue for Asian Americans was finally resolved in 1952 when the McCarran-Walter Act rescinded the racial restrictions of the 1790 Naturalization Law. It had taken over 160 years for U.S. leaders to decide that naturalized citizenship would not be restricted to whites. The Japanese American Citizens League played an active role in eliminating the white-only provisions in immigration laws. A Japanese American Citizens League member, Harry Tagaki, commented after the passage of the McCarran-Walter Act, "The bill established our parents as the legal equal of other Americans; it gave the Japanese equality with all other immigrants, and that was a principle we had been struggling for from the very beginning."

The educational experiences of Asian Americans paralleled their public image in the United States. By public image, I mean the representation of Asian Americans that appears in the popular press and media dominated by European Americans. In his study of the portrayal of Asian Americans in U.S. popular culture, Robert Lee identified five major images of Asians—"the coolie, the deviant, the yellow peril, the model minority, and the gook." As he points out, each image, including that of the model minority, has presented some threat to "the American national family."

Prior to World War II, educational discrimination and segregation resulted from images held by many European Americans of Asian Americans as coolies, deviants, and yellow peril. The coolie image was that of the servile Asian worker who was willing to work endless hours at low wages and accept substandard living conditions; this image was considered a threat to the standard of living of the white working-class family. The deviant image was that of the Chinese opium den and Asian sexual freedom and was considered a threat to the morality of the white family. The yellow peril image was that of Asian immigrants overrunning the United States.

The image of Asians as the model minority evolved during the civil rights movement of the 1960s and 1970s. In the popular mind of European Americans, Asians were not only the model minority but also the model student. This image is strikingly different from earlier images of coolie and yellow peril. However, the model minority image was used by European Americans to criticize African Americans and Hispanics. As writer Frank Chin said in 1974 regarding the model minority image, "Whites love us because we're not black."

Ironically, the stereotype of a model minority student has caused many educators to overlook the educational problems encountered by many Asian American students in U.S. schools. Part of the problem is the tendency for non-Asians to lump all Asian Americans together. In fact, Asian Americans represent a broad spectrum of different cultures and nations, including, as Valerie Ooka Pang indicates in her article "Asian American Children: A Diverse Population," "Cambodian, Chinese, East Indian, Filipino, Guamian, Hawaiian, Hmong, Indonesian, Japanese, Korean, Laotian, Samoan, and Vietnamese . . . [and] smaller Asian

American groups within the category of all other Asians." According to U.S. census classification there are 16 of these smaller Asian American groups.

Asian Americans faced many problems of educational discrimination. In *All Deliberate Speed*, Charles Wollenberg tells the story of the denial of equal educational opportunity to Asian Americans in California schools. With cries of yellow peril coming from the European American population, the state superintendent of public instruction in California, William Welcher, pointed out in 1884 that the state constitution called Chinese "dangerous to the well-being of the state" and, therefore, argued that San Francisco did not have "to undergo the expense of educating such people." Denied a public education for his daughter, Joseph Tape, an Americanized Chinese, challenged the decision in court. Judge Maguire of the municipal court ruled that since the daughter, Mamie, was an American citizen she could not be denied equal educational opportunity according to the Fourteenth Amendment to the U.S. Constitution. In addition, Judge Maguire argued that it was unjust to tax Chinese for the support of a school system that excluded Chinese children. State superintendent Welcher reacted angrily to the decision, declaring it a "terrible disaster," and asked, "Shall we abandon the education of our children to provide that of the Chinese who are thrusting themselves upon us?"

In reaction to the court decision, the California State Assembly passed legislation allowing school districts to establish segregated schools for Mongolians. This legislation empowered the San Francisco Board of Education to establish a segregated school for Asians. The courts affirmed this action in 1902, when Wong Him challenged the requirement of attending a segregated institution. Eventually, pressure from the Chinese American community brought an end to segregation. In 1921, Chinese American educator Mary Bo-Tze Lee challenged the segregation policy by showing that Chinese students scored as well as white students on IQ tests. As the Chinese population dispersed through the city, traditionally white schools were forced to open their doors to Chinese students. A study in 1947 found that formal school segregation had ended but that the original segregated Commodore Stockton School was still 100 percent Chinese.

Putting together a wide variety of cultures and languages under the label "Asian" continues to be problematic. The U.S. Department of Education's *The Condition of Education 2014* defines Asian as: "A person having origins in any of the original peoples of the Far East, Southeast Asia, or the Indian subcontinent, including, for example, Cambodia, China, India, Japan, Korea, Malaysia, Pakistan, the Philippine Islands, Thailand, and Vietnam." Adding to the confusion is the U.S. Department of Education combining this broadly defined group with Pacific Islanders defined in *The Condition of Education 2014* as "Native Hawaiian or Other Pacific Islander: A person having origins in any of the original peoples of Hawaii, Guam, Samoa, or other Pacific Islands." Thus, projected school enrollments from the fall of 2012 to 2013 were reported in *The Condition of Education 2014*: "the number of Asian/Pacific Islander students is projected to increase from 2.5 million to 2.9 million, and their enrollment share in 2023 is projected to be 5 percent."

EDUCATIONAL ATTAINMENT OF IMMIGRANTS

Immigrant groups arrive with a variety of educational backgrounds. For instance, studies of Chinese immigrants in New York City found a vast range of educational achievement. Those living in Chinatown arrived with primarily working-class backgrounds and limited exposure to formal learning. One study found that roughly 85 percent of Chinatown residents in New York, Boston, and San Francisco had not attended secondary school. The children of these immigrants often struggle in school because of language problems. On the other hand, many wealthy and well-educated Chinese immigrants, who in New York tend to live outside Chinatown, often send their children to elite universities. The educational level of immigrants reflects their social class backgrounds. In the case of the Chinese, some come from peasant backgrounds with little access to higher education; on the other hand, some come from professional classes and are engineers and college teachers. Therefore, the educational needs of immigrants must be assessed according to their social and educational backgrounds. These backgrounds vary widely within each immigrant group and between immigrant groups. For the purposes of this discussion, I focus on variations among Asian/Pacific Islander immigrants; however, similar differences exist among immigrants from other areas, particularly countries of the Commonwealth of Independent States.

Table 6.1 Educational Attainment of the Population Aged 25 and Older by Nativity: 2015

Educational Attainment	Native Born (%)	Foreign Born (%)
High school graduate or more	91.8	72
Some college or more	61.3	47.6
Associate's degree or more	43.3	37.6
Bachelor's degree or more	32.7	31.4
Advanced degree	11.9	12.5

Source: Camille L. Ryan and Kurt Bauman, *Educational Attainment in the United States: 2015*, Current Population Reports P20–578, U.S. Census Bureau, March 2016. Retrieved from www.census.gov/content/dam/Census/library/publications/2016/demo/p20-578.pdf on March 6, 2017.

Table 6.2 Educational Attainment of the Foreign-Born Population: 2012 (Aged 25 and Older by World Region)

Educational Attainment	Asia (%)	Europe (%)	Mexico (%)	Other Latin America (%)
Less than 9th grade	7.5	6.7	38.1	17.0
High school graduate	21.4	27.9	26.9	31.2
Bachelor's degree	29.6	23.9	4.5	14.6
Master's degree	14.3	11.5	1.0	4.8
Professional degree	2.4	2.3	0.3	1.1
Doctorate degree	3.9	3.7	0.1	0.8

Source: Adapted from U.S. Census Bureau, *Educational Attainment of the Foreign-Born Population 25 Years and Over by Sex and World Region of Birth: 2012.*

Tables 6.1 and 6.2 indicate variations in educational attainment among foreign-born Americans. In general, the educational attainment of foreign-born Americans is less than that of native-born Americans.

As indicated in Table 6.1, 91.8 percent of native-born citizens graduate from high school as compared to 72 percent of foreign-born Americans. On the other hand, the percentage of foreign born with advanced degrees was 12.5 percent, which was higher than the native-born percentage of 11.9.

Table 6.2 highlights an important problem facing U.S. schools. Some immigrants arrive with less than a ninth-grade education, particularly from Mexico (38.1%) and other Latin American countries (17%). It might be assumed families with less than a ninth-grade education lack the social capital to ensure success for their children in school. On the other hand, there are families from Asia (7.5%) and Europe (6.7%) with less than a ninth-grade education. Also, there are fewer foreign born with bachelor's degrees from Mexico (4.5%) and other Latin American countries (14.6%) as compared to Asia (29.6%) and Europe (23.9%).

As indicated in Table 6.3, the problems for foreign born from Mexico are compounded by poverty, with 27.8 percent living below the poverty level. On the other hand, it should be remembered that 72.2 percent of Mexican immigrants live above the poverty level. So it would erroneous to stereotype all Mexican immigrants as poor and uneducated. It would be equally wrong to think of all Asian immigrants as well educated and doing well economically. As indicated in Table 6.2, 7.5% of foreign-born Asians had less than a ninth-grade education, and 13.6% were living below the poverty level.

Table 6.3 Poverty Status of the Foreign-Born Population by World Region of Birth: 2011

Poverty Status	Asia (%)	Europe (%)	Mexico (%)	Other Latin America (%)
Below poverty level	13.6	9.7	27.8	18.1
At or above poverty level	86.4	90.3	72.2	80.6

Source: Adapted from U.S. Census Bureau, *Poverty Status of the Foreign-Born Population by Sex, Age, and World Region of Birth: 2011.* Retrieved from www.census.gov/population/foreign/data/cps2012.html on November 5, 2014.

The Pew Hispanic Center report, *The Improving Educational Profile of Latino Immigrants,* found that the educational profile of foreign-born Latinos is improving because many are receiving an education in the United States and the quality of education in their countries of origin is improving. The report concludes: "Levels of educational achievement have improved in sending countries, and those who choose to migrate to the United States are better educated than those who stay behind." However, there remains a crisis in the education of Latino immigrants. The Pew Hispanic Center reports, "Typically, Mexican and Central American immigrants are less educated than those from the Caribbean and South America. Immigrants from Mexico and Central America are less likely to have completed either secondary education or post-secondary education than are other Latino immigrants." However, according to *The Condition of Education 2014,* Latino educational attainment is improving, with the gap between white and Latino finishing high school narrowing from 32 to 18 percentage points from 1990 to 2013.

LANGUAGES AND SCHOOLS

Court rulings are quite clear that the primary task of the schools is to teach standard English and that other languages and black English are to be used as a means to achieve that goal. On the other hand, schools must provide special help to students who have limited use of English. The landmark case is the 1974 U.S. Supreme Court decision in *Lau et al. v. Nichols et al.* The case was a class-action suit brought for non-English-speaking Chinese students in the San Francisco school district. The complaint was that no special instruction for learning standard English was provided to these students. The complaint did not ask for any specific instructional methods to remedy this situation. In the words of the court decision: "Teaching English to the students of Chinese ancestry who do not speak the language is one choice. Providing instruction to this group in Chinese is another. There may be others." This point created a good deal of controversy in 1980, when the federal government issued regulations for a specific remedy to *Lau*. It was argued that specific remedies were not defined under the *Lau* decision. Those regulations were withdrawn in 1981.

The claim in *Lau* was that the lack of special instruction to help non-English-speaking students learn standard English provided unequal educational opportunity and therefore violated the Fourteenth Amendment to the Constitution. The court did not use the Fourteenth Amendment in its ruling, but relied on Title VI of the 1964 Civil Rights Act. This law bans discrimination based on "race, color, or national origin" in "any program or activity receiving Federal financial assistance." The Supreme Court ruled: "It seems obvious that the Chinese-speaking minority receives fewer benefits than the English-speaking majority from the respondents' school system that denies them a meaningful opportunity to participate in the educational program—all earmarks of the discrimination banned by the regulations." Although the court did not give a specific remedy to the situation, its ruling meant that all public-school systems receiving any form of federal aid must ensure that children from non-English-speaking backgrounds be given some form of special help in learning standard English so they may have equal educational opportunity.

The problem not addressed in *Lau* was that of specific remedies for the situation of children from non-standard-English backgrounds. A decision regarding this issue was made by the U.S. District Court in 1979 in *Martin Luther King Junior Elementary School Children et al. v. Ann Arbor School District*. The court was quite clear that the case was "not an effort on the part of the plaintiffs to require that they be taught 'black English' or that a dual language program be provided." As the court defined the problem, it was the ability to teach standard English to "children who, it is alleged, speak 'black English' as a matter of course at home and in their home community." The plaintiffs introduced into the case the testimony of expert witnesses who argued that attempts to teach standard English without appreciating the dialect used by the children at home and in the community could cause the children to be ashamed of their language and hinder their ability to learn standard English.

The court gave recognition to the existence of a bilingual culture within the African American community, in which individuals would speak African American English with peers and standard English with the larger community. In the words of the court, the African American children "retain fluency in 'black English' to maintain status in the community and they become fluent in standard English to succeed in the general society."

After reviewing the evidence and the expert testimony, the court argued that there was a possible relationship between poor reading ability and the school's not taking into account the home language of the children. This prevented the children from taking full advantage of their schooling and was a denial of equal educational opportunity. This argument was based on the reasonable premise that knowing how to read was one of the most important factors in achievement in school.

The court gave a very specific remedy to the situation, a remedy that might be used as a guide in future cases. The court directed the school system to develop within 30 days a plan that would "identify children speaking 'black English' and the language spoken as a home or community language." Second, the school system was directed to "use that knowledge in teaching such students how to read standard English."

LANGUAGES OF SCHOOL-AGE CHILDREN

The National Center for Education Statistics (NCES) report *The Condition of Education 2014* provides statistics on the number of English language learners (ELL) in public schools. The report provides this definition: "Students who are English language learners (ELL) participate in appropriate programs of language assistance, such as English as a Second Language, High Intensity Language Training, and bilingual education." Based on this definition, the percentage of ELL in public schools increased from 8.7 percent in 2002–2003 to 9.1 percent in 2011–2012. The highest concentration of ELL was in large cities (16.7%) as compared to small cities (10.9%).

What is the language of home? This could be an important factor influencing the learning of English. Based on the 2014 U.S. census report "English-Speaking Ability of the Foreign-Born Population in the United States: 2012," Table 6.4 indicates the percentage of homes that spoke languages other than English. As indicated in Table 6.4 the percentage of foreign born not speaking English is very high at 84.6% in 2012 up from 70.2% in 1980.

Table 6.4 Percentage of the Foreign-Born Population Who Spoke a Language Other Than English at Home: 1980 to 2012

Year	Percentage of the Foreign-Born Population Who Spoke a Language Other Than English at Home (%)
1980	70.2
1990	79.1
2000	83.0
2010	84.7
2012	84.6

Source: Adapted from U.S. Census Bureau, *English-Speaking Ability of the Foreign-Born Population in the United States: 2012*, June 10, 2014. Retrieved from www.census.gov/library/publications/2014/acs/acs-26.html on November 6, 2014.

Regarding ELL, the *Condition of Education 2016* states: "Students who are English language learners (ELL) are making up a growing share of public school students. In 2013–14, Spanish, Arabic, and Chinese were the most common languages spoken by ELL students." The same report stated the percentage of ELL in public schools was increasing:

The percentage of public school students in the United States who were English language learners (ELL) was higher in school year 2013–14 (9.3 percent) than in 2003–04 (8.8 percent) and 2012–13 (9.2 percent). In 2013–14, five of the six states with the highest percentages of ELL students in their public schools were located in the West.

Are ELL being taught in segregated schools? *The Condition of Education 2010* by the NCES reports:

The percentage of students who were limited-English proficient (LEP) was higher in high-poverty schools than in low-poverty schools. In 2007–08, about 25 percent of students attending high-poverty elementary schools were identified as LEP, compared with 4 percent of students attending low-poverty elementary schools. At the secondary level, about 16 percent of students attending high-poverty schools were identified as LEP, compared with 2 percent attending low-poverty schools.

Table 6.5 Ten Most Commonly Reported Home Languages of English Language Learner (ELL) Students: School Year 2013–2014

Home Language	Number of ELL Students	Percentage Distribution of ELL Students (%)	Number of ELL Students as a Percentage of Total Enrollment (%)
Spanish, Castilian	3,770,816	76.5	7.7
Arabic	109,170	2.2	0.2
Chinese	107,825	2.2	0.2
Vietnamese	89,705	1.8	0.2
Hmong	39,860	0.8	0.1
Haitian, Haitian Creole	37,371	0.8	0.1
Somali	34,472	0.7	0.1
Russian	33,821	0.7	0.1
Korean	32,445	0.7	0.1

Source: Adapted from National Center for Education Statistics, *The Condition of Education 2016* (Washington, DC: U.S. Department of Education, 2016), p. 94.

The number of ELL in U.S. schools continues to grow. *The Condition of Education 2018* reported:

> The percentage of public school students in the United States who were English language learners (ELLs) was higher in fall 2015 (9.5 percent, or 4.8 million students) than in fall 2000 (8.1 percent, or 3.8 million students). In fall 2015, the percentage of public school students who were ELLs ranged from 1.0 percent in West Virginia to 21.0 percent in California.

In addition, the 2018 report stated, "In fall 2015, a greater percentage of public school students in lower grades than of those in upper grades were ELL students. For example, 16.3 percent of kindergarteners were ELL students, compared to 8.2 percent of 6th-graders and 6.6 percent of 8th-graders."

ARE U.S. TEACHERS PREPARED FOR LANGUAGE DIVERSITY?

In 2014, the National Council on Teacher Quality, according to *Education Week* reporter Lesli A. Maxwell, found that 75 percent of elementary teacher-preparation programs are failing to prepare teachers to work with ELL. What the National Council on Teacher Quality defines as the "low bar" in this evaluation are teacher-preparation programs that simply expose teacher candidates to different strategies for English language learners. That fact that 75 percent of teacher-preparation programs are failing is a shocking number when compared to statistics given prior on the increasing number of ELL in public schools.

Another problem is the potential cultural clash between a predominantly white teaching staff and a student body with high percentages of cultural minorities. This problem is reflected in Table 6.6, which shows that 80 percent of teachers are white.

Table 6.6 Percentage Distribution of Full-Time Teachers in U.S. Public Elementary and Secondary Schools by Race/Ethnicity, 2015–2016

	Percentage Distribution of Teachers (%)
White	80
Black	8
Hispanic	6
Asian	2
American Indian/Alaska Native	1
Two or more races	1

Source: National Center for Education Statistics, *The Condition of Education 2018* (Washington, DC: U.S. Department of Education, 2018), p. 89.

CONCLUSION

The diversity of the student population raises important questions regarding culture and language. The history of Mexican American, Asian American, and Native American schooling highlights serious issues regarding the responsibility of the schools to preserve language and cultural traditions. Consider the following set of questions:

- Should public schools consciously attempt to eradicate the language of non-English-speaking students in a manner similar to that used with Mexican American and Native American students?
- Should public schools attempt to preserve the home language of non-English-speaking students?
- Should public schools consciously attempt to change or Americanize the culture of immigrant students?
- Should public schools preserve the cultures of immigrant, Native American, and Mexican American students?

SUGGESTED READINGS AND WORKS CITED IN CHAPTER

Chin, Frank, et al., eds. *Aiiieeeee! An Anthology of Asian-American Writers*. Washington, DC: Howard University Press, 1974. In this anthology, Chin criticizes the view of Asian Americans as the model Americans.

Coleman, Michael C. *Presbyterian Attitudes Toward American Indians, 1837–1893*. Jackson: University of Mississippi Press, 1985. This is a good history of missionary attempts to change Native American cultures.

Committee on Labor and Public Welfare, U.S. Senate 91st Congress, 1st Session. *Indian Education: A National Tragedy—A National Challenge*. Washington, DC: U.S. Government Printing Office, 1969. This is the report that set the stage for recent efforts in Native American education.

Donato, Ruben. *The Other Struggle for Equal Schools: Mexican Americans During the Civil Rights Era*. Albany: State University of New York, 1997. This is the best study of the Mexican American civil rights movement and its impact on education.

Flores, Juan, and George Yudice. *Living Borders/Buscando America: Languages of Latino Self-Formation, Latinos and Education*, edited by Antonia Darder, Rodolfo D. Torres, and Henry Gutierrez. New York: Routledge, 1997. Deals with language issues among Latinos.

Fox, Geoffrey. *Hispanic Nation: Culture, Politics, and the Constructing of Identity*. Tucson: University of Arizona Press, 1996. I relied on this book for my discussion of the meaning of "Hispanic" and "Latino/Latina."

Fry, Richard. *The Role of Schools in the English Language Learner Achievement Gap*. Washington, DC: Pew Hispanic Center, 2008. Study demonstrates the effect on English learners of attending overcrowded schools serving low-income families.

Gonzales, Manuel. *Mexicanos: A History of Mexicans in the United States*. Bloomington: Indiana University Press, 1999. Gonzales provides a good introductory history of Mexican Americans.

Gonzalez, Gilbert. *Chicano Education in the Era of Segregation*. Philadelphia: Balch Institute Press, 1990. This is a history of when Chicanos were segregated in U.S. schools.

Hartocollis, Anemona. "The Harvard Bias Suit by Asian-Americans: 5 Key Issues." *The New York Times* (December 20, 2018). www.nytimes.com/2018/12/20/us/harvard-asian-american-students-discrimination.html on December 24, 1918. Suit against Harvard for discrimination against Asians.

Jordan, Miriam. "Family Separation May Have Hit Thousands More Migrant Children Than Reported." *The New York Times* (January 17, 2019). www.nytimes.com/2019/01/17/us/family-separation-trump-administration-migrants.html on January 19, 2019. The problem of illegal immigrant parents being separated from their children.

Lange, Jason, and Yeganeh Torbati. "U.S. Foreign-Born Population Swells to Highest in Over a Century." *Reuters* (September 13, 2018). www.reuters.com/article/us-usa-immigration-data/u-s-foreign-born-population-swells-to-highest-in-over-a-century-idUSKCN1LT2HZ on January 15, 2019. Discusses U.S. census report on increased foreign-born population in the United States.

Lee, Robert G. *Orientals: Asian Americans in Popular Culture*. Philadelphia: Temple University Press, 1999. This is an important study of the popular image of Asian Americans in the United States.

León, Concepción De. "'500,000 Students Are Affected by the L.A. Teachers Strike. Most Are Latino." *The New York Times* (January 18, 2019). www.nytimes.com/2019/01/18/style/la-school-strike-latino.html on January 19, 2019. The Los Angeles teacher strike and how it reflects the socioeconomic status of Latinos.

Low, Victor. *The Unimpressible Race: A Century of Educational Struggle by the Chinese in San Francisco*. San Francisco: East, West Publishing, 1982. This is the book to read to understand racism and segregation of Chinese in California.

Lowell, B. Lindsay, and Roberto Suro. *The Improving Educational Profile of Latino Immigrants*. Washington, DC: Pew Hispanic Center Report, 2002. This report contains statistics on the educational attainment of Latino immigrants to the United States and finds levels of educational attainment to be increasing.

Lyman, Rick. "Census Shows Growth of Immigrants." *The New York Times on the Web* (August 15, 2006). www.nytimes.com. This article discusses implications of immigration findings of the 2005 American Community Survey.

Maxwell, Lesli. "More Than 75 Percent of Elementary Teacher-Preparation Programs Are Failing When It Comes to Readying Future Teachers to Work Effectively with English-Language Learners, a New Report from the National Council on Teacher Quality Contends." *Education Week* (June 17, 2014). http://blogs.edweek.org/edweek/learning-the-language/2014/06/most_teacher_prep_falls_short_.html?qs=teachers+ell. Report on study showing teacher-training programs not preparing future teachers for ELL students.

———. "U.S. School Enrollment Hits Majority-Minority Milestone." *Education Week* (August 20, 2014). www.edweek.org/ew/articles/2014/08/20/01demographics.h34.html. A report on the number of "nonwhite" students exceeding the "white" students in U.S. public schools.

Nakanishi, Don T., and Tina Yamano Nishida, eds. *The Asian American Educational Experience*. New York: Routledge, 1995. This is an excellent collection of articles on Asian American education.

Pang, Valerie Ooka. "Asian American Children: A Diverse Population." *The Educational Forum* (Fall 1990), pp. 49–66. This is a good discussion of diversity in the Asian American population in the United States.

Philip, John Mollenkopf, Mary C. Waters, and Jennifer Holdaway. *Inheriting the City: The Children of Immigrants Come of Age*. Cambridge, MA: Harvard University Press, 2008. A study of immigrant youth in New York City.

Pitt, Leonard, and Ramon Gutierrez. *The Decline of the Californios: A Social History of Spanish-Speaking Californios, 1846–1890*. Berkeley: University of California Press, 1999. This is an important history of the resident population of California when the United States took the area from Mexico.

Prucha, Francis Paul. *Documents of United States Indian Policy*. Lincoln: University of Nebraska Press, 1990. This volume contains reprints of all the important laws, court cases, and reports affecting Native American education.

Republican Platform 2016. https://gop.com/platform/ on November 23, 2016. States goal of curbing illegal immigration and deporting illegal immigrants.

Reyhner, Jon, and Jeanne Eder. *A History of Indian Education*. Billings: Eastern Montana College, 1989. The authors provide a short introduction to the history of Native American education.

Ryan, Camille L., and Kurt Bauman. *Educational Attainment in the United States: 2015 Current Population Reports P20–578, U.S. Census Bureau* (March 2016). www.census.gov/content/dam/Census/library/publications/2016/demo/p20-578.pdf on March 6, 2017. Provides educational attainment for native and foreign-born U.S. population.

San Miguel, Guadalupe, Jr. *"Let All of Them Take Heed": Mexican Americans and the Campaign for Educational Equality in Texas, 1910–1981*. Austin: University of Texas Press, 1987. This is a good history of the events and court cases surrounding efforts by Mexican Americans to end segregation.

State of Washington, Office of Superintendent of Instruction. *Immigrant Students' Rights to Attend Public Schools*. www.k12.wa.us/MigrantBilingual/ImmigrantRights.aspx on March 2, 2017. Details rights of undocumented children in U.S. public schools.

Szasz, Margaret. *Education and the American Indian: The Road to Self-Determination, 1928–1973*. Albuquerque: University of New Mexico Press, 1974. Szasz provides a good history of the revolution in Native American education in the twentieth century.

Takaki, Ronald. *A Different Mirror: A History of Multicultural America*. Boston: Little, Brown, 1993. This is the single-best history of multiculturalism in the United States.

———. *Strangers from a Different Shore: A History of Asian Americans*. New York: Penguin Books, 1989. Takaki writes an excellent history of Asian Americans.

Ujifusa, Andrew. "Senate Proposals Dealing With 'Dreamers' Go Down to Defeat." *Education Week* (February 15, 2018). https://blogs.edweek.org/edweek/campaign-k-12/2018/02/senate_DACA_proposals_defeated_dreamers.html on January 1, 2019. Defeat of Dreamers legislation.

Ujifusa, Andrew, and Corey Mitchell. "Educating Migrant Children in Shelters: 6 Things to Know." *Education Week* (June 20, 2018). www.edweek.org/ew/articles/2018/06/20/6-things-to-know-about-the-trump.html on January 6, 2019. Discussion of education in shelters holding illegal immigrant children.

U.S. Census Bureau. *2005 American Community Survey; C05006. Place of Birth for the Foreign-Born Population; and B05007, Place of Birth by Year of Entry by Citizenship Status for the Foreign-Born Population, Using American FactFinder*. http://factfinder.census.gov on May 16, 2008. Provides data on countries of origin of immigrants to the United States.

———. *American Community Survey, Puerto Rico Community Survey: 2006 Subject Definitions*. Washington, DC: U.S. Census Bureau, 2006. Definitions and problems associated with racial categories used by the Census Bureau.

———. *English-Speaking Ability of the Foreign-Born Population in the United States: 2012 American Community Survey Reports*. www.census.gov/content/dam/Census/library/publications/2014/acs/acs-26.pdf. This report provides statistics on the number of foreign born in the United States and their English-speaking abilities.

———. *Population Estimates*. www.census.gov. Population projections into the next century are listed.

———. "Selected Social Characteristics in the United States: 2005." *2005 American Community Survey*. Washington, DC: U.S. Census Bureau, 2005. This census survey contains statistics on foreign-born peoples and language spoken in the home.

U.S. Department of Education. *The Condition of Education 2018*. Washington, DC: U.S. Department of Education, 2018. This report provides the most recent statistics on public schools.

Walsh, Mark. "School's Ban on U.S. Flag Shirts on Cinco de Mayo Upheld." *Education Week* (February 27, 2014). http://blogs.edweek.org/edweek/school_law/2014/02/schools_ban_on_us_flag_shirts_.html?qs=mexican+students. This blog discusses continuing tensions that can exist in schools between descendants of Mexicans and white students.

Weinberg, Meyer. *Asian American Education: Historical Background and Current Realities.* Mahwah, NJ: Lawrence Erlbaum, 1997. Weinberg presents an excellent history of the Asian American educational experience in the United States.

Wollenberg, Charles M. *All Deliberate Speed: Segregation and Exclusion in California Schools, 1855–1975.* Berkeley: University of California Press, 1976. This is a landmark study of segregation in the education of Asian Americans, Mexican Americans, and Native Americans in California.

Zehr, Mary Ann. "The Role of Schools in the English Language Learner Achievement Gap." *Education Week on the Web* (June 26, 2008). Report on the Pew Hispanic Center study, which found that English learners are negatively affected by attending overcrowded schools serving low-income families.

CHAPTER 7

Multicultural and Multilingual Education

This chapter discusses multicultural and multilingual education. As explained in Chapter 6, there is currently a global migration of peoples that has raised issues in national school systems regarding multicultural and multilingual student populations. Most nations of the world face the issue of multiculturalism caused by the growth of an international labor market, multinational corporations, the search for better economic and political conditions, and displacement by war. As the host country of the largest number of global migrants, Americans have engaged in a broad spectrum of debates about the type of multicultural and multilingual education in schools.

The issue of basic cultural differences in worldviews is part of the discussion of multicultural and multilingual education. Also, some of the multicultural proposals embrace issues of racism and sexism. In this context the following issues are discussed:

- Global migration of the world's peoples
- Cultural differences in seeing and knowing the world
- Biculturalism, or the ability to move easily between two cultures
- Dominated cultures
- Different forms of multicultural education
- Racism and sexism
- Different forms of language education
- Language rights

GLOBAL MIGRATION OF THE WORLD'S PEOPLES

Multiculturalism and multilingualism are pressing global issues with the world migration of peoples. A small number of countries host 75 percent of the world's international migration. While wealthier nations have only 16 percent of the world's workers, they have over 60 percent of global migrants. The report of the Global Commission on International Migration declared:

> International migration has risen to the top of the global policy agenda. . . . In every part of the world, there is now an understanding that the economic, social and cultural benefits of international migration must be more effectively realized, and that the negative consequences of cross—border movement could be better addressed.

As reported by the 2017 report of the Global Commission on International Migration:

> There are now almost 200 million international migrants, a number equivalent to the fifth most populous country on earth, Brazil. It is more than double the figure recorded in 1980. . . . Migrants are now to be found in every part of the globe, some of them moving within their own region and others travelling from one part of the world to another. Almost half of all migrants are women, a growing proportion of whom are migrating independently. More people than ever are living abroad.

The United Nations' Population Division 2017 report stated that migrants are from poorer to richer nations: "Overall, between 1950 and 2015, the regions of Europe, Northern America and Oceania were net receivers of international migrants, while Africa, Asia and Latin America and the Caribbean were net senders, with the volume of net migration generally increasing over time."

The pattern of global migration becomes clearer when it is broken down by country. A small number of countries host 75 percent of the world's international migrants. In 2013, the United States had the largest number of international migrants with 46 million, about equal to 19.8 percent of the total world migrants. Second was the Russian Federation with 11 million. It is important to note that the high percentage of global migrants in the Russian Federation is a result of the 1991 disintegration of the Union of Soviet Socialist Republics (USSR). This is an example of how political changes can affect citizenship. The high number in the Russian Federation is a result of the reclassification of citizens after the dissolving of the USSR. Prior to 1991, there were large numbers of internal migrants who moved from former parts of the USSR to what is now the Russian Federation. After 1991 these formerly internal migrants were reclassified as international migrants.

As a result of global migration, many populations have difficulty adjusting to the culture of their host countries. Some countries experience "brain drain" as the more educated move to other countries. However, in their host country people might find their educational qualifications underutilized. This is referred to as "brain waste." The classic story of brain waste in the United States is of immigrant New York taxi drivers with engineering degrees earned in their country of origin. There is also the issue of language. Should migrants retain their own languages and have them taught in schools? As a result of these cultural and language problems, many immigrant populations have higher rates of unemployment.

In the United States, multicultural problems are compounded by the existence of dominated populations, as discussed in Chapter 6. These formerly enslaved and conquered populations, such as descendants of enslaved Africans and conquered Mexicans along with Native Americans, Puerto Ricans, Native Hawaiians, and Alaskan Natives, continue to face cultural and linguistic domination. Consequently, multicultural education involves both immigrant groups and the legacy of dominated populations. Over the years there have been many education proposals to help groups adjust to American culture and learn English. It is important for teachers to understand differences in ways of knowing and seeing the world among recent immigrant populations. I will discuss this in the next section.

CULTURAL DIFFERENCES IN KNOWING AND SEEING THE WORLD

A fundamental aspect of multicultural education is that different students have different ways of knowing and seeing the world. The pioneer work in this field is Richard E. Nisbett's *The Geography of Thought: How Asians and Westerners Think Differently . . . and Why*. Working with social psychologists from Japan and China, Nisbett concluded that Japanese and Chinese students have a holistic worldview while U.S. students tend to see the world as made up of discrete categories of objects that can be defined by a set of rules. Nisbett states that Japanese and Chinese students see

> The world in holistic terms. They see a great deal of the field, especially background events; they are skilled in observing relationships between events. . . . Modern Westerners . . . see the world in analytic, atomistic terms; they see objects as discrete and separate from their environments.

These differences were exemplified in a number of psychological experiments. For example, in an experiment conducted at Japan's Kyoto University and at the University of Michigan in the United States, students were shown eight colored animated scenes of underwater life with one or more "focal" fish that were brighter and larger than the others. The fish were shown swimming around plants, rocks, and bubbles. Similar to the results of many other experiments conducted by Nisbett, the results of this experiment indicate that after 20 seconds of viewing the scene, Japanese students remembered many details of the whole scene while the American students primarily remembered the focal fish. In other words, Japanese students looked at the whole scene while the Americans looked at the parts—particularly the most noticeable parts. In responding to questions, Japanese students began by describing the total environment ("It looked like a pond . . .") whereas the Americans began by describing the focal fish.

In another experiment, American and Chinese children were presented with a series of illustrations depicting three objects. The children were asked to place two of the objects together. One illustration showed a chicken, a cow, and grass. American children grouped the chicken and cow together because they are both animals. Chinese children grouped the cow and grass together because the cow eats grass. In fact, the cow and chicken ordinarily have no experiential relationship: If a human were introduced into the illustration and children were asked to group three objects together, one might hypothesize that both American and Chinese children would group the cow, the chicken, and the human together, but for different reasons. The American children would put the three together because they are all animals, while the Chinese children would put the three together because the human eats chickens and drinks cows' milk. Nisbett and two Chinese colleagues conducted a similar experiment yielding similar results using college students in the United States, Taiwan, and the People's Republic of China. They gave the participants three words and asked which two of the words were related. One set of words included "panda," "monkey," and "banana." As can be inferred from the previous discussion, the American college students tended to see the closest relationship between the panda and monkey because they are animals, and the Chinese students grouped the monkey and banana together because monkeys eat bananas.

Differences in "seeing" a forest is one way to illustrate the differences between American and Japanese or Chinese worldviews. Americans are inclined to see a forest in taxonomic categories. Those seeing a forest through the lens of taxonomic categories, which is what many people call Western "seeing," would observe groups of trees, bushes, animals, birds, insects, moss, flowers, and so on. In contrast, those seeing the forest through a holistic lens of relationships, which is what many people might call the Asian way of seeing, would view an interrelated world of birds eating berries and insects, moss growing on trees and the earth, animals eating the moss and leaves, bees pollinating flowers, bushes sheltering animals, and so on. Of course a Westerner could understand the interdependence of the forest, but, according to the preceding discussion, the Westerner would initially focus on separate objects having common characteristics. Nisbett argues that these differences in knowing and seeing the world can be traced back to differences in the original philosophical underpinnings of Western and what he identifies as Confucian-based societies: "Confucian-based societies" refers to communities guided by an ethical system first articulated by the Chinese scholar Confucius (c. 551–c. 479 BCE). The major Confucian-based nations are Korea, Japan, and China.

Nisbett asserts that Westerners developed a belief that knowledge could exist separate from human experience. He traced the belief back to the ancient Greeks, who distrusted knowledge gained through the senses and favored abstract thought. The Greeks believed they could study an object in isolation from its total environment. Isolated, Greeks tried to discern the disparate parts of the object. This approach to seeing the world, he argues, set the stage for the later Western development of the scientific method and the use of science to search for the basic matter of the universe, such as the atom, rather than focusing on how the whole universe works.

In Confucian-based societies, people see the world as made up of relationships based on some form of contact or interaction between objects. In contrast to ancient Greek thought, which favored abstract forms of human behavior, Confucius focused on a person's relationship to others. For Confucius, people were interdependent and inextricably bonded to others through emotional ties. For this reason, modern-day Confucianism maintains a sense of responsibility to others along with a holistic view of society. People in Confucian-based societies demonstrate a greater sense of social responsibility and conformity to group wishes than those in the individualistically oriented Western society.

BICULTURALISM: COLLECTIVIST AND INDIVIDUALIST SOCIETIES

An important understanding in multicultural education is that people can be bicultural in knowing and viewing the world. This is particularly important for understanding the learning processes of students who have recently arrived in the United States. In general, Americans are highly individualistic, with a worldview, as demonstrated in the previously discussed experiments, that favors seeing the parts in contrast to the whole. However, people can be bicultural, switching from a holistic to a Western worldview. This is what many children from Confucian-based and other collectivist societies must learn when entering U.S. schools. They must learn to be bicultural.

There are many societies other than Confucian-based ones that have a collectivist view of social relationships. The differences between individualist and collectivist cultures center around personal orientation to self and others. In individualist cultures, behavior is primarily determined by personal attributes and feelings. People focus on their own individual freedom and personal goals. Social psychologist Eunkook M. Suh writes, "Psychological characteristics [in individualist cultures] commonly associated with mental health . . . portray the personal qualities of a highly independent, self-reliant individual who is capable of transcending the influences of others and the society."

In collectivist societies, people rely on their relationships to others to judge their own happiness. Success in a collectivist society is measured by fulfillment of one's duties and obligations toward one's in-group. In collectivist societies, Suh writes, "discussion of the individual starts with the Confucian assumption that the person exists in relationship to others. The individual is viewed as being fundamentally socially oriented, situation centered, interdependent, and inextricably bonded to others through emotional ties."

In researching the differences between Western and Confucian ways of knowing, Nisbett found that Hong Kong Chinese, who were influenced by British schools and traditions as well as Chinese culture, could be prompted to think according to a Confucian or Western perspective; they are bicultural in their ways of seeing the world. Biculturalism results from what is referred to as hybridity of cultures. For example, many immigrants from collectivist cultures to the United States and Europe must undergo some adaptation to the individualist culture of the host society. Social psychologists Daphna Oyerman, Izumi Sakamoto, and Armand Lauffer write:

> Hybridization involves the melding of cultural lenses or frames such that values and goals that were focused on in one context are transposed to a new context. . . . Cultural hybridization may be said to occur when an individual or group is exposed to and influenced by more than one cultural context.

These researchers found that some immigrant cultures in the United States retained their parental culture in their private lives while taking on the values of the host culture in their public lives. Regarding hybridization, they found that among Asian American students, individualist cultural values were included in the in-group "without a loss of the social obligation that is built into collectivism."

International studies yield the following rankings between collectivist and individualist nations. These rankings also indicate that it is wrong to think of collectivist societies being Asian or Confucian when many are in South America and Africa. I suspect that high collectivist ratings for countries in South America and Africa are a result of indigenous cultures.

The 10 most collectivist nations in rank order beginning with the most collectivist are as follows:

1. China
2. Colombia
3. Indonesia
4. Pakistan
5. Korea
6. Peru
7. Ghana
8. Nepal
9. Nigeria
10. Tanzania

The following list of individualist nations are primarily Western. The one exception is South Africa, which, despite the existence of indigenous peoples, might be considered dominated by a European culture.

The 10 most individualist nations in rank order beginning with the most individualist are as follows:

1. United States
2. Australia
3. Denmark
4. Germany
5. Finland
6. Norway
7. Italy
8. Austria
9. Hungary
10. South Africa

In conclusion, American multicultural education must consider the transition of immigrant children from collectivist societies to the individualist orientation of U.S. society. This transition involves learning to be bicultural. The immigrant child from a collectivist society learns to know and view the world in individualistic terms while still being able to switch to a collectivist view. Often, the child from a collectivist society learns to think in individualistic terms when dealing with American schools and institutions but switches to a collectivist view when interacting with family and the surrounding immigrant community.

THE DIFFERENCES AMONG DOMINANT, DOMINATED, AND IMMIGRANT CULTURES

In multicultural education, distinctions are made among *dominant*, *dominated*, and *immigrant* cultures. The *dominant culture* is the prevailing culture, which is European American in the United States. This is the culture brought to the colonies and the United States by immigrants from Europe and modified by the social and political conditions in America. Traditionally, the curriculum of public schools has been based on European American traditions. In this sense, European American culture is the dominant culture of public schools.

Dominated cultures, as discussed in Chapter 6, refer to groups that were forcefully incorporated into the United States. For instance, Africans were forcefully brought to the United States as slaves, and their cultures were changed by the domination of European American culture to produce an African American culture. Similarly, Native American tribes were conquered by the United States and "Americanized." Mexicans living in the Southwest were forcefully made part of the United States with the signing in 1848 of the Treaty of Guadalupe Hidalgo, and a new Mexican American culture emerged. Finally, the Spanish-American War of 1898 resulted in the forceful annexation of Puerto Rico to the United States; therefore, Puerto Ricans represent another dominated culture.

Immigrant cultures refer to the first generation of groups who freely decided to come to the United States. *First generation* refers to adults and children who are born in another county and then emigrate to the United States. European American immigrants are included in this category. Immigrants have a variety of educational, cultural, and linguistic backgrounds. The diversity of immigrant languages and cultures presents a complex problem for schoolteachers. In *The Inner World of the Immigrant Child*, Cristina Igoa provides questions designed to help teachers do research into the educational background of immigrant children. I strongly recommend that all teachers of immigrant children read Igoa's invaluable book. Igoa's list of questions includes the following:

- Were the children schooled or unschooled before they came into the country?
- Was their education fragmented?
- Are the children dependent on the teacher for learning? Do they have any independent learning skills?
- Did they learn English abroad?

- How much of their own language did they learn, orally and in writing, receptively and productively?
- What is the educational attainment of their parents?

DOMINATED CULTURES: JOHN OGBU

Anthropologist John Ogbu concludes that the historical experience of dominated groups resulted in the development of a basic distrust of the major institutions in American society. For instance, a history of forced subjugation and slavery, segregation, discrimination, and harassment by police and government officials left many members of the African American community with the feeling that the government works primarily to benefit European Americans. This general distrust of institutions includes public schools. Segregation and second-generation segregation have left many African Americans feeling that public schooling is organized to keep them at the bottom rungs of America's social and economic system. Mexican Americans and Puerto Ricans encountered the hostility of segregation and second-generation segregation as well as attempts to keep them from speaking Spanish. Similarly, many Native Americans, as discussed in Chapter 6, feel a strong hostility toward schools because of the deculturalization programs they experienced in government-operated boarding schools. For instance, Mick Fedullo, in his wonderful book on Indian education, *Light of the Feather: Pathways through Contemporary Indian America*, recounts a discussion with an Apache bilingual education teacher, Elenore Cassadore, about Apache attitudes toward schools. As she tells Fedullo, many Apache parents were sent to Bureau of Indian Affairs boarding schools where they "came to believe that their teachers were the evil ones, and so anything that had to do with 'education' was also evil—like books." Now, she explains, they send their children to school only because of compulsory-education laws. "But they tell their kids not to take school seriously. So, to them, printed stuff is white-man stuff."

According to Ogbu, these historical conditions created a *cultural frame of reference* among dominated groups that is quite different from that of many immigrants and European Americans. As discussed earlier in the chapter regarding collectivist and individualist cultures, cultural frames of reference refer to the manner in which people interpret their perceptions of the world. In the case of dominated groups, I am concerned with that part of a person's cultural frame of reference that is formed, in part, by his or her family's historical experience. For instance, an African American child might not have witnessed a lynching of a black person by a white mob, but knowledge of these incidents might be passed on to the child through the recounting of family history and experience in the

United States. A Mexican American child might not have experienced discrimination in employment, but he or she might frequently hear about it through family conversations. The history told by families and a person's experiences play a major role in shaping one's cultural frame of reference.

Differences in cultural frames of reference can result in differing interpretations of the same event. For instance, a European American might perceive school as an institution that is benign and helpful. In contrast, a member of a dominated group might perceive school as an institution not to be trusted. The actions of a disgruntled server in a restaurant might be interpreted through the cultural frame of reference of a European American as resulting from the server not feeling good about his job. On the other hand, the cultural frame of reference of African Americans, Native Americans, Mexican Americans, and Puerto Ricans might lead members of these groups to interpret the server's actions as hostile and prejudicial. Also, differences in cultural frames of reference can result in differences in action in particular situations. For instance, in the preceding example, a European American might give little attention to the actions of a disgruntled server. On the other hand, members of a dominated group might act in a hostile manner to what they perceive to be the prejudicial actions of the server. Low academic achievement, Ogbu argues, results from dominated cultures holding negative feelings about schools. Ogbu identifies six ways this can occur:

1. Some members of dominated groups believe they must act white to succeed in school. This feeling is exemplified by the previous quotation from the Apache teacher.
2. Some students from dominated cultures may fear that doing well in school will symbolize a rejection of their own culture.
3. Peer pressure against acting white might result in students actually avoiding academic achievement.
4. The feelings of hostility some students from dominated cultures might feel toward school can result in conflicts with European American administrators, teachers, and other students. Of course, these conflicts might be in response to real feelings and actions displayed by school officials and other students.
5. Conflicts with school personnel and other students can heighten distrust of school and a rejection of school rules. The open rejection of school rules leads to suspension, expulsion, and other forms of school punishment.
6. Some students from dominated cultures might begin school disillusioned about their ability to achieve. This can result in little effort being put into academic work.

These six reactions to school cause, according to Ogbu, *low academic effort syndrome* and *counteracademic attitudes and behaviors*. Low academic effort syndrome refers to lack of effort in doing schoolwork, which results from peer pressure, conflict, and disillusionment. Counteracademic attitudes and behaviors refers to actions that are hostile toward the school and its rules. Obviously, many students from dominated groups succeed in school and do not display a low academic effort syndrome or adopt counteracademic attitudes and behavior. Despite their success in school, many of these students still interpret their educational experience through a cultural frame of reference that is quick to note prejudice and unfair treatment. This type of cultural frame of reference can be found in Jake Lamar's autobiography, *Bourgeois Blues: An American Memoir*. Although his father was a successful businessperson who could afford to live in wealthy neighborhoods in New York City and send his children to elite private schools, Jake discovered that racism was still a major factor in his life. Richard Rodriguez interprets his own academic success through the cultural frame of reference of a Mexican American in his autobiography, *Hunger of Memory: The Education of Richard Rodriguez*. Key to understanding the problems of students from dominated cultures is the pain Rodriguez felt as his academic success widened the gap between him and his family culture.

It is important to remember that many students of dominated cultures do succeed in school and in the economic life of the United States. Advocates of multicultural education programs argue that educational programs supporting cultural diversity can help students from dominated cultures who might be experiencing low academic effort syndrome and exhibiting counteracademic attitudes and behaviors. These multicultural programs are described in the next section.

EMPOWERMENT THROUGH MULTICULTURAL EDUCATION: JAMES BANKS, SONIA NIETO, AND CRITICAL PEDAGOGY

Leaders of the multicultural education movement, such as James Banks, Christine Sleeter, Carl Grant, and Sonia Nieto, are concerned with empowering oppressed people by integrating the history and culture of dominated groups into public school curricula and textbooks. In general, their goal is to reduce prejudice, eliminate sexism, and equalize educational opportunities. *Empowerment* is concerned with ethnic studies and raising consciousness. Within this context, the term means providing the intellectual tools for creating a just society. Usually the concept of empowerment is contrasted with benevolent helping, such as welfare programs, family assistance, and other forms of aid. These programs, it is argued, keep people in a state of dependence. Empowerment gives people the ability to break out of these dependent states. Ethnic studies can empower dominated and oppressed immigrant cultures by creating an understanding of the methods of cultural domination and by helping build self-esteem. For instance, the study of African American, Native American, Puerto Rican, Hawaiian American, and Mexican American history serves the dual purpose of building self-esteem and empowerment. In addition, the empowerment of women and people with disabilities involves, in part, the inclusion of their histories and stories in textbooks and in the curriculum.

As one aspect of social empowerment, ethnic studies have influenced textbooks and classroom instruction in the United States. The ethnic studies movement resulted in the integration of content into the curriculum dealing with dominated and immigrant cultures, women, and people with disabilities. Multicultural educator James Banks worries that many school districts consider content integration as the primary goal of multicultural education. He states, "The widespread belief that content integration constitutes the whole of multicultural education might. . . [cause] many teachers of subjects such as mathematics and science to view multicultural education as an endeavor primarily for social studies and language arts teachers."

The best example of multicultural education for empowerment is Sonia Nieto's *Affirming Diversity: The Sociopolitical Context of Multicultural Education*. Growing up as a Puerto Rican in New York City, Nieto felt the tension between the language and culture of her family and the language and culture of the school. The school made her feel there was something deficient with her background. She states, "We learned to feel ashamed of who we were, how we spoke, what we ate, and everything else that was 'different' about us." For Nieto, the goal of multicultural education should be to bridge the gap between the culture of the family and the culture of the school so children of immigrant and dominated families do not have to suffer the pain and shame she experienced. In her words, "Our society must move beyond causing and exploiting students' shame to using their cultural and linguistic differences to struggle for an education that is more in tune with society's rhetoric of equal and high-quality education for all students."

Multiculturalism for social empowerment attempts to maintain cultural identity while promoting values of social justice and social action. In her book, Nieto presents a chart displaying the seven characteristics of this form of multicultural education.

1. The school curriculum is openly antiracist and antidiscriminatory. An atmosphere is created where students feel safe about discussing sexism, racism, and discrimination. In addition, the curriculum includes the history and cultural perspectives of a broad range of people. Students are to be taught to identify and challenge racism in society.

2. Multicultural education is considered a basic part of a student's general education, which means that all students become bilingual and all students study different cultural perspectives.
3. Multiculturalism should pervade the curriculum by being included in all aspects of the curriculum and in the general life of the school, including bulletin boards, lunchrooms, and assemblies.
4. Multicultural education is considered important for all students.
5. Schools should teach social justice by preparing students to overcome racism and discrimination against various cultures.
6. Learning should emphasize asking the questions why, how, and what if. When these questions are asked regarding issues of social injustice, they can lead to a questioning of the very foundations of political and economic institutions. This makes multicultural education a combination of content and "process."
7. Multicultural education should include critical pedagogy as the primary method of instruction. With critical pedagogy, in Nieto's words, "students and teachers are involved in a 'subversive activity' and decision making and social action skills are the basis of the curriculum."

In the framework of this approach to multicultural education, critical pedagogy helps students understand the extent to which cultures can differ. In addition, these differences are to be affirmed and given equal treatment. Also, critical pedagogy will help students understand cultural domination and how they can end it.

Missing from multicultural education for social empowerment is an analysis of the intersection of different cultures. It is assumed that an understanding of oppression and discrimination will provide a common theme in critical pedagogy that will prepare all students to struggle for social justice. But there are important and deep differences in values among cultures. Does social justice mean giving a person an opportunity to achieve within the framework of English or Native American values? Or does it mean creating a whole new set of values for the world?

EMPOWERMENT THROUGH MULTICULTURAL EDUCATION: COMBATING RACISM

Advocates of multicultural education for empowerment include in their agenda ridding the world of racism. *Racism* can be defined as prejudice plus power. Racism refers to acts of oppression of one racial group toward another. One form of oppression is economic exploitation. This definition of racism distinguishes between simple feelings of hostility and prejudice toward another racial group and the ability to turn those feelings into some form of oppression. For instance, black people might have prejudicial feelings toward white people, but they have little opportunity to express those prejudicial feelings in some form of economic or political oppression of white people. On the other hand, prejudicial feelings white people might have toward blacks can turn into racism when they become the basis for discrimination in education, housing, and the job market. Within this framework, racism becomes the act of social, political, and economic oppression of another group.

When discussions of racism occur in my multicultural education classes, white students complain of a sense of hostility from black students and, consequently, accuse black students of racism. Black students respond that their feelings represent prejudice and not racism because they lack the power to discriminate against whites. The troubling aspect of this response is the implication that if these black students had the power, they would be racist. One black student pointed out that there are situations where blacks can commit racist acts against whites. The black student used the example of a black man killing white passengers on a commuter railroad several years ago. The evidence seemed to indicate the killer was motivated by extreme hatred of whites that the newspapers labeled "black rage." This was a racist act, the black student argued, because the gun represented power. Racism is often thought of as whites oppressing people of color. Of course, there are many problems with this definition. If one parent is black and another white, are their children considered black or white? Can a white-skinned child of this marriage be considered white while a dark-skinned child is considered black?

Jake Lamar recalls how the confusion over skin color sparked the development of his racial consciousness at the age of three. Jake was sitting at the kitchen table when his Uncle Frank commented "about how obnoxious white people were." Jake responded, "But Mommy's white." His uncle replied that his mother was not white but was "just light-skinned." Jake then said that he thought his father, brother, and himself were black while his sister and mother were white. His mother then explained that they had many white ancestors that caused the variation in skin color, but they were still "all Negroes." Thinking back on this incident, Lamar reflected, "Black and white then meant something beyond pigmentation . . . so my first encounter with racial awareness was at once enlightening and confusing, and shot through with ambiguity."

Keeping in mind the complexities of racial classification and the importance of social class, certain generalities can be made about the racial attitudes of whites at the end of the twentieth century. In *Prejudice and Racism*, social psychologist James Jones summarizes the racial attitudes of some whites:

- Whites feel more negatively toward blacks than they do toward Hispanics, Asians, and legal and illegal immigrants.
- Whites perceive blacks as lazy, violent, and less intelligent than Hispanics, Asians, and legal and illegal immigrants.
- Whites believe blacks are receiving more attention from the government than they deserve.
- Whites believe blacks are too demanding in their struggle for equal rights.
- High levels of antiblack racism are correlated with white beliefs that police and the death penalty make streets safe and white attitudes that oppose assistance to the poor.
- Antiblack and anti-Hispanic racism are correlated with whites' opposition to open immigration and multilingualism.

TEACHING AN ANTI-BIAS AND TOLERANCE CURRICULA

It is sometimes difficult to teach anti-bias and tolerance curricula when schools are becoming more segregated. Even in racially integrated schools there is sometimes a push back from white students who feel they are being blamed in discussions about racism. One excellent book that deals with this issue is Beverly Daniel Tatum's *Why Are All the Black Kids Sitting Together in the Cafeteria: A Psychologist Explains the Development of Racial Identity*. Educator and African American activist Beverly Tatum worries about the loss of white allies in the struggle against racism and the hostility she feels from white college students when teaching about racism. Reflecting on her teaching experiences, she writes, "White students . . . often struggle with strong feelings of guilt when they become aware of the pervasiveness of racism. . . . These feelings are uncomfortable and can lead white students to resist learning about race and racism." Part of the problem, she argues, is that seeing oneself as the oppressor creates a negative self-image, which results in withdrawal from a discussion of the problem. What needs to be done, she maintains, is to counter the guilt by giving white students a positive self-image of whites fighting against racism. In other words, she wants to create a self-image among whites of being allies with people of color against racism.

A popular antiracist curriculum for preschool children is the National Association for the Education of Young Children's "Anti-Bias Education for Young Children and Ourselves." The authors of the association's anti-bias curriculum, Louise Derman-Sparks and Julie Olsen Edwards, provide the following examples of intolerance in classrooms:

"I don't want to sit next to her. She talks funny," comments a 3-year-old, regarding a new teacher who speaks English with a strong accent.

"I don't want to!" defiantly states a 4-year-old from a single-mom family when the teacher announces they are making cards for Father's Day.

"You can't be the princess! Princesses have blond hair!" announces a White 4-year-old to an African American friend.

"No girls allowed. No girls allowed. We're big. We're superheroes. No girls, no girls," chant three 5-year-old boys from the top of the climbing structure.

These are laced with intolerance against second-language speakers of English, family structures, racial features, and gender. It is not within the scope of this book to cover all details of the National Association for the Education of Young Children's anti-bias curriculum. Interested readers should visit their Website: https://www.naeyc.org/resources/topics/anti-bias-education/overview or purchase Louise Derman-Sparks and Julie Olsen Edwards' book *Anti-Bias Education for Young Children and Ourselves*. In this book, the two authors establish the following goals. They provide methods and lessons on how to achieve these goals.

- Goal 1 Each child will demonstrate self-awareness, confidence, family pride, and positive social identities.
- Goal 2 Each child will express comfort and joy with human diversity; accurate language for human differences; and deep, caring human connections.
- Goal 3 Each child will increasingly recognize unfairness, have language to describe unfairness, and understand that unfairness hurts.
- Goal 4 Each child will demonstrate empowerment and the skills to act, with others or alone, against prejudice and/or discriminatory actions.

Teaching Tolerance has been a project of the South Poverty Law Center since 1991. Its latest publication is *Perspectives for a Diverse America: A K-12 Literacy-Based Anti-Bias Curriculum*. The Teaching Tolerance Project began after a group of teenage skinheads attacked and beat to death an Ethiopian man on a street in Portland, Oregon, in 1988. After this incident, members of the Southern Poverty Law Center decided it was time to do something about teaching tolerance. Dedicated to pursuing legal issues involving racial incidents and denial of civil rights, the law center sued, for the man's family, the two men who were responsible for teaching violent racism to the Portland skinheads. These two men—Tom Metzger, the head of the White Aryan Resistance, and his son—became symbols of racist teachings in the United States. In a broad sense, the Teaching Tolerance Project is designed to provide information about teaching methods and materials that will counter the type of racist teachings represented by Metzger and his son.

There is not enough space in this chapter to discuss all the details of Teaching Tolerance's *Perspectives for a Diverse America: A K-12 Literacy-Based Anti-Bias Curriculum.* Readers should visit http://www.tolerance.org/sites/default/files/general/Perspectives%20for%20a%20Diverse%20America%20User%20Experience.pdf/ for more details. The curriculum is aligned with the Common Core State Standards for literacy and integrates into these literacy standards what they call an "Anti-bias Framework" consisting of four domains:

1. Identity: Students will understand the multiple facets of their identities, know where those traits come from, and feel comfortable being themselves in a diversity of settings.
2. Diversity: Students will recognize the diversity of people in the world, be able to identify differences and commonalities, express interest in the lived experiences of others and develop genuine connections with others.
3. Justice: Students will be aware of bias and injustice, both individual and systemic, will understand the short and long-term impact of injustice, and will know about those who have fought for more fairness and justice in our world.
4. Action: Students will feel confident that they can make a difference in society and will commit to taking action against bias and injustice even when it is not popular or easy.

EMPOWERMENT THROUGH MULTICULTURAL EDUCATION: COMBATING SEXISM

In the classic study *Failing at Fairness: How America's Schools Cheat Girls*, Myra and David Sadker (1995) summarize current research on educational discrimination against girls. One surprising result of their research and analysis of other data was that girls are equal to or ahead of boys in most measures of academic achievement and psychological health during the early years of schooling, but by the end of high school and college, girls have fallen behind boys on these measurements. On entrance examinations to college, girls score lower than boys, particularly in science and mathematics. Boys receive more state and national scholarships. Women score lower than men on all entrance examinations to professional schools.

An explanation for the decline in test scores is that girls suffer a greater decline in self-esteem than boys from elementary school to high school. (Of course, an important general question about the following statistics is why both boys and girls decline in feelings of self-esteem.) As a measure of self-esteem, the Sadkers rely on responses to the statement, "I'm happy the way I am." The Sadkers report that in elementary school 60 percent of girls and 67 percent of boys responded positively to this statement. By high school these positive responses declined to 29 percent for girls and 46 percent for boys. In other words, the decline in self-esteem for girls was 31 percentage points as compared with 21 percentage points for boys. Why is there less self-esteem and a greater decline in self-esteem among girls as compared with boys?

To answer the question, the Sadkers asked students how their lives would be different if they suddenly were transformed into members of the opposite sex. Overall, girls responded with feelings that it wouldn't be so bad and that it would open up opportunities to participate in sports and politics. In addition, girls felt they would have more freedom and respect. Regarding self-esteem, girls expressed little regret about the consequences of the sex change. In contrast, boys expressed horror at the idea, and many said they would commit suicide. They saw themselves becoming second-class citizens, being denied access to athletics and outdoor activities, and being racked with physical problems. Concerning self-esteem, and in contrast to girls, boys expressed nothing but regret about the consequences of the sex change.

Contributing to the lack of self-esteem among girls, the Sadkers argue, are modes of classroom interaction, the representation of women in textbooks and other educational materials, and the discriminatory content of standardized tests. In one of their workshops with classroom teachers, the Sadkers illustrate classroom sex bias by asking four of the participants—two men and two women—to act like students in a middle school social studies classroom. The lesson is about the American Revolution and begins with an examination of homework. Acting as the teacher, David Sadker perfunctorily tells one woman that two of her answers are wrong and comments to the group on the neatness of the other woman's homework. He tells one man that two of his answers are wrong and, unlike his response to the woman with wrong answers, urges the man to try harder and suggests ways of improving his answers. David then states to the other man that he failed to do his homework assignment. In contrast to the woman with the neat paper, this man illustrates what the Sadkers call the "bad boy role."

David Sadker then continues the lesson by discussing battles and leaders. All the Revolutionary leaders are, of course, male. During the lesson he calls on the males 20 times each while only calling on one woman twice and completely ignoring the other woman. The one woman called on misses her question because she is given only half a second to respond. When questioning the men, David Sadker spends time giving hints and probing. At the end of this demonstration lesson, the Sadkers report, one woman commented that she felt like she was back in school. She often had the right answer but was never called on by the teacher.

What this workshop demonstration illustrates, based on the Sadkers' findings on classroom interaction, is that boys receive more and better instruction. Boys are more often called on by the teacher, and boys interact more with the teacher than do girls. In a typical classroom situation, if both boys and girls have their hands raised to answer a question, the teacher is most likely to call on a boy. A teacher will spend more time responding to a boy's question than to a girl's question. In other words, girls do not receive equal educational opportunity in the classroom.

It is most likely that the treatment received by girls in the classroom and in textbooks contributes to their low self-esteem and to their decline, as compared with boys, in performance on standardized tests from elementary school to high school. The lowering of self-esteem and content bias may contribute to the significant gender gap in scores on standardized college entrance examinations and entrance examinations to professional schools. For instance, the widely used Scholastic Assessment Test (SAT) has demonstrated a major gap between male and female scores on the math test. In 2012 the gap was 32 points, and in 2013 it was 33 points, according to the analysis of American Enterprise scholar Mark Perry. He concludes:

> Even though female high school students are better prepared academically on many different measures than their male classmates, both overall and for mathematics specifically, female high school students score significantly lower on the SAT math test, and the +30-point differences in test scores favoring males has persisted for generations.

In 2014, studies were still reporting bias against females in science classrooms similar to what the Sadkers had found. In an *Education Week* article, Liana Heitin reported about a study that asked science teachers about the best students in their classes, and they described more males than females. In one case, a science teacher could not remember the name of even one female student. When science teachers were asked to describe the characteristics of their best students, the researchers reported: "When you compare the list of characteristics, for boys it was always things like,

'He's really curious, inquisitive, a good thinker,' all intellectual [descriptions]. Girls were described as they work really hard, they always turn in homework, they get papers in on time, their papers are really neat."

The low test scores in math and bias against females in science courses raises issues regarding the present push of STEM (science, technology, engineering, and mathematics) courses in public schools. Writing about "Effective STEM Courses for Adolescent Girls," Harriet S. Mosatche, Susan Matloff-Nieves, Linda Kekelis, and Elizabeth K. Lawner review three effective programs and conclude that an important element is providing girls with positive role models: "When role models show that they have interesting lives outside their labs or other work environments, they begin to dispel girls' negative stereotypes about scientists and engineers. The most effective role models are likely to be those who come from backgrounds similar to those of the participants."

EDUCATING FOR ECONOMIC POWER: LISA DELPIT

Lisa Delpit is more interested in directly instructing children of dominated groups in the culture of power. She believes that advocates of multicultural education often fail to reveal to children the requirements for economic advancement. She does not reject the importance of critical thinking, but she does think children should be directly told about the standards for acceptable speech and behavior for social mobility.

Working at the University of Alaska, she criticized what she called liberal educators for primarily focusing on native culture while instructing native Alaskans. These liberal educators, she claimed, were damaging students by not preparing them for success in the broader society. She was also critical of traditional instructors for ignoring native traditions. From her perspective, native culture needed to be considered when preparing students to achieve in the real world. Delpit encountered the same issues when working with teachers of black children in Philadelphia schools. White teachers often thought they knew what was best for black students. Usually this meant some form of progressive instruction designed to enhance critical thinking and imagination. While not denying the importance of these goals, Delpit found white teachers neglecting the instruction of black students in standard English. One complaining black parent told her, "My kids know how to be black—you all teach them how to be successful in the white man's world." Several black teachers suggested to Delpit that the " 'progressive' educational strategies imposed by liberals upon black and poor children could only be based on a desire to ensure that the liberals' children get sole access to the dwindling pool of American jobs." According to Delpit, there are five important aspects that need to be addressed when preparing dominated children for access to power.

1. "Issues of power are enacted in classrooms." It is important to examine, Delpit argues, the power of teachers and government over students, textbook publishers, and curriculum developers. This examination can be considered preparation for understanding the exercise of power in the world of work.
2. "There are codes or rules for participating in power; that is, there is a 'culture of power.'" In the classroom, this means direct instruction in linguistic forms and presentation of self, including ways of talking, writing, dressing, and interacting.
3. "The rules of the culture of power are a reflection of the rules of the culture of those who have power." For Delpit, the culture of the school is the culture of the middle and upper classes. Therefore, it is important for children from dominated groups to participate in and learn school culture.
4. "If you are not already a participant in the culture of power, being told explicitly the rules of that culture makes acquiring power easier."
5. "Those with power are frequently least aware of—or least willing to acknowledge—its existence. Those with less power are often most aware of its existence."

From Delpit's perspective, white liberal educators are uncomfortable admitting they are part of the culture of power. On the other hand, students from dominated groups are aware of white power and would like the parameters of power clearly stated.

ETHNOCENTRIC EDUCATION

In ethnocentric education subjects are taught from the perspective of a particular culture. Obviously, this is what U.S. public schools have always done. The curriculum of public schools is organized around the cultural frame of reference of European Americans while the curriculum of new ethnocentric schools is organized around the cultural frames of reference of African Americans, Native Americans, and Hispanics.

The purpose of these new ethnocentric schools is twofold. First, these schools want to overcome among some children of dominated cultures the resistance to schooling that results in low academic effort and counteracademic attitudes and behaviors. Second, these schools want to preserve the cultural traditions of each dominated group. The preservation of culture is considered important because of what are believed to be some shortcomings of European American culture. For instance, many Native Americans feel European Americans show little respect for nature and are primarily concerned with the control of nature. The result of these attitudes is massive environmental destruction. What Native American culture can contribute is an understanding of how to live with nature and an attitude that shows respect for nature and desires its preservation.

There are proposals for Hispanic and Afrocentric schools that are designed to redirect resistance cultures and build student self-esteem. A major source of inspiration for ethnocentric schools comes from the work of Jawanza Kunjufu, president of the Chicago-based African American Images. African American Images serves as a publishing house for Kunjufu's books and other books and videos focused on the teaching of African American culture. African American Images also offers a model curriculum called SETCLAE: Self-Esteem Through Culture Leads to Academic Excellence. The stated goals of the curriculum are to improve academic achievement, discipline, and school climate while transmitting racial pride and enhancing students' knowledge of culture and history and its significance to contemporary living. Kunjufu's discussion of the experience of African American students is similar to John Ogbu's. Kunjufu argues that for most African American students, being successful in school means acting white. Kunjufu exemplifies this situation by an exchange between African American students about two other academically successful African American students in his book *To Be Popular or Smart: The Black Peer Group*:

"Girl, she thinks she's something, making the honor roll."

"I know, she's beginning to act like Darryl. They both think they're white, joining the National Honor Society."

Molefi Kete Asante, chairperson of the Department of African American Studies at Temple University and one of the proponents of an Afrocentric curriculum, argues that Afrocentricity is a transforming power involving five levels of awareness. On the first four levels of this transforming experience individuals come to understand that their personalities, interests, and concerns are shared by black people around the world. Afrocentricity is achieved on the fifth level when a people struggle against foreign cultures that dominate their minds. At this stage, Asante argues in his book *Afrocentricity*, "An imperative of will, powerful, incessant, alive, and vital, moves to eradicate every trace of powerlessness. Afrocentricity is like rhythms; it dictates the beat of your life."

By purging images given by white culture of African Americans as stupid and powerless, African American students can, according to the arguments of those advocating Afrocentricity, gain a new image of themselves as people of ability and power. In this sense, Afrocentricity is considered a curriculum of empowerment. In addition, the students lose the lenses that filter the world through a white Eurocentric perspective and replace them with a set of Afrocentric lenses.

Therefore, ethnocentric curriculums in the United States create a cultural battle at two levels. At one level, an ethnocentric curriculum is an attempt to give equal value to different cultural traditions. At the second level, it means purging a Eurocentric view of the world from Native American, Hispanic, and African American children's minds and replacing it with a different cultural frame of reference. The purpose of this cultural battle is to empower Native American, Hispanic, and African American children so they believe they can succeed in the world and so they are not self-destructive. From this perspective, getting ahead in the economic and social system is not a matter of being white but of learning to believe in oneself and one's cultural traditions.

Ethnocentric education is one method for helping children from dominated groups succeed in school. Bilingual education is another. Bilingual education, as I discuss in the next section, is particularly important for Native Americans, Mexican Americans, and Puerto Ricans because of the conscious attempt by public schools in the past to destroy their languages.

BILINGUAL EDUCATION AND ENGLISH LANGUAGE ACQUISITION: NO CHILD LEFT BEHIND

The No Child Left Behind Act of 2001 transformed the original goals of the bilingual education movement. Bilingual education is a means for protecting minority languages while teaching English to non-English speakers. It is part of the effort to protect language and cultural rights. Some Americans object to public schools protecting minority languages and believe the primary goal should be the acquisition of English.

The No Child Left Behind Act clearly places the federal government's support on the side of English acquisition as opposed to bilingual education. One part of the legislation is titled "English Language Acquisition, Language Enhancement, and Academic Act." This part of the legislation symbolically changes the name of the federal government's Office of Bilingual Education to the Office of English Language Acquisition, Language Enhancement, and Academic Achievement for Limited English Proficient. Its shorter title is simply the Office of English Language Acquisition. The director of bilingual education and minority languages affairs is now called the director of English language acquisition.

To understand the significance of these changes, we need to consider the arguments *for* bilingual education. Bilingual education refers to teaching a person to be proficient in the use of two languages. For instance, Native American students can be taught to be proficient in the use of their own native languages and English, while a Mexican American or Puerto Rican child can be taught to be proficient in Spanish and English.

In addition, there are several specific types of a bilingual education, including maintenance bilingual, transitional bilingual, and two-way bilingual. As the term suggests, *maintenance bilingual* programs are designed to maintain the ability to speak, read, and write in the student's language while learning English. For instance, a student might enter school speaking only Spanish with little knowledge of English. The ability to speak Spanish does not necessarily mean the child knows how to read and write in Spanish. Similarly, most English-speaking students entering school do not know how to read and write in English. During the early years, maintenance bilingual education programs conduct classes in the language of the student while also teaching English. Therefore, during the period when students are learning English, they are also learning the content of the curriculum, including how to read and write, in their native tongue. This avoids the problem of learning being delayed until students know English. After learning English, students continue to receive lessons in both their native languages and in English.

One of the strongest arguments for maintenance bilingual education is that students are better able to learn English if they know how to read and write in their native language. In *Affirming Diversity*, Sonia Nieto argues that children who know how to read and write in their native language will be more successful in school than children whose language is neglected by the school and who do not become literate in their native tongue.

In contrast, *transitional bilingual* does not have the goal of making the student literate in two languages. The student's native tongue is used in class until the student learns English. After the student learns English, classes are taught only in English.

Two-way bilingual programs include both English-speaking and non-English-speaking students. By conducting class in two languages, English-speaking students can learn the language of the non-English speakers, while the non-English speakers learn English. The goal is for all students to become bilingual in English and another language.

Of course, language is linked to culture. Many Mexican Americans, Puerto Ricans, and Native Americans believe maintenance bilingual education programs are essential for the retention of their cultures. As discussed earlier in this chapter, many deculturalization programs were directed at stamping out the use of Spanish and Native American languages. In addition, a person's cultural frame of reference is directly related to attitudes regarding the use in the United States of languages other than English.

THE END OF BILINGUAL AND MULTICULTURAL EDUCATION: ENGLISH LANGUAGE ACQUISITION ACT OF 2001 AND THE COMMON CORE STATE STANDARDS

The English Language Acquisition Act and the Common Core State Standards replaced efforts to maintain languages other than English in schools, and the Common Core State Standards ended meaningful discussions of multiculturalism by imposing the same educational standards on all cultural groups. Curriculum standards by their very nature standardize what is taught for all students. As I explain, students might learn about other cultures, but the content is taught from the perspective of Common Core State Standards and not from the differing cultural perspectives of students. Also, the Common Core State Standards are designed to prepare workers for the global economy and therefore emphasize getting along with other cultures in the workplace.

In 2001, a majority of Congress and President George W. Bush opposed bilingual education and stood firmly for the principle that the primary objective of U.S. schools should be the teaching of English without any attempt to preserve minority languages. The limited exception was for Native Americans and Puerto Ricans. While recognizing programs designed to maintain Native American languages and Spanish, the major thrust of these programs is English proficiency. The legislation declares:

> Programs authorized under this part that serve Native American (including Native American Pacific Islander) children and children in the Commonwealth of Puerto Rico may include programs . . . designed for Native American children learning and studying Native American languages and children of limited Spanish proficiency, except that an outcome of programs serving such children *shall be increased English proficiency among such children.*

(emphasis added)

The English Language Acquisition Act's nine major purposes clearly spell out the antibilingual education agenda. Just as the Office of Bilingual Education became the Office of English Language Acquisition, the goals focus on teaching English in the context of state academic standards and high-stakes testing. In fact, the first stated purpose of the legislation reads:

> (1) to help ensure that children who are limited English proficient, including immigrant children and youth, attain English proficiency, develop high levels of academic attainment in English, and meet the same challenging State academic content and student academic achievement standards as all children are expected to meet.

The next eight legislative purposes support this first goal, including (2) to prepare for learning core academic subjects; (3) to develop language instructional programs for limited-English-proficient students; (4) to design instructional programs that prepare limited-English-proficient children to enter all-English instruction settings; (5) to continue English instruction for limited-English-proficient children; (6) to provide language instruction programs for the parents and communities of limited-English-proficient children; and (7) to streamline the grant programs for English language acquisition.

The eighth purpose gives the federal government supervisory power to ensure states comply with the intent of the legislation. Even if a state government supports bilingual education, it is now faced with the problem of having to refuse any federal money granted under this legislation. Further, the legislation requires that state governments measure English proficiency. Specifically, the federal government will:

> Hold State educational agencies, local educational agencies, and schools accountable for increases in English proficiency and core academic content knowledge of limited English proficient children by requiring—(A) demonstrated improvements in the English proficiency of limited English proficient children each fiscal year.

The ninth and final purpose uses the language of "scientifically based research" to ensure schools do not use bilingual education methods to teach English proficiency.

The larger question is whether politicians and the federal government should ever have been involved in the struggle to protect minority languages. The English Language Acquisition Act of 2001 replaces the goals and programs of the Bilingual Education Act of 1968. Will some future federal legislation resurrect federal involvement in bilingualism? Imagine the waste of time and money in replacing the Office of Bilingual Education with the Office of English Language Acquisition! Of course, there will continue to be a struggle between the advocates of English only and those wanting to protect minority languages. This issue will persist in debates about American education.

In addition to the triumph of English in the school, differing cultural perspectives in instruction are negated by the very existence of a common curriculum. The Common Core State Standards explicitly state that the goal of teaching about other cultures, which is different than teaching from the cultural perspectives of students, is to prepare for a multicultural workplace. The standards state:

> Students [will] appreciate that the twenty-first-century classroom and workplace are settings in which people from often widely divergent cultures and who represent diverse experiences and perspectives must learn and work together. Students actively seek to understand other perspectives and cultures through reading and listening, and they are able to communicate effectively with people of varied backgrounds.

While the goal is preparing for a multicultural workplace, there is little multicultural content in the proposed literature for the standards. In the kindergarten to fifth-grade standards under "Range of Text Types for K–5: Students in K–5 apply the Reading standards to the following range of text types, with texts selected from a broad range of cultures and periods" is stated "Stories—Includes children's adventure stories, folktales, legends, fables, fantasy, realistic fiction, and myth." There is nothing in the standards that suggests students should read these stories from differing cultural perspectives or that they should be linked to the culture of the students or that they should teach about relationships of power as recommended by Lisa Delpit. The goal is not maintenance of differing cultures but creating a harmonious workplace.

GLOBALIZATION: LANGUAGE AND CULTURAL RIGHTS

The issues surrounding the language and culture of schools are present in most of the world's nations, as most nations are now multicultural and multilingual. As a result, there has been a call for international recognition of language and cultural rights. A longtime champion of these international rights, Tove Skutnabb-Kangas proposes a universal covenant protecting linguistic human rights as part of the protection of cultural rights. Key to her proposal is the definition of a mother tongue. A mother tongue, she writes, can be distinguished as "the language one learned first (the language one has established the first long-lasting verbal contacts in)" or "the language one identifies with/as a native speaker of; and/or the language one knows best."

Of fundamental importance to Tove Skutnabb-Kangas's Universal Covenant of Linguistic Human Rights is the stress on bilingual education if the student's language is not the official national language or the language of global culture and economics, which at this time is English. Bilingualism resolves the problem of maintaining the mother tongue and associated culture while ensuring the student has access to the world's knowledge. According to her Universal Covenant, everybody has the right to:

- Identify with his/her mother tongue(s) and have this identification accepted and respected by others
- Learn the mother tongue(s) fully, orally (when physiologically possible), and in writing
- Profit from education mainly through the medium of their mother tongue(s) and within the state-financed educational system
- Use the mother tongue in most official situations (including schools)

In reference to other languages, the covenant states that those

whose mother tongue is not an official language in the country where s/he is resident. . . [have the right] to become bilingual (or trilingual, if s/he has 2 mother tongues) in the mother tongue(s) and (one of) the official language(s) (according to her own choice).

Additionally, "any change. . . [in] mother tongue. . . [should be] voluntary (includes knowledge of long-term consequences) . . . [and] not imposed."

Applied to the United States, this covenant would mean that students whose mother tongues were not English would have the right to receive instruction in their mother tongues but would not have to exercise that right. In other words, students could choose to be instructed in English. The covenant also guarantees that all children will learn English, the dominant language of the United States. Essentially, students would have the right to a bilingual education if they wanted. Some constitutions of other nations specifically recognize language rights. For instance, the Italian Constitution states, "The Republic shall safeguard linguistic minorities by means of special provisions." The Indian Constitution provides specific protection for minority language rights. The Indian Constitution states:

350. **Facilities for instruction in mother-tongue at primary stage:** It shall be the endeavor of every State and of every local authority within the State to provide adequate facilities for instruction

in the mother-tongue at the primary stage of education to children belonging to linguistic minority groups.

Should the government be required to provide classes in a mother tongue that is spoken by only one or two students in a community? Realistically, the educational rights of minority languages can only be exercised when there is a sufficient number of students speaking a language. This is particularly a problem in a country like the United States with a high number of immigrants. Considering this problem, an international agreement on language rights might state: "Everyone has a right to an education using the medium of their mother tongue within a government-financed school system when the number of students requesting instruction in that mother tongue equals the average number of students in a classroom in that government financed school system."

Of equal importance is learning the dominant or official language of society. Therefore, an addition to the right to learn minority languages might state: "Everyone has the right to learn the dominant or official language of the nation. The government-financed school system will make every effort to ensure that all students are literate in the dominant or official language of the country."

Cultural rights are an important issue for indigenous peoples such as Native Americans. The United Nation's International Labor Office defines indigenous peoples as "tribal peoples in independent countries whose social, cultural and economic conditions distinguish them from other sections of the national community, and whose status is regulated wholly or partially by their own customs or traditions." In addition, the definition includes those groups who identify themselves as indigenous. This definition of indigenous includes, for example, Native Americans and Hawaiians in the United States, Aborigines in Australia, Mayans in Guatemala, Maoris in New Zealand, and Hmongs in Laos. The World Commission on Culture and Development estimates that in 1995, indigenous peoples composed 7 percent of the population of China and India (80 and 65 million, respectively). In the Americas, the largest numbers of indigenous peoples are in Peru (8.6 million) and Mexico (8 million). In Africa, the number is 25 million. The international group Worldwatch estimates that there are at least 300 million indigenous people worldwide and that between 4,000 and 5,000 of the 6,000 world languages are spoken by indigenous peoples. A Declaration of Indigenous Peoples' Rights has been proposed to the United Nations. The declaration asserts, with regard to human rights and development,

That the indigenous peoples have been deprived of their *human rights and fundamental freedoms*, resulting . . . in their colonization and dispossession of their lands, territories, and resources, thus preventing them from exercising, in particular, *their right to development in accordance with their own needs and interests.*

(emphasis in original)

Regarding the right to education, the declaration asserts that indigenous children have a right to education in their own language and according to cultural practices. Article 15 states:

Indigenous children have the right to all levels and forms of education of the State. All indigenous peoples also have this right and the right to establish and control their educational systems and institutions providing education in their own languages, in a manner appropriate to their cultural methods of teaching and learning. Recognition of these rights in the United States would guarantee that Native Americans would have the right to operate their own schools according to the principles of their cultures and using their languages.

GLOBAL RESPONSES TO EDUCATION OF LINGUISTIC AND CULTURAL MINORITIES

Table 7.1 outlines general global policies regarding linguistic and cultural minorities. I presented this outline at a conference at Minzu University, Beijing, in September 2012. The conference focused on multicultural education, which is a concern in China because of its large number of minority cultural groups. Minzu University is the central Chinese university for educating ethnic minorities.

As indicated in "1. Immersion of Children of Minority Cultures into the Dominant Culture and Language of the Nation" of Table 7.1, one possible school policy is immersion of linguistic and cultural minorities into the dominant culture and language of a nation. There would be no attempt by schools to protect minority linguistic and cultural traditions. This could be a planned by national political leaders shared by all citizens and loyal to a national language and culture. Students would be discouraged from speaking their mother tongues. The majority dominant language would be used in all classroom instruction. There would be no instruction in minority languages, history, and culture.

Table 7.1 Global Responses to Schooling Minority Cultures and Languages

---

1. **Immersion of Children of Minority Cultures into the Dominant Culture and Language of the Nation**

  · Classroom instruction is only in the dominant language of the nation
  · No special help in learning the dominant language is provided for linguistic and cultural minority students
  · Minority students are discouraged from speaking their mother tongues
  · Language of the classroom would be the language of the majority or dominant population
  · The curriculum would reflect the history and culture of the majority or dominant population

---

2. **Boarding Schools for Minority Languages and Cultures**

  · Removal of minority student from family and community
  · Students are not allowed to speak minority language at boarding school
  · Students are not allowed to wear traditional clothes or practice traditional culture at boarding school
  · Students are not allowed to practice their traditional religions at boarding school
  · Language and cultural practices of boarding school, including classroom instruction, would be that of the majority or dominant culture and language

---

3. **Planned Assimilation**

  · Special classes and programs to help minority linguistic and cultural students learn the majority or dominant language
  · Bilingual programs to help students learn the majority or dominant language, but would not be used to preserve minority languages and cultures
  · The curriculum would include instruction about other cultures for purpose of maintaining social cohesion, but not for maintaining minority cultural traditions

---

4. **Unity through Diversity**

  · Schools teach minority cultures and languages to cultural and linguistic minority students
  · Classroom instruction using the language of the family
  · The teaching of a shared national culture and language to create national unity
  · Curriculum materials that include a variety of cultural perspectives

---

5. **Religious Schools**

  · Parents given choice of religious school at government expense
  · Each religious school would reflect the culture and language of the local members of that religion

---

6. **Cultural Autonomy and Control**

  · Each cultural group would determine the content and methods of instruction
  · Each cultural group would determine the language of instruction

---

7. **Cosmopolitanism**

  · Education for global citizenship
  · Educated to be able to move easily among the world's peoples
  · Educated to understand differences between world's languages and cultures
  · Allegiance to humanity and not a particular nation

In "2. Boarding Schools for Minority Languages and Cultures" of Table 7.1, minority students are removed from their families and communities and placed in boarding schools where they are not allowed to speak their family language, wear traditional dress, or practice traditional cultures and religions. The language and teaching methods of the classroom would be the dominant national language and teaching methods preferred by the dominant culture. By isolating children from their families and communities, it is considered easier to replace minority cultures and languages with the dominant culture and language.

In "3. Planned Assimilation" of Table 7.1, government schools would provide special programs and classes to help minority cultures assimilate to the dominant culture and learn the dominant language. There would be no instruction in minority languages and cultures. Students would be assisted in learning the dominant language, which might include bilingual education programs. These bilingual programs would *not* be for the purpose of preserving minority languages and cultures. The programs would only assist students in learning the dominant national language. The curriculum would include instruction about other cultures to reduce tensions between cultural groups.

Teaching about other cultures is not the same as trying to maintain different cultures. The purpose would not be to preserve minority cultures but rather to maintain social cohesion and reduce social tensions. The goal would be to maintain the dominant position of the majority culture and language.

Under "4. Unity through Diversity" of Table 7.1, schools would maintain minority cultures and languages while at the same time creating unity through a shared national culture and language. Bilingual education would be for the purpose of maintaining minority languages while also teaching the dominant language. Parents might have the choice of sending their children to schools where the family's mother tongue is used in classroom instruction. Schools using the mother tongue of the parents for instruction would center the curriculum on the cultural background of the students. There would be required instruction in the national language and culture, including the country's history, government, and cultures. This approach might be called unity through diversity where everyone feels united by sharing a learned national language and an understanding of the nation's attempt to maintain a multicultural society.

Another approach, "5. Religious Schools" in Table 7.1, is government support of religious schools. Parents have a choice to send their children to a particular religious school. In a nation with Buddhist, Christian, Hindu, and Muslim populations, one could assume the cultural traditions of the population are reflected in their religious practices. Choice of school based on religion might be a means of ensuring a multicultural society. Of course, language is still an issue. Would each religious school use the language of its particular religious culture for instruction? The answer is dependent on the circumstances of the various religions and whether or not there are cultural and language differences within each religious group.

In "6. Cultural Autonomy and Control" of Table 7.1, each cultural group controls their own schools and uses their own language in classroom instruction and the traditional educational methods of their culture. This is the United Nations' proposal for protecting the rights of indigenous peoples. The school curriculum would reflect the culture of the group in control and would make every effort to maintain cultural traditions including religious traditions. In this scenario, the goal of the educational system is to maintain a multicultural and multilingual society.

Embodied in some of these scenarios is the idea of choice, such as parents choosing to send their children to a school that teaches in their mother tongue or to one associated with their religious beliefs. Should educational choice be financially supported by the government? In most cases choices can only be meaningful if parents have the economic freedom to send their child to a particular type of school. Financed by the government, educational choice might be one way for schooling to maintain multilingual and multicultural societies.

There is also the issue of control. Should national governments control the content of instruction, or should that be left to the school or local community? On the other hand, should the religious community associated with the school determine the curriculum?

Another option is "7. Cosmopolitanism" of Table 7.1. Rather than educating for submission to the will of a nation, students might be educated as global citizens where they learn to move easily among the world's peoples with an acceptance of differences in cultures and languages. In this case, education would not attempt to ensure allegiance to a particular nation-state but would try to create an allegiance to humanity and a concern for the welfare of all people.

PRESIDENT TRUMP AND AMERICA FIRST

President Donald Trump and the 2016 Republican platform advocated economic and cultural nationalism and the idea of American exceptionalism. This approach emphasized the preservation of traditional American culture over changes that might be caused by globalization and immigration. The preamble to the 2016 Republican platform states the theme of American exceptionalism:

We believe in American exceptionalism.

We believe the United States of America is
unlike any other nation on earth.

We believe America is exceptional because of
our historic role—first as refuge, then as defender,
and now as exemplar of liberty for the world to see. . .

We believe political freedom and economic
freedoms Every time we sing, "God Bless America," we are asking for help. We ask for divine help that our country can fulfill its
promise. We earn that help by recommitting ourselves to the ideas
and ideals that are the true greatness of America.

This strong statement of patriotism and American exceptionalism
was accompanied by an English-only policy. The 2016 Republican platform stated: "To ensure that all students have access to the mainstream
of American life, we support the English First approach and oppose
divisive programs that limit students' ability to advance in American
society."

CONCLUSION

The struggle over issues of language and culture will continue as dominated
groups struggle for equality of opportunity and as new immigrant groups
adjust to American society. On a global scale, issues of multicultural, ethnocentric, bicultural, and bilingual education will become increasingly
important with the development of a global economy and the internation-
alization of the labor force. The United States is not the only country confronting these issues. Many European countries have begun multicultural
education programs because of the influx of foreign workers.

In the United States, conflict will continue between those who want
to maintain the supremacy of English and European American traditions and dominated cultures whose members want to protect and
maintain their cultural traditions. Many Native Americans, African
Americans, and Hispanics reject the image of European American culture at the head of a dinner table ruling over other cultures. In addition,
many immigrant groups might not be willing to give up their cultural
traditions to a European American model. But whatever the conclusion
of this conflict, American public schools will never be the same after
the impact of the cultural and language demands of dominated groups
and after the adjustment of educational programs to meet the needs of
new immigrants.

The discussion of multiculturalism generates the following set of questions:

- Should public schools teach a common culture to all students?
- Should that common culture be based on a Eurocentric culture?
- Should English be the official language of the United States?
- Should students have the right to learn their mother tongue and the dominant language?
- Should students have the right to receive instruction in their own culture?
- Should the major goal of instruction about different cultures be the teaching of appreciation of other cultures?
- Should public schools teach non-Eurocentric cultural traditions to maintain those cultural traditions?
- Should multicultural education attempt to change the dominant culture by incorporating values from other cultures?

SUGGESTED READINGS AND WORKS CITED IN CHAPTER

Advisory Board for the President's Initiative on Race. *One America in the 21st Century: Forging a New Future.* Washington, DC: U.S. Government Printing Office, 1998. Report predicting future of race relations in the twenty-first century.

Anyon, Jean. *Ghetto Schooling: Political Economy of Urban Educational Reform.* New York: Teachers College Press, 1997. This book demonstrates how the combination of politics and economics creates segregated and underfunded urban schools.

Asante, Molefi Kete. *Afrocentricity.* Trenton, NJ: Africa World Press, Inc., 1988. This is an important discussion of the philosophy of Afrocentricity.

Banks, James. "Multicultural Education: Historical Development, Dimensions, and Practice." In *Review of Research in Education,* edited by Linda Darling-Hammond. Washington, DC: American Educational Research Association, 1993, pp. 3–50. This article is an excellent introduction to the development of the field of multicultural education.

Common Core State Standards Initiative. *Common Core State Standards for English Language Arts & Literacy in History/Social Studies, Science, and Technical Subjects.* www.core standards.org/wp-content/uploads/ELA_Standards.pdf. These standards standardize the cultural perspective of the classroom.

Delpit, Lisa. *Other People's Children: Cultural Conflict in the Classroom.* New York: New Press, 1995. Delpit provides a strong argument for utilizing a student's culture to prepare him/her for success in the economic power structure of the United States.

Derman-Sparks, Louise, and Julie Olsen Edwards. *Anti-Bias Education for Young Children and Ourselves.* Washington, DC: National Association for the Education of Young Children, 2010. This book describes the National Association of Young Children's anti-bias curriculum.

Estrich, Susan. "For Girls' Schools and Women's Colleges, Separate Is Better." *The New York Times Magazine* (May 22, 1994), p. 39. Estrich argues against coeducation.

"Exit Polls on the June 2nd Vote on Proposition 227." *Los Angeles Times/Washington Edition* (June 4, 1998). www.latimes.com. Results of voting on bilingual issue in California are provided.

Fedullo, Mick. *Light of the Feather: Pathways Through Contemporary Indian America.* New York: William Morrow, 1992. Fedullo provides a beautiful description of the development of bicultural education among Native Americans.

Global Commission on International Migration. *Migration in an Interconnected World: New Directions for Action.* Geneva: Global Commission on International Migration, 2005. This report provides information of the global migration of the world's peoples.

Hacker, Andrew. *Two Nations: Black and White, Separate, Hostile, Unequal.* New York: Scribner's, 1992. This is a study of racial divisions in the United States.

Heitin, Liana. "Science Teachers Favor Males in Class, Study Finds." *Education Week* (March 27, 2014). http://blogs.edweek.org/edweek/curriculum/2014/03/study_science_teachers_ inadver.html?qs=gender+bias. This is a report of a study that shows continuing bias against females in science courses.

Heller, Carol, and Joseph Hawkins. "Teaching Tolerance: Notes from the Front Line." *Teachers College Record* (Spring 1994), pp. 1–30. A history and description of the Teaching Tolerance project is presented.

Ignatiev, N., and John Garvey. *Race Traitor.* New York: Routledge, 1996. This important book for antiracist education is based on the idea of the importance of deconstructing and reconstructing "whiteness."

Igoa, Cristina. *The Inner World of the Immigrant Child.* Mahwah, NJ: Lawrence Erlbaum, 1995. This is an invaluable guide to instructing immigrant children and dealing with their educational and psychological problems.

Jones, James. *Prejudice and Racism.* New York: McGraw-Hill, 1996. This is an excellent introduction to the psychology of racism.

Kunjufu, Jawanza. *Countering the Conspiracy to Destroy Black Boys.* Chicago: African American Images, 1985. This book provides a strong argument for the necessity of an Afrocentric curriculum.

———. *To Be Popular or Smart: The Black Peer Group.* Chicago: African American Images, 1988. This is a discussion of the attitudes of African American youth regarding education.

———. *SETCLAE: Self-Esteem Through Culture Leads to Academic Excellence.* Chicago: African American Images, 1991. This is a model Afrocentric curriculum.

Lamar, Jake. *Bourgeois Blues: An American Memoir.* New York: Penguin, 1992. This powerful contemporary autobiography details the racism encountered by an upper-middle-class African American.

Mosatche, Harriet S., Susan Matloff-Nieves, Linda Kekelis, and Elizabeth K. Lawner. "Effective STEM Courses for Adolescent Girls." *ERIC* (2013). http://files.eric.ed.gov/fulltext/ EJ1003839.pdf. Explores three programs designed to encourage female students in STEM courses.

Nieto, Sonia. *Affirming Diversity: The Sociopolitical Context of Multicultural Education.* White Plains, NY: Longman, 1992. This is a good introduction to issues in multicultural education.

Nisbett, Richard E. *The Geography of Thought: How Asians and Westerners Think Differently . . . and Why.* New York: Free Press, 2003. This is the pioneer study contrasting different ways of seeing and knowing the world.

Ogbu, John. "Class Stratification, Racial Stratification, and Schooling." In *Class, Race, & Gender in American Education,* edited by Lois Weis. Albany: State University of New York Press, 1988, pp. 163–183. In this article, Ogbu outlines his basic theory for the development of resistance to schooling among dominated cultures in the United States.

Oyerman, Daphna, Izumi Sakamoto, and Armand Lauffer. "Cultural Accommodation: Hybridity and the Framing of Social Obligation." *Journal of Personality and Social Psychology,* Vol. 74 (1998), pp. 1606–1616. This article explains the concept of cultural hybridity as related to different beliefs about social obligations.

Perry, Mark. "2013 SAT Test Results Show That a Huge Math Gender Gap Persists with a 32-Point Advantage for High School Boys." *American Enterprise Institute 2013.* www.aei. org/publication/2013-sat-test-results-show-that-a-huge-math-gender-gap-persists-with-a- 32-point-advantage-for-high-school-boys/. Article provides information on the continuing low scores of females on the SAT math test.

Perry, Pamela. *Shades of White: White Kids and Racial Identities in High School*. Durham, NC: Duke University Press, 2002. Perry performs an important study of how white high school students form their racial identities.

Porter, Rosalie Pedalino. *Forked Tongue: The Politics of Bilingual Education*. New York: Basic Books, 1990. Porter attacks maintenance bilingual education programs. The book is a good introduction to the controversy surrounding bilingual education.

Public Law 107-110, 107th Congress, January 8, 2002 [H.R. 1]. *No Child Left Behind Act of 2001*. Washington, DC: U.S. Government Printing Office, 2002. This federal legislation contains the English Acquisition, Language Enhancement, and Academic Achievement Act, which overturns the 1968 Bilingual Education Act.

Republican Platform 2016. https://gop.com/platform/ on November 23, 2016. Platform stresses American exceptionalism and America First doctrines.

Rodriguez, Richard. *Hunger of Memory: The Education of Richard Rodriguez*. New York: Bantam Books, 1982. This is an important autobiography of the emotional and social struggles of a successful Mexican American student.

Sadker, Myra, and David Sadker. *Failing at Fairness: How America's Schools Cheat Girls*. New York: Scribner's, 1995. This is the landmark study on the treatment of women in American schools.

San Miguel, Guadalupe, Jr. *"Let All of Them Take Heed": Mexican Americans and the Campaign for Education Equality in Texas, 1910–1981*. Austin: University of Texas Press, 1987. This is a landmark book on the Mexican American struggle for equality of education.

Skutnabb-Kangas, Tove. *Linguistic Genocide in Education or Worldwide Diversity and Human Rights?* Mahwah, NJ: Lawrence Erlbaum, 2000. This publication is the most comprehensive study of language rights issues.

Spring, Joel. *Education and the Rise of the Global Economy*. Mahwah, NJ: Lawrence Erlbaum, 1998. This book describes the process of globalization of education through colonialism and current economic policies.

———. *Globalization and Educational Rights: An Intercivilizational Analysis*. Mahwah, NJ: Lawrence Erlbaum, 2000. This book discusses educational rights in the context of Confucian, Muslim, Hindu, and Western civilizations and as provided for in the constitutions of the world's nations. The book offers a statement of educational rights that could be included in national constitutions.

———. *The Universal Right to Education: Justification, Definition, and Guidelines*. Mahwah, NJ: Lawrence Erlbaum, 2000. This book provides a justification for the universal right to education provided by the Universal Declaration of Human Rights. The book discusses cultural, lingual, and child rights and provides examples of human rights teaching.

Suh, Eunkook. "Self, the Hyphen Between Culture and Subjective Well-Being." In *Culture and Subjective Well-Being*, edited by Ed Diener, and Eunkook M. Suh. Cambridge, MA: MIT Press, 2000. This article describes the differences between collectivist and individualist societies, particularly regarding a sense of subjective well-being.

Tatum, Beverly Daniel. *Why Are All the Black Kids Sitting Together in the Cafeteria? A Psychologist Explains the Development of Racial Identity*. New York: Basic Books, 1997. This landmark book on antiracist education discusses methods of creating positive antiracist models for white students.

Teaching Tolerance. *"Perspectives for a Diverse America: A K-12 Literacy Based Anti-Bias Curriculum." A Project of the Southern Poverty Law Center*. http://perspectives.tolerance.org/. This is an anti-bias curriculum by a well-respected organization.

Trueba, Henry, et al. *Myth or Reality: Adaptative Strategies of Asian-Americans in California*. New York: Falmer Press, 1993. This is a study of Asian American adjustments to social life in California.

United Nations. *"World Population Prospects: The 2017 Revision." Department of Economic and Social Affairs: Population Division*. New York: United Nations, 2017. This document provides statistics on world migration.

PART 2

POWER AND CONTROL IN AMERICAN EDUCATION

CHAPTER 8

Local Control, Choice, Charter Schools, and Home Schooling

This chapter examines the complicated question: Who controls American education? If schools are considered a major disseminator of knowledge to children and youth, the bigger question is: Who decides what knowledge is of most worth to teach to students? These questions are directly linked to the goals of education discussed in Chapters 1 to 4. For instance, take the goal of developing human capital to ensure the United States remains competitive in the global economy. Who decides if this should be the goal of schools? Who decides what should be taught to attain this goal? Who decides how teachers should teach the knowledge considered necessary for educating workers for the global workforce?

There are several ways political control is exercised over schools. One way is through voting for representatives in the federal and state governments that legislate education policies. The second is through voting for local school boards. A third way is through parents voting with their feet by deciding to exercise choice regarding what school their children attend or if they want to keep their children out of school and educate them at home.

The first section of this chapter, "The Education Chair," asks a central question regarding the control of education: Who should decide what knowledge should be taught to public-school students? Should it be national politicians, federal administrators, state politicians, state administrators, local school boards, teachers, or parents? This question is important in light of recent debates about the teaching of evolution in science courses and sexual abstinence education. Who should decide whether a student should learn evolutionary theory and/or alternative theories in science courses? Who should decide the content of instruction regarding birth control instruction and/or abstinence education?

The second section, on local school boards, is followed by a discussion of the choice plans embodied in the federal legislation No Child Left

Behind. This legislation not only impacts local control but also encourages school choice, charter schools, and for-profit education. After discussing the basic provisions of No Child Left Behind, I discuss school choice, charter schools, home schooling, and for-profit education.

THE EDUCATION CHAIR

One way of thinking about the problem of control is to imagine yourself sitting in what I will call the education chair. Imagine that at a flick of a lever this chair has the power to shape your morality, to control your behavior, and to teach you any subject. This education chair can be considered a public school that works. After all, the goals of public schooling include moral instruction, shaping behavior, and transmitting knowledge.

Now the question is: Who should control this education chair? In other words, who should decide your morality, behavior, and knowledge? You? Your parents? Your professor of education? Elected officials? How you answer this question will reflect the political values you have regarding the control of public schools.

Currently, the debate over who should control education has ranged from the business community to religious organizations to minority parents. Many groups have a stake in the outcomes of public schooling. The business community wants graduates with knowledge and behaviors that conform to its needs. Some religious organizations want schools to teach their versions of morality. In fact, a major controversy in recent years has involved fundamentalist Protestant churches accusing the public schools of teaching a morality that is destructive to their religious principles. In a similar manner, minority parents complain that public schools are damaging to their children because they teach the culture and values of the white elite. Understanding the concept of representation is important for answering the question of who should control American education. The United States is primarily composed of representative forms of government; that is, people elect government officials to represent them on school boards, in state legislatures, and in Congress. In only a few situations, such as voting on local property taxes, are decisions made by a direct vote.

While reading this chapter, you should keep in mind the following questions:

- Who should decide what knowledge should be taught in public schools?
- Do you think public schools should let parents decide what should be taught to their children?
- Should parents receive government funding to send their children to a private secular school, a religious school, or a for-profit school?

- Do you think the government should finance only parental choice of public schools?
- Should state charter school laws finance private secular schools, religious schools, or for-profit schools?

SCHOOL BOARDS

Traditionally, local communities exercise control over public schools by electing representatives to local school boards. In turn, the school board appoints the superintendent of schools who functions as the chief executive officer of the school district. Usually the superintendent of schools works out of the central office of the school district. School principals report directly to the central office and the superintendent.

This traditional district organization is criticized for its lack of responsiveness to the desires of parents. School board members are criticized for not representing the interests of the parents. The central office and superintendent are criticized for being bureaucratic barriers to any real change in the school district. (As I discuss later in this chapter, home schooling, school choice, and charter schools are promoted as giving power to parents when faced with unrepresentative school boards and an entrenched bureaucratic structure in the central office.)

Boards of education are criticized for being dominated by white members despite the fact that in 2014, as discussed in Chapter 6, for the first time the "nonwhite" population of U.S. public schools exceeded the number of whites. However, Frederick Hess and Olivia Meeks in *School Boards Circa 2010: Governance in the Accountability Era* found, as noted in Table 8.1, 80.7 percent of school board members are white while 12.3% are African American and 3.1% are Hispanic. There are more males on school boards (56%) than females (44%), as indicated in Table 8.2. Frederick Hess and Olivia Meeks conclude, as indicated in Tables 8.3 through 8.5:

> On the whole, board members are substantially better educated than the general adult population. Nearly three-fourths of board members have at least a bachelor's degree, far exceeding the 29.5 percent of American adults over age 25 who hold at least a B.A. In large districts, 85 percent of board members have at least a B.A., and more than half report that they have earned an advanced degree of some kind. Politically, a plurality of board members place themselves in the center of the ideological spectrum. When asked to identify their general political views, 47.3 percent respond as moderates, 32.3 percent as conservatives, and 20.4 percent as liberals.

Table 8.1 Race/Ethnicity of U.S. School Board Members

White	80.7
African American	12.3
Hispanic	3.1
Asian	7.0
Native Hawaiian or other Pacific Islander	1.0
American Indian or Alaska Native	10
Other	1.7

Source: Frederick Hess and Olivia Meeks, *School Boards Circa 2010: Governance in the Accountability Era*, National School Boards Association, 2010, p. 38. Retrieved from www.nsba.org/sites/default/files/SBcirca2010_WEB.pdfon November 11, 2014.

Table 8.2 Gender Composition of U.S. School Boards

Male	56%
Female	44%

Source: Frederick Hess and Olivia Meeks, *School Boards Circa 2010: Governance in the Accountability Era*, National School Boards Association, 2010, p. 38. Retrieved from www.nsba.org/sites/default/files/SBcirca2010_WEB.pdf on November 11, 2014.

Table 8.3 Annual Household Incomes of U.S. School Board Members

Less than $25,000	1.6%
$25,000—$49,999	8.1
$50,000-$99,999	41.8
$100,000-$200,000	39.1
More than $200,000	9.5

Source: Frederick Hess and Olivia Meeks, *School Boards Circa 2010: Governance in the Accountability Era*, National School Boards Association, 2010, p. 40. Retrieved from www.nsba.org/sites/default/files/SBcirca2010_WEB.pdf on November 11, 2014.

Table 8.4 Educational Attainment of U.S. School Board Members

Did not graduate high school	0.1%
High school graduate or GED	5.1
Some college or other postsecondary education/training	20.6
Bachelor's degree	27.7
Advanced degree	38.3

Source: Frederick Hess and Olivia Meeks, *School Boards Circa 2010: Governance in the Accountability Era*, National School Boards Association, 2010, p. 40. Retrieved from www.nsba.org/sites/default/files/SBcirca2010_WEB.pdf on November 11, 2014.

Table 8.5 General Political Philosophy of School Board Members

Political Philosophy	Percentage of School Board Members (%)
Liberal	20.3
Moderate	49.3
Conservative	30.3

Source: Frederick Hess and Olivia Meeks, *School Boards Circa 2010: Governance in the Accountability Era*, National School Boards Association, 2010, p. 41. Retrieved from www.nsba.org/sites/default/files/SBcirca2010_WEB.pdf on November 11, 2014.

SCHOOL CHOICE

As mentioned in previous chapters, the 2016 Republican platform and President Donald Trump strongly support school choice and alternative ways of financing schools.

> We support options for learning, including homeschooling, career and technical education, private or parochial schools, magnet schools, charter schools, online learning, and early-college high schools. We especially support the innovative financing mechanisms that make options available to all children: education savings accounts (ESAs), vouchers, and tuition tax credits.

Prior to the 2016 national elections, Arianna Prothero's blog for *Education Week* headlined "GOP Leaders in Congress Make School Choice Top Priority." School choice has been widely debated since the 1950s when economist Milton Friedman declared public schools monopolies and suggested that competition would break the monopoly and improve quality. Since then charter schools have moved to the forefront in choice discussions.

School choice gives parents the power to vote with their feet by allowing them to select a school for their children. However, there have been proposed a variety of school choice plans. Some involve parental choice of only public schools while others include private schools. Those advocating parental choice of public or private schools often include the use of vouchers. Parents take a voucher from the government to the school and the school is reimbursed. Charter schools, now the biggest factor in choice plans, will be discussed in another section of this chapter.

The following is a list of different types of choice plans:

1. *Public-School Choice:* Under this type of choice plan, parents of students are free to choose any public school in their district or in the state. Traditionally, students are assigned to schools in their districts,

and if they wish to attend school in another district, then they are often required to pay tuition.

a. Types of public-school choice plans

 i. Open enrollment among schools in a district or among districts

 ii. Magnet schools designed to attract students and integrate schools; some restrictions are made to balance enrollment.

 iii. Alternative schools within a school district

 iv. Public charter schools (described later in this chapter)

2. *Public-Private Choice:* Parents of students can choose between a public or private school with the tuition at the private school being paid for by a government or privately issued voucher. Traditionally, students have the choice of private and public schools without government support. Government support of private school choice, some argue, provides the opportunity for children from low-income families to attend private schools.

3. *Failing-School Choice:* Under No Child Left Behind, parents of students in schools not making adequate yearly progress can choose another school for their children. The policies surrounding this choice plan are discussed in the following section of this chapter: "National Public-School Choice Plan: No Child Left Behind Act of 2001."

4. *Low-Income Private School Vouchers:* Taxpayer dollars are used to pay for all or part of the cost for students from low-income families to attend private, often religious, schools.

The original proposal by economist Milton Friedman is very similar to the choice provisions of the No Child Left Behind Act of 2001. Both Friedman's proposal and recent legislation provide parents with children in low-performing schools the opportunity to send their children to another public school. Friedman's original proposal called for the government to give parents monetary vouchers that could be used to purchase an education for their children at any school. Parents would give the vouchers to the school that enrolled their child. The school would then turn over the voucher to the government for reimbursement. Vouchers are another method for distributing tax dollars to schools. As a free-market economist, Friedman blamed the poor quality of public schools on the lack of competition. Also, he argued that impoverished parents are often trapped in poor school systems because they cannot afford to move to the school districts with better schools.

The free-market aspects of Friedman's plan appealed to many school reformers. The assumption of free-market economics is that competition will produce the best products. Advocates argue that if parents can choose between schools, the schools will be forced to improve to remain competitive. Schools are like any other product in the marketplace. If a large number of parents don't choose a particular school, that school would be forced to either change or shut down. If the school that is least attractive to parents wants to survive, it will probably model itself after a school that is attractive to parents or create an entirely new educational package. Imagine the production of cars: If no one buys a particular car model, the company must either discontinue the model or improve it.

Of course, schools differ from automobiles in that they are produced by the government and by private groups. The mix of public and private schools adds another dimension to choice plans.

- Should government issued vouchers be redeemed only at public schools?
- Or should government issued vouchers be redeemed at both public and private schools?

Many supporters of religious schooling and free-market advocates support the public-private model of choice. Supporters of private Catholic schools argued from the nineteenth century that it is unfair for them to pay for the education of public-school students while paying for their children to attend a religious school. In addition, Catholics and Protestant fundamentalists complain that the moral values taught in public schools are destructive to the values of Christianity and that their only choice is to send their children to private religious schools. The rapid growth of private Catholic schools occurred in the nineteenth and early twentieth century, while privately operated fundamentalist Protestant schools grew rapidly in the latter half of the twentieth century.

SCHOOL CHOICE AND RELIGION

Government support of religious schools is a contentious issue regarding school choice. Should parents be allowed to choose a religious education for their children at government expense? In 2002, the U.S. Supreme Court issued a landmark decision on school vouchers and religious schools. In *Zelman v. Simmons-Harris*, the primary issue was the use of government-funded vouchers by students to attend schools with religious affiliations. Was the use of these government vouchers a violation of the Establishment Clause ("Congress shall make no law respecting an establishment of religion") of the First Amendment?

The state of Ohio's Pilot Project Scholarship Program provides tuition aid vouchers to families residing in the Cleveland City school district. These vouchers can be used to attend any accredited private school or public schools in other school districts adjacent to the Cleveland City school district. The Establishment Clause became an issue because, as stated in the U.S. Supreme Court decision, "82% of the participating private schools had a religious affiliation, none of the adjacent public schools [in other school districts] participated, and 96% of the students participating in the scholarship program were enrolled in religiously affiliated schools." Clearly, religious schools were receiving the bulk of the voucher money provided under the Pilot Project Scholarship Program.

In the decision regarding Ohio's Pilot Project Scholarship Program, the U.S. Supreme Court relied on a previous decision, *Mueller v. Allen* (1983), which dealt with a Minnesota law that allowed state taxpayers to take deductions from gross income for expenses incurred for "tuition, textbooks, and transportation" for dependents attending elementary and secondary schools. The majority of beneficiaries (96 percent) of the Minnesota law were parents of children attending religious schools. In *Mueller*, the U.S. Supreme Court argued that the law did not violate the Constitution because "the deduction is available for educational expenses incurred by all parents, including those whose children attend public schools and those whose children attend nonsectarian private schools or sectarian private schools." The court reasoned that the intent of the law was primarily secular, it did not advance religion, and it did not cause an excessive entanglement between the government and religion.

What about the fact that under both the Minnesota and Ohio laws the majority of the government benefits went to parents sending their children to religious schools? Wasn't this a violation of the Establishment Clause? No, the U.S. Supreme Court answered, because the intent of the law was secular. The fact that the majority of benefits went to religious institutions was the result of the choices made by parents. In the words of the U.S. Supreme Court decision regarding Ohio's Pilot Project Scholarship Program, "The amount of government aid channeled to religious institutions by individual aid recipients was not relevant to the constitutional inquiry."

Based on the preceding reasoning, the court concluded that Ohio's Pilot Project Scholarship Program was not a violation of the Establishment Clause. However, the decision left many questions unanswered. In reality, Cleveland parents were limited in choice to private schools because none of the surrounding school districts were willing to participate in the program. This fact highlights efforts by suburban school districts to protect their educational advantages.

The guiding principle for court decisions regarding government support of education and religion is a 1971 U.S. Supreme Court case, *Lemon v. Kurzman*, which established a three-part test for determining the constitutionality of government programs that benefit religion. The case involved laws in Rhode Island and Pennsylvania that provided salary supplements to teachers in private religious schools. Under the *Lemon* test, government aid to religious schools:

- Must have a secular purpose
- Must not inhibit or advance religion
- Must not cause excessive entanglement of government in religion

In another indirect way of funding religious schools, the U.S. Supreme Court upheld in 2011 an Arizona law allowing taxpayers to receive a tax credit of $500 (or $1,000 for married couples) on state income-tax returns for contributions to "school tuition organizations," or STOs. In turn these STOs can give grants to students to attend religious or other schools. In 2008, the overwhelming amount of money ($54 million) went to religious schools. Writing for the majority, Justice Anthony M. Kennedy argued:

> Private citizens create private [school tuition organizations]; STOs choose beneficiary schools; and taxpayers then contribute to STOs. While the state, at the outset, affords the opportunity to create and contribute to an STO, the tax-credit system is implemented by private action and with no state intervention. Objecting taxpayers know that their fellow citizens, not the state, decide to contribute and in fact make the contribution. These considerations prevent any injury the objectors may suffer from being fairly traceable to the government.

In 2013, the Indiana State Supreme Court ruled in favor of a state voucher law that, unlike most states, was not limited to low-income students. A key issue was the use of state vouchers at private religious schools. Reflecting previous court decisions based on the child benefit theory, *Education Week* reporter Alyssa Morones reported the court's decision as "that the law does not violate the Indiana Constitution's guarantee of religious freedom, nor does it violate a ban on using state funds for religious institutions. *Rather, the primary benefits of the program went to parents by giving them a choice in their children's education*" (author's emphasis).

NATIONAL PUBLIC-SCHOOL CHOICE PLAN: NO CHILD LEFT BEHIND ACT OF 2001

The No Child Left Behind Act requires local school districts to implement a public-school choice plan for parents with children in unsafe and/or failing schools. The U.S. Department of Education in its guide *Choice Provisions in No Child Left Behind* provides that students in unsafe situations be allowed to transfer to other, safer public schools. Transfers must be allowed for two reasons: (1) when a school is determined to be "persistently dangerous" and (2) when a student becomes the victim of a violent crime at a school.

The Unsafe Schools Choice Option also requires states to determine "persistently dangerous" schools by using objective criteria such as the number of times a firearm has been brought into a school, the number of fights, and so on within the current or most recent school year. Furthermore, if a student becomes the victim of a violent criminal offense at school, the local education authority (LEA) must allow the student the choice to transfer to another public school.

Parents of students in failing schools are given the option of sending their children to another school in the same school district. A *failing school* is defined as one that does not make adequate yearly progress (AYP). According to the U.S. Department of Education, a school or district achieves AYP when each group of students meets or exceeds the statewide annual objective. Further, for each group, 95 percent of students enrolled must participate in the assessments on which AYP is based.

Schools not achieving AYP are given the time line shown in Table 8.6 for school improvement. If the school fails to make adequate yearly progress two years in a row, in the following year the school must be provided with technical assistance for improvement and parents must be allowed the choice of another public school within the same public-school district. In the next year, supplemental educational services such as tutoring must be provided to students along with technical assistance and public-school choice. It should be noted that supplemental educational services can be from for-profit organizations.

Table 8.6 Improvement Time Line for Schools Not Making Adequate Yearly Progress

Year	Assessment	Action Taken
1	Baseline established for measuring yearly progress	
2	Fail to make adequate yearly progress	
3	Fail to make adequate yearly progress	
4	First year of school improvement	Technical assistance; public-school choice
5	Second year of school improvement	Technical assistance; public-school choice; supplemental educational services

Source: Adapted from Cheri Pierson Yecke and Laura O. Lazo, "Sample School Timeline," in *Choice Provisions in No Child Left Behind* (Washington, DC: U.S. Department of Education, 2002).

According to the U.S. Department of Education, any school offered as a choice option must have higher academic performance than the school of origin and may not be identified for improvement. That is, students may not transfer to any schools that have been identified for improvement, corrective action, or the planning year of restructuring or that have been identified by the state as persistently dangerous. In addition, the choice option can include public charter schools within the boundaries of the local education authorities. However, local education authorities cannot disregard entrance requirements, such as evidence of specific academic ability or other skills, when identifying transfer options for students. For example, students wishing to transfer to a fine arts magnet school or to a school for gifted students would still need to meet the requirements to attend those schools.

Finally, what if no schools are available for choice by parents whose children are in unsafe schools or schools not making adequate yearly progress? Parents must be offered the option of supplemental services, such as tutoring, and/or the school system can make a cooperative agreement with another school district to receive choice students.

CHARTER SCHOOLS

Charter schools bypass the control of local school boards and their educational bureaucracies. In recent years both Democratic and Republican national leaders have advocated an expansion of charter schools. The idea was first proposed by educator Ray Budde in the 1970s and then promoted by American Federation of Teachers (AFT) president Albert Shanker in the 1990s. Minnesota and California had the first charter school laws in 1991 and 1992, respectively.

What is a charter school? The No Child Left Behind Act defines a charter school as:

(1) CHARTER SCHOOL.—The term "charter school" means a public school that—

    (A) in accordance with a specific State statute authorizing the granting of charters to schools, is exempt from significant State or local rules that inhibit the flexible operation and management of public schools, but not from any rules relating to the other requirements of this paragraph;

    (B) is created by a developer as a public school, or is adapted by a developer from an existing public school, and is operated under public supervision and direction;

(C) operates in pursuit of a specific set of educational objectives determined by the school's developer and agreed to by the authorized public chartering agency;

(D) provides a program of elementary or secondary education, or both;

(E) is nonsectarian in its programs, admissions policies, employment practices, and all other operations, and is not affiliated with a sectarian school or religious institution;

(F) does not charge tuition;

(G) complies with the Age Discrimination Act of 1975, title VI of the Civil Rights Act of 1964, title IX of the Education Amendments of 1972, section 504 of the Rehabilitation Act of 1973, and part B of the Individuals with Disabilities Education Act;

(H) is a school to which parents choose to send their children, and that admits students on the basis of a lottery, if more students apply for admission than can be accommodated;

(I) agrees to comply with the same Federal and State audit requirements as do other elementary schools and secondary schools in the State, unless such requirements are specifically waived for the purpose of this program.

As stated in the prior definition, charter schools are public schools. They are different from regular public schools in that they are, as stated in section (A), "exempt from significant State or local rules." This exemption is supposed to foster innovative teaching, curriculum, and school organization. Also, as stated in section (B), a charter school can be developed as a new public school or created from "an existing public school." According to federal legislation, as stated in section (F), they cannot charge tuition. Charter schools, per sections (E) and (G), cannot be affiliated with a religious institution, and they cannot discriminate on the basis of age, race, gender, religion, ethnic origin, or disability. In addition, according to section (L), which is not shown here, charter school students must take any state-required tests.

Some states allow a variety of agencies to charter schools, while others allow only a single state agency to grant charters. In some states only public schools are allowed to convert to charter schools, whereas in other states the establishment of new schools is also allowed. States vary in their requirements for charter school compliance with state education regulations. Most states have granted automatic waivers to most of the state education code, but in a few states, charter schools must follow most of the state education code.

While chartered by state governments, the federal government has supported the expansion of charter schools through No Child Left Behind and later by President Barack Obama's program Race to the Top. The U.S. Department of Education has officially defined a successful charter school in its report titled *Successful Charter Schools*, which states:

> The promise charter schools hold for public school innovation and reform lies in an unprecedented combination of freedom and accountability. Underwritten with public funds but run independently, charter schools are free from a range of state laws and district policies stipulating what and how they teach, where they can spend their money, and who they can hire and fire. In return, they are held strictly accountable for their academic and financial performance.

What is the general mission of charter schools? The National Alliance for Public Charter Schools uses a human capital economic argument as discussed in Chapter 4 to highlight what they consider to be the importance of the charter school movement:

> In today's global economy, students are no longer competing against just local peers for positions in higher education and the workforce. They are competing with students across the globe. More than ever, it is critical that our K–12 public education system provide our students with an internationally rigorous education.

According to the National Center for Education Statistics report *The Condition of Education 2018*, as indicated in Table 8.7:

> In school year 2015–16, over two-thirds of traditional public schools (69 percent) were elementary schools, compared to 56 percent of public charter schools. The percentages of traditional public and public charter schools that were secondary schools were similar (25 and 23 percent, respectively).

Table 8.7 Percentage Distribution of Traditional Public Schools and Public Charter Schools, by School Level: School Year 2015–2016

Percentage of traditional schools that were elementary schools	Percentage of charter schools that were elementary schools	Percentage of traditional schools that were secondary schools	Percentage of charter schools that were secondary schools
69%	56%	25%	23%

Adapted from National Center for Education Statistics, *The Condition of Education 2018* (Washington, DC: U.S. Government Printing Office, 2018), p. 78.

There are a wide variety of charter schools serving different populations. As I will discuss, there are sharp differences between an elite charter school like the Peak to Peak Charter School and charter schools operated to serve low-income families like a major national system of charters, the KIPP academies. Peak to Peak Charter School was identified as one of the best schools in the world by the National Alliance for Public Charter Schools.

The National Alliance for Public Charter Schools identified several charter schools in which students received high scores on the international test PISA (Programme for International Student Assessment) administered by the Organization for Economic Co-operation and Development (OECD). Five charter schools that participated in this testing (which is only a small percentage of the total number of charter schools) scored higher than the national average, with Peak to Peak Charter School in Colorado scoring higher than students in Shanghai, China, who had the highest global scores. National Alliance for Public Charter Schools identified the characteristics of these high scoring schools, which included the charter schools Peak to Peak Charter School (Lafayette, Colorado), NYOS Charter School (Austin, Texas), Sturgis Charter Public School (Hyannis, Massachusetts), and University Laboratory School (Honolulu, Hawaii).

> [Each has] no more than 150 students per grade level and often substantially fewer. Data are used for decision-making and continual improvement at all of these public charter schools. Each school has been in operation for at least 14 years and focuses on creating a school environment that is safe and supportive. In addition to these common traits, each of these public charter schools has drawn on its location, student needs, and school mission to create a thriving school culture.

The one issue that could be raised by these high scoring charter schools identified by the National Alliance for Public Charter Schools is that their demographics do not match those of other charter schools. Table 8.8 provides the national enrollment percentages in charter schools by race and ethnicity.

Charter schools tend to have more high-poverty students compared to regular public schools. According to *The Condition of Education 2016*:

> In school year 2013–14, the percentage of students attending high-poverty schools—schools in which more than 75 percent of students qualify for free or reduced-price lunch (FRPL) under the National School Lunch Program—was higher for charter school students (37 percent) than for traditional public school students (24 percent).

Table 8.8 Percentage of Traditional Public Schools and Public Charter Schools, by Racial/Ethnic Concentration: School Years 2000–2001 and 2015–2016

	Percentage of Traditional Public Schools by Racial/Ethnic Concentration 2000–2001 (%)	Percentage of Traditional Public Schools by Racial/Ethnic Concentration 2015–2016 (%)	Percentage of Charter Public Schools by Racial/Ethnic Concentration 2000–2001 (%)	Percentage of Charter Public Schools by Racial/Ethnic Concentration 2015–2016 (%)
More than 50% white	71	58	52	34
More than 50% black	11	9	25	23
More than 50% Hispanic	9	16	11	25

Adapted from National Center for Education Statistics, *The Condition of Education 2018* (Washington, DC: U.S. Government Printing Office, 2018), p. 79.

Table 8.9 Student Race at Peak to Peak Charter School

White	78
Asian–Pacific Islander	11
Hispanic	10
Black	1
Free and reduced lunch eligibility	8

Source: National Association of Charter Schools, *On Top of the World: Public Charter Schools and International Benchmarking, 2013–14.* Retrieved from www.publiccharters.org/wp-content/uploads/2014/11/NAPCS-OECD-Report-04-REV.pdf on November 21, 2014.

Now contrast the demographics in Table 8.8 with the top Peak to Peak Charter School. Peak to Peak Charter School enrolls 150 students in each high school grade level. Based on Table 8.9 one might call Peak to Peak Charter School an elite school, with only 8 percent of its students eligible for free and reduced-price lunch (free and reduced-price lunches is a standard measure of the number of low-income students in a school) and the overwhelming majority of the students (78%) classified as white. The National Alliance for Public Charter Schools provides this description of Peak to Peak Charter School:

Peak to Peak Charter School has a liberal arts curriculum with a focus on college acceptance. It has one campus with elementary, middle, and high school programs serving 1,440 students in grades K–12. Peak to Peak Charter School students' OECD Test for Schools scores were on par with the top educational system on PISA 2009. In

2000, Peak to Peak Charter School established the goal of becoming one of the top 100 high schools in the United States and since 2008 has been consistently ranked among the top 50 on both Newsweek's and U.S. News & World Report's high school ranking lists.

The elite nature of the Peak to Peak Charter School is highlighted when compared to one of the largest national systems of charter schools, the KIPP academies, which reports: "KIPP currently serves 58,000 students in 162 schools around the country. Over 88 percent of our students are from low-income families and eligible for the federal free or reduced-price meals program, and 95 percent are African American or Latino." This number of 88 percent receiving free or reduced-price lunches is in sharp contrast to the Peak to Peak Charter School's 8 percent, as is the differences in the number nonwhite students.

Also in contrast to Peak to Peak Charter School's use of a liberal arts curriculum throughout its grades, KIPP academies combine behavioral development with the use of the Common Core State Standards. As stated on the KIPP Website: "In order to truly prepare students for college, we must create classrooms and schools that not only deliver rigorous academics but also help students develop their character." KIPP's character work focuses on "seven highly predictive character strengths that are correlated to leading engaged, happy and successful lives: zest, grit, optimism, self-control, gratitude, social intelligence, and curiosity."

KIPP's emphasis on character development reflects a belief that low-income students lack character traits needed to be successful in school and in the world. In contrast, Peak to Peak, with its more elite student body, sees character developing out of learning a traditional liberal arts curriculum. Its Website claims:

A liberal arts education has been recognized throughout history for its broad benefits and its appropriateness as a foundation for future learning. By focusing on a liberal arts college preparatory program, Peak to Peak achieves two important objectives: it prepares students to successfully meet the educational challenges of higher education and to be well-educated citizens in an increasingly complex world.

Differences in charter schools are highlighted by KIPP and Peak to Peak Charter School, with one providing a curriculum geared to low-income students and the other providing a liberal arts curriculum for a relatively elite student body. However, Peak to Peak's relatively high-income students, with only 8 percent receiving free and reduced-priced lunches, is more the exception than the rule.

Are charter schools creating a new form of racial and economic segregation? The trend is for charter schools to serve primarily minority and low-income students. Have charter schools been successful? There are conflicting research results on the effectiveness of charter schools. According to the Center for Public Education in 2010, the variety of charter schools makes it difficult to make a conclusive statement about their success:

> Given the varied nature of charter schools, it's logical that any evaluation of their overall impact would be difficult. Rigorous charter school research is, in fact, still in its infancy. . . . Given the nature of the research base, drawing broad conclusions about charter schools and achievement across the nation may be premature.

FOR-PROFIT GLOBAL EDUCATION CORPORATIONS

For-profit corporate involvement in education is now global. In 2014, Natasha Singer reported in the *New York Times* that the education software market was worth an estimated $7.9 billion for products designed for prekindergarten through high school. This $7.9 billion doesn't include profits gained from the sale of online and tutoring services, hardware, tests, and course and administrative management systems to schools. With the rush to comply with Common Core States Standards, companies began marketing tablets loaded with Common Core adapted material, such as Amplify, McGraw-Hill, and Ready-Curriculum Associates.

Take the case of the for-profit company K[12], which describes its products as such:

> At K[12], we deliver individualized learning for each and every student. Many children simply cannot get the individually focused and flexible learning they need in a traditional classroom. Parents and educators who choose K[12] understand the great potential of an individualized education.

In its 2014 annual report, "Putting Students First K12," the company reported: "Fiscal year 2014 was an exceptional year for the Company. We increased revenues to $919.6 million, a growth rate of 8.4%." It made this money selling online learning to partner schools, many of them virtual schools. The company's annual report described the extent of its business:

> In June, 2014 more than 6,000 high school students graduated from online and blended schools using the award-winning K[12] education

program. The high level of academic performance for the K^{12} class of 2014 earned graduates millions of dollars in academic scholarships and acceptance to some of the nation's top colleges and universities. This represents a 50% increase over the 4,000 students who graduated in 2013.

K^{12} is only one example of the multitude of global for-profit education companies. I provide detailed coverage of other global for-profit education in my book *The Globalization of Education* (2015). Of particular importance is the British-based company Pearson, which has made a great deal of money in the United States publishing tests aligned with the Common Core State Standards and teacher evaluation products like edTPA. Pearson boasts that it "is the world's leading education company. From pre-school to high school, early learning to professional certification, our curriculum materials, multimedia learning tools and testing programmes help to educate millions of people worldwide—more than any other private enterprise." Pearson provides this description of its global reach: "Though we generate approximately 60% of our sales in North America, we operate in more than 70 countries. We publish across the curriculum under a range of respected imprints including Scott Foresman, Prentice Hall, Addison-Wesley, Allyn and Bacon, Benjamin Cummings and Longman."

In *Global Education Inc.*, British sociologist Stephen J. Ball writes that Pearson in its advertising offers solutions to:

National policy of raising standards and achieving educational improvements linked to both individual opportunity and national competitiveness . . . [it] is a globalizing actor . . . through its publishing, assessment . . . [and] English language teaching and administration and management products.

The global reach of McGraw-Hill Education into 44 countries and with publications in 60 languages proudly announced on its Website:

McGraw-Hill Education partners around the world with students, educators, administrators and other professionals to deliver engaging, adaptive and personalized solutions that improve performance and results. We combine proven, research-based content with the best emerging digital technologies to guide assessment, teaching and learning to achieve the best possible outcome for students, instructors and institutions. McGraw-Hill Education employs more than 6,000 people in 44 countries and publishes in more than 60 languages.

In 2013, McGraw-Hill Education was sold to "to investment funds affiliated with Apollo Global Management, LLC." In the same year it jumped on the technology bandwagon by offering an adaptive e-book called SmartBook, declaring it "the world's first ever adaptive e-book, which revolutionizes college reading by focusing students on content most critical to their learning."

Another indication of the growing importance of for-profit education is the Education Industry Association (EIA), which advertises:

> Why Join EIA? Do yourself and your business an enormous service: Join EIA. Meet the people and make the connections that matter. Keep up with education industry trends, policy developments and network with other CEOs. Feel the impact of our collective national voice. Accelerate your business growth.

EIA lists, as two of the services provided:

1. Access to successful CEOs who can provide insight and guidance to developing companies, including companies seeking business opportunities with other EIA members;
2. More open and fair access by companies to the public education marketplace, while making the school purchasing process more efficient through our Private Ventures for the Public Good—Procurement Campaign.

This discussion of the education industry is only the tip of the iceberg. Education companies, particularly software companies, are inundating school with computer tablets, software, course management platforms, and behavioral control systems. A great deal of public money is going to these companies without state or federal regulation of the products. There is also concern about the data being collected by these products and their use by other education businesses and government agencies.

HOME SCHOOLING

Home schooling appears to be growing in popularity. It is one answer for parents who want to take charge of their children's education and avoid federal and state control of their children's education. The head of the Home School Legal Defense Association, J. Michael Smith, announced in 2013:

> Approximately 1,770,000 students are homeschooled in the United States—3.4% of the school-age population . . . [and] that among children who were homeschooled, 68 percent are white,

15 percent are Hispanic, 8 percent are black, and 4 percent are Asian or Pacific Islander.

In reporting national school enrollments, the U.S. Department of Education's *The Condition of Education 2013* noted that "the slight decline for youth ages 7–13, from 99 percent in 1970 to 98 percent in 2011, reflects an increase in the rate of homeschooling."

In 2014, the number of home-schooled children in North Carolina outnumbered those attending private schools. Citing parental reaction to the Common Core State Standards as a possible cause, *Education Week*'s Karla Scoon Reid reported that in North Carolina:

There were 98,172 home schoolers in 2013–2014, while 95,768 students attended private schools. State figures also showed a 14.3 percent increase in the number of home schools over the previous year. There were 60,950 home schools in North Carolina in 2013–2014.

In the same year Fox News headlined: "Opposition to Common Core Spurs Jump in Homeschooling." Fox News reporter Perry Chiaramonte stated: "The home-schooling boom is getting a new push due to opposition to Common Core, the controversial national education standard that some parents claim is using their children's public-school lessons to push a political agenda, according to critics of the Washington-backed curriculum." And in Pennsylvania a legislative bill was introduced that would eliminate review of home schoolers by local superintendents. For the Home School Legal Defense Association, the major advocate for home schooling, the legislation was a triumph after a decade lobbying to free home schoolers from review by local school districts.

The extent of state regulation and state laws are available on the Website of the Home School Legal Defense Association (www.hslda. org). This organization was established to provide legal defense to home schoolers. It divides states by those with no requirements that parents contact government authorities when deciding to home school; those requiring only that parents notify appropriate government authorities; those with moderate regulation of home schoolers; and those with extensive regulation of home schoolers. One can find the various state requirements for home schooling on the Home School Legal Defense Association's Website.

Why do families choose to home school their children? A survey conducted by the Home School Legal Defense Association cited the following reasons:

- Religious convictions: 49 percent
- Positive social environment: 15 percent
- Academic excellence: 14 percent
- Specific needs of the child: 12 percent
- Curriculum choice: 5 percent
- Flexibility: 5 percent

Home schooling is now a global movement. Writing for the *Washington Times*, Andrea Billups reports, "Home schooling is rapidly expanding worldwide as families abroad search for options to guide their children's education amid growing concerns over lax educational standards and increasing violence in government-run schools." The Home School Legal Defense Association claims it has been contacted by home educators from 25 countries for information on legalization of home schooling. In fact, Christopher J. Klicka, senior lawyer at the association, traveled to Germany and Japan in the summer of 2000 to work with families to gain legal protection.

Home schooling represents a rejection of traditional arguments for public schooling. Originally, common-school reformers believed all children should attend public schools, where they would learn to get along with others and learn a common morality and culture. Public schools were to educate good citizens. Public schools were to create a community spirit. By the twentieth century, schools required certified teachers based on the belief that good teachers needed to be trained.

Home schooling tosses all those arguments out the window. By educating their children at home, advocates reject the belief that children should obtain a common morality and culture through the public schools. In fact, many fundamentalist Christian parents, a major source of support for home schooling, feel public schools are both immoral and irreligious. They don't want their children exposed to the values taught by public schools. Others, such as politically liberal parents, home school their children because they reject the conservative economic and political philosophy of public schools. Some choose home schooling because of what they perceive to be the factory-like instruction of public schools.

Home schooling raises the issue of parental competence as teachers. This issue came to the forefront of home-schooling concerns when the Second District Court of Appeals, in Los Angeles, ruled on February 28, 2008, in a child-welfare case that a particular family's home-schooling arrangement required their children to be taught by a parent or tutor holding a teaching certificate. In an March 18, 2008, *Education Week* article, "Home-School Advocates Push to Blunt, Reverse California Ruling," Linda Jacobson reported California governor Arnold Schwarzenegger issued a statement after the ruling: "Parents should not be penalized for acting in the best interests of their children's education. This outrageous ruling must be overturned by the courts, and if the courts don't protect parents' rights then, as elected officials, we will." Home School Legal Defense Association immediately issued a statement: "We believe that the court erred in ruling . . . this is how home-schoolers have been home schooling for over 20 years."

Teachers' unions and some members of the educational establishment believe anyone teaching students should be certified by the government. Can you trust parents to be good teachers? Do good teachers require special training and certification? Another frequently asked question is whether home schoolers develop social skills. The Home School Legal Defense Association provides the following answers to this question:

- Home-school support groups organize field trips, teaching co-ops, and tutoring services.
- Home-schooled youngsters are active in community sports, scouting, church activities, political volunteering, community service, and more.
- Home schoolers are taken to museums, parks, libraries, and other educational institutions.

James Dobson, a columnist for the *Washington Times*, writes,

The great advantage of home schooling, in fact, is the protection it provides to vulnerable children against the wrong kind of socialization. When children interact in large groups, the strongest and most aggressive children quickly intimidate the weak and vulnerable. I am absolutely convinced that bad things happen to immature and "different" boys and girls when they are thrown into the highly competitive world of other children.

ONLINE AND DISTANCE LEARNING

The U.S. Department of Education defines distance learning as "courses that are credit-granting, technology-delivered, have either the instructor in a different location than the students and/or have the course content developed in, or delivered from, a different location than that of the students." In other words, distance learning involves online learning. As indicated in Table 8.10, the number of students taking online courses jumped dramatically.

Table 8.10 Number of Public High School Student Enrollments in Distance Education Courses: School Years 2002–2003 and 2009–2010

Year	Number of Public High School Students Enrolled in Distance Learning
2002–2003	222,000
2009–2010	1,349,000

Adapted from National Center for Education Statistics, *The Condition of Education 2012*, Figure 15.1 (Washington, DC: U.S. Department Of Education, 2012), p. 47.

Enrollments in distance learning in colleges also increased. According to the *Condition of Education 2014*:

> In fall 2012, about 4.6 million undergraduate students participated in distance education, with 2.0 million students (11 percent of total undergraduate enrollment) exclusively taking distance education courses . . . a higher percentage of students at private for-profit institutions (46 percent) exclusively took distance education courses than did students at public institutions (8 percent) and private non-profit institutions (10 percent).

A major advocate for online learning is the Foundation for Excellence headed by Jeb Bush, former governor of Florida and brother of ex-president George W. Bush. As governor of Florida, Bush supported the work of the Florida Virtual School (FLVS) as an important part of school reform. The Florida Virtual School exemplifies similar efforts in other states. Florida's Virtual School was founded in 1997 as the first statewide system of K–12 online instruction. The courses are offered globally with Florida residents taking the courses for free while non-Florida residents pay tuition.

A major issue regarding distance learning/online instruction is how many online courses a student can take in a given year and for graduation. In Florida the number of online courses is not limited. Florida's legal requirements are explained by Florida's commissioner of education Eric Smith in a January 8, 2009, memorandum, "school districts may not limit student access to FLVS courses," stating that there are "no limits on the number of credits a student may earn at FLVS during a single school year or multiple school years."

Distance/online learning is sometimes used to ease budget problems, particularly if new teachers need to be hired. In other words, online instruction can reduce the number of teachers employed by local school districts. Florida law allows for the use of the Florida Virtual Schools by local school districts "to help ease overcrowding."

Exemplifying the legal changes that must be made in state laws to expand distance learning/online instruction are those proposed by Jeb Bush's Foundation for Excellence in Education. The Foundation's action report *Digital Learning Now* lists in its "10 Elements of High Quality Digital Learning" actions that should be taken by lawmakers and policymakers. These actions include states passing laws providing online courses to students in K–12 and providing access to online courses from public charter schools, not-for-profit organizations, and for-profit companies. These laws will require that online courses are aligned with the Common Core curriculum and that all providers are treated equally, meaning that for-profit companies will be treated the same as public schools. The foundation's action plan calls for states to not place limits on the number of credits earned online, to allow students to take all or some of their courses online, and to make online instruction all year and at any time.

Will distance learning/online instruction replace brick and mortar schools? Will education be completed at home or in a computer center?

Figure 8.1 is my model of online instruction that might replace the traditional school. The school as a social center provides spaces for both student learning and community activities. The model completely changes traditional school organization with students being divided into separate classes by age. One section of the school center contains computers where students of any age can learn through online instruction. There are no classrooms. Students would enter the social center and at their own volition or at a set time go to the computer center and access their assigned online instruction materials. The teacher functions as a consultant, helping students with online instruction problems and other social and psychological issues.

The school center provides meeting rooms and offices to community groups along with medical, dental, social, and psychological services. The teacher would also help with any organizational problems faced by community groups. There is also a section of the school center that provides a gym, pool, and club offices for students that could be used at any time by students or at specific times. In this model students and community members cross paths with the possibility of face-to-face interchange. Medical, dental, social, and psychological services might be provided only for students, or they could, in the spirit of building a sense of community, be provided to all community members. A central responsibility of the teacher-consultant would be to ensure integration of students and community members and building a sense of community cooperation.

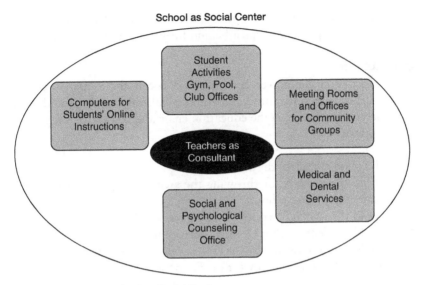

School as Social Center

Student Activities Gym, Pool, Club Offices

Computers for Students' Online Instructions

Meeting Rooms and Offices for Community Groups

Teachers as Consultant

Medical and Dental Services

Social and Psychological Counseling Office

Figure 8.1 Online Learning in a Social Center

U.S. SECRETARY OF EDUCATION BETSY DEVOS AND REPUBLICAN SUPPORT OF SCHOOL CHOICE AND VOUCHERS

As mentioned earlier in this chapter and in previous chapters, the 2016 Republican platform and President Donald Trump's secretary of education, Betsy DeVos, support school choice and, in particular, the use of vouchers and innovated funding methods, such as education savings accounts (ESAs) and tuition tax credits.

Supporting school choice, the Heritage Foundation describes ESAs:

> Through ESA options, states deposit a portion of the money that the state would have spent on a child in a public school into a parent-controlled, restricted-use savings account. Parents can then use those dollars to pay for any education-related service, product, or provider, including private school tuition, online learning, special education services and therapies, textbooks, curricula, and college courses, among other education expenditures. Notably, parents can roll over unused funds from year to year to save for anticipated future education-related expenses, such as high school or college tuition.

The idea of for-profit schools competing in a marketplace supported by government funds, particularly as vouchers or as charter schools, was highlighted by President Donald Trump's speech on September 8, 2016, at the for-profit charter school Cleveland Arts and Social Science Academy.

In the speech, President Trump praised the owner, Ron Packard, as representing the entrepreneurial spirit behind for-profit charter schools.

CONCLUSION

After considering the power and politics of local school boards, choice, charter schools, privatization, and commercialization, you should again imagine you are sitting in the education chair and answering the following questions:

- Who should control the switch?
- Should the options for throwing the switch be determined by petitioners for charter schools?
- Should the switch be controlled by parental choice?
- Should an elected school board control the switch?
- Should it be controlled by the educational bureaucracy?
- Should it be controlled by for-profit companies?

Whatever your answers, the important thing is for you to understand that the political structure of education determines the content of education that in turn directly affects what a student learns. Often students don't question why they are subjected to a particular curriculum or textbook. The content of learning in public schools is determined by a political process. But local politics of education is only one part of the process.

SUGGESTED READINGS AND WORKS CITED IN CHAPTER

American Federation of Teachers. *The Many Names of School Vouchers.* www.aft.org/topics/vouchers/index.htm on September 12, 2008. AFT's statement of opposition to vouchers for private schools.

———. *School Vouchers: Myths and Facts.* Washington, DC: American Federation of Teachers, 2006. The American Federation of Teachers (AFT) Website. www.aft.org, provides a list of the major criticisms the AFT has of public–private choice. In addition, the statement has a list of research on voucher plans.

Archer, Jeff. "Private Charter Managers Team Up." *Education Week on the Web* (February 4, 2004). www.edweek.org. Archer's article describes the creation of the National Council of Education Providers by six for-profit education companies.

Arizona Virtual University. www.AZVA.org. A free online public school that pays for the services of the for-profit education company K^{12}.

Ball, Stephen J. *Global Education Inc.: New Policy Networks and the Neo-Liberal Imaginary.* London: Routledge, 2012. This book provides a survey of the interconnections between global education corporations.

Belfield, Clive. *The Business of Education.* National Center for the Study of Privatization in Education. New York: Teachers College Press, 2004. The Website www.ncspe.org provides a summary of trends in for-profit education services.

Billups, Andrea. "Home School Movement Goes Global." *The Washington Times* (September 19, 2000). www.hslda.org.

Blair, Julie. "Doing It Their Way: Teachers Make All Decisions at Cooperative Venture." *Education Week on the Web* (July 27, 2002). www.edweek.org. This article features Minnesota's EdVisions Cooperative, which establishes charter schools based on teacher control.

Bloomberg News. "Edison Reaches Contract on Philadelphia Schools." *The New York Times on the Web* (August 1, 2002). www.nytimes.com/2002/08/01/business/edison-reaches-contract-on-philadelphia-schools.html. This story discusses the contract reached by Edison to manage 20 elementary and middle schools in Philadelphia.

Bracey, Gerald. *Charter Schools* (October 12, 2000). www.uwm.edu/Dept/CERAI. This report was written for and distributed by the Center for Education Research, Analysis, and Innovation.

Braun, Henry, Frank Jenkins, and Wendy Grigg. *A Closer Look at Charter Schools Using Hierarchical Linear Modeling.* Washington, DC: United States Department of Education, 2006. This study found no significant differences in achievement in reading and math between public charter schools and regular public schools.

———. *Comparing Private Schools and Public Schools Using Hierarchical Linear Modeling.* Washington, DC: U.S. Department of Education, 2006. This study found no significant differences in student achievement between public and private schools.

———. *Comparing Private Schools and Public Schools Using Hierarchical Linear Modeling.* Washington, DC: U.S. Department of Education, July 2006. Supports the use of public–private school vouchers.

Center for Educational Reform. www.edreform.com. This Website is an important source for information about school choice and charter schools.

———. *What the Research Reveals About Charter Schools.* www.edreform.com. This report summarizes 53 research-based studies on charter schools.

Chiaramonte, Perry. "Opposition to Common Core Spurs Jump in Homeschooling." *Fox News* (November 25, 2014). www.foxnews.com/us/2014/11/25/opposition-to-common-core-spurs-jump-in-homeschooling/. This article relates the increasing number of home schoolers in opposition to the Common Core State Standards.

Chubb, John E., and Terry Moe. *Politics, Markets & America's Schools.* Washington, DC: The Brookings Institution, 1990. This important study of the relationship between political control and student achievement supports choice as a means of improving student achievement.

Dobson, James. *Dobson Writes Many Articles on the Advantages of Home Schooling for the Home Schooling Legal Defense Association.* www.hslda.org.

Edison Project. www.edisonproject.com. This Website provides ongoing information about Edison school projects and financial reports.

Education Industry Association. www.educationindustry.org/. This group lobbies for increased support of the for-profit education industry.

Education Week. This excellent weekly newspaper contains news about local, state, and federal politics of education.

Fairlie, Robert. *Racial Segregation and the Private/Public School Choice.* New York: National Center for the Study of Privatization in Education, 2006. This study concludes that private schools are racially segregated and that private school vouchers could either increase this segregation or reduce segregation by allowing children of low-income families to attend private schools.

Florida Virtual School. *About Us.* www.flvs.net/areas/aboutus/Pages/default.aspx on May 9, 2011. The Florida Virtual School is a pioneer in providing complete online instruction to state public school students.

Foundation for Excellence in Education. *Digital Learning Now.* www.excelined.org/DOCS/Digital%20Learning%20Learning%20Now%20Report%20For%20Governors.pdf on April 19, 2011. This foundation is active in trying to change state laws to allow for more online instruction.

Heritage Foundation. *Education: Recommendations.* http://solutions.heritage.org/culture-society/education/?_ga=1.167443774.1611892490.1480956937 on December 5, 2016. These recommendations include a description of education savings accounts.

Hess, Frederick, and Olivia Meeks. *School Boards Circa 2010: Governance in the Accountability Era*. National School Board Association, 2010. www.nsba.org/sites/default/files/SBcirca2010_WEB.pdf. This study provides statistics on the characteristics of school board members.

Home School Legal Defense Association. www.hslda.org. This is the best source for information on the home-schooling movement and different state laws governing home schooling.

Jacobson, Linda. "Home-School Advocates Push to Blunt, Reverse California Ruling." *Education Week on the Web* (March 18, 2008). www.edweek.org. Report of California ruling and reaction that home-schooled pupils must have a certified teacher.

KIPP Public Charter Schools. Http://www.kipp.org/. This is one of the largest charter school networks.

K[12]. http://ww2.k12.com/mod/exp12/. This company sells online courses and services.

———. *Putting Students First K12: 2014 Annual Report*. This report describes the company's revenues, business structure, and number of schools buying its products.

McGraw-Hill Education. *About Us*. www.mheducation.com/about/about-us This Website provides a history of the for-profit company and its educational products.

Morones, Alyssa. "Indiana Supreme Court Upholds Voucher Law." *Education Week* (April 3, 2013). www.edweek.org/ew/articles/2013/04/03/27brief-b1.h32.html?tkn=ZMSFaL-0rhIQsTcs6CBOeQpa9Jktf7YzhyTDT&print=1. Article describes Indiana Supreme Court decision allowing vouchers to be used at religious schools.

Nathan, Joe. *Charter Schools: Creating Hope and Opportunity for American Education*. San Francisco: Jossey-Bass, 1996. Nathan describes the struggle for charter schools and provides help in organizing a charter school.

National Alliance for Public Charter Schools. *On Top of the World: Public Charter Schools and International Benchmarking, 2013–14*. www.publiccharters.org/wp-content/uploads/2014/11/NAPCS-OECD-Report-04-REV.pdf. This report provides statistics on the success of a small number of charter schools on the international test PISA.

National Assessment of Educational Progress. *America's Charter Schools: Results from the NAEP 2003 Pilot Study*. Washington, DC: U.S. Department of Education, 2005. This report found no significant difference between the achievement of students in public charter schools and other public-school students.

National Center for Education Statistics. *The Condition of Education 2016*. Washington, DC: U.S. Government Printing Office, 2014. Provides statistics on charter school enrollment.

———. "Indicator 6: Homeschooled Students." *The Condition of Education 2009*. Washington, DC: National Center for Education Statistics, 2009. Statistical information on number of students being homeschooled.

———. "School Choice: Parental Choice of Schools." *The Condition of Education 2006*. Washington, DC: National Center for Education Statistics, 2006. This report gives the percentage of parents exercising choice options.

National Center for the Study of Privatization in Education. *Cyber and Home School Charter Schools: How States Are Defining New Forms of Public Schooling*. New York: Teachers College Press, 2004. www.ncspe.org. A summary of trends in home- and cyberschooling is provided.

National Council of Education Providers. *"Home" and "Our Goals"*. www.educationproviders.org. Organization of seven for-profit school companies whose goal is to serve charter schools around the country.

National Education Association. *Can Corporate Management Solve the Challenges Facing America's Public Schools?* www.nea.org. Teachers' union's concerns about private management of public schools.

———. *Five Talking Points on Vouchers*. www.nea.org/vouchers/talkingpoints.html on September 12, 2008. NEA's opposition to school vouchers.

———. *National School Voucher Legislation Announced by Congressional Leaders and Education Secretary: Bill Will Mislead Parents and Funnel Money Away from Public Schools.* Washington, DC: National Education Association, 2006. This press release can be found on www.nea.org and contains the National Education Association's negative response to the proposal for America's Opportunity Scholarships for Kids Act.

———. *Research Undercuts Case for Private Schools.* Washington, DC: National Education Association, 2006. This press release can be found on www.nea.org. The organization's press release hails the study by Henry Braun et al. *Comparing Private Schools and Public Schools Using Hierarchical Linear Modeling,* as proof that government money should not be used to support private school choice plans.

———. *Vouchers.* Washington, DC: National Education Association, 2006. This article can be found on www.nea.org and lists the organization's objections to vouchers.

Nelson, Howard, Bella Rosenberg, and Nancy Van Meter. *Charter School Achievement on the 2003 National Assessment of Educational Progress.* Washington, DC: American Federation of Teachers, August 2004. This study shows poor achievement scores for charter school students in comparison to students in regular public schools.

Patrinos, Harry, and Shobhana Sosale, eds. *Mobilizing the Private Sector for Public Education: A View from the Trenches.* Washington, DC: World Bank, 2007. Articles provide an introduction to the World Bank's sponsorship of for-profit education.

Peak to Peak Charter School. www.peaktopeak.org/pages/PeaktoPeakCS. Students at this charter school receive the top scores on international tests.

Pearson. www.pearson.com/about-us.html. It is worth exploring the Website of this for-profit mega-education corporation and examining its various products.

Public Law 107-110, 107th Congress, January 8, 2002 [H.R. 1]. *No Child Left Behind Act of 2001.* Washington, DC: U.S. Government Printing Office, 2002. This federal legislation contains important provisions supporting public-school choice and charter schools.

Reid, Karla Scoon. "Districts Spar with Ed. Dept. Over Tutoring: Chicago, Boston Argue They Should Be Allowed to Help." *Education Week* (November 3, 2004), p. 3. This article describes how Boston and Chicago were forced by No Child Left Behind to hire for-profit companies to provide tutoring services to students in failing schools instead of using their own school services.

———. "Number of N.C. Home Schoolers Exceeds State's Private School Enrollment." *Education Week* (August 15, 2014). http://blogs.edweek.org/edweek/parentsandthepublic/2014/08/number_of_nc_homeschoolers_exceeds_states_private_school_enrollment.html?print=1. Reports on the increase of home schoolers with suggestions it was being caused by the Common Core State Standards.

Republican Platform 2016. https://gop.com/platform/ on November 23, 2016. Platform emphasizes educational choice using vouchers, tuition tax credits, and educational savings account.

Rethinking Schools: An Urban Educational Journal Online. www.rethinking schools.org. This is an important source of information on urban school reform, including school choice, charter schools, and multicultural education.

Ring, Trudy. "Trump Picks Right-Wing Activist Betsy DeVos for Secretary of Education." *Advocate* (December 6, 2016). www.advocate.com/politics/2016/11/23/trump-picks-antigay-activist-betsy-devos-secretary-education on December 11, 2016. Describes reasons for Trump's selection of Betsy DeVos as U.S. secretary of education and their support of for-profit charters schools.

Schemo, Diana Jean. "Nation's Charter Schools Lagging Behind, U.S. Test Scores Reveal." *The New York Times on the Web* (August 17, 2004). www.nytimes.com. This article revealed data discovered buried at the U.S. Department of Education showing that charter school students were doing worse than regular public-school students on achievement tests. The article raised serious doubts about the effectiveness of charter schools.

Smarthinking. www.smarthinking.com. For-profit online education company that provides tutoring to students in schools, colleges, and government agencies. Uses tutors located in foreign countries.

Smith, Eric. *Florida Department of Education: Florida Virtual School as School Choice Option* (January 8, 2009). http://info.fldoe.org/docushare/dsweb/Get/Document-5250/dps-2009-07.pdf. Outlines Florida state laws regarding online instruction.

Smith, J. Michael. *U.S. Department of Education: Homeschooling Continues to Grow!* www.hslda.org/docs/news/2013/201309030.asp. The president of the Home School Legal Defense Association hails the increase in the numbers of home schoolers.

Spellings, Margaret. *Press Releases: Statement by Secretary Margaret Spellings on Release of NCES [National Center for Education Statistics] Study on Charter Schools.* Released on August 22, 2006 on the U.S. Department of Education. www.ed.gov/news/pressreleases/2006/08/08222006a.html. U.S. Secretary of Education Spellings defends charter schools after a report shows students in public charter schools have significantly lower achievement scores in reading and math than those in public noncharter schools.

Spring, Joel. *Educating the Consumer-Citizen: A History of the Marriage of Schools, Advertising, and Media.* Mahwah, NJ: Lawrence Erlbaum, 2003. Spring provides a history of the commercialization of schools and American society.

————. *Globalization of Education: An Introduction.* New York: Routledge, 2015. This book contains a detailed analysis of for-profit education corporations.

————. *Political Agendas*, 6th edition. New York: Routledge, 2018. This book, among other things, discusses the religious and political attitudes of U.S. Secretary of Education Betsy DeVos.

Stutz, Terence. "Charters Score Below Public Schools, Exclusive: At 235 Texas Campuses, Passing Rate Was 42 Percent." *The Dallas Morning News* (October 21, 2004). www.dallasnews.com. Stutz gives the report by the Texas Education Agency on the poor performance of charter schools.

U.S. Department of Education. *The Condition of Education 2012.* Contains statistics on charter schools and distance learning.

————. *The Condition of Education 2013.* Contains enrollment statistics on home schooling.

————. *Successful Charter Schools* (2004). www.uscharterschools.org/pub/uscs_docs/scs/toc.htm on 20 September 2010. Provides examples of successful charter schools.

Walsh, Mark. "Businesses Flock to Charter Frontier." *Education Week on the Web* (May 22, 2002). www.edweek.org. This article surveys the operation of the major companies trying to make a profit from the development of charter schools, including National Heritage Academies Inc.

————. "Edison Outlines Strategies to Reassure Wall Street." *Education Week on the Web* (August 7, 2002). www.edweek.org. Walsh provides an analysis of Edison Schools, Inc.'s financial maneuvering.

————. "Education Inc." *Education Week on the Web* (October 4, 2000). www.edweek.org. This article describes Nobel Learning Communities, Inc.'s planned investment in for-profit schools in China.

————. "High Court Tax-Credit Ruling Could Offer New Momentum to School Choice Supporters: Arizona Program Benefiting Religious Schools Survives Challenge." *Education Week* (April 19, 2011). www.edweek.org/ew/articles/2011/04/20/28scotus-2.h30.html?tkn=YYRFn4wMq0BYvyJz6ZPLkEmGRlorHxuEtFhW&print=1. Article describes court decision allowing school tuition organizations to provide grants to students to attend religious schools.

Weiner, Rebecca. "San Diego Charter School a Model for Technology Leaders." *The New York Times on the Web* (November 1, 2000). www.nytimes.com. Weiner provides a description of the founding and operation of High Tech High charter schools.

Wilgorin, Jodi. "School Days Are Rule Days in Bronx Charter Classrooms." *The New York Times on the Web* (October 30, 2000). www.nytimes.com. Wilgorin gives a description of the Bronx Preparatory Charter School.

Wyatt, Edward. "Educational Company Says Its Scores Rise." *The New York Times on the Web* (August 10, 2000). www.nytimes.com. Edison report that test scores in its schools are improving.

———. "Investors Are Seeing Profits in Nation's Demand for Education." *The New York Times on the Web* (November 4, 1999). www.nytimes.com. This is an important article on investment in for-profit education companies.

———. "Union Study Finds for-Profit Schools No Better." *The New York Times on the Web* (October 19, 2000). www.nytimes.com. The AFT disputes an Edison school report that its test scores are improving in comparison to traditional public-school students.

U.S. Charter Schools. www.uscharterschools.org. This is the official Website on charters operated by the U.S. Department of Education.

Yecke, Cheri Pierson, and Laura O. Lazo. *Choice Provisions in No Child Left Behind*. Washington, DC: U.S. Department of Education, 2002. This is the official government interpretation of the choice provisions of No Child Left Behind.

Zimmer, Ron, and Richard Buddin. *Charter School Performance in Urban Districts: Are They Closing the Achievement Gap?* Santa Monica, CA: Rand Corporation, 2005. This study, available online at www.rand.org/education, found no significant achievement differences between students in public charter schools and those attending noncharter public schools.

CHAPTER 9

Power and Control at State and National Levels

During the 2016 national elections, both Republicans and Democrats criticized federal involvement in local schools. There is nothing in the U.S. Constitution about education; consequently, it is a responsibility given to state governments. State constitutions and laws contain provisions for creating and regulating public schools. However, in recent years the federal government has exercised dramatic control over schools by funding No Child Left Behind and the Race to the Top section of the American Recovery and Reinvestment Act of 2009. Resulting from these laws were highly controversial requirements for testing students, calls for using student test scores to evaluate teachers, the Common Core State Standards, and efforts to create student data systems.

When President Donald Trump appointed Secretary of Education Betsy DeVos, there was a new direction given to the federal government's education policies, one that emphasized school choice. As discussed at the end of Chapter 8, DeVos believes school choice is a panacea for U.S. schools. In a 2017 interview with *Education Week*'s Alyson Klein, DeVos reiterated her support for school choice. Klein wrote, "For now, it sounds like DeVos will be relying on another important tool of her office—the bully pulpit—to put a focus on states, schools, and districts that are using choice in a way she thinks is working for students."

Directing her attention to state governments to provide choice plans, DeVos demonstrates the connections between federal influence over local school policies. She told Klein:

> The reality is that most of the momentum around this, and frankly most of the funding around it, comes at the state level. More and more states are adopting programs that embrace a wide range of choices. And I expect that to continue apace.

One consequence of federal involvement in local education is the inclusion of education issues in campaigns for federal offices. Even national presidential campaigns address school issues ranging from sex education to testing of students.

This chapter examines the following issues:

- Source of federal influence over local school policies
- Categorical federal aid
- Increasing state involvement in schools
- No Child Left Behind
- Student privacy and big data
- Common Core State Standards

FEDERAL INFLUENCE OVER LOCAL SCHOOL POLICIES

Federal influence over state education and local schools is primarily through categorical aid. *Categorical aid* is money provided to support specific federal programs and legislation such as No Child Left Behind and Race to the Top. Once states or local school districts accept federal money, they have to accept the regulations and requirements that accompany the funding. Most states and local school systems find it difficult to refuse the money provided by the federal government. Consequently, the federal government has increased its influence over local schools despite the fact that the actual amount of money from federal sources is only a small percentage of the money local schools spend on students.

Since 1989, there has been a decline in the total revenue for public elementary and secondary education from local sources and an increase in funding from the federal government. The state percentage has remained about the same. This shift in funding reflects the growing role of the federal government in local schools. The federal legislation No Child Left Behind and Race to the Top are examples the how the increase in categorical federal aid has affected local school systems. *The Condition of Education 2018* reports:

> In school year 2014–15, elementary and secondary public school revenues totaled $664 billion in constant 2016–17 dollars. Of this total, 8 percent, or $56 billion, were from federal sources; 47 percent, or $309 billion, were from state sources; and 45 percent, or $299 billion, were from local sources.

The 2018 report noted that there was a "7 percent increase in total elementary and secondary public school enrollment, from 47 million students in 2000–01 to 50 million students in 2014–15."

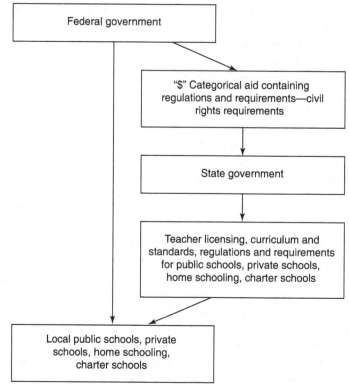

Figure 9.1 Relationship between Federal and State Governments and Local Schools

CATEGORICAL FEDERAL AID

Beginning in the 1950s, the federal government began using requirements attached to funding to influence local school policies. During the 1950s, there was a debate about whether the federal government should give money to local school systems and let them determine how to use it or whether the federal government should specify how the money should be used. With passage of the 1958 National Defense Education Act (NDEA), Congress targeted funds for specific purposes, such as improving mathematics, science, and foreign language instruction. The next major federal educational legislation, the 1965 Elementary and Secondary Education Act (ESEA), also tied education to national policy objectives; in this case it was the War on Poverty. Funds were targeted for reading and arithmetic programs that would supposedly provide equality of educational opportunity for students from low-income families.

Regulatory control is exemplified by Title VI of the 1964 Civil Rights Act, which applies to federal education legislation. Any school agency receiving federal funds must comply with Title VI, which requires the mandatory withholding of federal funds from institutions practicing racial, religious, or ethnic discrimination. Title VI states that no person, because of race, color, or national origin, can be excluded from or denied the benefits of any program receiving federal financial assistance. Also, any educational agency receiving federal funds must comply with Title IX of the 1972 amendments to the Higher Education Act. Title IX states: "No person in the United States shall, on the basis of sex, be excluded from participation in, be denied the benefits of, or be subjected to discrimination under any education program or activity receiving Federal Assistance."

The federal government, therefore, exerts considerable indirect influence over education by:

- Providing federal money to support a particular educational program (categorical aid)
- Attaching federal regulations to federal programs
- Forcing schools to comply with civil rights legislation to receive federal money
- Funding educational research

NO CHILD LEFT BEHIND

Theoretically, No Child Left Behind, which was a reauthorization of the 1965 ESEA, tried to balance federal and state power by allowing states to determine their own academic standards and testing programs. The ESEA was again reauthorized 2015 as the Every Student Succeeds Act (ESSA). Both pieces of legislation give states federal funds to create academic standards and testing programs, require public reporting of test scores, and to identify and improve schools failing to meet adequate yearly progress.

ESSA includes provisions designed to help students and schools succeed. As described by the U.S. Department of Education, the law:

1. Advances equity by upholding critical protections for America's disadvantaged and high-need students.
2. Requires—for the first time—that all students in America be taught to high academic standards that will prepare them to succeed in college and careers.
3. Ensures that vital information is provided to educators, families, students, and communities through annual statewide assessments that measure students' progress toward those high standards.
4. Helps support and grow local innovations—including evidence-based and place-based interventions developed by local leaders and educators.

5. Maintains an expectation that there will be accountability and action to effect positive change in our lowest-performing schools, where groups of students are not making progress, and where graduation rates are low over extended periods of time.

In 2017, Secretary of Education Betsy DeVos approved state plans submitted under the ESSA. As stated in the approval announcement by the U.S. Department of Education:

> The Every Student Succeeds Act pushes states to move beyond test scores in gauging school performance and gives them all sorts of new flexibility when it comes to funding, turning around low-performing schools, and more. But states still have to submit an accountability roadmap—including long-term goals for student achievement—to the U.S. Department of Education for approval.

STUDENT PRIVACY AND BIG DATA

A major concern is the possible hacking of data required by No Child Left Behind and ESSA. They contain provisions for "Building data systems that measure student growth and success, and inform teachers and principals about how they can improve instruction." with the part of the National standards, in contrast to individual state standards, would make it possible to link a national data bank of student test scores to individual teachers and eventually to the institutions that trained each teacher. This trend has raised concerns about hacking into massive student data banks that contain not only student test scores but other student characteristics.

These big data sets could be used to create what is called personalized learning in which past student data is used to adapt instructional materials to meet students' abilities. It would also be used to evaluate teachers and teacher-education programs. Given student and teacher geographic mobility, the analysis of teacher-education programs would not be possible without national standards and testing. As Secretary of Education Arne Duncan stated in a speech on teacher education, "The draft Race to the Top criteria would also reward states that publicly report and link student achievement data to *the programs where teachers and principals were credentialed*" (emphasis in original). The criteria for selection of state grants under Race to the Top included whether or not states were willing to participate in creating national standards, common tests, and a data bank of student scores to be used to evaluate teachers and support charter school expansion.

Writing for *Education Week*, Benjamin Herold describes the use of $4.8 million from the National Science Foundation to create a big data set that would include "learning and behavioral information that students generate when they use digital-learning tools," including "every mouse click a student makes when using a software program and information demonstrating a student's thought process when attempting to solve a problem in an online simulation." This data would be shared with multiple institutions, including third-party and for-profit vendors. Concerns were immediately raised about student privacy with the sharing of this data with outside vendors and the possibility of it being hacked. There was also concern about who owned the data.

Similar concerns are raised about student privacy regarding the Data Quality Campaign funded by organizations committed to using big data to solve social problems, such as the Bill and Melinda Gates Foundation and the Michael & Susan Dell Foundation. The Data Quality Campaign is creating a system of data sharing between states. The organization's publication "Paving the Path to Success: Data for Action 2014" describes its objectives as more than collecting student test scores:

> The Data Quality Campaign (DQC) is dedicated to helping everyone with a stake in education, including parents, teachers, education leaders, and policymakers, effectively and appropriately understand and use education data. DQC helps parents and educators understand the value of data—why data matter and how they can help students be successful in the classroom and beyond. Data are more than just test scores, and by effectively accessing and using different types of data—such as attendance, grades, and course-taking—teachers, parents, and school and district leaders can help ensure that every student is on a path for success every day, not just at the end of the school year.

Data Quality Campaign recognizes the problem of protecting student data but provides no assurance it will be protected. Its report "Paving the Path to Success: Data for Action 2014" states that "in 2014, many states sought to safeguard student data privacy by introducing legislation. In total, 36 states considered 110 bills directly addressing student data privacy."

COMMON CORE STATE STANDARDS

Representing another form of federal influence on state education policies is the adoption of the Common Core State Standards released on June 2, 2010, by the National Governors Association Center for Best Practices (NGA Center) and the Council of Chief State School

Officers (CCSSO). By 2014, the Common Cores State Standards were adopted by 43 states, the District of Columbia, four territories, and the Department of Defense Education Activity. As discussed at the beginning of Chapter 1, there is already a great deal of controversy about the literacy standards in the Common Core State Standards. Controversy occurs anytime you try to define an academic field by creating learning standards.

It is impossible in this text to review all the Common Core State Standards for K–12. However, all the standards are available on the Website of the Common Core State Standards Initiative at www. corestandards.org/. The Website provides answers to these commonly asked questions about the standards:

What are educational standards?

- Educational standards help teachers ensure their students have the skills and knowledge they need to be successful by providing clear goals for student learning.

Why do we need educational standards?

- We need standards to ensure that all students, no matter where they live, are prepared for success in postsecondary education and the workforce.
- Common standards will help ensure that students are receiving a high-quality education consistently, from school to school and state to state.
- Common standards will provide a greater opportunity to share experiences and best practices within and across states that will improve our ability to best serve the needs of students.
- Standards do not tell teachers how to teach, but they do help teachers figure out the knowledge and skills their students should have so that teachers can build the best lessons and environments for their classrooms.
- Standards also help students and parents by setting clear and realistic goals for success. Standards are a first step—a key building block—in providing our young people with a high-quality education that will prepare them for success in college and work. Of course, standards are not the only thing that is needed for our children's success, but they provide an accessible roadmap for our teachers, parents, and students.

Readers of this book may be teaching a variety of courses and grade levels. The important thing to remember is that you might not agree with the standards for a particular grade and subject. As discussed at the beginning of Chapter 1, these standards are directed at preparing students for work and college. Consequently, the literacy standards discussed in Chapter 1 increase the amount of nonfiction and reduce the amount of fiction read by students. Questions about personal feelings and relationship to the text are avoided. The idea is to prepare students to write corporate memos and college essays.

FEDERAL AND STATE CONTROL THROUGH HIGH-STAKES TESTS AND ACADEMIC STANDARDS

High-stakes testing mandated in NCLB and supported by ESSA can provide direct control over student learning, particularly if teachers teach to the test. Tests based on the Common Core State Standards represent another form of control of the content of student learning. The No Child Left Behind Act of 2001 mandates a schedule, target populations, and reporting procedures for high-stakes testing and academic standards. Test data are used to determine which schools are making adequate yearly progress; those that are not can receive funds for school improvement and educational services, and parents of children at those schools will be allowed school choice. Theoretically, the purpose of test data is to spur school improvement by identifying low-performing schools and motivating teachers and school administrators to achieve state standards. The combination of state report cards for each school district and district report cards for each school results in every level of school administration and all teachers being judged by student performance.

Also, to highlight any possible discrimination of schools and school districts, states must make available to the public a list of elementary and secondary schools receiving funds for school improvement because they have, according to state standards, been failing for two years. This public list must include "the percentage of students in each school from families with incomes below the poverty level." In addition, the state must report students "by race, ethnicity, gender, disability status, migrant status, English proficiency, and status as economically disadvantaged."

The high-stakes testing required under NCLB and embodied in ESSA can have consequences for how teachers and principals are paid, real estate prices, instructional time in the classroom, and profits for corporations making the tests, and it contributes to the nationalization of public schools. Student testing affects the evaluation of teachers and administrators. In 2006, the Houston Board of Education approved a $14.5 million program that rewards teachers and administrators according to the scores of their students on standardized tests. Teachers can receive up to $3,000 annually for their students' improved test scores and administrators up to $25,000 for the improved performance of students in their schools. New York City School Chancellor Joel Klein announced near the opening of the 2002–2003 school year that district superintendents would receive bonuses up to $40,000—about a quarter of their base salaries—if test scores improved in their districts. School principals were already receiving bonuses for improved scores in their schools. In March 2004, Denver teachers voted 59 to 41 percent for a merit pay system using student achievement test scores. The Denver plan provides several methods for teachers to gain pay raises. The most important method is for pay hikes to be based on student academic growth as measured by test scores. Denver teachers under the plan would also be able to gain salary increases by being evaluated as satisfactory, improving their education, or teaching in high-poverty schools.

High-stakes test scores are now news items that even affect the real estate market. For instance, a July 26, 2006, *Education Week* headline reveals, "Scores Linked to Home Prices." In the article, economics professor Donald Haurin reports that "a 20 percent increase in a district's pass rate on the state tests translated to a 7 percent increase in the home prices in the district."

Some people worry that testing is taking away from instructional time. "Time Devoted to Testing Surprises New Teacher" is what the editors of *Education Week* titled a April 5, 2006, letter from Cindy Mulvey of La Quinta, California. Mulvey asks, "Is it true that our students are tested more than 85 out of 180 days?" She explains her experience as a long-term third-grade substitute:

> I . . . spent more time testing my 3rd graders . . . than I did instructing them. In addition to daily multiplication quizzes, the students took a weekly spelling test, a weekly Houghton Mifflin Reading test, a chapter math test every two weeks, a theme skills test once a month, a unit math test once a month, a writing-prompt test every trimester, several county and state exams, and a physical-fitness test.

Testing is a for-profit industry. McGraw-Hill and Pearson are the two largest makers of tests. An example of the testing industry was presented in an August 28, 2006, article in the popular *Newsweek* magazine titled "Test Wars: The SAT [Scholastic Assessment Test] vs. the ACT [American College Testing Program]." The article reveals the big business aspect of high-stakes testing in the struggle between SAT and ACT to control the college entrance exam market. High school counselors are advising some students to take both tests, but some colleges are dropping both tests as an entrance requirement. In 2005, 1.2 million students took the ACT compared to 1.5 million taking the SAT. The SAT suffered serious public relations problems in October 2005 when its hired, for-profit scoring company, Pearson Educational Measurement, allowed scoring sheets to be damaged by moisture. The result: 4,411 test takers had scores reported to colleges that were lower than they should have been. It was a nightmare for these students when college rejections began to arrive in the mail. Embarrassed by the scoring errors and feeling the competitive heat from the makers of the ACT, the president of the SAT's College Board, Gaston Capteron, a former business executive and two-term governor of West Virginia, is trying to increase revenue for the College Board, which is technically a nonprofit organization. The College Board is marketing new products including English and math curricula for grades 6 through 12 along with the management of schools. By 2007 it plans to open 11 College Board public schools. In 2006, the College Board reported revenues of $530 million and Caperton's annual compensation as $639,000 with a $110,000 expense account.

Current test usage places a burden on the testing industry. "All testing companies are overwhelmed by the burdens of writing, scoring, and reporting vastly more federal tests than in the past under No Child Left Behind," declares the Washington think tank Education Sector in a 2006 report. The report complains that the testing industry is overwhelmed by "trying to test vastly greater numbers of students under very tight timelines and under highly competitive conditions." In an *Education Week* article, Vaishali Honawar writes, "Watchdogs of the testing industry—dominated by CTB/McGraw, Harcourt Assessment, and Pearson—warn that errors could become only too common as standardized testing in schools multiplies under federal and state mandates."

Finally, many argue that if money is going to be invested in education, there must be some means of measuring its effectiveness. Of course, tests provide the easiest measure to report. Test results can be published in local newspapers or distributed by state agencies. But accountability based on test scores can potentially contribute to greater inequality among school districts. Real estate agents, as I discussed in Chapter 3, are reporting that home buyers are arriving at their offices with lists of school test scores to use in selecting houses. And, as was previously suggested, real estate prices can be correlated with school district test scores. Though there is no proven causal relationship, school districts reporting high test scores might be the most attractive to home buyers with school-age children.

What is the controlling power of standards and tests? First, state academic standards determine what will be taught in the classroom. For instance, state science standards establish the content of instruction in science. Second, state high-stakes tests ensure that teachers teach the content specified in the state's academic standards. The state tests are constructed around the state's academic standards. If students do poorly on high-stakes tests, teachers and school administrators are blamed. Consequently, teachers and administrators are motivated to ensure that classroom instruction complies with academic standards and provides students with the specific knowledge and skills required by the tests.

FEDERAL AND STATE MANDATED TESTS AND EQUALITY OF OPPORTUNITY

The NCLB creates a high-stakes testing model of equality of opportunity as discussed in Chapter 3. Simply put, high-stakes testing means there are important consequences for students and educators resulting from test performance—and also, it appears, for local housing prices. For students, high-stakes tests might determine promotion between grades or graduation from high school. For teachers and school administrators, the results of student test scores can be used to measure their performance or determine their salary increases. For individual schools, test results might determine their continued existence. Low-stakes testing means there are no significant consequences resulting from student test performance.

There is concern that standardized tests cannot be objective in measuring student learning. There are such things as test skills that can be learned. In fact, many private agencies offer courses in test-taking. Also, the wording of questions can reflect particular cultural knowledge. I remember being stumped on a question in a standardized math test because I did not know the meaning of a word. I excelled at math but missed this test item because of my limited cultural knowledge. Writing in *Education Week*, test expert W. James Popham contends:

> If you were to review the actual items in a typical standardized achievement test, you'd find many items whose correct answer depends heavily on the socioeconomic status of a child's family. There are also many items that measure the verbal, quantitative, or spatial aptitudes that children inherit at birth. Such items are better suited to intelligence tests. Clearly items dependent either on the affluence of a student's family or on a child's genetic inheritance are not suitable for evaluating schools.

The testing approach shifts the discussion from the conditions of learning to motivation to learn. By conditions of learning, I mean students having well-trained teachers, complete sets of textbooks, small classes, and school buildings in good repair. The threat of failure on high-stakes tests will, it is assumed, overcome any major obstacles to learning. According to this reasoning:

- Fear of failure will cause students to study.
- Worried about their evaluations by school administrators, teachers will focus on instruction to keep their students from performing poorly on high-stakes tests.
- Worried about their evaluations, principals will work to ensure that teachers prepare students for high-stakes tests.
- Worried about their jobs and public images, superintendents will work to ensure that each school receives high test scores by preparing principals and teachers to ready their students for testing.

DOES FEDERALLY MANDATED HIGH-STAKES TESTING WORK? IS THERE A LACK OF LONGITUDINAL RESEARCH?

There are important research unanswered questions regarding the effects of mandated testing, particularly tests based on the Common Core State Standards. There are no longitudinal studies on the consequences of mandated testing and the Common Core State Standards. For instance, assume that a state education agency adopts the Common Core State Standards in 2012. If a student first experiences the Common Core State Standards in the first grade in 2012, that student would graduate from high school around 2024. This would mean that the consequences of the Common Core State Standards and tests based on those standards could not be fully evaluated and researched until after 2024. Should the Common Core State Standards and related tests have been implemented without longitudinal research on their consequences?

There are many questions regarding high-stakes testing. Does it simply mean improved performance on other tests? Any meaningful determination would require a longitudinal study of the impact of high-stakes testing on a person's life. Does high-stakes testing, which often leads to teachers teaching to the test, reduce students' creativity and their willingness to take risks? It is important to remember that the goal of implementing high-stakes testing is to educate people who can compete in a global labor market. How can this be measured?

There are contradictory research findings about the value of high-stakes testing. In a 2002 study, University of Arizona researchers Audrey Amrein and David Berliner report that high-stakes testing does not improve achievement and might worsen academic performance and increase dropout rates. They find little gain in performance on college entrance examinations by students in high-stakes testing states. Their study was sharply criticized by Stanford researchers Margaret Raymond and Eric Hanushek, who accuse Amrein and Berliner of faulty research methods. Raymond and Hanushek find that the average gain for fourth and eighth graders in mathematics was higher in states using high-stakes testing compared to states not giving much weight to test scores. The Stanford study measures only performance on tests and not the long-term consequences of an educational system centered on test performance. It could be that where standardized testing is used for promotion between grades or for high school graduation, students pay closer attention to learning better test-taking skills.

Contrary to the Stanford study, a 2004 report by Henry Braun of the Educational Testing Service concludes that "comparisons slightly favor the low-stakes testing states." Braun's conclusions were based on a reanalysis of an earlier study by Amrein and Berliner. In other words, students in states with high-stakes testing did not perform any better on college entrance examinations than students in states with low-stakes testing. (Recall that low-stakes testing means there are no significant consequences resulting from student test performance.)

In a 2005 article by Sharon Nichols, Gene Glass, and David C. Berliner's titled "High-Stakes Testing and Student Achievement: Problems for the No Child Left Behind Act," the authors conclude that high-stakes testing disproportionately affects minority students and increases dropouts. Their analysis reveals the following:

- States with greater proportions of minority students implement accountability systems that exert greater pressure. This suggests that any problems associated with high-stakes testing will disproportionately affect America's minority students.
- High-stakes testing pressure is negatively associated with the likelihood that 8th and 10th graders will move into 12th grade.
- Studies suggest that increases in testing pressure are related to larger numbers of students being held back or dropping out of school.
- Increased testing pressure produced no gains in National Assessment of Educational Progress reading scores at the fourth- or eighth-grade levels.
- Prior increases in testing pressure were weakly linked to subsequent increases in NAEP math achievement at the fourth-grade level.

None of these conflicting studies examine the issue that caused the movement for high-stakes testing: Does high-stakes testing improve the ability of American workers to compete in the global labor market? It would be difficult to design a research study to answer this question that includes all possible causal factors. This research problem raises another question: Should politicians impose an educational reform for which there exists no evidence—in fact, there appears to be conflicting evidence—that it will improve the skills of American workers?

DOES FEDERAL TESTING POLICY PROMOTE UNETHICAL BEHAVIOR? IS TEST CHEATING INCREASING?

"An astonishing amount of cheating is taking place on the tests . . . under the federal No Child Left Behind," asserts W. James Popham, an emeritus professor in the Graduate School of Education at the University of California–Los Angeles (UCLA) in a 2006 commentary for *Education Week*. "And the cheating I'm referring to isn't coming from the kids," he continues. Popham identifies the following forms of cheating:

- School administrators erasing incorrect responses on students' answer sheets and substituting correct answers.
- Teachers allowing more time than test instructions require.
- Teachers supplying students with hints about which answers are correct.
- Test preparation sessions using actual test items.

The reasons for the cheating, he argues, are (1) possible embarrassment to school personnel when test scores are reported in local newspapers, (2) fear that the school will not meet adequate yearly progress (AYP) standards, and (3) fear that the school will be designated for improvement.

As Popham indicates, cheating is a major problem in any situation using high-stakes exams. For instance, college entrance exams have always been closely monitored to reduce the possibility of cheating. Now professional staffs are being monitored as high-stakes testing is used to evaluate teachers and school administrators. For example, Texas has been the scene of widespread cheating. Texas administrators and teachers have been accused of erasing student answers and adding correct answers.

There are many other examples. In 1999, teachers and administrators in 32 schools in New York City were accused of erasing wrong answers and doing corrective editing on student answer sheets. A total of 47 principals, teachers, and staff members were implicated in the scandal. Examples of cheating included a seventh-grade teacher who left a sheet of answers to a citywide math test near a pencil sharpener and then urged students to sharpen their pencils while she was out of the room. A fourth-grade teacher discovered an essay question concerning Cubist art on the state English test and then devoted a lecture to Cubism right before the test. But these were somewhat minor compared to the corrective editing of tests by teachers and administrators. In 2000, Houston Public Schools fired a teacher and reprimanded two principals after test tampering was discovered. In Austin, Texas, school officials were accused of raising state accountability ratings through test tampering. One Austin staff member was forced to resign. An elementary school teacher was fired after it was discovered the teacher had used an answer key to change student answers. In addition, Austin school officials changed student identification numbers so students with low scores would not be factored into the school system's accountability ratings.

In Rhode Island, state education officials were forced to cancel the administration of English and mathematics tests for 2000 when it was discovered that many teachers had kept copies of the previous year's exams to use with students as part of the test preparation. The problem was that both years' exams contained the same questions. "It became clear that the scope of the breach was extensive," said Commissioner of Education Peter J. McWalters, "and that the assessment results would be invalid." Also in 2000, officials at one of the best schools in affluent Potomac, Maryland, were accused of cheating—the school's principal resigned and a teacher was suspended. The principal was accused of allowing students extra time to complete state examinations, coaching them on questions, and changing incorrect answers. In Fairfax County, Virginia, charges were brought against a middle school teacher for improper coaching of students for state examinations.

Finally, in 2004, the famed Bracey Report gave its annual Gold Apple award to Steve Orel, who discovered that schools in Birmingham, Alabama, when "threatened with a state takeover, had 'administratively withdrawn' 522 students just before the state tests were administered. The district acknowledged Orel's keen powers of observation by firing him."

"There's no way to tell how much cheating there actually is," claims Monty Neill, director of FairTest, a private education group opposed to the use of standardized tests, "but I get the sense nobody is looking too hard for abuses." Neill believes that because of high-stakes testing, "Schools are turning into test coaching centers, caught up in this frenzy of trying to look their best."

The future of high-stakes testing depends on the resolution of the problems associated with the cost, the effect on students from low-income families, the increasing residential segregation based on test scores, the increasing classroom time devoted to test preparation and test-taking, the emphasis on lower-order thinking, the evaluation of teachers and school administrators, and cheating. These are not minor problems. In addition, there is now in place a testing industry that depends on schools using high-stakes testing for accountability. The testing industry is a major lobbyist for state and national testing. The final resolution of the issues raised by high-stakes testing will depend on the actions of politicians, school officials, and the testing industry.

CONCLUSION

State and federal politicians are increasingly involved in issues of curriculum, methods of instruction, testing, and teacher certification. The trend is for more federal and state involvement in these areas. Should there be a nationalized system of schooling? A pressing issue for the future is deciding whether there should be limits to political involvement in public schooling. Should federal and state politicians determine the content and methods of instruction? What will be the long-term effect of testing based on the Common Core State Standards?

SUGGESTED READINGS AND WORKS CITED IN CHAPTER

Amrein, A. L., and D. C. Berliner. *The Impact of High-Stakes Tests on Student Academic Performance: An Analysis of NAEP Results in States with High-Stakes Tests and ACT, SAT, and AP Test Results in States with High School Graduation Exams.* Educational Policy Studies Laboratory, Education Policy Research Unit, 2002. www.edpolicylab.org. This study shows little gain in performance on college entrance examination by students in high-stakes-testing states.

Archer, Jeff. "R.I. Halts Exams in Wake of Wide-Scale Security Breaches." *Education Week* (March 17, 2000). www.edweek.org. This is a discussion of the Rhode Island scandal over cheating on standardized tests.

Arenson, Karen W. "For SAT Maker, a Broader Push to the Classroom." *The New York Times* (August 16, 2006). www.nytimes.com. This article describes the effort by the SAT maker to increase revenues and expand into other educational services.

Belluck, Pam. "Students Accused of Plotting Mass Slaying." *The New York Times* (November 17, 1998). www.nytimes.com. This is the story of the plot in Burlington, Wisconsin, to kill students and the principal.

Blumenthal, Ralph. "Houston Ties Teachers' Pay to Test Scores." *The New York Times* (January 13, 2006). www.nytimes.com. This article reports on policies in Houston and other school districts to link teachers' and administrators' pay to student scores on high-stakes tests.

Bracey, Gerald. "The 14th Bracey Report on the Condition of Public Education." *Phi Delta Kappan* (October 2004), pp. 149–167. Bracey gives an insightful report on annual events in education. Here, the Gold Apple award is given to a whistle-blower who pointed out that school administrators in Birmingham, Alabama, cheated on state tests.

Braun, Henry. "Reconsidering the Impact of High-Stakes Testing." *Education Policy Analysis Archives*, Vol. 12, no. 1 (January 5, 2004). http://epaa.asu.edu/epaa/v12n1. This study finds that students in states with high-stakes testing do not perform any better than students in states with low-stakes testing on college admission examinations.

Cavanagh, Sean. "Testing Officials Again Tackle Accommodations and Exclusions for Special Student Populations." *Education Week* (July 16, 2008). www.edweek.org. Discusses the wide variations between states and cities on the accommodation of English learners and students with disabilities in tests mandated by No Child Left Behind.

Clines, Francis. "Cheating Report Renews Debate Over Use of Tests to Evaluate Schools." *The New York Times* (June 12, 2000). www.nytimes.com. This is a national report on the effect of cheating on the use of high-stakes tests.

Common Core State Standards Initiative. www.corestandards.org/. This Website provides the Common Core Standards for subjects and grades.

Data Quality Campaign. *Paving the Path to Success: Data for Action 2014.* www.dataqualitycampaign.org/files/DataForAction2014.pdf. Report on efforts to create a central student data bank between states.

Dillon, Sam. "McCain Calls for Limited U.S. Role in Schools." *The New York Times* (September 10, 2008). www.nytimes.com. Republican presidential candidate John McCain believes education is more a state and local responsibility than a federal responsibility.

———. "States Mold School Policies to Win New Federal Money." *The New York Times* (November 11, 2009). www.nytimes.com. Describes how states shape their educational policies to meet federal demands.

Democratic Party Platform (July 21, 2016). www.presidency.ucsb.edu/papers_pdf/117717.pdf on January 10, 2017. Contains Democratic support of the opt-out movement from standardized tests and no support of the Common Core State Standards.

Education Week. www.edweek.org. This weekly newspaper is one of the best sources of information on national educational politics.

Goodman, Ken. *Ten Alarming Facts About No Child Left Behind.* www.sosvoice.org on Monday, July 26, 2004. The father of the whole-language movement attacks No Child Left Behind, particularly for imposing national methods for teaching reading and math.

Goodnough, Abby. "If Test Scores of Students Swell, So May Superintendents' Wallets." *The New York Times* (September 25, 2002). www.nytimes.com. Goodnough describes bonus system for school superintendents based on student test scores.

Haney, Walt. "The Texas Miracle in Education." *Education Policy Analysis Archives: Center for Education, Research, Analysis, and Innovation* (August 21, 2000). http://epaa.asu.edu/epaa/v8n41.

Hartocollis, Anemona. "9 Educators Accused of Encouraging Students to Cheat." *The New York Times* (May 3, 2000). www.nytimes.com. This article reports on the New York City cheating scandal.

Herold, Benjamin. "'Big Data' Research Effort Faces Student-Privacy Questions." *Education Week* (October 21, 2014). www.edweek.org/ew/articles/2014/10/22/09learnsphere.h34.html. Article discusses concern about the collection of big data about student behaviors.

Honawar, Vaishali. "SAT Glitches Prompt Broader Testing Worries." *Education Week* (March 22, 2006). www.edweek.org. After the incorrect scoring of SAT tests in 2005 and other mishaps in the testing industry, this article reports on continuing concerns about the ability of companies to handle the demands placed on schools to use high-stakes tests.

Hu, Winnie. "9 Fired and 11 Others Face Dismissal in Cheating Scandal." *The New York Times* (December 12, 1999). www.nytimes.com. This article reports on the New York City testing scandal.

Johnston, Robert. "Texas Presses Districts in Alleged Test-Tampering Cases." *Education Week* (March 15, 2000). www.edweek.org. Johnston discusses the testing scandal in Texas.

Kaufman, Phillip, et al. "Indicators of School Crime and Safety: 2000." *Education Statistics Quarterly* (February 2001). Indicators of school crime.

———. *Indicators of School Crime and Safety: 2001.* Washington, DC: U.S. Departments of Education and Justice. NCES 2002–113/NCJ—190075, 2001. This is a recent survey of school crime and violence.

Keller, Bess. "Next Pay-Plan Decision Up to Denver Voters." *Education Week* (March 31, 2004). www.edweek.org. Denver teachers vote for merit pay plan based on student test scores.

Klein, Alyson. "Race to the Top Winners, Meeting in D.C., See Challenges Ahead." *Education Week* (September 1, 2010). www.edweek.org. Quotes U.S. Secretary of Education Arne Duncan's remarks to winners of the Race to the Top.

Lawton, Millicent. "Facing Deadline, Calif. Is Locked in Battle Over How to Teach Math." *Education Week* (March 12, 1997). www.edweek.org. This article discusses California's political battle over the best method for teaching math.

Lessinger, Leon. *Every Kid a Winner: Accountability in Education.* Chicago: Science Research Associates College Division, 1970. Lessinger presents the classic justification for accountability standards in American education.

Manzo, Kathleen Kennedy. "Limitations on Approved Topics for Reading Sessions Rile Teacher Trainers." *Education Week* (November 5, 1997). www.edweek.org. This is a discussion of the California state law restricting the use of whole-language methods to teach reading.

Mathews, Jay. "Test Wars: The SAT vs. the ACT." *Newsweek* (August 28, 2006), pp. 78–80. This article describes the struggle between SAT and ACT to control the college entrance examination market.

Mulvey, Cindy. "Time Devoted to Testing Surprises New Teacher." *Education Week* (April 5, 2006). www.edweek.org. In a letter to the editor, a third-grade teacher complains about the amount of the school year devoted to testing.

National Center for Education Statistics. "Indicator 33: Public School; Revenue Sources." *The Condition of Education 2010*. Washington, DC: U.S. Department of Education, 2010, p. 54. Provides information on percentages of revenue supporting local schools from the federal, state, and local governments.

———. *Violence and Discipline Problems in U.S. Public Schools: 1996–97*. Washington, DC: U.S. Department of Education, 1998. This is a sweeping survey of violence in U.S. schools.

National Commission on Excellence in Education. *A Nation at Risk*. Washington, DC: U.S. Government Printing Office, 1983. This is the report that launched the current standards and testing movement to prepare American workers for a global workforce.

Nichols, Sharon, Gene Glass, and David Berliner. *High-Stakes Testing and Student Achievement: Problems for the No Child Left Behind Act*. Arizona State University, Education Policy Studies Laboratory (September 2005). http://edpolicylab.org.

Popham, W. James. "Educator Cheating on No Child Left Behind Tests: Can We Stop It." *Education Week* (April 19, 2006). www.edweek.org. Popham argues that tests that impact teacher and administrator salaries and affect calculations of adequate yearly progress tempt teachers and school administrators to cheat in both giving tests and reporting test scores.

———. "Standardized Achievement Tests: Misnamed and Misleading." *Education Week* (September 19, 2001). www.edweek.org. A leading expert on test making, Popham criticizes the idea that standardized tests measure only achievement.

Portner, Jessica. "Clinton Releases Findings of School Violence Survey." *Education Week* (March 25, 1998). www.edweek.org. President Clinton's comments on school violence are reported.

Public Law 107-110, 107th Congress, January 8, 2002 [H.R. 1]. *No Child Left Behind Act of 2001*. Washington, DC: U.S. Government Printing Office, 2002. This federal legislation deals with high-stakes testing, reading, and school violence, among other issues.

Raymond, Margaret, and Eric Hanushek. "High-Stakes Research: The Campaign Against Accountability Brought Forth a Tide of Negative Anecdotes and Deeply Flawed Research." *Education Next* (Summer 2003). www.educationnext.org. This article disputes the findings of Amrein and Berliner that found little gain in performance on college entrance examination by students in high-stakes testing states.

Report of the Platform Committee. *Renewing America's Promise*. Washington, DC: Democratic National Committee, 2008. Contains education planks of the Democratic platform.

Report Roundup. "Test Scores Linked to Home Prices." *Education Week* (July 26, 2006). www.edweek.org. Economist finds that a 20 percent increase in test scores in a district results in a 7 percent increase in housing prices in that district.

Republican Platform 2016. https://gop.com/platform/ on November 23, 2016. Contains Republican statement on rejection of the Common Core State Standards.

Richardson, Lynda. "Time-Zone Caper: Suspect Is Arrested in Testing Scheme." *The New York Times* (October 29, 1996), pp. 1, B17. Richardson reports on an example of one cheating scheme on high-stakes tests.

Spring, Joel. *Conflict of Interests: The Politics of American Education*, 5th edition. New York: McGraw-Hill, 2004. This book provides an analysis of educational politics in the United States.

———. *Political Agendas for Education: From the Christian Coalition to the Green Party*, 3rd edition. New York: Routledge, 2005. This is a concise guide to the educational platforms of the major political organizations in the United States.

Toch, Thomas. *Margins of Error: The Testing Industry in No Child Left Behind ERQ.* Washington, DC, Education Sector Reports, 2006. www.educationsector.org. Report on problems facing the testing industry.

U.S. Department of Education. *The Condition of Education 2018.* Washington, DC: U.S. Department of Education, 2018. This publication provides information on sources of school revenues.

———. *Every Student Succeeds Act (ESSA): Approved ESSA Plans: Explainer and Key Takeaways From Each State.* www.ed.gov/ESSA on January 22, 2019. Highlights state plans submitted under ESSA.

———. *Modified Academic Achievement Standards: Non-Regulatory Guidance* (July 20, 2007). www.ed.gov/policy/speced/guid/nclb/twopercent.doc.

———. *Race to the Top Fund-Executive Summary Notice; Notice of Proposed Priorities, Requirements, Definitions, and Selection Criteria* (July 29, 2009), p. 1. Criteria for Race to the Top. http://www/ed/gov/programs/racetotop/executive-summary.pdf on September 24, 2009.

———. "Spellings Announces New Special Education Guideline, Details Workable, 'Common-Sense' Policy to Help States Implement No Child Left Behind." *U.S. Department of Education Press Release* (May 10, 2005). www.ed.gov/news/pressreleases/2005/05/05102005.html. These are the guidelines for testing students with disabilities under the requirements of No Child Left Behind.

———. *Statistics of State School Systems; Revenues and Expenditures for Public Elementary and Secondary Education; and Common Core of Data Surveys* (May 2001). This is a historical review of the proportion of revenues from local, state, and federal sources.

Wilgorin, Jodi. "National Study Examines Reasons Why Pupils Excel." *The New York Times* (July 26, 2000). www.nytimes.com. This is a report on the Rand Corporation study on factors that contribute to high performance on high-stakes examinations.

Yardley, Jim. "Critics Say a Focus on Test Scores Is Overshadowing Education in Texas." *The New York Times* (October 2000). www.nytimes.com. This is a summary of criticisms of the Texas government's emphasis on test scores as a method of improving education.

Zehr, Mary Ann. "New Era for Testing English-Learners Begins." *Education Week* (July 12, 2006). www.edweek.org. This is a report on 44 states that have developed English proficiency tests aligned with state English language proficiency standards. These tests are required under No Child Left Behind.

———. "State Testing of English-Language Learners." *Education Week* (June 15, 2005). www.edweek.org. Zehr reports complaints by school districts about states not providing tests in students' native languages and the effect on calculating adequate yearly progress.

———. "U.S. Cites Problems in California Testing." *Education Week* (November 9, 2005). www.edweek.org. Zehr reports on the U.S. Department of Education's criticism of California for accommodating English language learners in the state's testing program.

CHAPTER 10

The Profession of Teaching

U.S. Secretary of Education Betsy DeVos declared in a speech to the Heritage Foundation on January 23, 2019, that teachers' unions are the greatest impediment to school choice. She made the statement just days after the Los Angeles teachers' union, representing the second largest school district in the United States, reached a settlement that included capping the number of charter schools that would be allowed. The Los Angeles union had protested that charter schools were draining money away from public-school systems. In addition, Los Angeles teachers complained about the amount of class time given to required testing.

New York Times reporters Jennifer Medina and Dana Goldstein summarized the final agreement:

> The deal includes caps on class sizes, and hiring full-time nurses for every school, as well as a librarian for every middle and high school in the district by the fall of 2020. The union also won a significant concession from the district on standardized tests: Next year a committee will develop a plan to reduce the number of assessments by half. The pro-charter school board agreed to vote on a resolution calling on the state to cap the number of charter schools. Teachers also won a 6 percent pay raise, but that was the same increase proposed by the district before the strike.

During the year preceding the Los Angeles teacher walkout, there were strikes in West Virginia, Oklahoma, Arizona, and Kentucky. These strikes were over low teacher salaries and the decline in state school funding.

Writing for the *New York Times*, Dana Goldstein reported that the 2018 Arizona strike was prompted by cuts in the state school budget:

> The state [Arizona] has cut approximately $1 billion from schools since the 2008 recession, while also cutting taxes. It

spent under $7,500 per pupil annually in 2015, the last year for which census data was available; only Utah and Idaho spent less ... many districts in Arizona are facing teacher shortages in subjects like math, science and special education.

In West Virginia, teachers in 2018 struck for higher pay. Citing the success of the West Virginia strike, Oklahoma teachers went on strike, circling the state Capitol and chanting, "No funding, no future!" Oklahoma teachers are among the poorest paid in the United States, with many reported as fleeing to Texas, which has higher teacher salaries. In Kentucky, the issue was the state teacher retirement plan. A bill introduced into the Kentucky state legislature would change the teacher retirement from a defined-benefit pension to a hybrid of plans, such as 401(k) accounts and reduction of cost-of-living increases for retirees. Teacher retirement systems have been one of the benefits attracting people to the teaching profession.

These recent teacher strikes highlight the complex nature of teaching. In this chapter I will discuss the following issues related to the teaching profession:

- The changing roles of teachers in the United States
- Teachers and No Child Left Behind and Race to the Top
- Teachers' salaries and turnover
- Teachers' unions
- Attempts to reduce the power of teachers' unions
- Performance pay
- Teachers' rights and liabilities

THE CHANGING ROLES OF AMERICAN TEACHERS

What is an American teacher? Guardian of morality and American character? Civilizer of Western mining and ranching towns? Saint of freed slaves? Social worker in urban slums? Americanizer of immigrants? Protector against fascism and communism? Warrior against poverty? Champion of the global economy? As educational goals change, so has the image and training of teachers.

Today, the emphasis is on teachers as a key element in educating workers for the global economy. Protecting the U.S. role in the global economy continues the messianic vision of teachers as the saviors of society. In the nineteenth century, the development of professional teacher training paralleled the changing image of a teacher from laughable weakling to the protector of American morality and character. In the 1830s, Horace Mann's declaration that common schools eliminate crime and morally reform society required the recruitment and training of moral teachers. The key was the feminization and professional training of the teaching force. Addressing the New York legislature in 1819, Emma Willard, founder of the Troy Female Seminary, whose main purpose was to educate teachers, declared the saving grace of female teachers:

> Who knows how great and good a race of men may yet arise from the forming hands of mothers, enlightened by the bounty of that beloved country, to defend her liberties, to plan her future improvements and to raise her to unparalleled glory.

In 1839, Mann supported establishment of a teacher-training institution in Lexington, Massachusetts. Called a *normal school*, this institution trained teachers for the elementary grades. Mann quickly recognized the value of recruiting women into the teaching force. He wrote in 1846: "Reason and experience have long since demonstrated that children under 10 or 12 years of age can be more genially taught and more successfully governed by a female than by a male teacher." As protectors of morality, Mann emphasized the importance of teachers being "of pure tastes, of good manners, [and] exemplary morals." He charged local school committees with the responsibility of seeing that no teacher cross the school "threshold, who is not clothed, from the crown of his head to the sole of his foot, in garments of virtue."

Others echoed the sentiment that female teachers would be guardians of American morality. Teachers were to save Western mining and cow towns from lawlessness and immorality. Through the Board of National Popular Education, Catherine Beecher recruited teachers to civilize the West. Writing in the 1840s, Beecher envisioned:

> In all parts of our country, in each neglected village, or new settlement, the Christian female teacher will quietly take her station . . . teaching . . . habits of neatness, order, and thrift; opening the book of knowledge, inspiring the principles of morality, and awakening the hope of immortality."

After the Civil War, female teachers rushed into the South with a mission of creating social equality and political rights for freed slaves.

However, female teachers were often demeaned and exploited. Even into the twentieth century, most school districts did not allow female teachers to marry. In addition, teaching contracts warned female teachers not to be seen in public with men other than their fathers or brothers. Female teachers were to be moral models for their communities. In addition, female teachers were paid less than male teachers. The Boston Board of Education in 1841 urged the hiring of female teachers because:

> As a class, they [women] never look forward, as young men almost invariably do, to a period of legal emancipation from parental control, when they are to break away from the domestic circle and go abroad into the world, to build up a fortune for themselves; and hence, the sphere of hope and of effort is narrower, and the whole forces of the mind are more readily concentrated upon present duties.

Willard S. Elsbree, in *The American Teacher: Evolution of a Profession in a Democracy*, reports that from the 1830s up to the Civil War, increasing numbers of women entered teaching. The Civil War, with its demands for military manpower, completed the evolution of elementary school teaching from a male occupation to a primarily female occupation. For example, Elsbree states that in Indiana the number of male teachers in all grades dropped from 80 percent in 1859 to 58 percent in 1864; in Ohio the number of male teachers went from 52 percent in 1862 to 41 percent in 1864. The second-class citizenship of women in the nineteenth century made it possible to keep teachers' salaries low and contributed to the continuing low status of teaching as it became professionalized.

The growth of urban centers and immigration changed the image of a teacher from protector of morality to that of social welfare worker and vocational trainer. Teachers were enlisted to fight urban problems of crowding, epidemics, drugs, and crime. In addition, they were to prepare students for work in the modern factory. As the United States transformed from a rural to an industrialized nation in the late nineteenth and early twentieth centuries, teachers became workers in large educational bureaucracies. It was during this period, as I discuss later in the chapter, that teachers, following the lead of other workers, began to unionize.

Paralleling the new role of teachers as workers and defenders of industrial life, the professionalization of teaching moved from local control to the bureaucratic confines of state governments. Nineteenth-century teachers were usually certified by taking an examination administered by the employing school system or the county board of education. Licensing, or the granting of certificates to teach, was based primarily on examination and not on the number of education courses taken. Elsbree reports that in 1898 only 4 states had centralized certification or licensing at the state level. By 1933, 42 states had centralized licensing at the state level; the primary requirement for gaining a teacher certificate was the completion of courses in teacher education and other fields.

The centralization of certification and the dependence on teacher-education courses led to a rapid expansion of normal schools and colleges of education in the early twentieth century. State certification laws and expanded training in education completed the professionalization of teaching. Since 1933, this pattern of professionalization has continued, with many normal schools becoming college and university departments of education. Course requirements in most states have generally increased, and there has been greater monitoring of teacher-education programs. From the 1920s to the 1950s, teachers were asked to promote 100 percent Americanism against the threat of fascist and communist ideas. During this period, many states required teachers to take loyalty oaths. Organizations such as the American Legion and Daughters of the American Revolution helped purge schools of teachers with leftist ideas. When it appeared in the 1950s that the United States was slipping behind the Soviet Union in the military arms race and conquest of space, American teachers were called on to educate a generation of students to win the technological race. As worries shifted to poverty and race relations in the 1960s, teachers became warriors in War on Poverty programs. As unemployment and high inflation gripped the nation in the 1970s and 1980s, teachers were called on to guide students into the labor market.

Now, No Child Left Behind and Race to the Top are pushing the certification of teachers to new levels of control and hierarchy, but some age-old questions about the profession of teaching still remain:

- Should teacher education change as the goals of schooling change?
- Should teacher education be focused on the imperatives of the global economy?
- Should teachers be trained to meet the special needs of children growing up in poverty, children from differing cultural backgrounds, children with special needs, and gay/lesbian students?
- Should teacher-education programs prepare teachers for training future citizens and inculcating moral and social values?
- Who should control teacher certification?

NO CHILD LEFT BEHIND AND RACE TO THE TOP: HIGHLY QUALIFIED TEACHERS

No Child Left Behind and Race to the Top are new phases in the history of U.S. teachers involving the federal government directly in the training and certification of teachers. No Child Left Behind requires that public-school teachers be "highly qualified." The legislation's Title II—Preparing, Training, and Recruiting High-Quality Teachers—

proposes increasing student academic achievement through strategies such as improving teacher and principal quality and increasing the number of highly qualified teachers in the classroom and highly qualified principals and assistant principals in schools.

Race to the Top emphasizes new methods for evaluating teachers and the collection of student test score data to evaluate teacher-education programs. Speaking to members of the National Education Association, Secretary of Education Arne Duncan explained the issues and goals:

> We created seniority rules that protect teachers from arbitrary and capricious management, and that's a good goal. But sometimes those rules place teachers in schools and communities where they won't succeed, and that's wrong.
>
> We created tenure rules to make sure that a struggling teacher gets a fair opportunity to improve, and that's a good goal. But when an ineffective teacher gets a chance to improve and doesn't—and when the tenure system keeps that teacher in the classroom anyway—then the system is protecting jobs rather than children. That's not a good thing. We need to work together to change that.
>
> Data can also help identify and support teachers who are struggling. And it can help evaluate them. The problem is that some states prohibit linking student achievement and teacher effectiveness.

THE REWARDS OF TEACHING

Why do some college students pursue a teaching career when they could earn more in other occupations requiring a college education? One answer is that teachers find their greatest reward in interacting with students. In *A Place Called School*, John Goodlad reports from his survey that the top reasons given by students for entering teaching are "having a satisfying job" and liking and wanting to help children. Despite these altruistic reasons, most students in the survey faced critical comments from family members and friends. Some parents rejected the decision and refused to support their child's schooling in teacher education.

Also, in comparison with many corporate and factory jobs, teachers enjoy a great deal of autonomy in the classroom. It has been estimated that teachers make more than 200 decisions an hour in their classrooms. These decisions range from curricular and teaching problems to behavioral problems. Unlike routine work, teaching involves creative decision making. In a national survey, "Teachers' Working Conditions," Susan

Choy found that "the vast majority of teachers thought that they had a good deal of control in their own classroom over practices such as evaluating and grading students, selecting teaching techniques, and determining the amount of homework to be assigned."

Other ancillary rewards of teaching are attractive to many individuals. A popular reward is the time for extended vacations and travel provided by the long summer vacation and other school holidays. Second to vacation time is the security of income and position. In most states, teacher tenure laws provide a security not often found in other jobs.

Table 10.1 is the National Education Association's 2016 report on average teacher salaries. Of course, average teacher salaries vary from state to state. According to the 2016 National Education report:

> In 2015–16, the salary in the state with the highest average annual salary of classroom teachers is expected to be 85.5 percent higher than that in the state with the lowest salary. The dollar gap has grown from $25,116 in 2005–06 to $35,932 in 2015–16.

A 2013 report by the American Federation of Teachers on "International Perspectives: Teacher Recruitment and Retention" bemoaned the low U.S. teacher salaries and status compared to other countries with school systems sometimes ranked similar to the United States. The report states:

> The cost of college to potential teachers in Finland and Singapore is virtually nothing, and the cost of higher education in South Korea is significantly less than in the United States. Teachers in all three countries are paid relatively higher salaries than teachers in the United States. In fact, South Korean teachers rank between doctors and engineers in terms of salary potential.

Table 10.1 Ten-Year Trend in Average Annual Salaries for Public-School Classroom Teachers, Select Years between 2006 and 2016

School Year	Elementary ($)	Secondary ($)	All ($)
2005–2006	48,579	49,492	49,088
2008–2009	53,988	54,800	54,354
2010–2011	55,160	56,436	55,586
2013–2014	56,368	56,999	56,648
2015–2016	57,598	59,568	58,064

Adapted from National Education Association, "Rankings and Estimates: Rankings of the States 2015 and Estimates of School Statistics 2016," May 2016, p. 78. Retrieved from www.nea.org/assets/docs/2016_NEA_Rankings_And_Estimates.pdf on March 7, 2017.

TEACHER TURNOVER

Do working conditions cause teachers to leave the profession? The 2013 MetLife "American Teacher" survey found, "Principal and teacher job satisfaction is declining. Principals' satisfaction with their jobs in the public schools has decreased nine percentage points since it was last measured in 2008." The report continues:

> Teacher satisfaction has dropped [since 2008] precipitously by 23 percentage points, including a five-point decrease in the last year, to the lowest level it has been in the survey in 25 years. A majority of teachers report that they feel under great stress at least several days a week, a significant increase from 1985 when this was last measured.

Dissatisfied teachers often leave the profession. The following provides the job satisfaction statistics in the MetLife survey:

Profile of Teachers with Lower Job Satisfaction

Personal Characteristics

- More than twice as likely to feel under great stress several days a week or more (65% vs. 28%)
- More likely to be mid-career teachers (6 to 20 years' experience) (56% vs. 48%)
- Less likely to be new teachers (16% vs. 27%)

School Characteristics

- More likely to teach in schools with two-thirds or more low-income students (42% vs. 33%)
- Just as likely to teach in urban schools (31% vs. 26%)
- Just as likely to teach in schools with two-thirds or more minority students (32% vs. 26%)
- Just as likely to teach at the elementary school level (49% vs. 53%), middle school level (16% vs. 17%), or high school level (28% vs. 24%)

Student Achievement, Curriculum, and Instruction

- Less likely to report that all or most of their students are performing at or above grade level in English language arts and mathematics (50% vs. 61%)
- More likely to say it is very challenging or challenging for a school's leaders to address the individual needs of diverse learners (81% vs.

73%) and create and maintain an academically rigorous learning environment (66% vs. 56%)

- Just as likely to say it is very challenging or challenging for a school's leaders to implement the Common Core State Standards (61% vs. 57%)

TEACHERS' UNIONS AND TEACHER POLITICS

There are two teachers' unions. One is the National Education Association (NEA), and the other is the American Federation of Teachers (AFT). Both unions have traditionally been active in supporting a wide variety of measures to benefit teachers and schools. In her speech "Why Teachers Should Organize," Margaret Haley, the first woman to ever speak from the floor of a national meeting of the NEA, declared, "Two ideals are struggling for supremacy in American life today: one the industrial ideal, dominating thru [sic] supremacy of commercialism . . . the other, the ideal of democracy, the ideal of educators." Inviting teachers to organize to protect the interests of children, workers, and democracy, Haley exhorted, "It will be well indeed if the teachers have the courage of their convictions and face all that the labor unions have faced with the same courage and perseverance." Delivered in 1904, Haley's speech marked the rise of teacher unionism and the eventual founding of the NEA's rival organization—the AFT.

In 1998, echoing Haley's idealism, Mary Kimmel bemoaned the continued rivalry between the NEA and AFT: "How can students learn if they don't have a full stomach and a safe environment? I don't know how we as educators can battle foes of public education if we're still fighting against ourselves." While struggling to overcome the differences between the two teachers' unions, organized teachers fulfilled Haley's dream of becoming an important force in American education and politics. Even national politicians paid attention to the power of the teachers' unions.

Both teachers' unions, the AFT and the NEA, actively participate in national elections. They work for both presidential and congressional candidates. Over the last two decades, they have given most of their support to candidates from the Democratic Party. This has created a split between the two national political parties over teachers' unions. Overall, Republicans oppose the work of teachers' unions, while Democrats are supportive. Of course, like other aspects of American politics, these alliances can vary from state to state. In recent years, the Democratic and Republican Parties, much to the consternation of the two unions, have supported revision of state teacher tenure and dismissal laws.

Besides working in election campaigns, both unions have full-time Washington lobbyists who try to ensure that federal legislation does not jeopardize the welfare of teachers. Also, both unions maintain lobbyists at the state level and work for candidates to the state legislature. At the local level, teachers' unions have increasingly supported and campaigned for candidates in local school board elections. The involvement of teachers' unions in national, state, and local politics has made them a powerful political force.

In 2014, faced with political attacks on both unions and changes resulting from federal intervention, the agendas of both unions were very similar. Writing for *Education Week*, Stephen Sawchuk and Liana Heitin reported that both unions:

> Attacked the prominence of standardized-test scores in judging both students and teachers. And in recent months, both unions have qualified their support for the Common Core State Standards, especially as it pertains to implementation. . . [and] pressure brought by internal factions that have urged the unions to take a tougher stance against market-based education policies.

A BRIEF HISTORY OF THE NEA

Founded in 1857, the NEA adopted the goal of nationalizing the work of state education associations. This would be one of its major functions in the history of American education. The letter inviting representatives to the founding meeting states, "Believing that what state associations have accomplished for the states may be done for the whole country by a National Association, we, the undersigned, invite our fellow-teachers throughout the United States to assemble in Philadelphia."

The 1857 meeting in Philadelphia gave birth to an organization that in the nineteenth and early twentieth centuries had major influence over the shaping of American schools and contributed to the nationalizing of the American school system. From the platform of its conventions and the work of its committees came curriculum proposals and policy statements that were adopted from coast to coast. Until the 1960s, the work of the NEA tended to be dominated by school superintendents, college professors, and administrators. These educational leaders took the proposals of the NEA back to their local communities for discussion and possible adoption.

Examples of the work of the NEA include its major role in the shaping of the modern high school. In 1892, the NEA formed the Committee of Ten on Secondary School Studies under the leadership of Charles Eliot, the president of Harvard University. The Committee of Ten appointed nine subcommittees with a total membership of 100 to decide the future of the American high school. The membership of these committees reflected the domination of the organization by school administrators and representatives of higher education: 53 were college presidents or professors, 23 were headmasters of private schools, and the rest were superintendents and representatives from teacher-training institutions. The work of the Committee of Ten set the stage for the creation in 1913 of the NEA Commission on the Reorganization of Secondary Education, which in 1918 issued its epoch-making report, *Cardinal Principles of Secondary Education*. This report urged the creation of comprehensive high schools offering a variety of curricula, as opposed to the establishment of separate high schools offering a single curriculum, such as college preparatory, vocational, and commercial. The report became the major formative document of the modern high school.

The NEA also influenced the standardization of teacher training in the United States. The Normal Department of the NEA began surveying the status of institutions for teacher education in 1886, and debates began within the organization about the nature of teacher education. The official historian of the NEA, Edgar B. Wesley, stated in his *NEA: The First Hundred Years*: "By 1925 the training of teachers was rather systematically standardized." The Normal Department of the NEA can claim a large share of the credit for this standardization.

NEA conventions and meetings further became a central arena for the discussion of curriculum changes in elementary and secondary schools. During the 1920s and 1930s, many surveys, studies, yearbooks, and articles were published. In 1924, the Department of Superintendence began issuing what were to be successive yearbooks on various aspects of the curriculum at various grade levels. In 1943, the Society for Curriculum Study merged with the NEA Department of Supervisors and Directors of Instruction to form an enlarged department called the Association for Supervision and Curriculum Development (ASCD). The ASCD is still recognized as the major professional organization for the discussion of curriculum issues.

After the passage of the National Defense Education Act in 1958, the NEA's leadership role in the determination of national educational policy was greatly reduced as the federal government became the major springboard for national policy. The NEA became an organization whose central focus was teacher welfare and government lobbying. This shift was a result of several developments: the emergence of the leadership role of the federal government, demands within the NEA for more emphasis on teacher welfare, greater democratic control of the organization, and the success of the AFT in winning collective bargaining for its members (thus serving as a model for the NEA).

In 1962, the NEA's activities underwent a dramatic transformation when it launched a program for collective negotiations. This meant that local affiliates would attempt to achieve collective-bargaining agreements with local boards of education. This development completely changed the nature of local organizations and required the rewriting of local constitutions to include collective bargaining. Up to this point, local school administrators had controlled many local education associations, which used the local organizations to convey policies determined by the board and administration. Collective bargaining reversed this situation and turned the local affiliates into organizations that told boards and administrators what teachers wanted.

Collective bargaining created a new relationship between locals of the NEA and local boards of education. Traditionally, local units of the NEA might plead for the interests of their members, but they most often simply helped carry out policies of local school boards and administrators. Teachers bargained individually with the school board over salary and working conditions. With collective bargaining, teachers voted for an organization to represent their demands before the school board. Once selected as a representative of the local teachers, the organization would negotiate with the school board over working conditions and salaries. Many school boards were caught by surprise when their usually compliant local of the NEA suddenly demanded higher wages and better working conditions for all teachers.

The NEA's early approach to collective bargaining differed from that of the union-oriented AFT. The NEA claimed it was involved in professional negotiating and not in union collective bargaining. Professional negotiation, according to the NEA, would remove negotiation procedures from labor precedents and laws and would resort to state educational associations, rather than those of labor, to mediate or resolve conflicts that could not be settled locally. All pretense of the NEA not being a union ended in the 1970s, when the NEA joined the Coalition of American Public Employees (CAPE). CAPE is a nonprofit corporation consisting of the National Education Association; the American Federation of State, County, and Municipal Employees; the National Treasury Employees Union; the Physicians National Housestaff Association; and the American Nurses Association. These organizations represent about four million public employees. The stated purpose of CAPE is "to provide a means of marshaling and coordinating the legislative, legal, financial, and public relations resources of the member organizations in matters of common concern." The most important of these matters "is supporting legislation to provide collective-bargaining rights to all public employees, including teachers."

By the 1980s, support of collective-bargaining legislation became one of many legislative goals of the NEA; the organization by this time was also directing a great deal of its energies to lobbying for legislation and support of political candidates. The turning point for the NEA was its endorsement of Jimmy Carter in the 1976 presidential election. This was the first time the NEA had supported a presidential candidate. After this initial involvement, the NEA expanded its activity to support candidates in primary elections. In 1980, the NEA worked actively in the primaries to ensure the victory of Jimmy Carter over Edward Kennedy for the Democratic nomination. Through the 1990s, the NEA committed itself to the support of Democratic candidates for the White House.

Today, as discussed in the last section, the NEA is concerned with attacks on teacher unions, tenure laws, and standardized testing. In 2014, NEA president Lily Eskelsen García announced support of testing to guide instruction but stated that parents and educators know the "one-size-fits-all annual federal testing structure has not worked." In the same year, an NEA article announced, "NEA Survey: Nearly Half of Teachers Consider Leaving Profession Due to Standardized Testing."

A BRIEF HISTORY OF THE AFT

Unlike the NEA's origins as a national policymaking organization, the AFT began in the struggle by female grade-school teachers for an adequate pension law in Illinois. The first union local, the Chicago Teachers Federation, was formed in 1897 under the leadership of Catherine Goggin and Margaret Haley. Its early fights centered on pensions and teacher salaries. Because of its success in winning salary increases, its membership increased to 2,500 by the end of its first year. In 1902, with the urging of famous settlement-house reformer Jane Addams, the Chicago Teachers Federation joined the Chicago Federation of Labor, which placed it under the broad umbrella of the American Federation of Labor (AFL).

From its beginnings, the AFT placed teacher-welfare issues and improving public education in the more general context of the labor movement in the United States. In an interview titled "The School-Teacher Unionized" in the November 1905 issue of the *Educational Review*, Margaret Haley declared: "We expect by affiliation with labor to arouse the workers and the whole people, through the workers, to the dangers confronting the public schools from the same interests and tendencies that are undermining the foundations of our democratic republic." Those "same interests" referred to in Haley's speech were big business organizations, against which Haley felt both labor and educators were struggling. The early union movement was based on the belief that there was unity between the educators' struggle to gain more financial support for the schools from big business and labor's struggle with the same interests to win collective-bargaining rights. Haley went on to state:

> It is necessary to make labor a constructive force in society, or it will be a destructive force. If the educational question could be understood by the labor men, and the labor question by the educators, both soon would see they are working to the same end, and should work together.

Margaret Haley's comments highlighted the union's efforts to create mutually supportive roles between teachers and organized labor. On the one hand, teachers were to work for the interests of workers by fighting for better schools and working to remove antilabor material from the classroom. Teachers would fight to provide the best education for workers' children, and organized labor would provide the resources of its organization to support the teachers' struggle for improved working conditions and greater financial support for the schools. In addition, the type of education received by children in the schools would give children the economic and political knowledge needed to continue the work of the union movement, and teachers could share their knowledge with the adult members of the labor movement. Teachers would also increase their political and economic knowledge through their association with the labor movement.

In December 1912, the newly established magazine of the union movement, the *American Teacher*, issued a statement of the beliefs of the growing union movement in education. First, the statement argued that the improvement of American education depended on arousing teachers to realize that "their professional and social standing is far too low to enable them to produce effective results in teaching." Second, it was necessary for teachers to study the relation of education "to social progress, and to understand some important social and economic movements going on in the present-day world." Third, it was believed that teachers could use their experience in teaching to adjust education to the needs of modern living. Fourth, in one of the earliest declarations for the end of sexism in education, the statement called for high-quality teaching "without sex-antagonism."

In 1915, union locals from Chicago and Gary, Indiana, met and officially formed the AFT. In 1916, this group, along with locals from New York, Pennsylvania, Oklahoma, and Washington, DC, were accepted into the AFL. At the presentation ceremony, the head of the AFL, Samuel Gompers, welcomed the AFT to

> the fold and the bond of unity and fraternity of the organized labor movement of our Republic. We earnestly hope . . . that it may . . . give and receive mutual sympathy and support which can be prop-

erly exerted for the betterment of all who toil and give service—aye, for all humanity.

It was not until 1944 that the AFT exercised any organizational control over a local school system. In 1944, the AFT local in Cicero, Illinois, signed the first collective-bargaining contract with a board of education. The form of the contract was that of a regular labor-union contract. It recognized the local as the sole bargaining agent of the teachers and listed pay schedules and grievance procedures. At the annual convention of the AFT in 1946, a committee was assigned to study collective bargaining and its application to school management. In addition, material was to be collected from trade unions on the education of shop stewards and union practices. With the introduction of collective bargaining, the AFT entered a new stage in its development.

The involvement of the AFT in collective bargaining led naturally to the question of teacher strikes. Since its founding the AFT had a no-strike policy. In 1946, the use of the strike for supporting teachers' demands became a major issue at the annual convention. Those supporting the use of the strike argued it was the only means available to arouse an apathetic citizenry to the problems in American education. It was also the only meaningful leverage teachers had against local school systems. AFT members who favored retention of the no-strike policy argued that teachers were in a public service profession and that work stoppage was a violation of public trust. In addition, it was argued that a strike deprived children of an education and was counter to the democratic ideal of a child's right to an education.

The AFT maintained its no-strike policy in the face of growing militancy among individual locals. In 1947, the Buffalo, New York, Teachers Federation declared a strike for higher salaries. The strike was considered at the time the worst teacher work stoppage in the history of the country. Other local unions supported the strikers, with local drivers delivering only enough fuel to the schools to keep the pipes from freezing. The Buffalo strike was important because it served as a model for action by other teachers around the country. School superintendents, school board associations, and state superintendents of education condemned these actions by local teachers. The national AFT maintained its no-strike policy and adopted a posture of aid and comfort but not official sanction. As William Edward Eaton states in *The American Federation of Teachers, 1916–1961*, "Even with a no-strike policy, the AFT had emerged as the leader in teacher work stoppages."

The event that sparked the rapid growth of teacher militancy in the 1960s, and contributed to the NEA's rapid acceptance of collective bargaining, was the formation of the New York City local of the AFT, the

United Federation of Teachers (UFT). In the late 1950s, the AFT decided to concentrate on organizing teachers in New York City and to provide special funds for that purpose. After the organization of the UFT in 1960, there was a vote for a strike over the issues of a dues checkoff plan, the conducting of a collective-bargaining election, sick pay for substitutes, 50-minute lunch periods for teachers, and changes in the salary schedules. On November 7, 1960, the UFT officially went on strike against the New York City school system. The union declared the strike effective when 15,000 of the city's 39,000 teachers did not report to school and 7,500 teachers joined picket lines around the schools. In the spring of 1961, the UFT won a collective-bargaining agreement with the school system and became one of the largest and most influential locals within the AFT.

During the 1960s, teachers increasingly accepted the idea of collective bargaining and the use of the strike. This was reflected in the rapid growth of membership in the AFT. In 1966, the membership of the AFT was 125,421. By 1981, the membership had more than quadrupled to 580,000. This increased membership plus the increased militancy of the NEA heralded a new era in the relationship among American teachers' organizations and the managers of American education. With the coming of age of the strike and collective bargaining, teachers in the NEA and AFT proved themselves willing to fight for their own welfare and the welfare of American public schools.

However, the union struggle came into conflict with anti-union groups resulting in a convergence, as discussed in the last two sections, of goals between the NEA and AFT.

PERFORMANCE-BASED PAY

Recently the issue of performance pay has concerned both unions. The traditional pay scale, or what is called a democratic pay scale because everyone receives the same salary based on qualifications and seniority, provides salary increases based on years of service and level of education. A performance-based pay scale bases salary increases on some measure of teacher performance, usually student test scores.

Both unions agree that any change in the traditional salary scale should be a result of collective bargaining between the local teachers' union and the local school district. The AFT issued the following statement regarding pay scales. In the statement, the AFT declared: "Teachers reject being evaluated on a single test score [student scores on standardized tests]."

The American Federation of Teachers believes the decision to adopt a compensation system based on differentiated pay should be made by the local union leaders and district officials who know best what will work in their schools. Systems must be locally negotiated, voluntary, and school wide and must promote a collaborative work environment.

Well-designed compensation systems based on differentiated pay for teachers must include the following elements:

- Labor-management collaboration
- Adequate base compensation for all teachers
- Credible, agreed-upon standards of practice
- Support for professional development
- Incentives that are available to all teachers
- Easily understood standards for rewards
- Sufficient and stable funding
- Necessary support systems, such as data and accounting systems

In addition, AFT locals have developed school-wide differentiated pay based on a combination of academic indicators, including standardized-test scores, students' classroom work, dropout rates, and disciplinary incidents. Teachers reject being evaluated on a single test score.

ASSAULT ON TEACHERS' UNIONS' COLLECTIVE-BARGAINING RIGHTS

In 2011 Republican officials in Ohio, Idaho, Tennessee, Wisconsin, and other states sought to curb collective-bargaining rights to control education costs. *Education Week* reporter Sean Cavanagh quoted Michele Prater, a spokeswoman for the Ohio State Education Association, regarding the effort to curb collective bargaining of teachers' unions in Ohio, "It represents an anti-worker, anti-student, anti-education agenda."

The goal of this political movement was to restrict or eliminate the collective-bargaining rights of teachers and other public employees. Besides those calling for elimination of public employee collective-bargaining rights, there were those who want to limit collective bargaining to wage issues. In other words, teachers' unions would not be able to bargain over working conditions, evaluations, and other non-wage issues. In addition, Ohio Republicans support limiting bargaining rights to wages and end bargaining over class size and pension contributions.

Randi Weingarten, president of the American Federation of Teachers, criticized these attempts to limit collective bargaining as a means of reducing state budget deficits: "Don't let anyone tell you that robbing workers of voice will somehow repair deficits . . . collective bargaining is not the cause of our state budget crises, but it can be a part of the solution." In a news article released by the National Education Association, Cindy Long claims, "But trying to blame public employee salaries and pensions for budget shortfalls is a red herring. Republican-controlled legislatures around the country, from New Hampshire to Arizona to Florida, are attacking collective bargaining by scapegoating public employees for budget problems." In addition, she claims:

> When states try to reduce public salaries and pensions by eliminating collective bargaining, they take an economic hit in the long term. The lower the wages of public employees, the less discretionary income they have to spend in the local economy. The higher the wages, the higher the reinvestment into the economy. And research shows that most public employees stay—and spend—within the state after retirement.

Given this uproar about public employee unions, readers must ask themselves if they favor collective bargaining by teachers' unions. Should collective bargaining be limited to wages only?

TEACHERS' RIGHTS

During the nineteenth and early twentieth centuries, schoolteachers were expected to be models of purity. Pressure was placed on teachers to be circumspect outside the school regarding dress, speech, religion, and types of friends. Within the school, a teacher's freedom of speech was abridged at the whim of the school administrator. Some school administrators allowed teachers to discuss controversial topics freely within the classrooms; others fired teachers who spoke of things within the classroom that were not approved by the administration. Very often, teachers were fired for their political beliefs and activities.

During the last several decades, court actions, the activities of teachers' associations, and state laws granting teachers tenure expanded academic freedom in the public schools and protected the free speech of teachers. The expansion of academic freedom in the United States first took place at the college level and later in elementary and secondary schools. The concept of academic freedom was brought to the United States in the latter part of the nineteenth century by scholars who received their training in Germany. The basic argument for academic freedom was that if scientific research were to advance civilization, scholars had to be free to do research and to lecture on anything they felt was important. The advancement of science depended on free inquiry. In Germany this was accomplished by appointing individuals to professorships for life.

The concept of academic freedom was not immediately accepted in institutions of higher education in the United States. Many professors were fired in the late nineteenth and early twentieth centuries for investigating certain economic problems and for backing reforms such as child labor laws. College professors found it necessary to organize the American Association of University Professors (AAUP) to fight for academic freedom. The major protection of academic freedom in American universities is provided by tenure. The idea behind tenure is that after individuals prove they are competent as teachers and scholars, they are guaranteed a position until retirement if they do not commit some major act of misconduct.

Tenure and academic freedom are supported by the NEA and AFT as ways of protecting the free speech of public-school teachers. Many states adopted tenure laws for the express purpose of protecting the rights of teachers. Court decisions also played an important role in extending academic freedom. But there are major differences between the way academic freedom functions at the university level and how it functions at the secondary and elementary levels. The organizational nature of public schools and the age of children in them places some important limitations on the extent of teachers' academic freedom.

Before they teach in the public schools, teachers must understand their rights and the limitations of their rights. There are three major types of rights about which teachers must be concerned. The first deals with the rights and limitations of speech and conduct of teachers in relationship to administrators and school boards. The second deals with rights and limitations of the speech of teachers in the classroom. And the third deals with the rights of teachers outside the school.

The most important U.S. Supreme Court decision dealing with the rights of teachers in relationship to school boards and administrators is *Pickering v. Board of Education of Township High School* (1967). The case involved an Illinois schoolteacher who was dismissed for writing a letter to the local school board criticizing the district superintendent and school board for the methods being used to raise money for the schools. The letter specifically attacked the way money was being allocated among academic and athletic programs and stated that the superintendent was attempting to keep teachers from criticizing the proposed bond issue. In court it was proved there were factually incorrect statements in the letter.

The U.S. Supreme Court ruled that teachers could not be dismissed for public criticism of their school system. In fact, the Court argued in *Pickering*:

> Teachers are, as a class, the members of a community most likely to have informed and definite opinions how funds allotted to the operation of the schools should be spent. Accordingly, it is essential that they can speak out freely on such questions without fear of retaliatory dismissal.

Here, the participation of teachers in free and open debate on questions put to popular vote was considered "vital to informed decision making by the electorate."

The court did not consider the factual errors in the public criticism grounds for dismissal; it did not find that erroneous public statements in any way interfered with the teacher's performance of daily classroom activities or hindered the regular operation of the school. "In these circumstances," the court stated, "we conclude that the interest of the school administration in limiting teachers' opportunities to contribute to public debate is not significantly greater than its interest in limiting a similar contribution by any member of the general public."

The *Pickering* decision did place some important limitations on the rights of teachers to criticize their school system. The major limitation was on the right to publicly criticize immediate superiors in the school system. In the words of the court, immediate superiors were those whom the teacher "would normally be in contact with in the course of his daily work." The court, however, did not consider the teacher's employment relationship to the board of education or superintendent to be a close working relationship. One could imply from the decision that teachers could be dismissed for public criticism of their immediate supervisor or building principal. But what was meant by close working relationship was not clearly defined in the decision. The court stated in a footnote:

Positions in public employment in which the relationship between superior and subordinate is of such a personal and intimate nature that certain forms of public criticism of the superior by the subordinate would seriously undermine the effectiveness of the working relationship between them can also be imagined.

There is a possible procedural limitation on a teacher's right to criticize a school system if the school system has a grievance procedure. This issue is dealt with in a very important book on teachers' rights published under the sponsorship of the American Civil Liberties Union (ACLU). The question is asked in David Rubin's *The Rights of Teachers*: "Does a teacher have the right to complain publicly about the operation of his school system even if a grievance procedure exists for processing such complaints?" The answer given by this ACLU handbook is "probably not." The handbook states that this issue has not been clarified by the courts, but there have been suggestions in court decisions that if a formal grievance procedure exists within the school system, a teacher must exhaust these procedures before making any public statements.

The Rights of Teachers also argues that a teacher is protected by the Constitution against dismissal for bringing problems in the school system to the attention of superiors. But, again, the teacher must first exhaust all grievance procedures. The example in the ACLU handbook was of a superintendent who dismissed a teacher because her second-grade class wrote a letter to the cafeteria supervisor asking that raw carrots be served rather than cooked carrots because of the higher nutritional value of the raw vegetable. In addition, when the drinking fountain went unrepaired in her classroom, her students drew pictures of wilted flowers and of children begging for water and presented them to the principal. The ACLU handbook states that the court decision found "the school policy was arbitrary and unreasonable and in violation of . . . First and Fourteenth Amendment rights of free speech and freedom peaceably to petition for redress of grievances."

Concerning freedom of speech in the classroom, one of the most important things for public elementary and secondary teachers to know is that the courts seem to recognize certain limitations. The three things the courts consider are whether the material used in the classroom and the statements made by the teacher are appropriate for the age of the students, related to the curriculum for the course, and approved by other members of the profession.

An example of the courts considering the age of students, given by the ACLU in *The Rights of Teachers*, is a case in Alabama where a high school teacher had been dismissed for assigning Kurt Vonnegut's "Welcome to the Monkey House" to her 11th-grade English class. The principal and associate superintendent of the school called the story "literary garbage," and several disgruntled parents complained to the school. School officials told the teacher not to use the story in class. The teacher responded that she thought the story was a good literary work and she felt she had a professional obligation to use the story in class. The school system dismissed her for insubordination. The first question asked by the court was whether the story was appropriate reading material for 11th-grade students. In its final decision, the court found that the teacher's dismissal was a denial of First Amendment rights since it had not been proved that the material was inappropriate for the grade level or that the story disrupted the educational processes of the school.

Another important issue is whether the classroom statements of a teacher are related to the subject matter being taught. One example given in *The Rights of Teachers* is of a teacher of a basic English class making statements about the Vietnam War and anti-Semitism although the lessons dealt with language instruction. The court found that his remarks had minimum relevance to the material being taught but might have been appropriate in courses such as current events and political science. What is important for teachers to know is that their freedom of speech in the classroom is limited by the curriculum and subject being taught.

Whether the method used by the teacher is considered appropriate by other members of the teaching profession might be another consideration of the courts. In a case in Massachusetts, an 11th-grade English teacher wrote an example of a taboo word on the board and asked the class for a socially acceptable definition. The teacher was dismissed for conduct unbecoming a teacher. The teacher went to court and argued that taboo words are an important topic in the curriculum and that 11th-grade boys and girls are old enough to deal with the material. The ACLU handbook states that the court ruled a teacher could be dismissed for using in good faith a teaching method "if he does not prove that it has the support of the preponderant opinion of the teaching profession or of the part of which he belongs."

In addition, officially stated school policies can limit the free speech of teachers in a classroom. A 1998 Colorado Supreme Court decision involved school regulations requiring teachers to get the principal's approval before using controversial materials in the classroom. A Jefferson County, Colorado, schoolteacher failed to get approval before showing the Bernardo Bertolucci film *1900* to his high school logic and debate class. The Colorado court upheld the firing of the teacher because the film depicted "full frontal nudity, oral sex, masturbation, profanity, cocaine abuse, and graphic violence." These scenes, according to the court, clearly fell under the school district's controversial-materials policy.

In another case, Cecil Lacks, a Missouri high school teacher, was fired for not complying with the school district's policy prohibiting profane language. She allowed students to use street language in writing plays and poetry dealing with sex, teenage pregnancy, gangs, and drugs. Other teachers defended her methods as being student centered, but the Eighth District Circuit Court supported the school district's firing of Lacks because she had willfully violated school board policies against the use of profane language in school.

Besides the question of academic freedom regarding curriculum and instruction, there is the issue of teachers' freedom of conscience. For instance, a New York high school teacher was dismissed from her job for refusing to participate in a daily flag ceremony. The teacher stood silently while a fellow teacher conducted the ceremony. In *Russo v. Central School District No. 1* (1972), a federal circuit court ruled in favor of the teacher. The U.S. Supreme Court refused to review the case, and, therefore, the circuit court decision was allowed to stand. The circuit court ruled that the teacher's actions were a matter of conscience and not disloyalty.

Although teachers do not have to participate in flag ceremonies or say the Pledge of Allegiance if it is a violation of their conscience, they cannot refuse to follow the curriculum of a school because of religious and personal beliefs. In *Palmer v. Board of Education* (1979), the U.S.

Court of Appeals decided, and the decision was later upheld by the U.S. Supreme Court, that the Chicago public schools had the right to fire a teacher for refusing to follow the curriculum because of religious reasons. The teacher was a Jehovah's Witness, and she informed her principal that because of her religious beliefs she refused "to teach any subjects having to do with love of country, the flag or other patriotic matters in the prescribed curriculum." The court declared, "The First Amendment was not a teacher license for uncontrolled expression at variance with established curricular content."

Can school districts require urine testing of teachers? In 1998, the U.S. Court of Appeals for the Fifth District struck down two Louisiana school districts' drug policies on testing teachers. The court argued that there has to be some identified problem of drug abuse before requiring tests. The ruling stated, "Despite hints of the school boards, the testing here does not respond to any identified problem of drug use by teachers or their teachers' aides or clerical workers."

In summary, teachers do not lose their constitutional rights when they enter the classroom, but their employment does put certain limitations on those rights. Important is the requirement that teachers follow the prescribed curriculum of the school. In addition, they must comply with any school policies regarding controversial materials and profane speech. Teachers have freedom of speech in the classroom if their comments are related to the curriculum, but when exercising their right to freedom of speech, teachers must consider whether their comments are appropriate for the age of the students and would be considered appropriate by other educational professionals. While teachers are required to follow a prescribed curriculum, they do not have to participate in flag ceremonies and other political ceremonies if it is a violation of their personal beliefs.

TEACHERS' LIABILITY

Is a teacher liable for monetary damages if a student is seriously injured by rocks thrown by another student? The answer in some situations is yes! In this example, Margaret Sheehan, an eighth-grade student, was taken along with other female students by her teacher to an athletic field. The teacher told the students to sit on a log while she returned to school. During her absence, a group of boys began throwing rocks at the girls, resulting in serious injury to Margaret's eye. In *Sheehan v. St. Peter's Catholic School* (1971), the Minnesota Supreme Court declared: "It is the duty of a school to use ordinary care and to protect its students from injury resulting from the conduct of other students under circumstances where such conduct would reasonably have been foreseen and could have been prevented by the use of ordinary care."

In *Teachers and the Law*, Louis Fischer, David Schimmel, and Cynthia Kelly state that teachers can be held liable for student injuries under the following conditions:

- Teachers injure the student or do not protect the student from injury.
- Teachers do not use due care.
- Teachers' carelessness results in student injury.
- Students sustained provable injuries.

The issue of teacher liability for student injuries is extremely important because of the potential for the teacher being sued for monetary damages. To protect themselves in these types of situations, teachers should carry some form of professional liability insurance. Often, this insurance coverage is provided by teachers' unions. In some cases, teachers might want to contact their insurance agents about coverage.

Now consider whether school districts should be liable for a teacher's sexual harassment of a student. In a small Texas school district, a high school teacher was fired after district officials discovered he was having an affair with one of his students. The student, Alida Gebser, testified that the teacher, Frank Walrop, began giving her special attention in 1991 when, as a 14-year-old, she attended an after-school Great Books discussion group. She stated that the 52-year-old teacher acted as a mentor; however, she became "terrified" when he made sexual advances. The following year, the teacher and student began having sexual relations until the police discovered them having sex in a wooded area. The teacher was barred from school and lost his state teaching certificate. The student and her mother sued the school district. The plaintiffs argued before the U.S. Supreme Court that the school district was responsible for the conduct of the teacher and that they should be awarded monetary damages under Title IX, which prohibits discrimination based on sex in any school receiving federal funds. Ruling that the school district was not liable in *Gebser v. Lago Vista Independent School District* (1998), Justice Sandra Day O'Connor stated in the majority opinion that school officials are liable only if they have "actual knowledge of discrimination . . . and fail adequately to respond."

Can gay or lesbian teachers inform students of their sexual orientation? In 1998, U.S. District Judge Bruce Jenkins ruled that Wendy Weaver could not be fired from coaching high school volleyball because she answered yes when asked by a student, "Are you gay?" The judge said her free speech and equal protection rights were violated. "Although the Constitution cannot control prejudices, neither this court nor any other court should, directly or indirectly, legitimize them," Judge Jenkins stated.

TEACHERS' PRIVATE LIVES

Another concern is teachers' activity outside the school. A controversial issue is whether a teacher's membership in a radical political organization is grounds for dismissal or denial of employment. The two most important U.S. Supreme Court decisions on this issue both originated in cases resulting from New York's Feinberg Law. The Feinberg Law was adopted in New York in 1949 during a period of hysteria about possible communist infiltration of public schools. The law ordered the New York Board of Regents to compile a list of organizations that taught or advocated the overthrow of the U.S. government by force or violence. The law authorized the board of regents to give notice that membership in any organization on the list would disqualify any person from membership or retention in any office or position in the school system.

The first decision concerning the Feinberg Law was given by the U.S. Supreme Court in *Adler v. Board of Education of New York* (1952). This ruling upheld the right of the state of New York to use membership in particular organizations as a basis for not hiring and for dismissal. The court argued that New York had the right to establish reasonable terms for employment in its school system. The court also recognized the right of a school system to screen its employees carefully because, as stated by the court, "A teacher works in a sensitive area in a schoolroom. There he shapes the attitude of young minds toward the society in which they live. In this, the state has a vital concern." The court went on to state that not only did schools have the right to screen employees concerning professional qualifications, but also:

> The state may very properly inquire into the company they keep, and we know of no rule, constitutional or otherwise, that prevents the state, when determining the fitness and loyalty . . . from considering the organizations and persons with whom they associate.

The *Adler* decision underwent major modification when the Feinberg Law again came before the U.S. Supreme Court 15 years later in *Keyishian v. Board of Regents of New York* (1967). Here a teacher at the State University of New York at Buffalo refused to state in writing that he was not a communist. This time the court decision declared the Feinberg Law unconstitutional. The reasoning of the court was that membership in an organization did not mean an individual subscribed to all the goals of the organization. The court stated: "A law that applies to membership, without the specific intent to further the illegal aims of the organization, infringes unnecessarily on protected freedoms. It rests on the doctrine of guilt by association which has no place here."

The *Keyishian* decision did not deny the right of school systems to screen employees or to dismiss them if they personally advocated the overthrow of the U.S. government. What the *Keyishian* decision meant was that mere membership in an organization could not be the basis for denial of employment or for dismissal.

Whether a teacher's private life can be a basis for dismissal from a school system has not been clearly defined by the U.S. Supreme Court. The ACLU argues in *The Rights of Teachers* that courts are increasingly reluctant to uphold the right of school authorities to dismiss teachers because they disapprove of a teacher's private life. Examples given by the ACLU include an Ohio court ruling that a teacher could not be dismissed for using offensive language in a confidential letter to a former student. The Ohio court ruled that a teacher's private actions are not the concern of school authorities unless they interfere with the ability to teach. The California Supreme Court ruled that a teacher could not be dismissed because of a homosexual relationship with another teacher. The court could not find that the relationship hindered the ability to teach.

It would appear that the major concern of the courts is whether teachers' private lives interfere with their professional conduct as teachers. But the difficulty of establishing precise relationships between private actions and ability to teach allows for broad interpretation by different courts and school authorities. Teachers should be aware that there are no precise guidelines in this area. The best protection for teachers is to develop some form of agreement between their teachers' organization and their school district regarding the use of private actions as a basis for dismissal and evaluation.

One limiting condition applied by the U.S. Supreme Court is that teachers' and students' actions cannot interfere with normal school activities. For instance, in *Board of Education v. James* (1972), the U.S. Supreme Court upheld a lower-court ruling that a teacher could not be dismissed for wearing an armband in class as a protest against the Vietnam War. The lower court reasoned that the wearing of the armband did not disrupt classroom activities and, therefore, there was no reason for school authorities to limit a teacher's freedom of expression.

CONCLUSION

The profession of teaching has changed greatly since the nineteenth-century model of teachers as paragons of morality. The changes in the profession parallel changes in the goals of U.S. schools. Essentially, the changes were from a moral to a global model. Teacher issues and concerns range from teacher education and licensing to high-stakes tests and classroom conditions.

Teachers are not passively manipulated by policymakers. Teachers' unions are a powerful force in American politics and in the formulation of educational policies. Unions protect wages and working conditions and allow for the voice of teachers in national and local educational policy decisions. However, teachers' unions are criticized for protecting poor-quality teachers and resisting performance pay based on student test scores.

In summary, there remain important questions about the profession of teaching.

- Who should determine the qualifications for entering the teaching profession? Teachers' unions? Politicians?
- Should teacher pay be based on some form of performance-based assessment?
- Should teachers strike?
- Which union best represents the interests of teachers?

SUGGESTED READINGS AND WORKS CITED IN CHAPTER

The best sources of current information about the teachers' unions can be found on their Websites. The NEA site is www.nea.org. The AFT site is www.aft.org. The information used in this chapter on recent NEA and AFT policies was taken from these sites.

American Federation of Teachers. *Differentiated Pay Plans* (undated). www.aft.org/pdfs/teachers/fs_diffpay0410.pdf. Provides the AFT's position on performance pay plans.

——. *International Perspectives Teacher Recruitment and Retention* (2013). www.aft.org/sites/default/files/pisa_recruitment2013.pdf. This report compares U.S. teacher salaries and status with that of other countries.

——. Press Release. March 28, 2011, Speech by AFT President Randi Weingarten: "Sharing Responsibility: Using Collective Bargaining as a Tool To Help Preserve Public Services in the Wake of State Fiscal Crises." www.aft.org/newspubs/press/2011/032811a.cfm.

——. *Resolution 2008: No Child Left Behind.* www.aft.org/about/resolutions/2008/nclb.htm. Resolution expresses concern that No Child Left Behind has done little to help schools serving low-income students.

——. *Standards* (2004). www.aft.org/topics/sbr/index.htm. The AFT recalls its history of support of the standards movement, its accomplishments, and its future needs.

——. *Survey and Analysis of Teacher Salary Trends 2005.* Washington, DC: American Federation of Teachers, 2007. Provides data and analysis of teacher salaries and teacher turnover.

——. *Teacher Salaries Remain Stagnant but Health Insurance Costs Soar, AFT Releases Annual State-by-State Teacher Salary Survey* (2004). www.aft.org/salary/index.htm. The annual teacher salary report is provided here.

Berube, Maurice. *Teacher Politics: The Influence of Unions.* Westport, CT: Greenwood Press, 1988. This is a very good introduction to the politics of teachers' unions.

Borrowman, Merle. *The Liberal and Technical in Teacher Education: A Historical Survey of American Thought.* New York: Teachers College Press, 1956. This is the classic study of the debates that have surrounded the development of teacher education in the United States. The book provides the best introduction to the history and issues regarding teacher education.

Duncan, Arne. *Address by the Secretary of Education to the National Education Association: Partners in Reform.* U.S. Department of Education (July 2, 2009). http://www2.ed.gov/

news/speeches/2009/07/07022009.html. Duncan outlines goals of Race to the Top regarding the profession of teaching.

Eaton, William E. *The American Federation of Teachers, 1916–1961*. Carbondale: Southern Illinois University Press, 1975. This is a good history of the development of the AFT.

Elsbree, Willard S. *The American Teacher: Evolution of a Profession in a Democracy*. New York: American Book, 1939. This is still the best history of the profession of teaching in the United States. Unfortunately, it traces the professionalization of teaching only to the 1930s.

García, Ekelsen. "NEA President Lily Eskelsen García: Trump Should Stand Up for Students and Families--Trump's Decisions and Policies Will Continue to Hurt Real People." *NEA Press Release* (February 28, 2017). www.nea.org/home/70065.htm on March 4, 2017.

Gay Teacher Faced Discrimination. *The New York Times* (November 26, 1998). www.nytimes.com. This article describes how the court supported a schoolteacher who told a student that she was a lesbian.

Goldstein, Dana. "Arizona Teachers Vote in Favor of Statewide Walkout." *The New York Times* (April 20, 2018). www.nytimes.com/2018/04/20/us/arizona-teacher-walkout.html on January 31, 2019. Discussion of why Arizona teachers decided to strike.

———. "Teachers in Oklahoma and Kentucky Walk Out: 'It Really Is a Wildfire'." *The New York Times* (April 2, 2018). www.nytimes.com/2018/04/02/us/teacher-strikes-oklahoma-kentucky.html on January 25, 2019. Discussion of the outbreak of teacher strikes around the country in 2018.

Hoffman, Nancy. *Woman's "True" Profession: Voices from the History of Teaching*. New York: Feminist Press, 1981. This is an important collection of essays on the history of women in teaching.

Honawar, Vaishali. "Labor Disputes Heating Up in Urban Districts, After Respite." *Education Week* (April 5, 2006). www.edweek.org. The increasing conflict between teachers' unions and big-city school administrations is reported.

———. "Teachers Achieving 'Highly Qualified' Status on the Rise: Poorer Schools Still Not Getting Their Share, State Data Shows." *Education Week* (June 11, 2008). www.edweek.org. Report on numbers of highly qualified teachers teaching core subjects.

Iasevoli, Brenda. "Survey Shows Support for an Oklahoma Teacher Strike." *Education Week* (March 6, 2018). https://blogs.edweek.org/edweek/teacherbeat/2018/03/survey_shows_support_for.html on January 24, 2019. Oklahoma teacher strike explained.

———. "West Virginia Teacher Strike Not Over Yet." *Education Week* (March 1, 2018). https://blogs.edweek.org/edweek/teacherbeat/2018/03/west_virginia_teacher_strike_not_over_yet.html on January 20, 2019. Description of West Virginia teacher strike.

Klein, Alyson. "DeVos: 'Teachers' Unions Are the Only Thing Standing in the Way' of School Choice." *Education Week* (January 23, 2019). https://blogs.edweek.org/edweek/campaign-k-12/2019/01/DeVos-voucher-Heritage-D.C.-choice-conservative.html on January 27, 2019. U.S. Secretary of Education Betsy DeVos speaks out against teachers' unions wanting to limit charter schools and other choice plans.

León, Concepción De. "500,000 Students Are Affected by the L.A. Teachers Strike. Most Are Latino." *The New York Times* (January 18, 2019). www.nytimes.com/2019/01/18/style/la-school-strike-latino.html on January 15, 2019. Discussion of issues in Los Angeles teacher strike.

Long, Cindy. *Behind the Right-Wing Attacks on Collective Bargaining, National Education Association*. http://neatoday.org/2011/03/04/whats-behind-right-wing-attacks-on-collective-bargaining/.

Lortie, Dan. *Schoolteacher: A Sociological Study*. Chicago: University of Chicago Press, 1975. This is the most complete study of the social interactions and world of the American teacher.

Mann, Horace. "Fourth Annual Report (1840)." In *The Republic and the School: Horace Mann on the Education of Free Men*, edited by Lawrence Cremin. New York: Teachers College Press, 1958. This report contains Horace Mann's ideas about teachers.

Medina, Jennifer. "At Los Angeles Teachers' Strike, a Rallying Cry: More Funding, Fewer Charters." *The New York Times* (January 17, 2019). www.nytimes.com/2019/01/17/us/lausd-strike-schools.html on January 21, 2019. Teacher strike where there is a call for caps on the number of charter schools allowed in Los Angeles.

Medina, Jennifer, and Dana Goldstein. "Los Angeles Teachers' Strike to End as Deal Is Reached." *The New York Times* (January 22, 2019). www.nytimes.com/2019/01/22/us/la-teacher-strike-deal.html on January 27, 2019. Discussion of conclusion to Los Angeles teacher strike and final agreement.

Metlife. *MetLife Survey of the American Teacher* (February 2013). www.metlife.com/assets/cao/foundation/MetLife-Teacher-Survey-2012.pdf. This survey focuses on the job satisfaction of teachers and principals.

Murphy, Marjorie. *Blackboard Unions: The AFT & the NEA*. Ithaca, NY: Cornell University Press, 1992. This is a good introduction to teacher unionism.

National Education Association. *NEA Survey: Nearly Half of Teachers Consider Leaving Profession Due to Standardized Testing* (November 2, 2014). http://neatoday.org/2014/11/02/nea-survey-nearly-half-of-teachers-consider-leaving-profession-due-to-standardized-testing-2/. Survey reveals teacher dissatisfaction with the amount of required standardized testing.

————. *No Annual Testing in ESEA Reauthorization, Urges NEA President* (January 12, 2015). http://neatoday.org/2015/01/12/no-annual-testing-esea-reauthorization-says-nea-president/. Call to end testing requirements of No Child Left Behind.

————. *Rankings and Estimates: Rankings of the States 2015 and Estimates of School Statistics 2016* (May 2016). www.nea.org/assets/docs/2016_NEA_Rankings_And_Estimates.pdf on March 7, 2017. Contains information on national teacher salaries and many other school statistics.

Paige, Rod. *Paige's Remarks at the National Press Club* (March 18, 2003). www.ed.gov/news/speeches/2003/03/03182003.html.

Robelen, Erik. "Federal Rules for Teachers Are Relaxed." *Education Week* (March 24, 2004). www.edweek.org. This article discusses problems of enforcing in rural areas and with veteran teachers the highly qualified teacher provision of No Child Left Behind.

Rubin, David. *The Rights of Teachers*. New York: Avon, 1972. This is the American Civil Liberties Union handbook of teachers' rights.

Sawchuk, Stephen. "Steep Drops Seen in Teacher-Prep Enrollment Numbers California and Other Big States Particularly Hard Hit, Raising Supply Concerns." *Education Week* (October 21, 2014). www.edweek.org/ew/articles/2014/10/22/09enroll.h34.htm. This article provides different explanations for the decline of enrollments in teacher education programs.

————. "Teacher Protections Violate Student Rights, Calif. Judge Finds." *Education Week* (June 11, 2014). www.edweek.org/ew/articles/2014/06/11/36vergara.h33.html?tkn=VTTFJrWDg0tmaAjg%2FLe47iJgjNnXQuEc73xo&print=1. This article discusses the teacher tenure and dismissal California lawsuit *Vergara v. California*.

Sawchuk, Stephen and Liana Heitin. "AFT, NEA Agendas Converge Amid External, Internal Pressure." *Education Week* (July 25, 2015). www.edweek.org/ew/articles/2014/07/25/37unions.h33.html?qs=vergara. Both unions adopt similar platforms reflecting attacks on unions and tenure laws.

Urban, Wayne. *Why Teachers Organized*. Detroit, MI: Wayne State University, 1982. This excellent history of teachers' unions argues that the primary reason for the formation of these unions was protection of wages and seniority.

U.S. Department of Education. *Highly Qualified Teachers for Every Child*. Available on the Department of Education Website. www.ed.gov. Issued in 2006, these are guidelines for achieving the "highly qualified teacher" requirements of No Child Left Behind.

————. *Meeting the Highly Qualified Teachers Challenge: The Secretary's Third Annual Report on Teacher Quality*. Washington, DC: U.S. Department of Education Office of Postsecondary Education, 2004. This report describes the meaning of highly qualified teachers as given in No Child Left Behind.

———. *Teacher Quality: Ensuring Excellence in Every Classroom.* www.ed.gov/offices/OIIA/stmresources/march/teacherquality.html. The department provides a Web guide to alternative certification and Troops to Teachers programs.

Weingarten, Randi. "AFT President Randi Weingarten on the Confirmation of Betsy DeVos." *AFT Press Release* (February 7, 2017). www.aft.org/press-release/aft-president-randi-weingarten-confirmation-betsy-devos on March 4, 2017.

———. "AFT President Randi Weingarten on Trump Visit to Florida Private School." *AFT Press Release* (March 2, 2017). www.aft.org/press-release/aft-president-randi-weingarten-trump-visit-florida-private-school on March 4, 2017. Weingarten criticizes Trump and DeVos for attempting to defund public schools and promote vouchers and private schools.

Wesley, Edgar. *NEA: The First Hundred Years.* New York: Harper and Brothers, 1957. This is the main source of information, in addition to original sources, about the early years of the NEA.

Will, Madeline. "Arizona Teachers Face Heavy Resistance as They Continue to Strike." *Education Week* (April 27, 2018). https://blogs.edweek.org/edweek/teacherbeat/2018/04/arizona_teachers_legal_threats.html on January 28, 2019. Discussion of Arizona teacher strike.

———. "West Virginia Teacher Strike Ends After Four Days, Governor Announces Pay Raise." *Education Week* (February 27, 2018). https://blogs.edweek.org/edweek/teacherbeat/2018/02/west_virginia_teacher_strike_e.html on January 22, 2019. Describes success of the West Virginia teacher strike.

CHAPTER 11

Globalization of Education

Almost all countries have adopted the Western model of schooling. The Western school model consists of an educational ladder that students climb from primary school grades to secondary school. As students move through these grades, they are taught a curriculum determined by government or other authorities. After graduation, students can enter some form of postsecondary education, including globalized forms of higher education. The model includes mass education of populations as a means of instilling nationalistic feelings and political and ethical values. Variations in the Western model result from national differences in religion, political power, family structures, and economic systems.

Since the nineteenth century, the Western school model has swept around the world, leaving in its trail "shop 'til you drop" consumerism, global urbanization, corporatism, nationalism, corporate English, environmental destruction, alienation from others, and a decline in spiritualism. Obviously, the school is not the single cause of these ills, but it is an important contributing factor.

As I discuss in *Global Impacts of the Western School Model: Corporatization, Alienation, Consumerism*, the Western school model fosters dreams of upward social and economic mobility. Ideally, schools would create a meritocracy in which people achieve their place in society through education and hard work in contrast to being given an ascribed social status at birth. However, the Western school model may also increase economic and social inequalities caused by differences in school achievement and access to schools or advanced schooling. The children of the poor may not have access to high-quality schools while the rich protect the schooling advantages of their children.

Early advocates of Western-styled schooling believed student obedience to school rules was preparation for obedience to government laws. Nationalism is developed through school rituals, such as flag pledges and singing anthems. In most cases, schooling is the first institution outside the family experienced by a child. The very process of sitting in organized classrooms governed by school officials and rules could also be considered preparation for working in factories and corporate hierarchies.

Grading under the schools' authority is often like ratings given by employers. Loyalty, teamwork, and team spirit, as taught in the school, could be transferrable to the workplace. I have compared American high school pep rallies to corporate sales meetings.

Not all the world's children are in school. UNESCO assumes the Western school model of primary to secondary grades in its *Education for All 2013/14* monitoring report. It states:

> By 2011, 57 million children were still out of school. Sub-Saharan Africa is the region that is lagging most behind, with 22% of the region's primary school age population still not in school in 2011. By contrast, South and West Asia experienced the fastest decline, contributing more than half the total reduction in numbers out of school. Girls make up 54% of the global population of children out of school. Almost half the children out of school globally are expected never to make it to school, and the same is true for almost two of three girls in the Arab States and sub-Saharan Africa.

A goal of Education for All is creating "a global commitment to provide quality basic education for all children, youth and adults."

SCHOOLING: AN ALIENATED CORPORATE-CONSUMER CULTURE

Today's well-schooled corporate workers leave their starkly furnished cubicles, walking with heads down, oblivious to others and their surroundings, staring at phones clasped in their hands. Feeling lonely, they seek others through social media. Their consumerist fantasies are flooded with world brands promising the good life, but, in the end, their shopping experiences result in desires to buy more. As our polluted earth crumbles around them, they want more money to buy more goods. Consumerism pervades most countries—communist, socialist, or capitalist—with school attendance promising high-paying jobs and, consequently, better shopping experiences.

Corporate workers are more concerned with their own careers (careerism) than what their corporations are actually making. Thus, worker satisfaction with a corporation's final products is greatly reduced and are replaced by desires to move up the corporate ladder like climbing the education ladder or finding a higher-paying job at another company. In other words, corporate workers are alienated from the social meaning of the products they make.

LONELINESS AND LOSS OF SPIRITUALITY

With the Western school model feeding dreams of greater consumption, there has been a loss of the spiritual feelings of compassion and empathy and an increase in feelings of loneliness. Until the rise of modern schooling, philosophers and religious teachers discussed what they thought were the best religious and ethical values for the good society. This was true in Confucian, Islamic, Hindu, Christian, and Buddhist schools. The loss of spiritual values makes it difficult to maintain cohesive communities. My definition of spiritual values includes the emotions, particularly compassion and empathy, that bind people together and provide ethical guidelines for behavior. These spiritual values, I believe, are felt and are part of human nature.

Without the guidance of spiritual values (a "moral compass"), political freedom and economic free markets result in destructive behavior, with people acting greedily and without concern for the welfare of others.

GLOBALIZATION OF THE WESTERN SCHOOL MODEL

Globalization of education refers to the worldwide discussions, processes, and institutions influencing local educational practices and policies. What comprises this global education superstructure? There are international organizations that directly and indirectly influence national school systems. There are multinational education corporations and schools. Government and professionals engage in global discussions about school policies. In the first issue of the journal *Globalisation, Societies and Education* (2003), Roger Dale and Susan Robertson state that globalization of education would be considered an intertwined set of global processes affecting education, such as worldwide discourses on human capital, economic development, and multiculturalism; intergovernmental organizations; information and communication technology; nongovernmental organizations; and multinational corporations.

The concept of globalized educational institutions and discourses developed after the term "globalization" was coined by the economist Theodore Levitt in 1985 to describe changes in global economics affecting production, consumption, and investment. The term was quickly applied to political and cultural changes that affect in common ways large segments of the world's peoples. One of these common global phenomena is schooling. As the opening editorial in the first edition of *Globalisation, Societies and Education*—the very founding of this journal indicates the growing importance of globalization and education as a field of study—states, "formal education is the most commonly found institution and most commonly shared experience of all in the contemporary world." However, globalization of education does not mean that all schools are the same as indicated by studies of differences between the local and the global.

The growth of worldwide educational discourses and institutions led to similar national educational agendas, particularly the concept that education should be viewed as an economic investment with the goal of developing human capital or better workers to promote economic growth. Consequently, educational discussions around the world often refer to human capital, lifelong learning for improving job skills, and economic development. Also, the global economy is sparking a mass migration of workers resulting in global discussions about multicultural education.

Intergovernmental organizations, such as the United Nations, the Organization for Economic Co-operation and Development (OECD), and the World Bank, are promoting global educational agendas that reflect discourses about human capital, economic development, and multiculturalism. Information and communication technology is speeding the global flow of information and creating a library of world knowledges. Global nongovernmental organizations (NGOs), particularly those concerned with human rights and environmentalism, are trying to influence school curricula throughout the world. Multinational corporations, particularly those involved in publishing, information, testing, for-profit schooling, and computers, are marketing their products to governments, schools, and parents around the world.

DOMINANT GLOBAL EDUCATIONAL IDEOLOGY: HUMAN CAPITAL AND CONSUMERISM

In Chapter 4 I discussed human capital economics as the dominant goal directing American and global education. As a reminder to the reader, human capital stresses education as a cause of economic growth and increased income. In this section, I link human capital economics to consumerism.

The triumph of consumerism was made possible by the related actions of schools, advertising, and media. Mass-consumer culture integrates consumerism into all aspects of life from birth to death, including, but not limited to, education, leisure-time activities, the popular arts, the home, travel, and personal imagination. Mass-consumer culture captures the fantasy world of people with brand names and fashions that promise personal transformation, the vicarious thrill of imagining the glamorous lives of media celebrities, and the promise of escape from hard work through packaged travel and cruises to an envisioned paradise.

The ideology of consumerism was articulated in the late nineteenth and early twentieth centuries with the appearance of industrial and agricultural abundance. As conceived by turn-of-the-century economist

Simon Patten, consumerism reconciled the Puritan virtue of hard work with the abundance of consumer goods. From the Puritan standpoint, the danger of abundant goods was more leisure time and possible moral decay. In Patten's 1907 book, *The New Basis of Civilization*, he argues that the consumption of new products and leisure-time activities would spur people to work harder. In Patten's words, "The new morality does not consist in saving, but in expanding consumption." Patten explains:

> In the course of consumption . . . the new wants become complex. . . [and as a result the] worker steadily and cheerfully chooses the deprivations of this week. . . . Their investment in tomorrow's goods enables society to increase its output and to broaden its productive areas.

The professionalization and expansion of advertising in the late nineteenth and early twentieth centuries were key contributions to the creation of a global mass-consumer culture. Advertising prompted desires for new products; it convinced consumers that existing products were unfashionable and, therefore, obsolete; and it made brand names into playthings in personal fantasies. The advertising profession transformed the capitalist model of buyers making rational choices in a free market into a consumerist model where the buyer was driven by irrational emotions associated with particular brand names and/or products.

Consumerism is strikingly different from other ideologies that place an emphasis on either social harmony or an abandonment of worldly concerns. Many religions value the denial of materialistic desires. Different branches of Islam, Hinduism, Buddhism, and Christianity reject the way of life represented by the consumer seeking personal transformation through the buying of goods. Confucianism emphasizes the importance of social harmony over individual pursuit of wealth.

Following is a list of the basic ideas that form the ideology of consumerism. Of course, consumerism is aligned with notions of human capital education.

Basic Ideas of Consumerist Ideology
- Work is a virtue, and it keeps people from an indolent life that could result in vice and crime.
- Equality means equality of opportunity to pursue wealth and consume.
- Accumulation of material goods is evidence of personal merit.
- The rich are rich because of good character, and the poor are poor because they lack virtue.

- The major financial goal of society should be economic growth and the continual production of new goods.
- Consumers and producers should be united in efforts to maximize the production and consumption of goods.
- People will want to work hard so they can consume an endless stream of new products and new forms of commodified leisure.
- Differences in ability to consume (or income) is a social virtue because it motivates people to work harder.
- Advertising is good because it motivates people to work harder to consume products.
- The consumer is irrational and can be manipulated in his/her purchases.
- The consumption of products will transform one's life.

SKILLS: THE NEW GLOBAL CURRENCY

The Common Core State Standards reflects the global trend to emphasize skills needed for success in employment and higher education. It is a skills-based curriculum in contrast to one emphasizing the learning of specific knowledge. "Skills have become the global currency of twenty-first century economies," declared the Organization for Economic Cooperation and Development's publication *Trends Shaping Education 2013*. As I discuss in my book *Economization of Education*, the OECD, the World Bank, and the World Economic Forum are globally promoting skill-based schooling, with many nations aligning their curricula to skills considered necessary for employment and economic growth.

Skills are divided into hard and soft, with hard skills usually referring to such things as literacy instruction and numeracy and soft skills referring to character traits that will help the worker succeed in the workplace. OECD defines skills as the "ability to do something," which could include the ability to operate a machine (hard skill) or the ability to get along with others (soft skill). Skill-based instruction, it is claimed, will solve most economic problems, including economic development and growth, unemployment, and inequalities in wealth. Preschool is now considered an important time to teach soft skills, such as grit and conscientiousness, for later success in school and work.

There are many questions surrounding the concept of skills. Are these skills to be general skills required by the economy or skills specifically related to a particular job or trade? What role do cultural differences make in teaching skills, or are skills to be global and unrelated to a specific culture? Will skill instruction solve other global problems, such as protection of human rights and the environment? And, most importantly, is there a global skills gap?

The World Economic Forum's report "Education and Skills 2.0" highlights the confusion over the question of a skills gap:

One arena in which accountability matters hugely is the effort to ensure that the skills imparted by an education system match those needed by employers. This issue has recently come to prominence because of the large number of reports from American National Association of Colleges and Employers who say they cannot find workers who have the skills needed to perform specific jobs even when pay levels are high. *Many economists, by contrast, say that the empirical evidence does not support the existence of any significant skills gap.* This is an issue that is unresolved in countries at all income levels.

(emphasis in original)

Despite these questions about the existence of a skills gap, globally schools are adopting skill-based curricula to meet the needs of future employers.

OECD AND HUMAN CAPITAL THEORY

OECD is a major force in global testing and in supporting human capital education for a knowledge economy. The OECD links education to economic growth. The OECD's 1961 founding document states as its goal "to achieve the highest sustainable economic growth and employment and a rising standard of living in Member countries, while maintaining financial stability, and thus to contribute to the development of the world economy." From its original membership of 20 nations, it has expanded to 30 of the richest nations of the world. In addition, the OECD provides expertise and exchanges ideas with more than 100 other countries, including the least-developed countries in Africa.

In keeping with its concerns with economic growth, the OECD promotes the role of education in economic development. Along with economic growth, OECD leaders express concern about nations having shared values to ensure against social disintegration and crime. The stated values of education according to the OECD are as follows:

Both individuals and countries benefit from education. For individuals, the potential benefits lay in general quality of life and in the economic returns of sustained, satisfying employment. For countries, the potential benefits lie in economic growth and the development of shared values that underpin social cohesion.

The OECD's global testing products, the Programme for International Student Assessment (PISA) and the Trends in International Mathematics and Science Study (TIMSS), are creating global standards for the knowledge required to function in what the OECD defines as the everyday life of a global economy. Also, the tests are serving as an "Academic Olympiad," with nations comparing the scores of their students with those of other nations. The result is national education policy leaders trying to plan their curriculum to meet the challenge of OECD testing, particularly preparation for TIMSS. Wanting to impress their national leaders, school officials hope their students do well on these tests in comparison to other countries. The consequence is a trend to uniformity in national curricula as school leaders attempt to prepare their students to do well on the test. Writing about the effect of PISA and TIMSS on world education culture, David P. Baker and Gerald K. LeTendre assert:

> After the first set of TIMSS results became public, the United States went into a kind of soul searching. . . . The release of the more recent international study on OECD nations called PISA led Germany into a national education crisis. Around the world, countries are using the results of international tests as a kind of Academic Olympiad, serving as a referendum on their school system's performance.

The potential global influence of PISA is vast since the participating member nations and partners represent, according to the OECD, 90 percent of the world economy. These assessments are on a three-year cycle beginning in 2000, with each assessment year devoted to a particular topic. For instance, international assessment of reading is scheduled for 2009, mathematics for 2012, and science for 2015. The OECD promotes PISA as an important element in the global knowledge economy: "PISA seeks to measure how well young adults, at age 15 and therefore approaching the end of compulsory schooling, are prepared to meet the challenges of today's knowledge societies—what PISA refers to as 'literacy.'"

The OECD is contributing to a world culture of schooling through its testing, research, and higher education programs.

THE WORLD BANK AND THE UNITED NATIONS

"Today," declares the 2007 official guide to the World Bank, "the World Bank Group is the world's largest funder of education." Founded in 1944, the World Bank provides educational loans to developing nations based on the idea that investment in education is the key to economic development. Educational improvement became a goal of the World

Bank in 1968 when its then president, Robert McNamara, announced, "Our aim here will be to provide assistance where it will contribute most to economic development. This will mean emphasis on educational planning, the starting point for the whole process of educational improvement." McNamara went on to explain that it would mean an expansion of the World Bank's educational activities. The World Bank continues to present its educational goals in the framework of economic development: "Education is central to development. . . . It is one of the most powerful instruments for reducing poverty and inequality and lays a foundation for sustained economic growth."

The World Bank and the United Nations share a common educational network. The World Bank entered into a mutual agreement with the United Nations in 1947 that specified that the Bank would act as an independent specialized agency of the United Nations and as an observer in the United Nations' General Assembly.

The World Bank supports the United Nations' Millennium Goals and Targets, which were endorsed by 189 countries at the 2000 United Nations Millennium Assembly. The Millennium Goals directly addressing education issues are:

- Goal 2 Achieve Universal Primary Education: Ensure that by 2015, children everywhere, boys and girls, will be able to complete a full course of primary schooling.
- Goal 3 Promote Gender Equality and Empower Women: Eliminate gender disparity in primary and secondary education, preferably by 2005, and at all levels of education no later than 2015.

These two Millennium Goals were part of the Education for All program of the United Nations Educational, Scientific, and Cultural Organization (UNESCO), which had established as two of its global goals the provision of free and compulsory primary education for all and the achieving of gender parity by 2005 and gender equality by 2015. Highlighting the intertwined activities of the World Bank and United Nations agencies is the fact that these two goals were a product of the 1990 World Conference on Education for All convened by the World Bank, UNESCO, United Nations Children's Fund (UNICEF), the United Nations Population Fund (UNFPA), and the United Nations Development Program (UNDP). This world conference was attended by representatives from 155 governments.

Nothing better expresses the World Bank's commitment to the idea of a knowledge economy and the role of education in developing human capital than its publication *Lifelong Learning in the Global Knowledge Economy*. The book offers a roadmap for developing countries on how to prepare their populations for the knowledge economy in order to bring about economic growth. The role of the World Bank is to loan money to ensure the growth of an educated labor force that can apply knowledge to increase productivity. These loans, according to World Bank policies, provide support to both public and private educational institutions.

GLOBAL BUSINESS AND GLOBAL TESTING SERVICES: STANDARDIZATION OF SUBJECTS AND GLOBAL INTERCULTURAL ENGLISH

In Chapter 8 I discussed the development of global education business, including for-profit schools, tutoring and test preparation centers, and the global publishing industry. Global education businesses are contributing a global uniformity of schooling. What is the cultural effect of this uniformity? What is the effect on students preparing for the same examinations? Does the global marketing of tests and testing programs of international organizations contribute to a uniformity of world education culture and promotion of English as the global language? Is worldwide testing leading to a global standardization of knowledge in professional fields? At this time any answer would have to be speculative since there is no concrete evidence about the effect of global testing programs. However, one could argue that if students worldwide are preparing for similar tests, they are being exposed to a uniform educational and professional culture that might contribute to creating a world culture.

The International Association for the Evaluation of Educational Achievement (IEA) first demonstrated the possibility of making comparisons between test scores of different nations. Founded in 1967 with origins dating back to a UNESCO gathering in 1958, the IEA initially attempted to identify through testing effective educational methods that could be shared between nations. According to the organization's official history, the original group of psychometricians, educational psychologists, and sociologists thought of education as a global enterprise to be evaluated by national comparisons of test scores. They "viewed the world as a natural educational laboratory, where different school systems experiment in different ways to obtain optimal results in the education of their youth." They assumed that educational goals were similar between nations but that the methods of achieving those goals were different. International testing, it was believed, would reveal to the world community the best educational practices.

Today, the IEA contributes to uniform worldwide educational practices. The organization's stated goal is to create global educational benchmarks by which educational systems can be judged. In fact, the following mission statement includes the creation of a global network of educational evaluators.

Global standardization of English, aided by the United States–based Educational Testing Service (ETS), is now necessary for the operation of worldwide industries. The trend to a global business English was reflected on a sign I saw in Shanghai that read, "Learn the English words your bosses want to hear!"

Until 2000, ETS primarily focused on the U.S. testing market. In 2000, business executive Kurt Landgraf became president and CEO, turning a nonprofit organization into one that looks like a for-profit, with earnings of more than $800 million a year. As part of Landgraf's planning, the company expanded into 180 countries. "Our mission is not just a U.S.-oriented mission but a global mission," Landgraf is quoted as saying in a magazine article. "We can offer educational systems to the world, but to do that, you have to take a *lesson from the commercial world*" (emphasis in original). The official corporate description of ETS's global marketing is:

> ETS's Global Division and its subsidiaries fulfill ETS's mission in markets around the world. We assist businesses, educational institutions, governments, ministries of education, professional organizations, and test takers by designing, developing and delivering ETS's standard and customized measurement products and services which include assessments, preparation materials and technical assistance.

An important role of the Global Division is standardizing English as a global language. Almost all its products are for English language learners. The division markets the widely used Test of English as a Foreign Language (TOEFL), Test of English for International Communication (TOEIC), and Test of Spoken English (TSE). TOEFL has long served as an assessment tool for determining the English language ability of foreign students seeking admission into U.S. universities. In 2002, ETS opened a Beijing, China, office and began marketing TOEIC along with TOEFL. In addition, the Global Division offers TOEFL Practice Online, which indirectly serves as a teaching tool for English instruction. In March 2007 ETS proudly announced that the service had been extended to its Chinese market. The Test of English for Distance Education (TEDE) is used worldwide to determine if a student has enough skills in English to participate in online courses conducted in English. Criterion is a Web-based online writing evaluation that promises to evaluate student writing skills in seconds. In 2007 ETS's Criterion won highest honors from the Global Learning Consortium. In addition to all these tests associated with global English, ETS offers ProofWriter, an online tool that provides immediate feedback on grammar and editing issues for English language essays.

In another major step in the global standardization of English, ETS and G2nd Systems signed an agreement in 2007 for G2nd Systems to join ETS's Preferred Vendor Network and to use TOEIC. G2nd Systems is promoting an intercultural form of English for use in the global workplace. "G2nd Systems defines the way people use non-culture-specific English in workplace environments as intercultural English, which is not the same as any national version of English that naturally includes cultural presumptions, idioms and local ways of communicating ideas," explains Lorelei Carobolante, CEO of G2nd Systems, in a news release from ETS. She continues:

> TOEIC test scores indicate how well people can communicate in English with others in today's globally diverse workplace. G2nd Systems recognizes that measuring proficiency in English speaking and writing capabilities allows business professionals, teams and organizations to implement focused language strategies that will improve organizational effectiveness, customer satisfaction and employee productivity.

In summary, the expansion of international testing might result in global standardization of school subjects, professional knowledge requirements, and English. It would be interesting to analyze the content of all the various tests offered by Pearson on the standardization of professional knowledge. By using online tests, Pearson is able to engage in global marketing. It seems hard to deny that, between ETS's range of English tests, its online services in English composition, and its connection with G2nd Systems, it is having a global impact on how English is spoken and written. Can English as a global language be standardized so it is not identified with a particular culture or nation?

THE SHADOW EDUCATION INDUSTRY AND CRAM SCHOOLS

Across the globe, from Japan to India to Cape Town to Buenos Aires to the United States, parents worry about their children's grades and test scores because they are thought to determine children's future economic success. Consequently, they seek out test preparation or cram schools and private learning services to help their children after school hours.

World culture theorists Baker and LeTendre label supplementary education providers as the "shadow education system." From the perspective of the twenty-first century, the authors see a global growth of the shadow education system as pressures mount for students to pass high-stakes tests and the world's governments attempt to closely link student achievement to future jobs. In their words, "Mass schooling sets the stage for the increasing importance of education as an institution, and to the degree that this process creates greater demand for quality schooling than is supplied, augmentation through shadow education is likely."

Baker and LeTendre predict that shadow education systems will continue to grow as nations embrace human capital forms of schooling. Simply put, as schooling is made more important for a child's future, families will invest more money in tutoring services for remedial education and for providing enhanced school achievement.

FRANCHISING THE SHADOW EDUCATION SYSTEM

Interested in joining the for-profit shadow education system? Sylvan Learning offers franchises requiring an initial investment of $179,000 to $305,000 to people having a minimum net worth of $250,000. By offering K–12 tutoring services, it is able to take advantage of government funds provided for for-profit educational services. Depending on the location, the franchise fee is from $42,000 to $48,000. Why might you choose Sylvan? The company advertises its sale of franchises by pointing out that it has served two million students since 1979 and was ranked 24 times in *Entrepreneur* magazine's Franchise 500 Ranking, number 61 overall in its 2009 Franchise 500 Ranking, and number 52 in the publication's Top Global Franchises ranking. It was ranked in *Bond's Top 100 Franchises* and was number 57 in the 2008 *Franchise Times'* Top 200 Systems. In addition, the Sylvan Learning franchise brand was selected the best educational provider in Nickelodeon's Parents Connect's First Annual Parents' Picks Awards and as Favorite Kids Learning Center by SheKnows.com. If you happen to be Hispanic, you might be tempted to invest in a franchise because Sylvan Learning was identified by *Poder Enterprise Magazine* as one of the Top 25 Franchises for Hispanics in April 2009.

Sylvan Learning's promotion of its franchises highlights the political stake it has in the continued government funding of for-profit supplementary education services. It functions like any corporation trying to expand its reach and profits. Like any corporation it relies on having a global brand name that is impressed on the public through its $40 million advertising and marketing program. In the midst of the 2010 recession the company claimed, "Despite the economy, now is the right time to enter the supplemental education industry. According to Eduventures, Inc., the current demand is strong and the market is projected to continue with double-digit growth." The company claimed that in 2008, when it decided to focus on "franchising to local entrepreneurs and business operators who can respond to the particular needs of each community while utilizing the tools, resources and brand equity of the Sylvan name," it grew by 150 percent.

Sylvan Learning is also a global company with tutoring services located in the Cayman Islands, the Bahamas, Hong Kong, Bahrain, Kuwait,

Qatar, and the United Arab Emirates. While this global reach is relatively small, it does indicate a potential future for Sylvan Learning as a major global education company.

Kumon Learning Centers has a vast number of global franchises, with over 25,000 franchises in other countries. The Kumon Learning Centers were founded in Japan in 1958 by Toru Kumon. In 2010 the company was ranked number 12 in a list of franchises that included, from the top, Subway, followed by McDonald's, 7-Eleven Inc., Hampton Inn, Supercuts, H&R Block, Dunkin' Donuts, Jani-King, Servpro, ampm Mini Market, and Jan-Pro Franchising International Inc. This is a pretty impressive list and indicates the growing global importance of the shadow education industry. In 2009, Kumon Learning Centers enrolled 4.2 million students in 46 countries.

Another global example is Kaplan, which started as a test preparation company and is now a global company operating for-profit schools along with test preparation and language instruction. Kaplan's operations in Singapore, Hong Kong, Shanghai, and Beijing are advertised as meeting "students' demand for Western-style education." In 10 European countries it offers test preparation and English language instruction. "In the UK," Kaplan states, "we are one of the largest providers of accountancy training and private higher education. We also operate the Dublin Business School, Ireland's largest private undergraduate college." Kaplan operates Tel-Aviv–based Kidum, the largest provider of test preparation in Israel. In Brazil, Colombia, Panama, and Venezuela, Kaplan operates English language and test preparation programs designed to prepare students for admission to schools in the United States.

In summary, the shadow education system is now an important player in national and global politics. The agenda of these supplementary education services focuses on increasing revenues by lobbying for government financial support and school policies supporting assessment systems that drive students into buying their services. These companies also seek to expand revenues through globalization of their products and by expanding into new areas such as for-profit schools and English language instruction.

TOMORROW'S SCHOOLS

Technology is changing classrooms around the world, but it is not impacting spirituality, government efforts to teach nationalism and submission to laws, and manipulation of national cultures and languages. Politicians and corporate bosses determine the content and purposes of schooling.

New classroom technology perpetuates the Western school model by preparing students for the technological world of global corporations. But will technologically oriented classrooms end the loneliness and alienation of workers who spend their days looking at computer screens or operating robotic machines? Workers leaving their corporatized workplaces, including office, service, and factory sites, leave their computers screens, robotic machines, or routinized service and hurry out after work while staring at their phone screens, oblivious to the world around them.

Classroom technology invites students to join the ranks of those addicted to smartphones and social media. Classrooms become advertising venues for corporate brands. There are "branded classrooms" that look like corporate spaces and advertise technology products. In "Silicon Valley Courts Brand-Name Teachers, Raising Ethics Issues," *New York Times* reporter Natasha Singer describes an entrepreneurial teacher, Kayla Delzer, who organized her classroom to resemble a Starbucks coffee shop. In the corporate-consumer environment of this Starbucks-like classroom, Delzer's third-grade students are required to open Twitter and Instagram accounts and to post daily on them. Delzer branded herself "Top Dog Teaching" and uses social media and workshops to sell the technological products used in her classroom.

Reporter Singer wrote:

> Ms. Delzer is a member of a growing tribe of teacher influencers, many of whom promote classroom technology. They attract notice through their blogs, social media accounts and conference talks. And they are cultivated not only by start-ups like Seesaw, but by giants like Amazon, Apple, Google and Microsoft, to influence which tools are used to teach American schoolchildren. Their ranks are growing as public schools increasingly adopt all manner of *laptops, tablets, math teaching sites, quiz apps and parent-teacher messaging apps.*
>
> (emphasis in original)

Will Starbucks-like classrooms foster empathy and compassion? What do you see when you walk into a Starbucks? A few people talking to each other, but most are sitting alone staring at computer or phone screens. There is little interaction in this corporate space, only consumers ingesting beverages as they type or fiddle with their phones. Delzer's classroom, or a Starbucks coffee shop, does not prepare students and customers to resist consumerism and corporate oppression or express compassion for the world's suffering people.

Are Starbucks or other corporations good models for classrooms? Corporations often try to create public images of how they help communities. Starbucks projects an image of concern for the environment. Their Website claims:

We have always believed Starbucks can—and should—have a positive impact on the communities we serve. One person, one cup and
one neighborhood at a time. As we have grown to now more than
25,000 stores in over 75 countries, so too has our commitment to
create global social impact.

What are they doing to "create global social impact"? Besides noting
their efforts to reduce their environmental footprint, Starbucks claims its
major contribution to communities are corporate careers: "We are committed to investing in paths to opportunity through education, training
and employment."

For cynics this could mean a debt-burdened college graduate can
always find work as a barista at a Starbucks. Starbucks promises this
corporate career track:

Gigantic possibilities lie ahead—to grow as a person, in your career
and in your community. To live the Starbucks mission and to be
a leader. It's the opportunity to become your personal best. To be
connected to something bigger. To be meaningful to the world. And
to be recognized for all of it. It's all here for you.

Sitting in Kayla Delzer's third-grade Starbucks-like classroom, do students
learn to see their future corporate careers as "something bigger. . . [and]
meaningful to the world?"

Corporate interest in expanding the use of classroom technology is
exemplified by the Australian Lumineer Academy, a primary school
established by Susan Wu. Referring to the Western school model, Ms.
Wu explains the reason for creating a new classroom organization using
technology: "Our current school models were built 100-plus years ago
for the Industrial Revolution. What they cared about were homogeneous
factories that produced a template of a kind of worker. The world has
changed." The Lumineer Academy almost sounds like a free school: "At
Lumineer Academy, a newly opened primary school in Williamstown,
Australia, there is no homework. There are no classrooms, uniforms or
traditional grades." Using new classroom technology, the overall goal
of the school is preparation for corporate work. "The Luminaria model
claims to balance hard S.T.E.M. [science, technology, engineering, and
math] subjects, like computer programing, with soft skills like emotional
intelligence and teamwork that *are increasingly sought by employers*"
(emphasis in original).

As illustrated by the Starbucks-like classroom and the Lumineer
Academy, classroom technology is often preparation for working alone,
in cubicles lining corporate offices, facing computer screens, handling

robotic machinery or as a service worker doing scripted routines using technology. As corporations tighten their controls, workers can be constantly rated by their computer inputs and keystrokes or, as in the case of our mail deliverer, monitored by GPS for time spent at each delivery site. This type of corporate workplace is depicted in the novel and movie *The Circle* about a major software company, possibly modeled on Google, described as the world's most powerful internet company linking emails, social media, banking, and shopping in a universal operating system. The recently hired Mae Holland, forced to work to pay off her college loans, is placed in a cubical facing an array of monitors. One screen gives Holland an instantaneously updated performance score, much like a computer game, to evaluate her work.

Mae Holland's continuous evaluation is intended to control her behavior and is like the instantaneous feedback received by students from online lessons. Thus, evaluation systems in technology-oriented classrooms prepare students for a similar process when they are employed. Referring to employer methods to motivate workers adapted from video games, *New York Times* reporter Noam Scheiber writes, "The methods have become increasingly sophisticated in an age when companies can collect more data about employee behavior than ever before, and as video game technology has proliferated."

Data collection and classroom technology will ensure the Western school model is increasingly central to economic and political systems. With a tightened feedback system between workplace needs and school curricula, classroom lessons can quickly be adapted to changing labor market needs. Student employment data can be shared with schools to enable continuous adjustment of teaching and curriculum. Corporate data on the adequacy of a graduate's work skills would be sent back to the schools and used to evaluate school staff and instruction.

Schools can collect data on student characteristics and correlate it with workplace success. For instance, does a student have the "grit" and stick-to-itiveness wanted by an employer? Developing "grit" in schools for successful employment is widely promoted by Angela Duckworth, whose book *Grit: The Power of Passion and Perseverance* is a best seller. Corporate data on fired and successful workers could be fed back to the school to plan methods for developing a student's character that will function well in a workplace environment. This feedback from corporations to schools can also be used to identify rebellious students who might not follow orders. Corporate obedience could be used to gauge potential political obedience and submission to the will of the nation-state. Schools could identify and try to correct personality traits that could hinder employment success and obedience to government laws.

CONCLUSION: LONG LIFE AND HAPPINESS

Human capital ideology dominates global education discourses. Human capital ideology supports the educational policies that will maximize profits for education businesses. Human capital ideology supports the testing companies and the shadow education industry because of the ideologies' emphasis on high-stakes testing to promote and sort students for careers and higher education and for evaluating teachers and school administrators. When schools put testing pressure on students, parents are willing to fork out extra money to the shadow education industry. Consequently, the shadow education system and multinational testing corporations are interested in public acceptance of human capital ideology and the legitimization of assessment-driven school systems.

In my book *A New Paradigm for Global School Systems: Education for a Long and Happy Life*, I offer an alternative to the current global focus on human capital education and consumerism. I propose that school policies be evaluated on their contribution to the social conditions that provide the conditions for human happiness and longevity rather than being judged by their contribution to economic growth and income. There is a great deal of international research on the social conditions that promote happiness and a long life. My work represents one effort to try and shift thinking about educational policies.

SUGGESTED READINGS AND WORKS CITED IN CHAPTER

Achieve, Inc. and National Governors Association. *America's High Schools: The Front Line in the Battle for Our Economic Future*. Washington, DC: Achieve, Inc. and National Governors Association, 2003. Illustrates human capital ideas related to the global economy.

Anderson Levitt, Kathryn, ed. *Local Meanings, Global Schooling: Anthropology and World Culture Theory*. New York: Palgrave Macmillan, 2003. Emphasizes local power over global education policies.

Baidawi, Adam. "Why This Tech Executive Says Her Plan to Disrupt Education Is Different." *The New York Times* (February 28, 2018). www.nytimes.com/2018/02/28/world/australia/school-tech-lumineer-academy-susan-wu.html on March 5, 2018. Discussion of the use of technology to change schools.

Baker, David P., and Gerald K. LeTendre. *National Differences, Global Similarities: World Culture and the Future of Schooling*. Palo Alto, CA: Stanford University Press, 2005. Classic statement of world theorists that global education is evolving according to a Western model.

Breton, Gilles, and Michel Lambert, eds. *Universities and Globalization: Private Linkages, Public Trust*. Quebec, Canada: UNESCO, 2003. Good discussion of the globalization of higher education.

Dale, Roger, and Susan Robertson. "Editorial: Introduction." *Globalisation, Societies and Education*, Vol. 1, no. 1 (2003), pp. 3–11. This introduction defines the field of educational globalization.

Dave, Eggers. *The Circle*. New York: Vintage Books, 2014. A novel about corporate control of workers.

Duckworth, Angela. *Grit: The Power of Passion and Perseverance*. New York: Scribner's, 2016. Teaching the soft skill of grit is considered important for educating future workers.

Educational Testing Service. *ETS Global.* http://www.ets.org/portal/site/ets/menuitrn.435c0b-d0ae7015d9510c3921509/?vgnextoid=d04b253b164f4010VgnVCM10000022f95190R-CRD on July 12, 2007. Profiles the global reach of Educational Testing Services.

Goldman, Michael. *Imperial Nature: The World Bank and Struggles for Social Justice.* New Haven, CT: Yale University Press, 2005. This book criticizes the programs of the World Bank.

International Association for the Evaluation of Educational Achievement. *Brief History of IEA.* www.iea.nl/brief_history_iea.html on January 28, 2008. A history of the early development of global testing programs.

Keeley, Brian. *Human Capital: How What You Know Shapes Your Life.* Paris: OECD Publishing, 2007. OECD's statement of human capital education.

Organization for Economic Co-operation and Development (OECD), Directorate for Education. *Trends Shaping Education 2013.* Paris: OECD Publishing, 2013. OECD's perspective on the future of global education systems.

———. *UNESCO Ministerial Round Table on Education and Economic Development: Keynote Speech by Angel Gurría, OECD Secretary—General Paris* (October 19, 2007). www.oecd.org/document/19/0,3343,en_2649_33723_1_1_1_1,00.html on November 13, 2010. Example of OECD's approach to education issues.

———. *The Well-Being of Nations: The Role of Human and Social Capital Education and Skills.* Paris: OECD Publishing, 2001. This book describes OECD's intention to use global schools to educate workers to meet the needs of global corporations.

Patten, Simon N. *The New Basis of Civilization.* Cambridge, MA: Harvard University Press, 1968. Early statement of consumerism as a driving force in the modern economy.

Pearson Vue. *About Pearson VUE: Company History.* www.pearsonvue.com/about/history on January 9, 2008. History of Pearson's involvement in testing.

Scheiber, Noam. "Workers Get 'Excitement,' Shareholders Get the Cash." *The New York Times* (March 12, 2018), p. B1. The use of technology to motivate workers.

Singer, Natasha. "Silicon Valley Courts Brand-Name Teachers, Raising Ethics Issues." *New York Times* (September 2, 2017). www.nytimes.com/2017/09/02/technology/silicon-valley-teachers-tech.html?ref=todayspaper&_r=0 on September 2, 2017. Describes teacher modeling her classroom on a Starbucks café.

Spring, Joel. *The Economization of Education.* New York: Routledge, 2015. Examines the increasing role of economists in influencing global education policies.

———. *Education and the Rise of the Global Economy.* Mahwah, NJ: Lawrence Erlbaum, 1998. A study of the globalization of human capital theories of education.

———. *Global Impacts of the Western School Model: Corporatization, Alienation, Consumerism.* New York: Routledge, 2019. A pessimistic interpretation of the negative impact of the Western school model.

———. *Globalization of Education: An Introduction Second Edition.* New York: Routledge, 2015. This book provides a global perspective on the development of contemporary education systems.

———. *Globalization and Educational Rights: An Intercivilizational Analysis.* Mahwah, NJ: Lawrence Erlbaum, 2001. This book calls for a global standard for educational rights.

———. *A New Paradigm for Global School Systems: Education for a Long and Happy Life.* New York: Routledge, 2007. This book advocates basing global education on the goals of happiness and longevity.

Starbucks. *Working at Starbucks.* www.starbucks.com/careers/working-at-starbucks on March 10, 2018. Starbucks defines its education and community purpose.

———. *What Is the Role and Responsibility of a for-Profit, Public Company?* www.starbucks.com/responsibility on March 10, 2018. Starbucks defines its education and community purpose.

Stromquist, Nelly P. *Education in a Globalized World: The Connectivity of Economic Power, Technology, and Knowledge.* Lanham, MD: Rowman & Littlefield, 2003.

Stromquist, Nelly P., and Karen Monkman, eds. *Globalization and Education: Integration and Contestation Across Cultures.* Lanham, MD: Rowman & Littlefield, 2000.

UNESCO. *Education for All (EFA) International Coordination: The Six EFA Goals and MDGs.* http://portal.unesco.org/education/en/ev.php-URL_ID=53844&URL_DO=DO_TOP-IC&URL_SECTION=201.html on October 5, 2007.

World Bank. *About Us: Organization: Boards of Directors.* http:www.worldbank.org on July 17, 2007, para. 1.

———. *Constructing Knowledge Societies: New Challenges for Tertiary Education.* Washington, DC: World Bank, 2002.

———. *A Guide to the World Bank Second Edition.* Washington, DC: World Bank, 2007.

———. *Lifelong Learning in the Global Knowledge Economy: Challenges for Developing Countries.* Washington, DC: World Bank, 2003.

World Economic Forum. *Education and Skills 2.0: New Targets and Innovative Approaches.* Geneva: World Economic Forum, January 2014. This report emphasizes the role of global school systems in teaching skills wanted by businesses.

World Trade Organization. *WTO Legal Texts: The Uruguay Round Agreements: Annex 1B General Agreement on Trade in Services (GATS).* www.wto.org/english/docs_e/legal_e/legal_e.htm#finalact on November 28, 2007.

INDEX

Note: Page numbers in *italic* indicate a figure and page numbers in **bold** indicate a table on the corresponding page.

classroom technology 296–299
Cleaver, Eldridge 17
Cleveland Arts and Social Science
    Academy 21, 227–228
Clinton, Bill 85–86
Clinton, Hilary 16
Coalition of American Public Employees
    (CAPE) 264
collective-bargaining rights 264,
    269–270
collectivist cultures 167–170
college education 9, 74, 84
Columbine High School 47
Committee of Ten on Secondary School
    Studies 262–263
Commodore Stockton School 151
Common Core States Standards
    219–220
Common Core State Standards 179,
    187–189, 222, 234, 239–241, 245, 288
common-school model 62–64, *63*
"concerted cultivation" 97–100
Condition of Education 2002, The 75
Condition of Education 2013, The 221
Condition of Education 2014, The
    151–152, 154, 156, 225
Condition of Education 2016, The 23,
    44, 48, 68, 157, 216
Condition of Education 2018, The 23,
    44, 47, 48, 104, 125, 158, 215, 235
consumerism 284, 286–288
Cook, Aleita 3, 4
corporate-consumer culture 284–285
Council for Exceptional Children
    (CEC) 124
Council of Chief State School Officers
    (CCSSO) 239–240
*counteracademic attitudes and
    behaviors* 173
Cox, Owen 140
cram schools 294–295
crime rate index 45
Criterion (online writing evaluation) 293
critical pedagogy 173–175
Crossroads Collaborative 42
Cruz, Nikolas 46
cultural capital 78, 96–100
cultural difference 165–167
cultural frame of reference 171–172
cultural rights 189–192
cyberbullying 49–51

Dale, Roger 285
Daniels, Mitch 21
data collection 238–239, 299
Data Quality Campaign (DQC) 239
Daughters of the American Revolution
    12, 257
Declaration of Independence 61
Decline of the Californios, The (Pitt and
    Gutierrez) 137
Deferred Action for Childhood Arrivals
    (DACA) 134–136
*Delgado v. Bastrop Independent School
    District* 140
Dell, Michael 89
Delpit, Lisa 182–183
Delzer, Kayla 297
Democratic platform (2012) 9
Depression 137
Derman-Sparks, Louise 177–178
desegregation of schools 117–119,
    117–118
Desilver, Drew 71
deskilling 87
DeVos, Betsy 20–22, 41, 227,
    234, 253
DeVos, Richard 20–21
Dewey, John 32–33
Dick and Betsy DeVos Family
    Foundation 20–21
Digest of Educational Statistics 24
digital divide 76–77
Digital Learning Now (action
    report) 226
distance learning 224–226
Ditch the Label 48
dominant culture 170
dominated cultures 170, 171–173,
    182–183
Down These Mean Streets (Thomas) 17
Dreamers 134–136
dropouts 75–76, 89, 90
Drug Abuse Resistance Education
    (D.A.R.E.) 53, 55
drug testing 53–55, 275
Duckworth, Angela 299
Due Process Clause 116–117
Duncan, Arne 145, 238, 258

early childhood education 144
Early Childhood Longitudinal
    Study 101

multicultural education: anti-bias and tolerance curricula 177–179; biculturalism 167–170; combating racism 175–177; combating sexism 179–182; critical pedagogy 173–175; cultural difference 165–167; *dominant culture* 170; *dominated cultures* 170, 171–173, 182–183; educating for economic power 182–183; ethnocentric education 183–185; global migration and 163–165; global responses to education of linguistic and cultural minorities 192–195; *immigrant cultures* 170

multilingual education: Common Core State Standards 187–189; English Language Acquisition Act 187–189; language and cultural rights 189–192; No Child Left Behind Act 185–187

Mulvey, Cindy 242

Naked Ape (Morris) 17

National Alliance for Public Charter Schools 215, 216

National Association for the Education of Young Children 177–178

National Center for Education Statistics (NCES) 48, 68, 75, 156, 157, 215

National Council on Teacher Quality 158

National Crime Prevention Council 48

National Defense Education Act 263

National Defense Education Act (NDEA) 236

National Education Association 271

National Education Association (NEA) 32, 37, 261–265

National Governors Association Center for Best Practices (NGA Center) 239

national health: efforts to curb drug and alcohol usage 53–55; improving nutrition of children 51–53

National Organization for Women Foundation 120

national standards 7

Nation at Risk, A (National Commission on Excellence in Education) 85

Native Americans 7, 32, 61, 110–111, 133, 141–147, 171–172, 183–184, 186, 187

Naturalization Act 61, 149

Naturalization Law 110, 147

naturalized citizenship 110, 147

NEA (Wesley) 263

Neill, Monty 248

New Basis of Civilization, The (Patten) 287

New Deal 21

Newdow, Michael 13

New Paradigm for Global School Systems, A (Spring) 300

Newsweek (magazine) 13, 242

New York (magazine) 21

New York Times (newspaper) 22, 42, 74, 219, 253, 297, 299

Nichols, Sharon 246

Nieto, Sonia 173, 174–175

Nineteenth Amendment, U.S. Constitution 25

Nisbett, Richard E. 165–166, 168

No Child Left Behind Act 36, 39, 86, 185–187, 208, 211–214, 234, 235, 237, 241, 244, 257–258

noncognitive abilities 91–92

nongovernmental organizations (NGOs) 286

normal school 255

Northwood University 21

Notes on the State of Virginia (Jefferson) 10

nutrition 51–53

NYOS Charter School 216

Obama administration 135

Obama, Barack 122, 146, 215

Obama, Michelle 52

Oberti, Rafael 128

Oberti v. Board of Education of the Borough of Clementon School District 128

O'Connor, Sandra Day 276

Office of Bilingual Education 187

Office of Economic Opportunity 144–145

Office of Education 118

Office of English Language Acquisition 187

Ogbu, John 171–173

Ohio Pilot Project Scholarship Program 209–210

Ohio State Education Association 269

33–36; school crime 44–51; student violence 46–49; types of 33

socialization 12

social relationships 167–168

social reproduction 77–78

socioeconomic status (SES) 75, 101–103

soft skills 91

sorting-machine model 64–65, *64*

Soul on Ice (Cleaver) 17

Southern Methodist University 16

Southern Poverty Law Center 178

spiritual values 285

Spoehr, Luther 3

standard English language 154–156

Starbucks 297–298

state educational agency (SEA) 130

Strauss, Valerie 15

student diversity: Asian Americans 147–152; Dreamers and DACA 134–136; educational attainment of immigrants 152–154; foreign-born population 133–134; Mexican immigrants 137–141; Native Americans 141–147

student privacy 53–55, 239

students with disabilities: background 123–124; charter schools 129–130; disability categories 125; Education for All Handicapped Children Act 124–125; inclusion 127–129; *individualized education plan* 126–127; students in schools **126**

student violence 46–49

Sturgis Charter Public School 216

"Summit Links Preschool to Economic Success" (Jacobson) 81

syphilis 40

Takao Ozawa v. United States 110–111

Tatum, Beverly Daniel 177

Taylor, Nathaniel 142

teachers: certification 256–257; changing roles of 254–257; female 255–256; liability 275–276; No Child Left Behind Act requirements 257–258; performance pay issues 268–269; private lives 277–278; Race to the Top program requirements 257–258; rewards of teaching 258–259; rights 270–275; strikes 253–254; turnover 260

Teachers and the Law (Fischer, Schimmel and Kelly) 276

teachers' unions: American Federation of Teachers 22, 259, 268–269, 271; collective-bargaining rights 264, 269–270; impact on school choice 253; National Education Association 32, 37, 261–265, 271; performance pay issues 268–269; United Federation of Teachers 268

"Teachers' Working Conditions" (Choy) 258–259

Teaching Tolerance Project 178–179

technology 296–299

"teenagers" 38

testing: controversial requirements for 234; global testing products 67–68, 290; global testing services 292–294; high-stakes testing 65–67, 244–246, 248; as key to global economic competition 7; as predictor of economic conditions 67–68

Test of English as a Foreign Language (TOEFL) 293

Test of English for Distance Education (TEDE) 293

Test of English for International Communication (TOEIC) 293–294

Test of Spoken English (TSE) 293

Texas Freedom Network 16

Texas State Board of Education 15–16

Texas State School Board 15

textbooks 14–16

Thomas B. Fordham Institute 16

Thomas, Piri 17

Tinker v. Des Moines Independent School District 18

Title IX, Education Amendments of 1972 120–123, 236–237, 276

Title VI, Civil Rights Act of 1964 118, 236–237

Title V, Welfare Reform Act 38–39

Toppo, Greg 47

Torbati, Yeganeh 134

transgender students 33–34, 41–42

transitional bilingual programs 186

Trends in International Mathematics and Science Study (TIMSS) 67–68, 290

Trial Lawyers for Public Justice 15

Tribally Controlled Schools Act 146

Windfern High School 14
Woessman, Ludger 68
Wolf Harlow, Caroline 46
Wollenberg, Charles M. 139, 151
working-class families 98–100
Workingman's Party 91
Work of Nations, The (Reich) 86
World Bank 286, 290–292

Wozniak, Steve 89
Wu, Susan 298

Yong, Chan 148–149

Zelman v. Simmons-Harris, 209
Zernike, Kate 22
"zero tolerance" policy 136

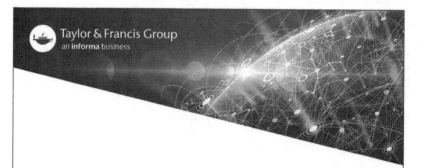